Chambers
Office Oracle

Chambers
Office Oracle

Consultant Editor: Doreen Sharp

Published in association with the
Royal Mail

Chambers

Published by W & R Chambers Ltd, Edinburgh, 1987

British Library Cataloguing in Publication Data

Chambers office oracle.
    1. Office practice—Dictionaries
    I. Sharp, Doreen
    651'.03'21   HF5547.5

ISBN 0 550 18075 3

Typeset by Blackwood Pillans & Wilson Ltd, Edinburgh

Printed by
Charles Letts & Co Ltd
London Edinburgh & New York

Acknowledgments
The Royal Mail
Tom Pinder, Consultant in Speech-in-Management
Inspector Waddington, Metropolitan Police Crime Prevention
   Service
Todd Research Ltd
Acco Company Ltd
SASCO
Business Education Service
Talisman Chauffeurs (defensive driving techniques)
British Telecom
Institute of Freight Forwarders Ltd
Trans Global Air Limited
British Standards Institution
British Rail
Susan Shatto

Contents

PART I:
Business Communication

Chapter 5
BUSINESS COMMUNICATION—*Written*

Chapter 6
ADVERTISING AND PUBLICITY

Chapter 7
GRAPHS, CHARTS AND VISUAL PLANNING

PART II:
Business Procedures

Chapter 8
BUSINESS ENTERTAINING

Chapter 9
MEETINGS

Chapter 10
PLANNING A CONFERENCE/EXHIBITION

Chapter 11
INTERVIEWING SKILLS

PART III:
Organisation and Finance

Chapter 12
BUSINESS STRUCTURES

Chapter 13
FINANCE AND BANKING

Chapter 14
SECURITY

Chapter 15
DISTRIBUTION OF GOODS

PART IV:
Government and Law

Chapter 16
GOVERNMENT IN THE UNITED KINGDOM

PART V:
Office Safety, Equipment and Services

Chapter 21
TELECOMMUNICATIONS

PART VI:
Useful Information

Chapter 22
GEOGRAPHICAL AND TRAVEL INFORMATION

Chapter 23
CALENDARS

Chapter 24
MAPS

Chapter 25
WEIGHTS AND MEASURES

Chapter 26
MEDIA

Chapter 27
GLOSSARIES

Chapter 28
ABBREVIATIONS IN COMMON USE

PART VII:
Dictionary

Consultant Editor   Doreen Sharp

Widely known and respected author, lecturer, examiner and moderator in Business Education. Formerly Head of Secretarial Studies, Department of Business and Social Sciences, Bromley College of Technology.

Author (and co-author) of 20 books on various aspects of business training for Pitman, McGraw-Hill and Macmillan including Pitman shorthand textbooks, *Electronic Keyboarding* and *The PA's Handbook* (Papermac 3rd edition 1986).

Founder member (Joint Chairman 1979–82) of the European Association of Professional Secretaries and member of the European Association of Teachers.

Presently a member of the Syllabus Committee of the Examinations Board of the London Chamber of Commerce and Industry (LCCI). Previously served on the Royal Society of Arts (RSA) Advisory Committee in Secretarial Subjects and the Secretarial Studies Committee of the Business and Technician Education Council (BTEC).

Editor   Virginia Tebbit

Contributors

Ian Derbyshire	Research Fellow at Cambridge University. Author of Chambers *Political Spotlights* series on modern world politics.
Pamela Forrester	Education Liaison Officer for the LCCI Examinations Board and Chief Examiner for the Meetings component of the LCCI Private and Executive Secretary's Diploma. Formerly in charge of secretarial training for British Petroleum. Has lectured in many parts of the world including Singapore, Lagos and Perth (Australia).
Doreen Lowe	Head of School of Information Processing, Wigan College of Technology. Author of four word processing textbooks (Wigantec).

Elizabeth McCall-Smith	General Medical Practitioner in Edinburgh.
Joan Moncrieff	Formerly Lecturer in Secretarial Studies, Mid-Warwickshire College of Further Education and Senior Lecturer in Business Studies, Bromley College of Technology. Co-author of *The PA's Handbook* (Papermac 3rd edition 1986). A member of the SIMpleton's Club (Speech in Management), for practice and promotion of Public Speaking.
Arthur Trimnell	Company Secretary/Accountant in the electrical industry before entering Further Education as Lecturer and Senior Lecturer in Business Studies at Bromley, Woolwich and Southwark Colleges. Examiner in Law and Accounts for professional bodies.
Doreen Trimnell	Formerly Principal Lecturer and Deputy Head of Department of Business Studies, Hackney College, 1976–86. Previously RSA Chief Examiner for Audio-Typewriting and presently Assessor for RSA Integrated Schemes. Co-author of textbooks on Keyboarding and Typewriting (McGraw-Hill) and Shorthand (Pitman).
Malcolm Wood	Solicitor working in private practice in Edinburgh.

Preface

Chambers Office Oracle provides a wide range of information and advice for staff in every type and size of office and has been designed to help office workers deal quickly and efficiently with many everyday queries—both common and uncommon—that can take time and effort to answer. *Chambers Office Oracle* is in fact one book and many books, blending up-to-date factual material with more general information *and* a handy Chambers dictionary.

Chambers Office Oracle represents the work of many individuals and organisations. In order to ensure the accuracy and usefulness of *all* the information in the book educational and business advisers have been consulted at each stage. The specialist sections have been written by experts in their fields.

The variety of information is mirrored in the variety of presentation. Articles, glossaries, lists, tables, charts, diagrams and maps have been used to guarantee ease of use and great flexibility.

Chambers Office Oracle will be an indispensable reference text no modern office can afford to be without.

The publishers welcome suggestions from readers for additional material which they would find useful in subsequent editions.

Part I
BUSINESS COMMUNICATION

1 English Standard Usage

2 Forms of Address

3 Business Communication
  Oral

4 Effective Speaking in Public

5 Business Communication
  Written

6 Advertising and Publicity

7 Graphs, Charts and Visual Planning

1 ENGLISH STANDARD USAGE

1.1 Clarity of expression

In business communication clarity of expression is all-important. The ability to communicate one's purpose, requirements and conclusions clearly and concisely saves time, money and unnecessary labour.

When composing a business letter, report or article, it is essential to keep its intended function in mind constantly and to be aware of how the structure and style of language works to fulfil that function. (See also Chapter 5.2.) Here are some helpful guidelines:

Structure

Before starting to write, establish and note down the objectives, the main points to be made and any firm conclusions to be conveyed; refer to those notes frequently.

Use a separate paragraph to deal with every major subject or idea; within each paragraph, make sure that every sentence connects logically with the preceding one.

Remember that every finite verb in a sentence marks a separate clause; each clause should be linked to the next by a conjunction, a colon or a semi-colon, rather than a comma.

In general, avoid forming sentences by joining a number of clauses with 'and' or 'but'.

Stay in one tense as far as possible.

Place descriptive phrases, adjectives and adverbs as close as possible to their subject.

Check that it is always clear what subject a pronoun refers to.

Style

Form sentences of different lengths and of varied structure.

Look for the most direct way of expressing your meaning; use clear and specific vocabulary, avoiding jargon, ambiguous phrases and unnecessarily technical language, e.g. 'I enclose' *not* 'Herewith please find enclosed', 'Soon' *not* 'In the near future'.

Make positive statements rather than negative ones.

Delete words that are not strictly necessary for meaning; they serve only to obscure the subject and lengthen the text, e.g. 'Though seriously ill, he came to the office daily' *not* 'In spite of the fact that he was seriously ill, he came to the office daily'.

Check that you have not repeated either vocabulary or subject
matter needlessly; if a word recurs frequently, · consult a
thesaurus for an alternative.

Ensure that major points are not swamped by minor details.

Accuracy

Check all facts and details carefully.

Consult a dictionary whenever there is any doubt about the
spelling or meaning of a word.

Consult an English usage dictionary if there is any doubt about
how a term should be used.

Finally, always re-read your work several times, revising it according
to these guidelines. Ensure that it fulfils its purpose concisely and
clearly, that the main points have been sufficiently emphasised, and
that no important facts have been omitted. If necessary, seek a second
opinion from a colleague who can offer constructive advice.

1.2 Correct grammatical usage

There are a number of areas in which grammatical errors are
commonly made in everyday English. Some simple rules can be
applied to avoid these errors.

Who and whom

(1)   Use *who* when the pronoun is the subject of a verb:

The man who *(subject)* phoned yesterday came to the office
today.

(2)   Use *whom* when the pronoun is the object of a verb:

The man whom *(object)* you *(subject)* phoned yesterday
came to the office today.

(3) Use *whom* when the relative pronoun is governed by a
preposition and try to keep the preposition and the relative pronoun
together:

The man *to whom* you spoke on the phone yesterday came
to the office today.

Like and as

(1) Use *like* to compare things or people, i.e. to qualify nouns or pronouns:

> Your *desk* is like *mine*.
> My electric *typewriter* is like *Anne's*.
> *He* looks like a *man* who has a lot of problems. (Here two people are compared.)

(2) Use *as* to compare actions, i.e. to join clauses and thus govern verbs (sometimes the verb is only implied):

> *You work* very much as *I do*.
> *Operate* the shift-key as I *told* you.
> We *shall give* the staff a bonus, as last year. (Here 'we *did*' is implied.)

Due to, owing to, because of

(1) Use *due to* only when preceded by some tense of the verb 'to be':

> My absence *was* due to illness.
> If mistakes occur they *will be* due to carelessness.

(2) Do not begin a sentence with *due to*.

(3) If a choice can be made between the phrases *because of, owing to* and *due to*, use the first. (*Owing to* and *due to* often cause ugly as well as dubious constructions.)

Shall and will, should and would

(1) When making a statement of fact without special emphasis *I* and *we* are usually followed by *shall* or *should* (not will or would):

> I should be glad if you would write to me without delay.
> We should be grateful if you would let us have a reply at once.

(2) *Shall* is used with *will* (future tense):

> I shall be glad if you will let me have a reply at once.
> If you will let us have your cheque we shall despatch the goods immediately.

Do not join a future tense to a conditional tense in one sentence.

I and me

(1) Use *I* as the subject of a sentence. Mistakes often occur when *I* or *me* is linked with another noun or pronoun. Avoid these mistakes by

mentally taking away the intervening noun or pronoun and checking the sense of what remains:

> The managing director and I will interview you.
>
> *not*
>
> Please meet the managing director and I for an interview. (*I* is wrongly used here instead of the object *me*. 'Please meet I for an interview' is obviously incorrect.)

(2)   Use *I* if the pronoun is linked to a following clause:

> It was I who wrote the report.

(3)   Use *me* after a preposition e.g. Come with me. Errors sometimes occur when the object of a preposition is two pronouns linked by 'and' e.g. Between you and me (*not* I), Like you and me (*not* I).

Either and or, neither and nor

(1)   Use *either* or *neither* with two persons or things:

> I have examined both machines and find that either (neither) will suit our purpose.

(2)   Use *either* or *neither* with the singular as they refer to one person or thing to the exclusion of the other:

> You will find that either (neither) of these typewriters *is* suitable.

(3)   Always follow *either* by *or*, and *neither* by *nor*, in a comparison:

> Either (Neither) Miss Brown or (nor) Miss Green is to take dictation in the Manager's office.

(4)   Always place *either* or *neither* next to the words they qualify:

> I shall buy either (neither) a magazine or (nor) a newspaper.
>
> *not*
>
> I shall either (neither) buy a magazine or (nor) a newspaper.

Each and none

Use *each* and *none* with the singular as they refer to one person or thing:

> Each of you *is* to receive a rise in salary next month.
>
> As none of the clerks *is* willing to work overtime we are behind schedule this week.

Using the infinitive

The infinitive has two forms; present and past:

e.g. to do (present infinitive)
to have done (past infinitive).

(1) Use the *present infinitive* after a past tense or any compound tense:

I meant *to telephone* you yesterday.

not

I meant to have telephoned you yesterday.

The staff would have preferred *to work* a five-day week.

not

The staff would have preferred to have worked a five-day week.

(2) Use the *past infinitive* when a present tense is followed by an infinitive which describes a past event:

Henry Ford *is* said *to have been* a millionaire by the age of forty.

The split infinitive

The infinitive of a verb consists of two words, e.g. to forecast, to announce, to move. The two words are a unity and should not be separated (split) by the insertion of additional words or phrases. Opinions differ on the gravity of this error but all agree that gross infringements of the rule should be avoided.

I should like, on behalf of all our members, *to move* a vote of thanks to the chairman.

not

I should like *to*, on behalf of all our members, *move* a vote of thanks to the chairman.

Comparative and superlative

(1) Use the comparative degree when two things are compared, and the superlative for more than two:

Mary has taken the *better* of the two typewriters and the *best* of the three dictating machines.

Which of these two cloths is the *more* hard-wearing?

(2) Use *less* for quantity or amount; use *fewer* for number:

The industry has bought *less* steel than it did last year and thus produces *fewer* cars. (Quantity and number)

I paid £3 *less* than the market price for a ton of cotton waste. (Amount)

5

(3) *Unique* means the only one of its kind and has *no comparative*. It should not be used casually to mean novel, scarce or rare. 'Almost unique' is allowable, but 'comparatively unique' or 'very unique' reduce the word to absurdity and should not be used.

Verbal nouns

In the following sentences the words in italic are nouns made from verbs (verbal nouns) and not participles:

>The chairman likes *travelling*.
>He hates *leaving* work unfinished.
>*Taking* a holiday is very refreshing.

(1) Qualify verbal nouns by possessive adjectives, not by pronouns (i.e. use *my, his, our, your, their* NOT *me, him, us, you, them*):

>The error was caused by *his typing* so carelessly.
>The supervisor criticised *our leaving* early.
>Do you agree to *my taking* a day's holiday.

(2) Similarly, use the possessive form for a noun qualifying a verbal noun:

>I don't object to *Mary's* talking provided she lowers her voice.
>He is unemployed because of the *firm's* going into liquidation.
>The department has been disorganised by the *Manager's* leaving.

1.3 Punctuation

A **full stop** (.) is used at the end of a statement and often after a command; a **question mark** (?) comes after a question and an **exclamation mark** (!) after an exclamation or interjection, and sometimes after a command:

>This is a useful report. Show it to the Chairman tomorrow.
>Would you make a copy for me? Cheerio! Don't forget what I said!

A **comma** (,) shows a slight break in a sentence. It is used:

(1) between two clauses joined by *but* or *or* if the second one has a subject:

> I'll come to see you tomorrow, but I don't know when I will arrive.

(2) after a subordinate clause:

> When he returned, I made a cup of tea.

(3) around the kind of relative clause that gives *additional information*:

> The salesman, who had driven from Southampton, was tired.

but *not* around the kind of relative clause that *identifies* a person or thing:

> Those people who would like tickets should write to the secretary.

(4) around a descriptive or explanatory phrase referring to a person or thing:

> Mrs Cook, our local councillor, has joined the committee.

(5) after introductory words, or around words which form a comment:

> However, I wasn't late after all.
> I must leave now, unfortunately.
> Philip, I'm sorry to say, has left the company.

(6) before *please*, after *yes* and *no*, and before or after the name of the person who is being spoken to:

> May I see the file, please?
> No, I'm sorry.
> Hurry up, Christopher.

(7) in a list of more than two things and often between adjectives preceding a noun, where there are two or more:

> a pen, a pencil and a rubber
> a busy, overcrowded room (but no commas in e.g. a *cheerful old man*, because *old man* is regarded as a single unit).

A **colon** (:) is used to introduce the answer that the first part of the sentence expects:

> There's one thing I'd really like: a new car.
> You'll need the following: passport, ticket, boarding pass.

A **semicolon** (;) separates parts of a sentence that are equally important and are not linked by *and, but, or*, etc. Sometimes a semicolon is used to separate items in a list:

> One tray of sandwiches will be sufficient; to prepare more would be wasteful.
>
> I have three ambitions: to set up my own business; to buy a boat and sail around the world; to live in Sydney.

Quotation marks (' ') or (" ") are used before and after direct speech; a **comma** is usually put before or after the direct speech:

> Mary said, 'You're late'.
>
> 'You're late', said Mary.

Both single and double quotes are correct, but modern usage prefers single quotes. However, if there is a quotation or highlighted passage within another quotation, both single and double quotes must be used:

> 'Did she say "You're late"?', John asked.

An **apostrophe** (') is used:

(1)   to form possessive nouns; it is placed before the *s* with singular nouns and with plural nouns not ending in —*s*, and after the *s* with plural nouns ending in —*s*:

> Anne's desk; the women's coats; the residents' car park.

(2)   in shortened forms, showing where part of a word has been left out:

> I've only two appointments today.
>
> Aren't you coming with us?

A **hyphen** (-) is used:

(1)   in many nouns (others are written as one word or as two words without a hyphen):

> air-conditioning (but *aircraft* and *air force*).

(2)   in compound adjectives placed before the noun:

> a six-page contract; a twenty-year-old building: a well-deserved award.

(3)   sometimes with a prefix:

> The votes must be re-counted.

1.4 Spelling rules

To a large extent the ability to spell English words correctly depends on becoming familiar with the *look* of them when they are spelt in the accepted way. Much help with spelling is given in the Dictionary (Part VII) and, in cases of doubt, words should always be looked up there.

There are, however, a few general rules *though one must always be on the watch for exceptions.*

Derivatives of words ending in -y

(1) The plural of a noun in -y, -ey (also -ay, -oy, -uy):

A noun in -y following a consonant has its plural in -ies.

baby	*babies*	*country*	*countries*

Nouns in -ey, etc., have their plural in -eys, etc.

donkey	*donkeys*	*valley*	*valleys*
day	*days*	*Monday*	*Mondays*
alloy	*alloys*	*guy*	*guys*

(2) The parts of a verb when the verb ends in -y, -ey (etc.):

The formation is similar to that of noun plurals in (1) above.

	cry	*cries*	*cried*
	certify	*certifies*	*certified*
but	*convey*	*conveys*	*conveyed*
	delay	*delays*	*delayed*
	destroy	*destroys*	*destroyed*
	buy	*buys*	

(3) Comparison of adjectives, or the formation of nouns or adverbs from them:

A rule similar to the above holds for words in -y, and in some cases for those in -ey (etc.).

	shady	*shadier*	*shadiest*	*shadiness*	*shadily*
	pretty	*prettier*	*prettiest*	*prettiness*	*prettily*
but	*grey*	*greyer*	*greyest*	*greyness*	*greyly*
	coy	*coyer*	*coyest*	*coyness*	*coyly*

There are, however, exceptions and irregularities for which a dictionary should be consulted.

Derivatives of words ending in -c

When a suffix beginning with a vowel is added, and the consonant still has a hard *k* sound, **-c** becomes **-ck**:

picnic	*picnicking*	*picnicked*	*picnicker*
mimic	*mimicking*	*mimicked*	*mimicker*

-k- is not added in words such as *musician, electricity,* etc., where the consonant has the soft sound of *sh* or *s*.

-ie- or -ei-?

i before *e*
except after *c*.

(This rule applies only to words in which the sound is long *ē*.)

e.g.	*belief*	*believe*	*grief*	*pier*	*siege*
	ceiling	*conceit*	*deceit*	*deceive*	

Exceptions are *seize, weird* and personal names (e.g. *Neil, Sheila*) and certain surnames.

The doubling of a final consonant before a following vowel

(1) In a word of one syllable with a short vowel, the final consonant is doubled:

e.g.	*man*	*manning*	*manned*	*mannish*
	red	*redder*	*reddest*	*redden*
	sin	*sinning*	*sinned*	*sinner*
	stop	*stopping*	*stopped*	*stopper*
	drum	*drumming*	*drummed*	*drummer*

(2) In a word of more than one syllable with a short final vowel, the final consonant is doubled only if the accent is on the final syllable:

e.g.	*entrap'*	*entrapping*	*entrapped*	
	regret'	*regretting*	*regretted*	
	begin'	*beginning*	*beginner*	
	occur'	*occurring*	*occurred*	*occurrence*
but	*en'ter*	*entering*	*entered*	
	prof'it	*profiting*	*profited*	
	gall'op	*galloping*	*galloped*	
	hicc'up	*hiccuping*	*hiccuped*	

(3)   In British English (but not in American) **-l** is doubled no matter where the accent falls:

e.g.	*compel'*	*compelling*	*compelled*
and also	*trav'el*	*travelling*	*travelled*	*traveller*

(4)   Some derivatives of words ending in **-s** can be spelt in two ways: e.g. *bias.*

Certain words ending in **-p** are not treated strictly in accordance with the rule stated in (2) above, e.g. *kidnap, handicap.*

Derivatives of words with final -e

(1)   Before a vowel (including **y**), **-e** is usually dropped:

e.g.	*come*	*coming*	*hate*	*hating*	*rage*	*raging*
	fame	*famous*	*pale*	*palish*	*use*	*usable*
	ice	*icy*	*noise*	*noisy*	*stone*	*stony*

Some exceptions are intended to distinguish one word from another:

e.g. *holey* (=full of holes), *holy; dyeing, dying.*

(2)   Before a consonant, **-e** is usually kept:

e.g.   *hateful*   *useless*   *movement*   *paleness*

but see *true, whole, judge* for exceptions.

(3)   **-e-** is kept after soft **-c-** or **-g-** before **-a, -o-**:

e.g.   *noticeable*   *traceable*   *manageable*   *advantageous*

Plural of words ending in -f

It is usual to add *s* to make the plural form, e.g. *roof, roofs,* but there are several exceptions, e.g. *calves, elves, knives, leaves.*

   Some words have optional spellings, e.g. *hoof* (*hoofs,* or *hooves*), *scarf, wharf, handkerchief.*

The suffix -ful

Take care in spelling adjectives formed by the addition of *-ful,* e.g.
            care+full=careful
            help+full=helpful

Irregular plurals

Where a noun has an irregular plural form it is usually shown in its entry in the Dictionary (Part VII).

1.5 Words confused and misused

accept	check	currant	fiancé
except	cheque	current	fiancée
access	choir	deduce	forceful
excess	quire	deduct	forcible
advice	chord	defective	foreward
advise	cord	deficient	forward
adverse	collaborate	deprecate	formally
averse	corroborate	depreciate	formerly
affect	complement	desert	gaol
effect	compliment	dessert	goal
allude	comprise	device	gild
elude	consist	devise	guild
allusion	concert	draft	gilt
delusion	consort	draught	guilt
illusion			
	concise	dual	gorilla
amend	precise	duel	guerrilla
emend	confidant	elicit	hangar
amoral	confident	illicit	hanger
immoral	confidante		
		eligible	hoard
aural	contemptuous	legible	horde
oral	contemptible		
	continual	emigrant	illegible
bail	continuous	immigrant	ineligible
bale			
berth	correspondent	eminent	imaginary
birth	co-respondent	imminent	imaginative
born	corps	ensure	imply
borne	corpse	insure	infer
breath	council	exceedingly	impractical
breathe	counsel	excessively	unpractical
cannon	councillor	exercise	inapt
canon	counsellor	exorcise	inept
canvas	credible	faint	ingenious
canvass	creditable	feint	ingenuous

interment	motif	pray	shear
internment	motive	prey	sheer
lair	naught	premier	stationary
layer	nought	première	stationery
lath	negligent	principle	storey
lathe	negligible	principal	story
lay	noxious	prophecy	straight
lie	obnoxious	prophesy	strait
licence	oculist	quiet	superficial
license	optician	quite	superfluous
lightening	official	raise	surplice
lightning	officious	raze	surplus
liqueur	peal	rare	swingeing
liquor	peel	unique	swinging
loath	persecute	recourse	team
loathe	prosecute	resource	teem
loose	personal	reverend	venal
lose	personnel	reverent	venial
metal	pore	review	veracity
mettle	pour	revue	voracity
meter	practice	sceptic	waive
metre	practise	septic	wave

2 FORMS OF ADDRESS

2.1 Correct forms of address

At some time you may wish to write to a peer of the realm or to a person holding some official title or position. You may be aware that etiquette requires the use of certain phrases such as 'His Grace' 'His Worship' or 'My Lord', but may be uncertain about which is the correct form to use.

To help with this problem, information is given below on how to address and begin a formal letter to such people, and also on how to address them when speaking to them. Where no form of spoken address is given, you may assume that no special style exists. *Note*: in the forms of address given below, 'S——' stands for surname and 'F——' for forename.

Air Force—see **Officers.**

Ambassador, British ——*Address on envelope*: 'His/Her Excellency' (HE) (in other respects according to the ambassador's rank), followed if desired by 'HM Ambassador'. *Note*: His/Her Excellency (HE) is not used in the United Kingdom. The wife of an ambassador is not entitled to the style 'Her Excellency'. *Begin*: 'Sir' or 'Madam' (or according to rank). *Close*: 'I have the honour to be, Sir/Madam (or according to rank) Your Excellency's obedient servant'. *Spoken address*: 'Your Excellency' at least once, thereafter 'Sir' or 'Madam', or by name.

Ambassador, foreign ——*Address on envelope*: 'His/Her Excellency the Ambassador of ——' or 'His/Her Excellency the —— Ambassador'. The wife of an ambassador is not entitled to the style 'Her Excellency'. *Begin*: 'Your Excellency', refer to as 'Your Excellency' once, thereafter as 'you'. *Close*: 'I have the honour to be, Sir/Madam (or according to rank), Your Excellency's obedient servant'. *Spoken address*: 'Your Excellency' at least once, thereafter 'Sir' or 'Madam', or by name.

Archbishop (Church of England and Churches in the Anglican Communion) ——*Address on envelope*: 'The Most Reverend the Lord Archbishop of ——'; the Archbishops of Canterbury and York are Privy Counsellors and should be addressed as 'The Most Reverend and Right Hon. the Lord Archbishop of ——'. *Begin*: 'Dear Archbishop' or 'My Lord Archbishop'. *Spoken address*: 'Your Grace'; begin an official speech 'My Lord Archbishop'.

Archbishop (Church of England, etc.) retired —— reverts to Bishop; see **Bishop (Church of England, etc.) retired.**

Archbishop (Roman Catholic) ——*Address on envelope*: 'His Grace the Archbishop of ——'. *Begin*: 'My Lord Archbishop'. *Close*: 'I remain, Your Grace, Yours faithfully' or 'Yours faithfully'. *Spoken address*: 'Your Grace'.

Archbishop (Roman Catholic) retired ——*Address on envelope*: 'The Most Reverend Archbishop [S——]'. Otherwise as for a Roman Catholic archbishop.

Archdeacon ——*Address on envelope*: 'The Venerable the Archdeacon of ——'. *Begin*: 'Dear Archdeacon' or 'Venerable Sir'. *Spoken address*: 'Archdeacon'; begin an official speech 'Venerable Sir'.

Army—see **Officers**.

Attorney-General—as for a Secretary of State.

Baron ——*Address on envelope*: 'The Right Hon. the Lord ——'. *Begin*: 'My Lord'. *Spoken address*: 'My Lord'.

Baroness (Baron's wife) ——*Address on envelope*: 'The Right Hon. the Lady [S——]. *Begin*: 'Dear Madam'. *Spoken address*: 'Madam'.

Baroness (in her own right) ——*Address on envelope*: either in the same way as a Baron's wife, or, if she prefers, as 'The Right Hon. the Baroness [S——]'. Otherwise as for a Baron's wife.

Baron's daughter ——*Address on envelope*: if unmarried, 'The Hon. [F—— S——]'; if married to a commoner, 'The Hon. Mrs [husband's surname]'; if married to a Baron or Knight, 'The Hon. Lady [husband's surname]'; if the wife of a peer or courtesy peer, address as such. *Begin*: 'Dear Madam', or according to rank. *Spoken address*: 'Miss/Mrs [S——]', or according to rank.

Baron's son ——*Address on envelope*: 'The Hon. [F—— S——]'; the eldest sons of Barons in the peerage of Scotland are usually addressed 'The Master of [peerage title]'. *Begin*: 'Dear Sir'. *Spoken address*: 'Mr [S——]' or 'Sir'; a Master may also be addressed as 'Master'.

Baron's son's wife ——*Address on envelope*: 'The Hon. Mrs [husband's forename and surname]'; if the daughter of a Viscount or Baron, 'The Hon. Mrs [husband's surname]'; if the daughter of a Duke, Marquess or Earl, address as such. *Begin*: 'Dear Madam', or according to rank. *Spoken address*: according to rank.

Baronet ——*Address on envelope*: 'Sir [F—— S——], Bt'. *Begin*: 'Dear Sir'. *Spoken address*: 'Sir [F——]'.

Baronet's wife ——*Address on envelope*: 'Lady [S——]'; if she has the title 'Lady' by courtesy, 'Lady [F—— S——]'; if she has the courtesy style 'The Hon.', this precedes 'Lady'. *Begin*: 'Dear Madam'. *Spoken address*: 'Madam'.

Bishop, Diocesan (Church of England and Churches in the

Anglican Communion) ——*Address on envelope*: 'The Right Reverend the Lord Bishop of ——'; the Bishop of London is a Privy Counsellor, so is addressed as 'The Right Rev. and Right Hon. the Lord Bishop of London'; the Bishop of Meath is styled 'The Most Reverend', not 'The Right Reverend'. *Begin*: 'Dear Bishop' or 'My Lord'. *Spoken address*: 'Bishop'; begin an official speech 'My Lord'.

Bishop (Church of England, etc.) retired ——*Address on envelope*: 'The Right Reverend [F—— S——]'; if a Privy Counsellor, 'The Right Rev. and Right Hon. [F—— S——]'. *Begin*: 'Dear Bishop', 'My Lord' or 'Right Reverend Sir'. *Spoken address*: 'Bishop'; begin an official speech 'My Lord' or 'Right Reverend Sir'.

Bishop (Episcopal Church in Scotland) ——*Address on envelope*: 'The Right Reverend [F—— S——], Bishop of ——'. Otherwise as for a bishop of the Church of England. The bishop who holds the position of Primus is addressed as 'The Most Reverend the Primus'. *Begin*: 'Dear Primus'. *Spoken address*: 'Primus'.

Bishop (Roman Catholic) ——*Address on envelope*: 'His Lordship the Bishop of ——' or 'The Right Reverend [F—— S——], Bishop of ——'; in Ireland, 'The Most Reverend' is used instead of 'The Right Reverend'; if an auxiliary bishop, address as 'The Right Reverend [F—— S——], Auxiliary Bishop of ——'. *Begin*: 'My Lord' or, more rarely, 'My Lord Bishop'. *Close*: 'I remain, My Lord (or, more rarely, 'My Lord Bishop'), Yours faithfully', or Yours faithfully'. *Spoken address*: 'My Lord' or, more rarely, 'My Lord Bishop'.

Bishop, Suffragan (Church of England and Churches in the Anglican Communion) ——*Address on envelope*: 'The Right Reverend the Bishop of ——'. *Begin*: 'Dear Bishop', 'My Lord' or 'Right Reverend Sir'; begin an official speech 'My Lord' or 'Right Reverend Sir'. Otherwise as for a Diocesan Bishop.

Bishop, US (1) **Protestant Episcopal Church** ——*Address on envelope*: 'The Right Reverend [F—— S——]'. *Begin*: 'Right Reverend Sir' or 'Dear Bishop'. *Spoken address*: 'Bishop [S——]'.

    (2) **Methodist Church** ——*Address on envelope*: 'The Reverend [F—— S——]'. *Begin*: 'Reverend Sir' or 'Dear Bishop'. *Spoken address*: 'Bishop [S——]'.

Cabinet Minister—see **Secretary of State.**

Canon (Church of England and Churches in the Anglican Communion) ——*Address on envelope*: 'The Reverend Canon [F—— S——]'. *Begin*: 'Dear Canon' or 'Dear Canon [S——]'. *Spoken address*: 'Canon' or 'Canon [S——]'.

Canon (Roman Catholic) ——*Address on envelope*: 'The Very

Reverend Canon [F— S——]'. *Begin*: 'Very Reverend Sir'. *Spoken address*: 'Canon [S——]'.

Cardinal —*Address on envelope*: 'His Eminence Cardinal [S——]'; if an archbishop, 'His Eminence the Cardinal Archbishop of —'. *Begin*: 'Your Eminence' or, more rarely, 'My Lord Cardinal'. *Close*: 'I remain, Your Eminence (or 'My Lord Cardinal'), Yours faithfully'. *Spoken address*: 'Your Eminence'.

Chairman of County Council, Regional Council, etc. —*Address on envelope*: 'The Chairman of the — Council'. *Begin*: 'Dear Mr Chairman', even if the holder of the office is a woman. *Spoken address*: 'Mr Chairman', even to a woman, or by name.

Clergy (1) **Church of England and Churches in the Anglican Communion.** *Address on envelope*: 'The Reverend [F— S——]'. *Begin*: 'Dear Sir' or 'Dear Mr [S——]'.

(2) **Roman Catholic** —*Address on envelope*: 'The Reverend [F— S——]'; if a member of a religious order, the initials of the order should be added after the name. *Begin*: 'Dear Reverend Father'.

(3) **Church of Scotland and other churches** —*Address on envelope*: 'The Reverend F—' S——. *Begin*: 'Dear Sir/Madam' or 'Dear Mr/Mrs etc. [S——]'.

Companion of an order of knighthood —the initials 'CB', 'CMG' or 'CH' (as it may be) follow the ordinary form of address.

Consul, British —*Address on envelope*: [F— S——], Esq., British Consul-General/Consul/Vice-Consul'; a Consul-General, Consul or Vice-Consul holding Her Majesty's Commission is addressed as 'HM Consul', etc., rather than as 'British Consul', etc.

Countess —*Address on envelope*: 'The Right Hon. the Countess of —'. *Begin*: 'Dear Madam'. *Spoken address*: 'Madam'.

Dame —*Address on envelope*: 'Dame [F— S——]', followed by the letters of the order; if a peeress or the daughter of a Duke, Marquess or Earl, 'Lady [F— S——]' followed by the letters of the order; if styled 'The Hon.' then this precedes 'Dame'. *Begin*: 'Dear Madam'. *Spoken address*: 'Madam'.

Dean (Anglican) —*Address on envelope*: 'The Very Reverend the Dean of —'. *Begin*: 'Dear Dean' or 'Very Reverend Sir'. *Spoken address*: 'Dean'; begin an official speech 'Very Reverend Sir'.

Doctor —physicians, anaesthetists, pathologists and radiologists are addressed as 'Doctor'. Surgeons, whether they hold the degree of Doctor of Medicine or not, are known as Mr/Mrs. In England and Wales, obstetricians and gynaecologists are addressed as Mr/Mrs, but in Scotland, Ireland and elsewhere as 'Doctor'. In addressing a letter to the holder of a doctorate, the initials DD, LLD, MD, MusD, etc., are placed after the ordinary form of address, as 'The Rev. John Smith, DD', 'John Brown, Esq., LLD', but 'The Rev. Dr Smith' and 'Dr John Brown' are also frequently used.

Dowager ——*Address on envelope*: on the marriage of a peer or baronet, the widow of the previous holder of the title becomes 'Dowager' and is addressed 'The Right Hon. the Dowager Countess of ——', 'The Right Hon. the Dowager Lady ——', etc. If there already is a Dowager still living, she retains this title, the later widow being addressed 'The Most Hon. [F——], Marchioness of ——', 'The Right Hon. [F——], Lady ——', etc. It should be noted, however, that many Dowagers prefer the style which includes their Christian names to that including the title Dowager. (*Begin*, etc. as for a peer's wife).

Duchess ——*Address on envelope*: 'Her Grace the Duchess of ——'. *Begin*: 'Dear Madam'. *Spoken address*: 'Your Grace'. (For Royal Duchess, see **Princess**).

Duke ——*Address on envelope*: 'His Grace the Duke of ——'. *Begin*: 'My Lord Duke'. *Spoken address*: 'Your Grace'. (For Royal Duke, see **Prince**).

Duke's daughter ——*Address on envelope*: 'Lady [F—— S——]', the surname being that of her husband if she is married. If married to a peer, she is addressed according to her husband's rank only; this, however, does not necessarily hold in the case of peers by courtesy. If married to a person with the style 'The Hon.', she does not adopt this but retains the title 'Lady'. *Begin*: 'Dear Madam'. *Spoken address*: 'Madam'.

Duke's eldest son and son's heir ——*Address on envelope*: A Duke's eldest son takes his father's second title. This courtesy title is treated as if it were an actual peerage (but see notes p 24). The son's eldest son takes his grandfather's third title, also being addressed as if a peer. (*Begin*, etc. according to rank).

Duke's eldest son's wife ——*Address on envelope*: as if her husband's courtesy title were an actual peerage (but see notes p 24).

Duke's younger son ——*Address on envelope*: 'Lord [F—— S——]'. *Begin*: 'My Lord'. *Spoken address*: 'My Lord'.

Duke's younger son's wife ——*Address on envelope*: 'Lady [husband's forename and surname]'. *Begin*: 'Dear Madam'. *Spoken address*: 'Madam'.

Earl ——*Address on envelope*: 'The Right Hon. the Earl of ——'. *Begin*: 'My Lord'. *Spoken address*: 'My Lord'. (For Earl's wife, see **Countess**).

Earl's daughter—as Duke's daughter.
Earl's eldest son and son's wife—as Duke's eldest son and son's wife.
Earl's younger son and son's wife—as Baron's son and son's wife.

Firms —*Address on envelope*: the term 'Messrs' is becoming archaic. It cannot be used with the name of a limited company, nor in addressing a firm (a) which does not trade under a surname, (b) whose name includes a rank or title, or (c) which bears the name of a woman. *Begin*: 'Dear Sirs'.

Governor of a colony or **Governor-General** —*Address on envelope*: 'His Excellency [ordinary designation], Governor (-General) of ——'. The Governor-General of Canada has the rank of 'Right Honourable' which he retains for life. The wife of a Governor-General is styled 'Her Excellency' within the country her husband administers. *Begin*: according to rank. *Close*: 'I have the honour to be, Sir (or 'My Lord' if a peer), Your Excellency's obedient servant'. *Spoken address*: 'Your Excellency'.

Judge, High Court —*Address on envelope*: if a man, 'The Hon. Mr Justice [S——]'; if a woman, 'The Hon. Mrs Justice [S——]'. *Begin*: 'Dear Sir/Madam'; if on judicial matters, 'My Lord/Lady'. *Spoken address*: 'Sir/Madam'; only on the bench or when dealing with judicial matters should a High Court Judge be addressed as 'My Lord/Lady' or referred to as 'Your Lordship/Ladyship'.

Judge, Circuit —*Address on envelope*: 'His/Her Honour Judge [S——]'; if a Knight, 'His Honour Judge Sir [F—— S——]'. *Begin*: 'Dear Sir/Madam'. *Spoken address*: 'Sir/Madam'; address as 'Your Honour' only when on the bench or dealing with judicial matters.

Judge, Irish—as English Circuit Judge.

Judge, Scottish—see **Lord of Session.**

Justice of the Peace (England and Wales) —when on the bench, refer to and address as 'Your Worship'. Otherwise according to rank. The letters 'JP' may be added after the person's name in addressing a letter, if desired.

Knight Bachelor—as Baronet, except that 'Bt' is omitted.

Knight of the Bath, of St Michael and St George, etc. —*Address on envelope*: 'Sir [F—— S——]', with the initials 'GCB', 'KCB', KCMG' (as it may be) added. *Begin*: 'Dear Sir'.

Knight of the Garter, or of the Thistle —*Address on envelope*: The initials 'KG' or 'KT' are to be added to the address. (*Begin*, etc. according to rank).

Knight's wife, (whether wife of a Knight Bachelor or of a Knight of an order of chivalry)—as Baronet's wife or according to rank.

Lady Mayoress ——*Address on envelope*: 'The Lady Mayoress of ——'. *Begin*: 'My Lady Mayoress'. *Spoken address*: '(My) Lady Mayoress'.

Lady Provost ——*Address on envelope*: 'The Lady Provost of ——'. *Begin*: 'My Lady Provost'. *Spoken address*: '(My) Lady Provost'.

Lord Advocate of Scotland ——*Address on envelope*: 'The Right Hon. the Lord Advocate, QC' or 'The Right Hon. [F—— S——], QC'. *Begin*: 'Dear Sir', or 'My Lord' if a peer. Otherwise according to rank.

Lord Chancellor ——*Address on envelope*: 'The Right Hon. the Lord Chancellor'. *Begin*: 'My Lord'. Otherwise according to rank.

Lord Chief Justice ——*Address on envelope*: 'The Right Hon. the Lord Chief Justice of England'. *Begin*: 'My Lord'. Otherwise according to his rank as a peer. The Lord Chief Justice of Northern Ireland is addressed in the same manner unless he is a knight, in which case he is addressed as 'The Right Hon. Sir [F—— S——], Lord Chief Justice of Northern Ireland'.

Lord High Commissioner to the General Assembly ——*Address on envelope*: 'His/Her Grace the Lord High Commissioner'. *Begin*: 'Your Grace'. *Close*: 'I have the honour to remain, Your Grace's most devoted and obedient servant'. *Spoken address*: 'Your Grace'.

Lord Justice-Clerk ——*Address on envelope*: 'The Hon. the Lord Justice-Clerk'; if a Privy Counsellor, 'The Right Hon.'. *Begin*: 'My Lord'. *Spoken address*: 'My Lord'; refer to as 'Your Lordship'. The wife of the Lord Justice-Clerk is styled and addressed in the same manner as the wife of a Lord of Session.

Lord Justice-General of Scotland ——*Address on envelope*: 'The Right Hon. the Lord Justice-General'. *Begin*: 'My Lord'. *Spoken address*: 'My Lord'; refer to as 'Your Lordship'. The wife of the Lord Justice-General is styled and addressed as for the wife of a Lord of Session.

Lord Justice of the Court of Appeal ——*Address on envelope*: 'The Right Hon. Lord Justice [S——]'. *Begin*: 'My Lord'. *Spoken address*: 'My Lord'; refer to as 'Your Lordship'.

Lord Mayor ——*Address on envelope*: The Lord Mayors of London, York, Belfast, Cardiff, Dublin and also Melbourne, Sydney, Adelaide, Perth, Brisbane and Hobart are styled 'The Right Hon. the Lord Mayor of ——'; other Lord Mayors are styled 'The Right Worshipful the Lord Mayor of ——'. *Begin*: 'My Lord Mayor', even if the holder of the office is a woman. *Spoken address*: '(My) Lord Mayor'.

Lord Mayor's wife—see **Lady Mayoress.**

Lord of Appeal in Ordinary and his wife—as Baron and Baroness. Their children are styled as those of a Baron.

Lord of Session in Scotland —*Address on envelope*: 'The Hon. Lord [S——]'; if a Privy Counsellor, 'The Right Hon.'. *Begin*: 'My Lord'. *Spoken address*: 'My Lord'; refer to as 'Your Lordship'. The wife of a Lord of Session is styled 'Lady' and is addressed as for the wife of a Baron, but without the prefix 'The Right Hon.'.

Lord Provost —*Address on envelope*: 'The Right Hon. the Lord Provost of Edinburgh/Glasgow', but 'The Lord Provost of Aberdeen/Dundee'. *Begin*: 'My Lord Provost'. *Spoken address*: 'My Lord Provost'.

Lord Provost's wife—see **Lady Provost.**

Marchioness —*Address on envelope*: 'The Most Hon. the Marchioness of ——'. *Begin*: 'Dear Madam'. *Spoken address*: 'Madam'.

Marquess —*Address on envelope*: 'The Most Hon. the Marquess of ——'. *Begin*: 'My Lord'. *Spoken address*: 'My Lord'.

Marquess's daughter—as Duke's daughter.

Marquess's sons and sons' wives—as Duke's sons and sons' wives.

Master—a title borne by the eldest son of a Baron or Viscount in the peerage of Scotland. See **Baron's son.**

Mayor —*Address on envelope*: 'The Worshipful the Mayor of ——'; in the case of cities and certain towns, 'The Right Worshipful'. *Begin*: 'Mr Mayor', even if the mayor is a woman, although some women prefer 'Madam Mayor'. *Spoken address*: 'Mr Mayor'.

Mayoress —*Address on envelope*: 'The Mayoress of ——'. *Begin*: 'Madam Mayoress'. *Spoken address*: 'Mayoress'.

Member of Parliament —*Address on envelope*: add 'MP' to the usual form of address. (*Begin*, etc. according to rank).

Moderator of the General Assembly of the Church of Scotland —*Address on envelope*: 'The Right Reverend the Moderator of the General Assembly of the Church of Scotland' or 'The Right Reverend [F—— S——]'. *Begin*: 'Dear Sir' or 'Dear Moderator'. *Spoken address*: 'Moderator'. Ex-moderators are styled 'The Very Reverend'.

Moderator of the General Assembly of the United Reformed Church —*Address on envelope*: 'The Right Reverend [F—— S——]'. *Begin*: 'Dear Moderator'. *Spoken address*: 'Moderator' or 'Mr Moderator'. Ex-moderators are styled 'The Reverend'.

Monsignor ——*Address on envelope*: 'The Reverend Monsignor [F——S——]'; if a canon, 'The Very Reverend Monsignor (Canon) [F——S——]'. *Begin*: 'Reverend Sir'. *Spoken address*: 'Monsignor [S——]'.

Officers in the Army, Navy and Air Force ——*Address on envelope*: the professional rank is prefixed to any other rank, e.g. 'Admiral the Right Hon. the Earl of ——', 'Lieut.-Col. Sir [F—— S——], KCB'; officers below the rank of Rear-Admiral, and Marshal of the Royal Air Force are entitled to 'RN' (or 'Royal Navy'), and 'RAF' respectively after their name. Army officers of the rank of Colonel or below may follow their name with the name of their regiment or corps (or an abbreviation thereof). Officers in the women's services add 'WRNS', 'WRAF', 'WRAC'. *Begin*: according to social rank.

Officers, retired and former ——*Address on envelope*: officers above the rank of Lieutenant (in the Royal Navy), Captain (in the Army) and Flight Lieutenant may continue to use and be addressed by their armed forces rank after being placed on the retired list. The word 'retired', or any abbreviation thereof, should not normally be placed after the person's name. Former officers in the women's services do not normally continue to use their ranks.

Pope ——*Address on envelope*: 'His Holiness, the Pope'. *Begin*: 'Your Holiness' or 'Most Holy Father'. *Close*: if a Roman Catholic, 'I have the honour to be, your Holiness's most devoted and obedient child' (or 'most humble child'); if not Roman Catholic, 'I have the honour to be (or 'remain') Your Holiness's obedient servant'. *Spoken address*: 'Your Holiness'.

Prebendary—as Church of England Canon.

Prime Minister ——*Address on envelope*: according to rank; the Prime Minister is a Privy Counsellor (see separate entry) and the letter should be addressed accordingly. (*Begin*, etc. according to rank).

Prince ——*Address on envelope*: if a Duke, 'His Royal Highness the Duke of ——'; if not a Duke, 'His Royal Highness the Prince [F——]', if a child of the sovereign, otherwise, 'His Royal Highness Prince [F——] of [Kent or Gloucester]' but see notes p 24. *Begin*: 'Sir'. Refer to as 'Your Royal Highness'. *Close*: 'I have the honour to remain (or be), Sir, Your Royal Highness's most humble and obedient servant'. *Spoken address*: 'Your Royal Highness' once, thereafter 'Sir'.

Princess ——*Address on envelope*: if a Duchess, 'Her Royal Highness the Duchess of ——'; if not a Duchess, the daughter of a sovereign is addressed as 'Her Royal Highness the Princess [F——]' followed by any title she holds by marriage; 'the' is omitted in addressing a princess who is not the daughter of a sovereign; a Princess by marriage is addressed 'HRH Princess [husband's forename] of —'; but see notes p 24. *Begin*: 'Madam'. Refer to as 'Your Royal Highness'. *Close*: as for Prince, substituting 'Madam' for 'Sir'. *Spoken address*: 'Your Royal Highness' once, thereafter 'Ma'am'.

Privy Counsellor —*Address on envelope*: if a peer, 'The Right Hon. the Earl of —, PC'; if not a peer, 'The Right Hon. [F— S—]', without the 'PC'. (*Begin*, etc. according to rank).

Professor —*Address on envelope*: 'Professor [F— S—]'; the styles 'Professor Lord [S—]', 'Professor Sir [F— S—]', etc. are frequently used but are deprecated by some people; if the professor is in holy orders, 'The Reverend Professor'. *Begin*: 'Dear Sir/Madam', or according to rank. *Spoken address*: according to rank.

Provost, Roman Catholic—as Roman Catholic Canon.

Provost, Town —*Address on envelope*: 'The Provost of —'. *Begin*: 'Dear Provost'. *Spoken address*: 'Provost'.

Queen —*Address on envelope*: 'Her Majesty the Queen'. *Begin*: 'Madam, with my humble duty' but see notes p 24. Refer to as 'Your Majesty'. *Close*: 'I have the honour to remain (or be), Madam, Your Majesty's most humble and obedient servant'. *Spoken address*: 'Your Majesty' once, thereafter 'Ma'am'; begin an official speech 'May it please Your Majesty'.

Queen Mother—as for the Queen, substituting 'Queen Elizabeth The Queen Mother' for 'The Queen'.

Queen's Counsel—append 'QC' to ordinary address, but not if addressing a letter to a person holding one of the higher legal appointments such as a High Court Judge or Lord of Appeal in Ordinary.

Rabbi —*Address on envelope*: 'Rabbi [initial and surname]' or, if a doctor, 'Rabbi Doctor [initial and surname]'. *Begin*: 'Dear Sir'. *Spoken address*: 'Rabbi [S—]' or 'Doctor [S—]'.

Secretary of State —*Address on envelope*: 'The Right Hon. [F— S—], MP, Secretary of State for —', or 'The Secretary of State for —'. Otherwise according to rank.

Viscount —*Address on envelope*: 'The Right Hon. the Viscount —'. *Begin*: 'My Lord'. *Spoken address*: 'My Lord'.

Viscountess —*Address on envelope*: 'The Right Hon. the Viscountess —'. *Begin*: 'Dear Madam'. *Spoken address*: 'Madam'.

Viscount's daughter, son and son's wife—as Baron's daughter, son and son's wife.

Some general notes

Closing a letter   The simplest correct way of closing a formal letter is 'Yours faithfully'. The longer very formal ceremonial styles are now seldom used, but they have been noted in the preceding list where they are still appropriate.

Courtesy titles   Holders of courtesy titles are addressed according to their rank, but without 'The', 'The Right Hon.' or 'The Most Hon.'.

Ranks   Ranks in the armed forces and ecclesiastical and ambassadorial ranks *precede* titles in the peerage, e.g. 'Colonel the Earl of ——' or 'The Rev. the Marquess of ——'.

Royal family   Although the correct forms of address are given in this section for use in communications addressed to members of the Royal family, it should be noted that it is more normal practice for letters to be addressed to their private secretary, equerry or lady-in-waiting.

For more detailed information, see especially Debrett's *Correct Form*, Black's *Titles and Forms of Address*, or contact the Foreign and Commonwealth Office's Protocol Department.

2.2 Orders, decorations and medals

General rules

The correct order for post-nominal letters is as follows:

1. Decorations and honours according to precedence.
2. Royal appointments (PC, ADC, QHP, QHS, QHDS, QHNS, QHC, QC, JP, DL). Of these only QC must be used in addressing. PC is rarely used, and JP and DL are only required if the letter concerns matters directly connected with that office.
3. University degrees.
4. Medical qualifications.
5. Fellowships and memberships (of professional bodies, societies etc.). Election to certain distinguished bodies should always be recognised, e.g. FRS, RA, ARA, RSA, FBA.
6. Appointments/offices, e.g. MP, WS.

Bt (for Baronet) must precede all other post-nominal letters; VC, GC and CV then take precedence over all other honours.

Kt (for Knight Bachelor) should never be used after the name.
PC (if used) follows KG.

British and Commonwealth honours

The following list shows British and Commonwealth honours in order of precedence. Any honours indicated by * carry the title 'Sir' or 'Lady', unless the holder has a higher rank e.g. Baron, which carries the title 'Lord'.

VC	Victoria Cross
GC	George Cross
CV	Cross of Valour (Aus.)
*KG	Knight of the Garter
*KT	Knight of the Thistle
*KP	Knight of the Order of St Patrick
*GCB	Knight/Dame Grand Cross of the Order of the Bath
*OM	Order of Merit
*AK	Knight of the Order of Australia
*AD	Dame of the Order of Australia
*GCSI	Knight Grand Commander of the Order of the Star of India
*GCMG	Knight/Dame Grand Cross of the Order of St Michael and St George
*GCIE	Knight Grand Commander of the Order of the Indian Empire
*CI	Imperial Order of the Crown of India
*GCVO	Knight/Dame Grand Cross of the Royal Victorian Order
*GBE	Knight/Dame Grand Cross of the Order of the British Empire
AC	Companion of the Order of Australia
CH	Companion of Honour
*KCB	Knight Commander of the Order of the Bath
*DCB	Dame Commander of the Order of the Bath
*KCSI	Knight Commander of the Order of The Star of India
*KCMG	Knight Commander of the Order of St Michael and St George
*DCMG	Dame Commander of the Order of St Michael and St George
*KCIE	Knight Commander of the Order of the Indian Empire
*KCVO	Knight Commander of the Royal Victorian Order
*DCVO	Dame Commander of the Royal Victorian Order

*KBE	Knight Commander of the Order of the British Empire
*DBE	Dame Commander of the Order of the British Empire
***Knight Bachelor**	
AO	Officer of the Order of Australia
CB	Companion of the Order of the Bath
CSI	Companion of the Order of the Star of India
CMG	Companion of the Order of St Michael and St George
CIE	Companion of the Order of the Indian Empire
CVO	Commander of the Royal Victorian Order
CBE	Commander of the Order of the British Empire
SC	Star of Courage
DSO	Companion of the Distinguished Service Order
AM	Member of the Order of Australia
LVO	Member (now Lieutenant) of the Royal Victorian Order (4th Class)
OBE	Officer of the Order of the British Empire
ISO	Companion of the Imperial Service Order
MVO	Member of the Royal Victorian Order (5th Class)
MBE	Member of the Order of the British Empire
RRC	Member of the Royal Red Cross (1st Class)
DSC	Distinguished Service Cross
MC	Military Cross
DFC	Distinguished Flying Cross
AFC	Air Force Cross
ARRC	Member of the Royal Red Cross (2nd Class)
GCStJ	Bailiff Grand Cross of the Order of St John of Jerusalem
AM	Albert Medal
DCM	Distinguished Conduct Medal
CGM	Conspicuous Gallantry Medal
GM	George Medal
BM	Bravery Medal (Aus.)
QPM	Queen's Police Medal for Gallantry
QFSM	Queen's Fire Service Medal for Gallantry
DSM	Distinguished Service Medal
MM	Military Medal
DFM	Distinguished Flying Medal
AFM	Air Force Medal
QGM	Queen's Gallantry Medal
BEM	British Empire Medal
QPM	Queen's Police Medal for Distinguished Service
QFSM	Queen's Fire Service Medal for Distinguished Service
Commendation for Brave Conduct	(Aus.)

Queen's Commendation for Brave Conduct
War Medals and Stars—in order of the date of campaign for which they were awarded
Polar Medals—in order of date
RVM   Royal Victorian Medal
Imperial Service Medal
Defence Force Service Medal
Reserve Force Decoration
Reserve Force Medal
National Medal
Coronation, Jubilee and other commemorative medals
Long Service Medals
VD   Victorian Decoration
ERD   Emergency Reserve Decoration
TD   Territorial Decoration
ED   Efficiency Decoration
RD   Royal Navy and Royal Marine Forces Reserve Decoration
AE   Air Efficiency Award
Foreign orders, decorations and medals (respectively)—in order of date

Commonwealth orders

The Order of Australia grades are shown in their appropriate positions in the above list, but for citizens of other Commonwealth countries the letters designating their own national orders should *precede* any other honours (other than VC or GC).

Thus, for Canadian citizens:

CC   Companion of the Order of Canada
OC   Officer of the Order of Canada
CM   Member of the Order of Canada

follow VC or GC and *precede* any other honours.

For New Zealand citizens:

QSO   Queens Service Order of New Zealand   *precedes* OBE.
QSM   Queens Service Medal of New Zealand   *follows* QGM.

3 BUSINESS COMMUNICATION
Oral

Good communication is the key factor in business. Despite the increasing application of microchip technology good relationships between people are built up through effective oral communication. It is important to develop a clear, natural speaking voice, a courteous manner and a tactful approach.

The spoken word is the least costly method of communication but to be effective demands the full attention of both the speaker and the hearer. Ideas can be exchanged, difficulties and problems solved, often more amicably by face-to-face conversation than by any other means. When sitting opposite one another personal reactions can be judged more precisely and a shift of emphasis or change of approach can often achieve the desired outcome. The main disadvantage of business deals transacted in this way is that there may be no record of the conversation. This can, of course, be overcome by a subsequent letter of confirmation.

Courteousness should always be maintained even in the most frustrating circumstances. In busy offices it is often necessary to interrupt other people at work but this is usually accepted with good grace if an apology introduces the request and a suitable tone of voice is adopted. Politeness between office personnel helps to make a more pleasant working atmosphere, although it is not always possible, of course, to like every member of staff.

A tactful manner should be cultivated. The ability to judge when and how to approach colleagues is an important asset in business life. When making a request, or discussing a new idea, choosing the right time can have a crucial effect upon the outcome.

How to address colleagues is a matter of protocol within each firm. Today first names seem to be the norm but it is wise to retain a degree of formality when addressing top executives, or people being introduced and met for the first time. An over-friendly manner may be misinterpreted and may not assist in promoting a good business relationship.

3.1 Reception of visitors to an office

Arrangements for receiving callers vary according to the size and type of organisation. Whether a full-time receptionist is employed or a secretary has to combine this role with other work, the receptionist is the first contact callers have with the firm.

Receptionist

Personal attributes of a receptionist:
> a pleasant personality and speaking voice
> a willingness to be helpful to visitors
> a smart appearance
> some work experience within the firm, in order to have gained a good understanding of its work.

To perform the role efficiently a receptionist needs:
> details of all employees i.e. name, status within the firm, department and telephone extension
> point of contact for executives i.e. personal assistant or secretary
> a copy of the daily appointments register (see p 30)
> up-to-date information on changes within the firm, i.e. movement of staff, absences, those on flexitime (if appropriate) and any other unusual occurrence which may affect callers
> a good internal communication system for contacting persons required by callers i.e. internal telephone, paging device, loudspeaker intercom (depending upon the requirements of the organisation).

Reception

The reception area or room should:
> be adequately furnished with comfortable chairs
> be well lighted, heated and ventilated
> contain magazines, as well as trade and company literature, if appropriate
> have facilities for refreshments if a caller is kept waiting.

Visitors

Visitors may be:
> people with appointments—business customers, clients or representatives, personal friends of executives/staff

members of the firm who need access to executives or managers (*Note:* This is sometimes arranged through a secretary.)

people without appointments—may be genuine contacts or 'time wasters'.

Procedure

(1) *Callers with appointments*

Welcome callers courteously; frequent visitors should be greeted by name.

Check the appointments register, which should list the names of expected visitors, time of arrival, and the persons they wish to see.

Contact any persons required to see if they are free. When using intercom devices speak slowly and clearly. Make sure names are pronounced correctly. Remember that what is said can be heard by the visitor. Never carry on a private conversation when attending to a visitor.

If the person required is available, ask the messenger (if one is employed), secretary or designated person to accompany the caller to the meeting place. Do not leave callers to find their own way.

If the person required is not immediately available, apologise and ask the caller to wait in reception.

If there is prolonged delay explain the reason and apologise again. At this stage it may be prudent to find another person to see the caller, or to arrange another appointment.

If a receptionist has a combined role (e.g. switchboard operator or typist) care should be taken to ensure that the visitor is given priority over other duties.

(2) *Callers without appointments*

These visitors require careful handling to discover if they are genuine or 'time wasting'.

Find out the purpose of the visit and if an immediate interview is necessary see if the person required is available.

It is the policy of some firms not to see casual callers and in this case an appointment should be made.

If the caller is an obvious 'time waster' the receptionist should say firmly but tactfully that there is no one available. Suggest that a message is left or an appointment made for another time.

Do not get involved in arguments with visitors. If they become hostile try to remain cool and courteous; seek the help of a senior member of staff if necessary.

3.2 Scheduling appointments

It is usually the secretary's role to prepare a daily appointments sheet for an executive and keep the desk diary up to date. A check should always be made to record any appointments booked directly by the executive. In the first instance appointments should be entered in the desk diary in pencil and inked in when confirmed.

Checklist for booking appointments:

avoid times allocated to routine tasks and meetings

space out appointments in case meetings and discussions run beyond the allotted time

confirm telephone appointments by letter, stating time and place

follow up when appointments are not kept and try to find out the reason

if appointments need to be cancelled through illness or unavoidable urgent business, do this by telephoning and making a new appointment.

3.3 Dictating correspondence

Shorthand

There are a number of advantages in having a shorthand secretary (or shorthand-typist) despite the economy of time in using an audio dictating machine. The personal contact provides greater interest and job satisfaction to the secretary; queries can be raised and settled quickly as they occur. A shorthand secretary should be well informed about the firm and able to advise and assist in many ways. A well-trained and experienced shorthand secretary should be capable of dealing with routine correspondence by composing letters from brief notes.

Guidelines for dictation to a shorthand-typist

Prepare notes for dictation before calling in the shorthand-typist.

Speak clearly. Do not try to dictate whilst smoking or eating.

An experienced shorthand-typist is able to punctuate and paragraph according to the sense of the passage and inflection in the dictator's voice. However, if there are individual preferences regarding punctuation it is as well to indicate them.

Give instructions regarding any special requirements, e.g. extra copies for distribution.

If there are interruptions during dictation (e.g. a difficult or confidential telephone call) signal the shorthand-typist to leave so that time is not wasted.

Avoid mistakes over names, specialist or technical data by giving the shorthand-typist relevant correspondence.

Audio

The use of a dictating machine saves time because recording can be done at any time most convenient to the dictator. A regular flow of small amounts of dictation throughout the day will help the audio-typist to achieve an even output of work. Where dictation tapes can be shared between several audio-typists this further improves the work flow. Dictation can also be recorded after office hours, at home or on the move, i.e. in a car, train or aircraft.

Other advantages of audio are:

the audio-typist is not interrupted by telephone or other calls whilst transcribing

the recording media can be mailed easily so that transcription need not wait until the dictator returns to the office

dictating machines can be used for other purposes: recording interviews and telephone conversations for later transcription; leaving instructions for work to be done during absence; dictating notes for the secretary to compose letters.

Guidelines for dictation to an audio-typist

Make sure the machine is working properly and the controls are understood.

Organise materials and thoughts before starting to dictate. Make any necessary notes to avoid mental blocks occurring during dictation.

Do not switch on until ready to start dictating as gaps in the recording will be confusing to the audio-typist. However, it is wise to leave a space between dictated passages in case it is necessary to insert instructions. Switch off when 'thinking' time is required.

Hold the microphone about 6″ from the mouth. Enunciate words carefully, emphasising word endings and plurals. Do not let the voice fade at the end of a sentence. Use the telephone phonetic alphabet for single letters which might be confused (see p 37).

The audio-typist must be able to understand quickly what is to be typed. Meaning and expression should be indicated by intonation of the voice. Vary the tone and speak more quickly when dictating instructions.

At the beginning of each passage indicate the length of the letter or document (i.e. short, medium or long), the number of copies required and any other particular requirements, e.g. distribution. Index strips are often used to indicate document lengths but it is helpful to the audio-typist in selecting stationery to be told on the recording medium also.

Dictate all punctuation marks and paragraphing, also any special requirements regarding headings, the use of capitals, brackets, etc. The audio-typist will not be able to produce good copy at the first typing unless clear instructions are given.

Erase errors by playing back and recording over.

Remote control system

This involves a pool of dictating machines. Dictators can dial over the internal telephone system, or a special circuit, to a bank of recording machines and dictate when convenient. It is preferable to record in small batches to spread the load in the audio centre. A supervisor controls and distributes the work between the audio-typists, and then arranges for the completed transcripts to be checked and returned to the originator. Although this is an impersonal system because the dictator and audio-typist may never meet, it is efficient and well suited to part-time employees and job-sharing.

3.4 Using the telephone

The telephone system provides a quick and easy form of instant communication between subscribers in homes, shops, offices, hospitals or factories situated almost anywhere in the world. All telephone subscribers are permanently connected to exchanges and exchanges can all be connected together. Via the exchange system, telephone calls are temporarily set up for the duration of the call.

General information

Dialling codes are needed to make calls to telephones on other exchanges and to call countries where there is direct dialling. Each telephone subscriber is given a booklet listing local, national and international dialling codes.

Telephone directories are issued free for a customer's own area. All customers are listed in strict alphabetical order, i.e. surname, initials, address. Directories explain how to get emergency services (on 999) and give details of operator and information services, e.g. directory enquiries.

Yellow page directories list all business subscribers under their respective trade or profession.

Telephone numbers in major cities are in all-figure form, e.g. 01-246 8071 (London). Elsewhere in the UK all telephone numbers have an exchange name associated with the number. The dialling codes for all exchanges in the UK are given in the dialling code booklet provided by British Telecom. Information on international dialling codes and tones is also given in the booklet.

Tones

Dial tone is a continuous purring or high pitched hum meaning that the equipment is ready for a call to be dialled.

Ringing tone is a repeated 'burr-burr' which indicates that the equipment is trying to call the dialled number.

Busy tone is a repeated simple tone meaning that the dialled number or British Telecom lines are in use.

Number unobtainable tone is a steady high pitched note indicating that the called number is unobtainable for one of the following reasons:

    the number was incorrectly dialled
    the number is a spare or ceased line
    the number is out of order
    the number is temporarily out of service.

No tone means a fault on the line or on the equipment. The code and number should be checked before re-dialling.

Pay-on-answer tone is a series of rapid pips telling the caller to insert money, and the called person that the call is from a payphone. Many coin boxes now require payment by credit card purchased from a post office.

Special information tone is a repeated series of three tones in ascending pitch indicating that a recorded message is about to be given.

Costs

All dialled telephone calls are charged in units. The time allowed per unit depends upon the time of day, day of the week, distance of the call and the destination. A map is available showing the extent of local call areas and calls within that area are all charged at local rate.

Monday to Friday

Cheap rate operates from midnight to 0800 and 1800 to midnight

Standard rate operates from 0800 to 0900 and 1300 to 1800

Peak rate operates from 0900 to 1300

Saturday and Sunday

Cheap rate operates over each 24 hours

Operator services

Operators help over difficulties and offer a range of services. See Chapter 21.3.

Guidelines

These give recorded information on specific topics and are obtained simply by dialling a special number (see p 218).

Making a telephone call

Check that the number and dialling code are correct. (Refer to telephone directory, dialling code booklet or directory enquiry service if necessary.)

Lift the receiver, listen for the dial tone (continuous purr or high pitched hum).

Dial code, if required, followed by the number. Dial carefully taking the dial right round to the finger stop and letting it return freely. For a press button telephone, press each button carefully to its full extent. Press at a steady rate. If a mistake is made replace the receiver for a moment or two and then re-dial.

When the call is answered ask for the person required and/or extension number if known, and give the caller's name.

Costs in time and money can be reduced if a note is prepared, in advance of making a telephone call, of the salient points for discussion or areas of enquiry. This is especially so when a message has to be left with a third party, or on an answering/recording machine (see p 37).

If a call is cut off replace the receiver for a few seconds before dialling again.

Answering a telephone call

Answer promptly and announce the number. If answering on an extension telephone announce your name or the department, whichever would be most helpful. Pick up the receiver with the hand not normally used to write with.

Keep a message pad and pencil by the telephone. A message should be repeated to ensure it is correct. Take the caller's name and telephone number. Make sure the message is given immediately to (or left for) the person for whom it is intended. If an enquiry involves collecting information, offer to call back and say what the delay is expected to be. An example of a useful message form is given below.

Telephone Message

FOR_____

DATE_____TIME_____

WHILE YOU WERE OUT

M_____

FROM_____

PHONE NO._____

TELEPHONED	PLEASE PHONE
RETURNED YOUR CALL	WANTS TO SEE YOU
CAME TO SEE YOU	WILL CALL AGAIN

MESSAGE_____

_____

_____

_____

_____

_____

_____

TAKEN BY

If an incoming call is cut off, replace the handset and wait for the other person to call again.

Using an answering/recording machine

The use of one of these machines when no-one is available to answer the telephone personally means that no calls or messages are missed. An announcement is recorded which invites the caller to leave a message. A bleep signifies when to start dictating the message. Business firms and private households have been quick to recognise the value and convenience of installing answering/recording machines and the majority of callers now find them acceptable.

The benefits of installing a machine, especially to the business user, are:

customers are not restricted to calling during normal office hours but can call when convenient to them

prospective customers can call immediately they read an advertisement, whether in the evening or during the week-end

incoming calls are spread so that congested lines are avoided during normally busy periods

if messages can be received before opening time it is possible to plan certain work schedules more economically, e.g. maintenance engineer, sales follow-up, ex stock goods delivery, staff absence

work flow is improved when outside staff can telephone in and indicate reports or messages for immediate action at any time of the day

meetings and work routines need not be interrupted by telephone calls at inconvenient times.

Pronunciation

Do not shout on the telephone; talk quietly but distinctly into the mouthpiece. Change the pitch of your voice and speak more slowly if there is difficulty in being heard. Clear and careful pronunciation prevents errors and aids efficiency. Use the telephone alphabet given below when spelling out words:

A	Alfred	J	Jack	S	Samuel
B	Benjamin	K	King	T	Tommy
C	Charlie	L	London	U	Uncle
D	David	M	Mary	V	Victor
E	Edward	N	Nellie	W	William
F	Frederick	O	Oliver	X	X-Ray
G	George	P	Peter	Y	Yellow
H	Harry	Q	Queen	Z	Zebra
I	Isaac	R	Robert		

Some numbers can be confused over the telephone. Here is a guide to pronunciation:

0	Long 'O'
1	Emphasise 'N'
2	Emphasise 'T' and long 'OO'
3	Slightly rolled 'R' and long 'E'
4	One syllable, long 'O'
5	Emphasise first 'F' pronounce as 'Fife'
6	Long 'X'
7	Two syllables
8	Long 'A' emphasise 'T' as in 'Ate'
9	One syllable, emphasise 'N' and long 'I'

When saying telephone numbers, groups of two or three numbers come most naturally; more than four can be confusing for the listener.

4 EFFECTIVE SPEAKING IN PUBLIC

The ability to speak fluently and effectively is a tremendous asset in business life and it carries no particular mystique. Contrary to popular belief everyone is capable of being a good speaker, providing sufficient attention has been paid beforehand to certain basic principles. Lack of confidence deters many people from volunteering to speak in public, but after the first time, and with practice, this becomes less and less of a problem.

Talks fall naturally into the following categories or combinations of these categories:

to inform

to persuade

to solve a problem

social speaking.

The first thing a prospective speaker must do, therefore, is to identify the main purpose of his or her talk.

4.1 Identification and purpose

To inform

This is the most straightforward type of talk, and the most effective way to deal with it is to find a sequence to build upon. For instance, an account of a journey provides its own sequence, so does a progression of events or ideas, or a description of someone's life and achievements.

If possible, build from basic facts which the audience already know to the new information to be imparted, working from the known to the unknown. Some kind of structural sequence can usually be found with a little thought.

Be absolutely certain that all your facts are accurate; it is not wise to risk a public correction from someone in the audience.

To persuade

A sales talk is one variety of this kind of talk ('Our products are the best'), or a call to action ('We want production figures doubled by next month') or simply a talk to the board to prove that your point of view is better than theirs. There can be many variations on the theme of persuasion. Barristers and politicians are experts in this technique. However, it is not effective just to state a point of view, a preference or even a strong belief and to expect your audience to agree. They need good reasons, if not absolute proof.

Bring in all the ammunition you can to support your argument. Use all your cunning to make your theme look attractive. If you are selling an idea, quote instances where similar ideas were successful. Set out the advantages to follow from the adoption of your proposals. Say what will happen if your advice is *not* adopted.

Quote references and sources of support. Your recommendations must be clear and understandable, and you must, of course, be totally convinced of the value of your cause. Anticipate any counter-objections that may come up and demolish them with sound argument before anyone has a chance to voice them (e.g. 'You may say that this is not going to work but I can prove that it will') and give your reasons with good examples.

Sound argument backed up by clear reasoning, combined with enthusiasm and conviction, should bring success; the more vitality and conviction you can show in your manner the more convincing you will be.

To solve a problem

You may already have the answer to the problem or, as in a committee meeting, you may hope to find it with the help of your audience.

To start with, muster all the information possible. Understand the different points of view that are held, so that the problem is clear in your own mind and you can explain it as simply as possible to your hearers. You should also know why the problem has arisen and the developments arising from it, and what may happen if it is *not* solved. You may suggest your own ideas for solving it, quote the various alternative ways put forward by others, and recommend a particular one if you have a preference.

This type of talk should be especially clear and constructive, with sensible suggestions put forward, and it may well have a set 'question time' afterwards, with general discussion and vote-taking in order to come to a final decision.

Social speaking

It is not unusual to be asked, sometimes at short notice, to propose a vote of thanks, open a new department, welcome a newcomer, say farewell to a colleague on retirement, propose a toast to a special guest or perform any other necessary social ceremony with grace and competence.

Between five and ten minutes is probably a suitable length for such speeches; more time could make them tedious. Keep the treatment light and amusing. Little anecdotes can be incorporated, provided that they have a bearing on the subject. Try to avoid saying 'And that reminds me of . . .' before bringing in a funny story, as it is usually obvious that this is not strictly the case.

Bring in personal but kindly references to those present (topical touches are appropriate) and mention familiar matters with which the audience can identify. All of these can combine to make a warm, humorous little speech. Risqué stories and controversial subjects must be avoided. You are there to contribute to the festive occasion and to combine the necessary formalities with a cheerful and light touch. Both speaker and audience should be enjoying themselves.

Two special variations on social speaking are set out below; the formula to introduce a guest speaker and the little vote of thanks that should follow.

To **introduce** a guest speaker:
>state the qualifications of the speaker
>remind the audience of the subject
>give the speaker's name
>give a signal that it is time to be quiet and attentive.

For instance (these are brief pointers and can of course be adapted):
>'Ladies and Gentlemen, it is my great pleasure this evening to welcome someone whose talents and achievements in the world of business are well known. He is the Principal of the Royal College of Commercial Communicators and he is going to tell us about the latest work they are doing there. He is the author of those two well-known books "Electronics for Everyone" and "Technical Analysis in Business" and I am sure we are going to hear a highly interesting talk. Ladies and Gentlemen, I am delighted to introduce . . .'

Pause slightly, give his name, look at him and smile, then sit down and start the clapping. The audience will clap, quieten down, and then settle down to listen.

To give a **vote of thanks**, stand up and say something on the following lines (again using your own adaptation):

> 'Ladies and Gentlemen, I am sure you would wish me, on your behalf, to thank Professor Peabody for her most interesting (amusing/instructive) talk. I was most interested to learn that (quote something appropriate that you have heard) and I am sure we are all now much the wiser about (whatever the subject was). I for one have enjoyed it tremendously, as I am sure we all have. Thank you, Professor Peabody, for a most interesting (exciting/informative) talk.'

Look at her, smile, start the clapping, and the audience will join in.

4.2 The audience

There may be only a few people present, as at a board meeting, or a vast number, as for a large formal lecture, and a speaker needs to know the size of group and the type of people who will make up their audience. Find out beforehand and plan your talk accordingly. Speak naturally, in your own style, but with proper consideration for those listening. Guard against appearing insufferably clever, and never talk down to an audience. A group of qualified engineers, for instance, will understand technical language but young trainee managers will need more general terms. The setting itself may be formal or informal and your manner and vocabulary should be adjusted sensibly to the occasion.

4.3 Content and construction

Theme

When you have decided on the type of talk you are going to give, take pen and paper and set down your main themes, with wide spacing between the lines for additions and notes. Then add notes to fill out your first draft, developing the headlines into paragraphs. Give your talk a beginning, a middle and an end. You might treat this as introduction, main theme(s) and conclusion. Adding a brief summary at the end is often useful, to remind the audience finally of your main points.

Develop your subject so that ideas move naturally from one to another in a way that makes it easy for your listeners to follow. Link ideas together; do not jump like a grasshopper from one subject to another unconnected one.

Timing

When your script is finally written out, read through it, revise and polish, and then talk it through, timing it carefully with a stopwatch. A tape-recorder is very helpful as you can play a recording back to yourself. Perhaps you have been asked to speak for twenty minutes; if you are speaking for twenty-five minutes prune carefully, tighten up the wording and re-record. If you are only speaking for fifteen minutes, add more material or suitably expand your existing paragraphs. Re-time, alter and adjust until your talk is exactly right for length at the rate at which you will be speaking. In this way you can make any talk fit exactly the time you wish it to take.

When rehearsing the talk, infuse an element of vitality and enthusiasm into what you are saying. This will bring the whole thing to life and make all the difference to the way your audience will receive it.

Check cards

The next step is to transfer the main paragraph headings onto a small card, to hold in your hand as a reminder while you are actually speaking. The main points should be written briefly in clear bold lettering, easy to pick up with a quick glance during your talk, to keep you on course, to ensure that you make your points in the right order, and to prevent you from omitting anything or actually drying up. It will not matter that you are seen to refer to your little card from time to time. If you need several, they can be held unobtrusively in a small pack, and you will be able to remove the top one from time to time and replace it at the back of the pack as you go confidently on your way.

Visual aids

If you are planning to use visual aids, make sure beforehand that they are in good order, and check that there will be no missing charts, non-existent projectors, chalkless blackboards or other embarrassments. Equipment must be up-to-date and in good working order, and of course this includes microphones. If you have an article to demonstrate, see that it will actually be there when you want it, that it works, and that you can anticipate and answer questions about it. It may be necessary to get to the hall or room early to see that everything is ready for you, or to check with your chairperson.

4.4 Presentation and delivery

Stance and gesture

Stand still and do not fidget. Keep gestures moderate and controlled. Do your best to appear relaxed. Do not pace restlessly up and down, jingle keys or coins in your pockets, toss a piece of chalk up and down, rub your nose, polish your spectacles or adjust your tie. Many people find it useful to hold something (check cards, for instance, or a pointer if you have slides or wallcharts to talk about). On the other hand, do not appear rooted to the spot or taut with nervous anxiety. Natural movement and an occasional gesture for emphasis are acceptable and quite sufficient.

Clarity

Speak clearly, perhaps a little more slowly than your natural conversational pace. If you are using a microphone, hold it a few inches away from your mouth, not too close or the sound will be loud and distorted. Try it out beforehand if you can. Should there be no microphone, pitch your voice as naturally and distinctly as you can, so that you can be heard at the back of the room or hall. There is no need to be self-conscious about a regional accent if you have one, but it *is* vitally important to be clear. Never mutter or mumble, and do not indulge in any ums and ers and y'knows, or any of the other irritating little clichés of sloppy and careless present-day speech.

Eye-contact

Remember that you have something to share with your audience and that your main purpose is to hold their interest and attention. Look at them, let your eyes make contact with different individuals, talk *to* them and not *at* them or beyond and past them. Be interested in your own talk and make that enthusiasm personal and infectious.

4.5 Interruptions

This is a difficult problem but it can be dealt with sensibly. Usually it is best for a speaker to ignore it altogether, relying on the chairperson to deal with it by having the offenders removed if necessary. A well-judged retort to a heckler may silence him or her temporarily and can make the heckler look foolish, but never do anything to start a slanging match. If you can score a point with good humour then do so, but to deal successfully with such nuisances is really a matter for the experts and the amateur is best advised to take as little notice as possible of rude interruptions, relying on the chairperson, or whoever has introduced them, to deal with the situation.

4.6 Conclusion and questions

Finish your talk definitely and finally. Do not tail off in a vague way so that the audience is uncertain whether you have finished or not. If the talk has been well constructed they will sense when you are coming to your conclusion, because you will be summarising or winding up your material. When you have done this and have reached the end, stop decisively and sit down.

To bring questions to an end when time is running out, say 'I think there is just time for one more question'. When this final question has been put and answered, the speaker can say 'I'm afraid that has to be the last one, as time has now run out', or the chairperson may do this for the speaker. There is no reason why talks and lectures should run overtime to the inconvenience of both speaker and audience.

4.7 Self-confidence

Self-confidence comes with good preparation and practice, and a self-confident speaker is usually a good one. Nervousness is every beginner's problem, but this need only be a temporary disadvantage if a speaker takes a little trouble to learn and persevere.

There are a number of excellent books on effective speaking, some of them listed below. You will find a selection on the shelves of your local public library.

Bibliography:
Stand and Deliver: Handbook for Speakers, Chairmen and Committee Members, by Kenneth P Brown. Pub. Thorsons Publishers Ltd, 1983.
The Art of Speaking Made Simple, Gondin & Mammen. Pub. Heinemann, 1983.
Tips on Talking. Pub. BACIE, 1960, 14th impr. 1983.

5 BUSINESS COMMUNICATION

Written

5.1 Business stationery

International paper sizes

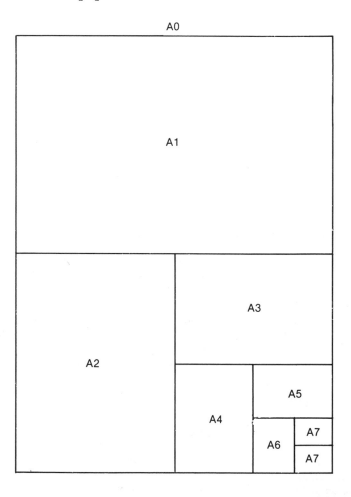

Sizes

A0 = 841 × 1189 mm	A4 = 210 × 297 mm
A1 = 594 × 841 mm	A5 = 148 × 210 mm
A2 = 420 × 594 mm	A6 = 105 × 148 mm
A3 = 297 × 420 mm	A7 = 74 × 105 mm

Types of paper

Bond A good quality paper which should not crease or tear easily. Usually white although pastel colours are obtainable. Used for top copy and business correspondence, when the firm's letter heading is printed at the top of the page. Normal weight 70–90 gsm (grammes per square metre).

Bank A flimsy paper used for carbon copies and sets of forms. White or coloured and weighing 40–45 gsm. When regular multi-person/department distributions are made, coloured copies can be used to identify specific areas.

Air mail A thin lightweight paper which reduces the cost of overseas air mail postage.

NCR (no carbon required) The reverse side of the top copy and top sides of subsequent sheets are treated with a special substance to produce copies.

Post Office Preferred (POP) envelopes and cards

There is a preferred range of sizes known as POP which is based on its suitability for Royal Mail equipment, and this range is recommended for all users, big and small. To fall within the POP range envelopes must be:

  no smaller than 90 × 140 mm
  no bigger than 120 × 235 mm
  oblong in shape, the longer side should be at least 1.4 times the
    shorter side
  made from paper weighing at least 63 gsm including contents.

The most widely-used International Standards Organisation envelope sizes fall within the POP range, i.e. DL (110 × 220 mm) and C6 (114 × 162 mm).

The above rules apply equally to window envelopes and cards. Rigidity is especially important for cards; to be sufficiently rigid they must not be less than 0.01 in. thick with a tolerance to an absolute minimum of 0.009 in.

Other types of envelope

A stock of the following shapes in varying sizes should be kept in the stationery store:

Banker		opens on the longer side
Pocket		opens on the shorter side
Window		a cut out address panel covered with transparent material
Aperture		a cut out address panel NOT covered with transparent material

Window and aperture envelopes save time as the name and address does not have to be typed twice, but care should be taken to position the window correctly so that no detail is lost. Enclosures must be secured so that they do not move and obscure the address.

Letterheads, business cards, compliment slips

Letterheads Most firms use a letter heading detailing:

> registered name
> registered office
> logo (if any)
> directors, company officials' or principals' names
> branch offices and/or subsidiary companies
> telephone number(s) and STD code
> telex number
> VAT number (if any).

The modern tendency is for the printed letterhead to be blocked to the left hand margin which then matches fully blocked letter layout. (See 5.2).

An advertising slogan may be incorporated on the headed notepaper. The quality and style of letterheading should reflect the firm's image and create in the public a feeling of confidence.

Business cards Standard size cards (88×55mm) are most popular as they fit easily into wallets and cardholders. Business cards may contain most of the information printed on the firm's letterhead, with the card owner's name displayed prominently.

Compliment slips Small pieces of paper which have details of the firm and *With Compliments* printed on them. These details are usually the same as those printed on the firm's letterhead. Compliment slips are used to accompany leaflets and small items where a letter is not considered necessary. They may be square or oblong. If printed as part of the firm's stationery order, i.e. on an A4 sheet, two thirds for the letter heading and one third for the compliment slip is the most economical layout.

Memoranda

Commonly called 'memos', these are used internally for sending messages to employees of a particular organisation, i.e. in the same building, or to representatives/agents based elsewhere in the country or abroad.

Printed forms are usual, specifying: To; From; Date; Reference; Subject heading.

No formal salutation or complimentary close is used. If there are enclosures ENC(S) should be marked at the end of the memo, against the left hand margin. A copy should be retained for filing.

5.2 Correspondence

Business letters—setting out

The most widely used and economical layout for a business letter is the fully blocked style with 'open' punctuation. All the parts of the letter are set against the left hand margin which should be aligned with the firm's printed letter heading. No punctuation is used except to ensure clarity in the address and text of the letter. Abbreviations do not need full stops.

Example showing letter parts and style:

Our reference	AD/DT (author's/typist's initials)
Date	12 April 198–
Addressee	Mr J Brown
	Brown, Green & Co Ltd
	3 Prince John Street
	LONDON N16 0RH
Salutation	Dear Sir
Subject heading	CHAMBERS OFFICE ORACLE
Text of letter: —introduction	I was very pleased to receive your letter of 8 April asking for an advance copy of our above publication to be released shortly.
—development	I am sending you two copies as requested so that you can circulate them amongst your staff and gauge their reaction to its suitability as an office reference book. I feel confident that they will find it the most comprehensive combined office manual and dictionary on the market today. The detailed index makes it very quick and easy to use.
—conclusion	I look forward to receiving your favourable comments in due course.
Complimentary close	Yours faithfully
Name of firm	W & R CHAMBERS LTD
Allow 5/6 line spaces for signature	
Signatory's name	(A N Other)
Signatory's designation	Sales Manager
Enclosure(s)	ENCS

Note: The usual salutation and complimentary close for a business letter is:

'Dear Sir(s)/Madam' followed by 'Yours faithfully'.

or

'Dear Miss, Mrs, Ms or Mr' followed by 'Yours sincerely'.

If a *For attention* line is used it should be inserted before or after the addressee's name and address. The letter, however, should be addressed to the company (i.e. Dear Sirs).

Letters should be typed on the company letterhead in single-line spacing, unless they are very short, when double-line spacing can be used. Continuation sheets are usually typed on plain matching paper with details of page number, date and addressee's name at the top of the page against the left hand margin.

Business letters—composing

A good business letter should be concise, courteous and correct in tone. It is usually set out in three paragraphs as indicated in the example above but that arrangement should not become artificial. Use the following logical arrangement for paragraphing:

(1) Introduction (one paragraph)	states subject of letter acknowledges a correspondent's letter (quotes date and reference, if any)
(2) Development (one or more paragraphs)	deals in a methodical way with the subject previously referred to in the introduction, i.e. lists facts or arguments, gives detailed explanation, outlines a course of action
(3) Conclusion (one paragraph)	usually kept for expressions of courtesy and goodwill which leave a favourable impression in the reader's mind.

The use of a subject heading, especially in a complicated matter, helps the letter to be correctly routed, gains the reader's interest and saves time.

Be specific and give full details, e.g. relevant dates, prices and description of articles, specification numbers and components.

Check that all the correspondent's queries have been answered.

Consider the letter from the reader's standpoint; what the writer takes for granted may not be obvious to the person receiving the letter.

Avoid opening the final sentence of the conclusion with a present participle such as hoping, trusting, wishing. For example, 'Thanking you for your prompt attention to our order, I am, Yours faithfully' ... This sentence would be incomplete without the words 'I am'. The plain statement 'We thank you for your prompt attention to our order' is preferable.

Style Keep sentences short and to the point. Paragraphs will vary; they should not consist of one short sentence, nor must they be too long. Long paragraphs are more difficult to read and to understand than short paragraphs. (See also Chapter 1.1).

Tone   Courtesy is more than the occasional use of a polite word or phrase. The reader's response should be borne in mind constantly and tactful phrasing sought. For example:

'May I clarify several points'

not

'You appear to have misunderstood several points'.

The tone of a letter reveals the writer's personality; a co-operative person writes a friendly, constructive letter.

'As we do not appear to have received . . .'

not

'As you forgot to enclose . . .'

Business letters help to create good public relations; they indicate an efficient organisation.

Direct mail—planning the letter

The four most common components of a direct mail package are: a letter; a reply service; an envelope; other inserts.

Direct mail tends to be a 'words' medium, an individual communication between advertiser and prospective customer, in which illustration and graphics are supportive of a message already expressed in words. The letter is the primary consideration in any mailing as it is the 'salesman'.

Construction and presentation

Write from the recipient's point of view, presenting the advantages and benefits to be gained from buying the product or service. Stress how it will help the prospective customer, what problems it will solve, why it is the most suitable product of its kind and the most cost-effective. A successful letter will:

gain attention by identifying a problem and offering to solve it

convince the recipient the product is the solution by describing how well it does what it is meant to do, how pretty it looks, how reasonably priced it is, etc.

stimulate desire to buy or find out more about the product (—case histories or glowing testimonies from people whose business efficiency or lifestyle the product has enhanced)

encourage immediate action (—include a reply card or envelope).

There are two key areas for attention in the presentation of a direct mail letter:

(1) *Salutation*   Use a name if possible, or 'Dear Gardener' or 'Dear

Wine Lover'. Avoid 'Dear Sir' and never use 'Dear Sir/Madam'. Consider a heading promoting the product's benefits.

(2) *After the complimentary close* A PS can enhance the response rates by, for example, announcing a discount or a special gift for people who reply before a certain date.

The body of the letter should be broken up into easy-to-read paragraphs, with sub-headings, indentations and underlinings to emphasise key points. Anything that makes the letter easier or more exciting to read will be advantageous.

Refer to Royal Mail leaflet *A Guide to Effective Direct Mail* for more detailed help. (See also Chapters 6.4 and 26.6).

Telemessages—composing

The telemessage is an electronic letter service which combines easy telecommunications access with reliable postal delivery. Telemessages can be sent from telephones, telex machines or the customer's own computer terminal equipment. Telemessages may be dictated from any telephone (with the sole exception of cardphones) by simply dialling 100 (190 in London) and asking for the Telemessage Service. Telex users should refer to the telex director for their access code.

Telemessages are printed on single sheets on A4 Telecom headed notepaper and delivered with the first class post on the next working day. They follow the format of a business letter with the sender's name and address, and the date printed in the top right hand corner. The text can be a short note, technical letter, lists with tabulating, or just a simple greetings message. The advice given on planning a business letter applies equally to telemessages. There is a limitation on the length of text (up to 35 lines). Telemessages are charged in blocks of 50 words at varying rates. Operators will help customers to lay out their message to achieve the desired impact.

A senders-copy service and business reply service are available.

5.3 Reports

In the business world a written report is often required for meetings and conferences or to summarise the result of an investigation. It provides information, reports on findings, puts forward ideas and may make recommendations. Reports must be carefully structured and the facts arranged logically so that the reader can grasp the meaning quickly and easily.

Reports deal with a wide range of topics and vary greatly in length, e.g. a single sheet of paper, a brochure, a book with chapter headings, footnotes, index and appendices.

It is important to note the difference between minutes and a report. Whereas minutes concentrate on recording decisions reached, a report analyses the reasons which lead to the decisions recorded.

Main types of report

Company This is a report required by statute to be made annually to shareholders. The Directors' Report, the audited statement of accounts and the Chairman's Annual Review are often contained in one booklet.

Annual (of a voluntary organisation) The Honorary Secretary usually presents this at the Annual General Meeting. It may also incorporate the Treasurer's accounts.

Committee A committee may be set up to study and report on a given problem. It will investigate, hear evidence and issue joint findings (e.g. Government Reports published by HMSO).

Conference A conference is usually held to exchange ideas, disseminate and/or formulate policy. A report is made setting out the factors involved and the reasoning which led to an acceptable solution.

Expert This is a report commissioned from one who possesses specialised knowledge (e.g. engineer, surveyor).

Unusual occurrences Fire, accident, theft: usually forms are used in the first instance to ensure that all the relevant information is given in a logical order. If an enquiry is later set up a report may be required setting out the findings.

Routine In industry and commerce all firms need a constant flow of up-to-date information on such matters as raw materials, stocks, liquid assets and sales. In the normal course of work, responsible persons may be asked to provide reports on problems within their organisation. These may be written out formally or, if short, may be in the form of a letter or memorandum. Reports required urgently may be given orally—face to face or as part of a telephone conversation.

Preparation

Subject Make sure of the concise terms of reference and be clear on the scope and purpose of the report.

Reader Bear in mind: (a) what the reader knows already and wants to know; (b) the terminology that will be understood; (c) how the report may be used.

Material Collect facts and ideas and file them under selected topics. Check for accuracy.

Structure

The following arrangement is frequently used:

terms of reference—statement of instructions/purpose
presentation of facts—analysed, then set out in the most effective order
conclusions—after study of the facts
recommendations—after study of the conclusions.

Method

Use this sequence in composing a report:

define the purpose briefly, then choose a suitable title
consider the facts and decide upon the conclusions and recommendations
select sufficient facts to support the conclusions and recommendations
arrange the material in logical order under appropriate headings
review and revise the material.

Style

Keep the following points in mind:

the tone should be impersonal and economical in wording
all views should be balanced and fair, free from bias
the facts should speak for themselves
keep the language: (a) brief, e.g. use 'if' not 'according as to whether'; (b) clear and definite, e.g. avoid expressions like 'in the region of'; (c) simple, e.g. use 'find out' not 'endeavour to ascertain'
use active constructions as they are more forceful and save words
avoid jargon and clichés—they will not impress the reader
keep sentences short, as involved sentences can impede understanding.

(See also Chapter 1.1).

Content

Checklist

Does the report state clearly: (a) subject and purpose?; (b) date?; (c) scope?; (d) by whom it was drawn up?

Does the main part of the report contain all the relevant facts?

Is the order of the main part of the report in logical sequence?

Is the problem clearly stated?

Is the main issue obscured by small details?

Are the sources of facts clearly set out?

Do the conclusions follow logically from the facts?

Have abbreviations and symbols been used consistently?

Are there any statements where the meaning is not quite clear?

Are all facts, figures and calculations accurate?

Format

Layouts vary widely. A routine report will not be set out in the same way as the findings of a conference, but this checklist covers the main requirements:

Is the layout clear and easy to follow?

Are the main parts of the structure in the most suitable order?

Do the headings stand out clearly?

Is the numbering of pages and paragraphs uniform?

Are the appendices clear and helpful?

Presentation

Reports should be accurately typed and attractively presented in a neat cover. If the report is to be duplicated or printed check the typescript carefully before it is submitted.

5.4 Summarising

The ability to summarise accurately is a valuable skill for noting messages, instructions, interviews with clients, dealing with correspondence and reports, and in minuting meetings.

A summary is a condensed form of verbal or written work. Brevity is secured by selecting the essentials and stating these tersely. However, a summary must remain faithful to the original work and must cover all essential points.

Skill in summarising requires:

> common sense
> an ability to listen
> careful reading
> frequent practice.

Using reported speech

For business purposes a summary is a record of a past event and is thus written in reported speech. When converting a passage to reported speech these guidelines should be followed:

> present tenses become past tenses
> verbs already in the past may need changing to the remoter past to keep the correct relationship
> future tenses must be changed to the conditional
> pronouns must be changed to the third person
> question marks and exclamation marks must not appear in reported speech.

> 'Are we all agreed that our next meeting will be held on the first Wednesday in March?' asked the chairman
> > *becomes*
> The chairman asked if members agreed that their next meeting should be held on the first Wednesday in March.

Note: The past tenses of 'may' and 'can' are 'might' and 'could'.

Basic technique for summarising

Read the document carefully several times so that the theme or central argument becomes clear.

Study each section in turn. Pick out the main points, underscore and number them.

All paragraphs may not be of equal importance, e.g. the introductory paragraph may have little to underscore whereas the central paragraphs may contain many important points.

Eliminate any repetition, lists, examples and detailed description. Retain technical terms or names.

Use your own words to note in short sentences the points underscored.

Check each point against the original passage making slight modifications if necessary.

Combine the notes into a continuous narrative, paragraphing appropriately. Be as brief as possible without changing the facts or sense.

Avoid disconnected statements and aim for a logical flow of sentences to provide continuity of thought.

Make sure that the summary is a clear and fair impression of the original and will make sense to the reader.

Summarising correspondence

Follow the basic summarising technique, using reported speech.

The layout should emphasise the following:

a title heading incorporating the names and addresses of correspondents
the subject of the correspondence
the date of each letter.

Keep to an active construction and avoid lengthy introductory statements, e.g.

'Bowes & Co complained . . .'

not

'Bowes & Co wrote saying that they wished to complain that . . .'.

5.5 Copy preparation and proof correction

There are certain basic rules for the preparation of manuscript for publication. A well prepared manuscript saves time and money.

Copy preparation

Style of presentation should be decided and adhered to consistently throughout the work.

Copy should be typed in double-line spacing on one side only of good quality A4 paper using a good quality black ribbon. A copy should be kept against loss of the original. Electronic typewriters and word processors allow for corrections and amendments to be made easily, and a variety of founts can be used quickly. Copy can also be prepared on disk for direct processing by the printer.

Headings—the importance of main, shoulder, side and sub-headings must be made clear to the editor and printer.

Margins should be kept uniform at top, base and sides. A quick estimation of the number of words per page or per chapter can then be made. A wide left-hand margin is usual so that the printer can add instructions for printing where necessary.

Punctuation marks and symbols, including use of single and double quotes, must follow a consistent pattern. Use open punctuation for abbreviations and acronyms.

Spelling should be kept consistent where dictionaries give alternatives for certain words.

Time—it is preferable to use the 24-hour clock (e.g. 1400 hrs not 2 o'clock or 2 pm).

Dates can be given as '1 November 1987' and 'in the 1980s' (no apostrophe). In tables and schedules months can be abbreviated to three letters.

Mathematical and scientific symbols should be inserted by hand if they cannot be typed exactly.

Metric system is now used almost worldwide (see Chapter 25.1). Use a written letter 'l' for litre as the typed 'l' could be confused with the figure '1'.

Footnotes add detail to the text and should be inserted at the end of the page carrying the text reference, at the end of the chapter, at the end of the completed work, or at the base of a tabulation. The standard symbols are * † ‡ § or superior numerals, with or without brackets, running serially throughout an article or chapter.

Illustrations should be kept separate from the main typescript but their exact position in the printed work should be clearly marked. As illustrations greatly increase the cost of printing their inclusion should be carefully considered. Photographs should not be folded, written on or clipped to a manuscript. Keep flat and pack carefully between stiff card if posted.

Pages should be numbered consecutively throughout the work. Attach a front page giving the name and address of the author(s) and title of the article or book. It is better not to staple or pin the completed manuscript.

Proof correction

The printer's readers check the proofs and mark any literal errors and queries before passing them on to the author. Alterations or corrections made by the author should be in a different colour from

Group B   Deletion, insertion and substitution

Note: The letters M and P in the notes column indicate marks for marking-up copy and for correcting proofs respectively.

Number	Instruction	Textual mark	Marginal mark	Notes
B1	Insert in text the matter indicated in the margin	$\wedge$	New matter followed by $\wedge$	M P Identical to B2
B2	Insert additional matter identified by a letter in a diamond	$\wedge$	$\wedge$ Followed by for example ⬩A⬩	M P The relevant section of the copy should be supplied with the corresponding letter marked on it in a diamond e.g. ⬩A⬩
B3	Delete	/ through character(s) or ⊢———⊣ through words to be deleted	⌒⌒	M P
B4	Delete and close up	/ through character or ⊢⌒⌒⌒⊣ through character e.g. chara͡cter chara͜cter	⌒⌒	M P
B5	Substitute character or substitute part of one or more word(s)	/ through character or ⊢———⊣ through word(s)	New character or new word(s)	M P
B6	Wrong fount. Replace by character(s) of correct fount	Encircle character(s) to be changed	⊗	P
B6.1	Change damaged character(s)	Encircle character(s) to be changed	✕	P
B7	Set in or change to italic	—————— under character(s) to be set or changed	⊔⌋	M P Where space does not permit textual marks encircle the affected area instead
B8	Set in or change to capital letters	≡≡≡≡≡ under character(s) to be set or changed	≡	

Extract from BS 5261 : Part 2 : 1976 reproduced by permission of the British Standards Institution. Complete copies can be obtained from BSI at Linford Wood, Milton Keynes, MK 14 6LE.

that used by the printer. Ideally corrections should be confined to misprints; alterations, other than minor adjustments, are very costly.

Standard correction marks   The British Standards Institution issue a classified list of standard marks for use in copy preparation and proof correction (BS 5261C:1976). An extract is shown opposite. Each correction is shown by a mark in the text with a corresponding mark in the left- or right-hand margin.

Return of proofs to printer   Clear written instructions should be made on the proofs in answer to any queries raised by the printer. If further page proofs are necessary, subject to the final corrections being made, the printer should be told. (For a glossary of printing terms see Chapter 27.5.)

6 ADVERTISING AND PUBLICITY

6.1 Choosing an advertising medium

The range of outlets available for successful advertising continues to increase and so reach a wider audience. The methods available to the businessman or private individual are specified below.

Broadcasting   Commercial television and independent local radio.

The Press   National and local newspapers; monthly and weekly magazines catering for every kind of interest; trade and technical journals.

Direct mail   e.g. Reader's Digest.

Outdoor advertising   All kinds of transport: rail, bus, underground, and stations; posters and signs on hoardings and shop fronts; aerial banners, etc.

Other   Cinema screen; exhibitions; point of sale.

Faced with this diverse range of options, the advertiser needs to formulate a clear set of principles upon which a choice can be based. In evaluating cost-effectiveness, the price of the product, the size of company and the type of operation required are all factors which should affect choice.

Target group
Define: the sex, age group and social economic group (e.g. high, middle or low income group, or retired) of readership or audience.

Media
Consider: which medium will reach the greatest number in the chosen target group, in the required depth, at the right time and in the right place

the advantages and disadvantages of each type

which media are used by competitors

the importance of speed and timing

the volume and frequency required

whether the various methods are easily available

whether surveys are available showing the effectiveness of the preferred medium.

Cost

Compare: the production costs

the comparative costs with other media

any rate concessions offered.

At the top end of the market, advertising at national level requires expert budgeting, planning, creation, placing, publishing and checking of advertising campaigns. This is a three-way operation involving the advertiser, advertising agency and media owners, as well as other ancillary services.

Advertising agencies

Advertising agencies are experts who prepare campaigns, known as 'accounts', for customers. They are media independents who plan and buy space and air time; they may arrange for other creative agencies to prepare materials. It is worth noting that whereas agents do not usually incur any liability on a contract, an advertising agent becomes responsible for paying the media and, should the need arise, may have to pursue the client for the debt.

Publicity

Publicity may not necessarily be bought but may be built up through good public relations. It is an important part of any business's marketing process. (See Chapter 12.6).

The press, radio and television are always keen to get a good story and the keen businessman should build up good relations with the media, using opportunities for news about his firm. This can be done by the firm issuing a **press release**, or employing a **public relations consultant** who can advise and prepare an appropriate campaign.

When issuing a press release make sure: that it is noticed (print *Press Release* across the letterhead); that it has eye appeal; that it has an attractive heading; that it is suitably brief; that it is simple in style; that it includes prices where applicable. If there is a human interest story involved this will add to the appeal.

A **press agency** will take a story or press release and distribute it. The timing of the release is vital; it is wise to get it to the editor early in the day, preferably on a Monday when news may be sparse. Allow ample time for consideration by the editor and for possible changes.

6.2 Independent broadcasting

Time can be bought on ITV, Channel 4, Independent Local Radio (ILR) and *Oracle* teletext just as space can be bought in newspapers. Independent broadcasting is financed in this way. Television advertising time is restricted to a total of six minutes in any hour averaged over the day's programmes, whilst radio advertising is normally limited to a maximum of nine minutes in each hour. Advertising breaks are carefully controlled: there must be a clear distinction between programmes and advertisements; they should occur in natural breaks, and there should be an even spread of advertising.

The Independent Broadcasting Authority enforces a strict code of advertising standards and practice by examining over 10 000 new television scripts and 8800 new radio scripts per annum. A copy of *The IBA Code of Advertising Standards and Practice* is available from IBA on request.

Television is an intimate form of advertising, reaching as it does millions of homes daily. This method of advertising is for the multi-national companies; production and air time costs are high. Expert advice and assistance is essential in the production of professional programmes in order to ensure customer appeal and impact.

Independent local radio is a powerful advertising medium which offers cost-effective advertising over 46 local radio stations. Charges are about one third of television costs for the same length of commercial. The programme style consists of news bulletins, short features and entertainment items, with music catering for all tastes across the musical spectrum. Each local radio station broadcasts programmes to suit local needs and interests. Listeners are encouraged to phone in to express opinions, seek advice on solving problems or participate in locally sponsored events, all of which suggests that commercials are likely to be well received. Radio is available all day—in the home, garden, car, street or at work.

ILR stresses listener loyalty. Its research shows that 73% of all radio listeners tune into one station and there are high levels of repeat listening. This produces an unusually stable audience around which it is easy to plan and buy advertising space. It is an immediate medium, peak listening time being early in the morning before people go shopping. With stations covering almost the whole country, radio offers flexibility in the selection of geographical markets suited to the needs of the individual advertiser.

Radio commercials offer low creative costs; they are quick to make and can be tested and varied easily, thus making them an attractive marketing opportunity. They do however require the assistance of experienced radio copy writers to achieve the greatest impact.

Advertising packages are available from stations to meet advertisers differing needs. For example, the advertiser can opt for evenly spaced spots throughout a broadcasting week, or a 'Target Group Plan' where a specified reach and frequency is guaranteed for target groups over seven days. There are only three buying points:

Broadcast Marketing Services
7 Duke of York Street, London SW1Y 6LA   Tel: 01-839 4151

Independent Radio Sales
86/88 Edgware Road, London W2 2EA   Tel: 01-258 0408

Capital Radio Sales
356 Euston Road, London NW1 3BW   Tel: 01-388 6801

Local advertisers can buy direct from their ILR station.

The *Radio Marketing Bureau* (259–269 Old Marylebone Road, London NW1 5RA. Tel: 01-258 3705) promotes independent radio to the advertising industry and is ready to give advice on all aspects of radio advertising. It has also developed various services to aid the planning of radio campaigns and these are available free of charge to enquirers.

Chapter 26 lists addresses of television and radio stations.

6.3 Press

National

Advertising in the national newspapers is a high cost operation but it has the advantage that people throughout the country will get the same advertising message in the same newspaper on the same day. Care must be taken to select the paper which will reach the right target group for the product or service offered. Some nationals have days and sections devoted to specific businesses (e.g. holiday, entertainment, cars, property). *British Rate and Data,* known as BRAD, is useful for studying the market. It is available in most libraries and lists different types of magazines, newspapers, etc., together with advertising rates and technical data, including circulation figures.

(For addresses see Chapter 26).

Regional

It is claimed that around 75% of adults in Britain see a local 'paid for' paper each week, as well as seeing one or more of the proliferation of free papers. This indicates that more people read a local paper than all the nationals put together. These statistics place the local press in an advantageous position for the advertiser. Local papers mirror the characteristics of their areas and so it is possible to plan advertising campaigns tailored to a particular section of the public. By using regional advertising it is easier to pin-point specific target groups geographically and less wastage occurs.

The *Regional Newspaper Advertising Bureau Ltd* (Grosvenor House, 141 Drury Lane, London WC2B 5TB. Tel. 01-836 8251) promotes national advertising in the regional press, covering some 1500 local papers. It keeps the advertising industry aware of its existence by selling the benefits of local and regional newspapers and providing services in the planning and use of the medium. Its computerised database and mapping facility has produced *Where,* a definitive guide to the regional press which has become an essential reference work in promoting and improving access to regional newspapers. The Bureau also operates a central booking facility for agencies who do not employ staff experienced in handling a booking service. The Co-operative Advertising Division is another expanding area of service to advertisers.

6.4 Direct mail

Direct mail has become increasingly popular in recent years for business and consumer advertising. It is now the third largest advertising medium in the United Kingdom, absorbing more of the total national advertising budgets than posters, cinema and radio put together. (See also Chapters 5.2, 26.6).

Developments within the industry have improved the quality of mailshots and made it a more effective advertising medium, either standing alone or as part of a multi-media campaign. However, unless direct mail is professionally organised it can result in wasted energy. Successful direct marketing is based on three factors: an accurate mailing list, correctly targeted to a potential target group of users; the product or service on offer; well-produced sales copy which carries impact and reflects the value of the product or service to the target group.

There are professional consultants who can provide a range of sophisticated services, e.g. a specially-generated marketing file validated against the National Household File, demographic data, response analysis and facilities for promotions to be enclosed and mailed. Royal Mail offer an extensive range of discount programmes which includes a free trial run for first time users of their Business Reply Service and Freepost. (See *The Guide to Effective Direct Mail* issued by Royal Mail).

The advantages of direct mail are that it can:

> select potential customers with great precision
>
> provide a choice of formats and creative approaches
>
> be directed personally to the target user.

Consumer direct mail

The most common uses for consumer direct mail are:

> selling direct to the customer without the need for middlemen
>
> generating sales where a product requires a meeting between customer and sales force (e.g. fitted kitchens, central heating)
>
> sales promotion of special offers with 'money off' vouchers
>
> seeking enrolment of club members (e.g. book and record clubs)
>
> mail order to recruit new customers and local agents
>
> fund raising by charitable organisations.

Business direct mail

Business markets usually consist of quite tightly defined groups of people for whom mass advertising is not suited. Direct mail can accurately pin-point different market sectors to suit different requirements such as launching a new industrial product or business service, sales lead generation to help minimise wasted calls, dealer support, conferences, etc.

The strategy of a well organised direct mail campaign comprises:

(1) *Initial planning* Decide the role direct mail will play within the overall marketing strategy.

(2) *List selection* Define the target market. If this is unknown employ market research consultants.

(3) *Designing and writing material*   Decide what is going to be said to the identified audience. (See p 52).

(4) *Printing*   Translate the words and pictures (if any) into print and production.

(5) *Mailing*   Physically collating all the items and despatching them. Except for small mailings this work is best done by a mailing house.

(6) *Response and fulfilling*   It is vital that this is carried out promptly, e.g. supplying goods, arranging for salesmen to call, etc.

(7) *Analysis of results*   The advantage of direct mail is that it is easily measurable, i.e. new business set against expenditure involved.

(See also Chapters 20.1, 26.6).

6.5 Outdoor advertising

Posters, cards and signs are the main media used in outdoor advertising. They are pasted on hoardings, inside and outside all kinds of transport, on sites at railway and bus stations, in bus shelters and at airports. Electric signs appear mostly in crowded urban streets, and on panels on the fascias of shops. In fact, any site can be used if planning permission has been granted for advertising purposes.

More specialised outdoor advertising can be by aerial means, e.g. trailing banners from aircraft, hot air and tethered balloons, airships, etc. There is also a developing advertising area known as *Newscaster* which uses an electronic device to show a moving strip of words; one application alternates news with advertisements. It has a versatile application ranging from signs on high buildings to a video strip in a shop window.

At Heathrow Airport Terminal Four underground station there is a video wall. Television monitors in banks of three are set into the cross-track wall of the single loopline station. Advertising time is sold in 60 or 30 second slots for up to twelve months, the advertiser's message being repeated every six minutes throughout the day.

Posters and signs are a mass advertising material which cannot be thrown away or turned off. They can be most effective when used to augment advertising in other media—television, radio or the press—by keeping a particular message or brand name constantly in the public eye. Success is dependent upon booking a selection of sites where there is a guaranteed audience.

Basic guidelines for posters are that they must be seen frequently and demand attention; the message must be brief, easily read and quickly understood by people on the move. Conversely, posters placed inside transport or in station waiting-rooms can be more informative; there the travelling public are a captive audience who have time to read more detailed copy. It is the place to give more information, to use illustrations or a series of posters, and to add some humour so that interest is maintained.

Posters and signs

Questions for consideration

What role will the poster play in the overall advertising strategy—remind or inform?

Does the size conform to the specification on the rate card?

Has colour been used for impact and realism?

Will the budget buy sufficient sites to ensure repetition value?

Are the best materials being used to give long life, and what is the possible replacement cost if one is mutilated?

What are comparative costs and can the scheme be tested?

Has geographical flexibility been utilised to ensure that the right kind of people see the poster?

Can a visit be made to assess the value of the site(s)?

Does the copy comply with the rules of advertising?

Poster Marketing (21 Tothill Street, London SW1H 9II. Tel: 01-222 7988) and *Outside Site Classification and Audience Research* (OSCAR) act together as a marketing bureau for the poster trade and will help and advise potential advertisers.

London Transport Authority (LTA)

London Transport Advertising offers extensive poster space distributed across the richest market-place in Britain—Greater London. It provides a comprehensive, versatile and sophisticated method of communicating with a potential daily advertising audience of over seven and half million consumers—residents, commuters and tourists. The LTA have analysed by demographics and life style their captive audience and the result is fully illustrated in their brochure *Advertising on the Move*. Details of costs and campaign planning are given in their brochure *Rate Card 18* together with information on eight campaigns which have produced impressive results.

Underground Research has shown that each year over 750 million passenger journeys are made on the London Underground. A recent survey of the attitudes to advertising by regular users of the Underground showed that the majority noticed posters and appreciated the impact, colour and information they provided. The average commuter stands face-to-face with a cross-track poster for at least three minutes before catching a train so can read and digest even the longest copy.

Buses LTA's fleet of double-decker buses is an advertising medium unique to the capital and moves for 18 hours every day through areas where it is often impossible to buy any other form of advertising. The campaign thus reaches passengers, pedestrians and motorists simultaneously. The high coverage and frequency offered make it equally effective as a single medium or as part of a mixed media schedule.

Recent research and development has produced a new technique in poster display on London buses. This has improved the quality of display and provided advertisers with a wider choice of format and more space. Posters are printed on vinyl or paper and mounted on tough, rigid, lightweight plastic boards. These boards are then slid into existing frames and locked tight to give all-round protection.

All over painted buses are available in Central London. The Cityrama fleet of 22 buses are advertising vehicles with an audience potential of commuters, London residents, overseas visitors and other UK tourists. Twelve open-top double-decker buses normally operate in the high tourist season, from May to September, and ten closed-top buses operate for twelve months of the year. They run exclusively on the London sightseeing tour which takes between one and a half and two hours to complete.

There are no design restrictions, all exterior bodywork of the bus, apart from the windows and destination blinds, being available. The interior of the bus can also be used for advertising, and leaflets or products distributed. Advertisers may also hire their painted bus for promotional purposes.

For further advice and information contact: The Sales Manager, London Transport Advertising, 10 Jamestown Road, Camden, London NW1 7BY. (Tel: 01-482 3000).

7 GRAPHS, CHARTS AND VISUAL PLANNING

There are many ways of presenting figures—from a small tabulated statement to a large display board. Graphic presentation of information is much more revealing than columns of figures. Whatever type of work is being conducted there are generally figures to be analysed— wages, exports, sales, prices, expenses, crime figures, births and deaths—the list is endless.

Obviously the method of presentation of facts must fit the purpose for which it is intended. Where figures are constantly fluctuating, perhaps weekly or even daily, an easily adjustable method needs to be used. Before selecting the type of graph or chart to be used it is important to identify the kind of comparison which is called for. Concentrate on key points and choose the chart form which brings out these points most graphically. Unnecessary detail weakens the impact.

Charts do not supersede other forms of records but they present existing records in pictorial form. There are many business areas where charting can considerably improve efficiency.

7.1 Line graphs

Much statistical information can be effectively displayed in line graph form—purchases of raw materials, sales figures for exports, monthly salary figures, daily temperature readings in the factory, orders for newly marketed products, etc.

The graph has a two-dimensional display of data. The two dimensions (axes) are the *index* (vertical axis) and the *scale* (horizontal axis). The graph is formed by plotting one against the other.

There are several points to remember when compiling a line graph:

give a suitable heading or title
annotate each axis adequately
time is usually shown on the horizontal scale, reading from left to right
the vertical scale must read from the base upwards and must be marked at regular intervals according to the data given; choose as large a scale as possible
plot each point carefully and join to the following point by a straight line

if possible draw on squared paper so that a set number of squares
can be given for each unit along each of the axes
multi-line graphs must have a key displayed showing the colour or
line formation adopted.

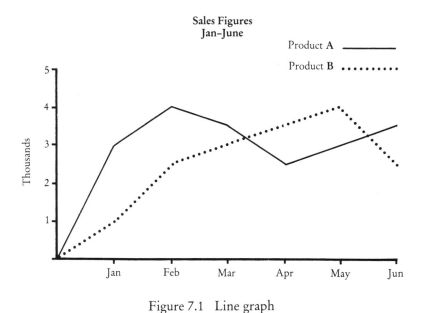

Figure 7.1   Line graph

7.2 Bar charts

A bar chart is the best way to display comparative figures, month by month or year by year. It can be displayed either vertically or horizontally.

Vertical

The information conveyed by the line graph (Fig. 7.1) could be given just as effectively in a bar chart (Fig. 7.2).

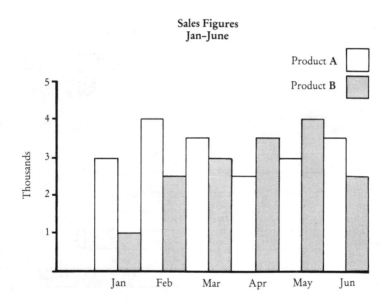

Figure 7.2   Vertical bar chart

Horizontal

Here the vertical dimension is not a scale but is merely used for labelling the items measured. The bars can therefore be used in any sequence.

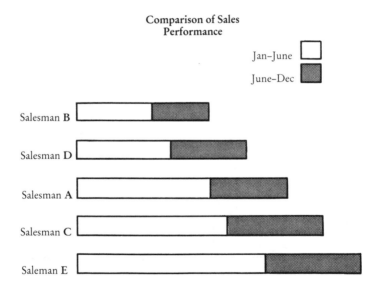

Figure 7.3   Horizontal bar chart

Deviation

Items are ranked in a rising scale from the least profitable to the most profitable. A vertical line separates the winners from the losers with the bars extending to the right of the centre line for winners and to the left for the losers.

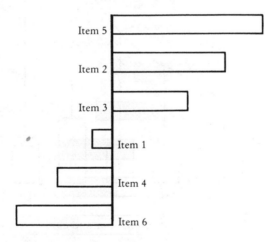

Figure 7.4   Deviation bar chart

Combined bar and curve

This type of chart shows both the fluctuation in each month's figures and the cumulative trend since the beginning of the year.

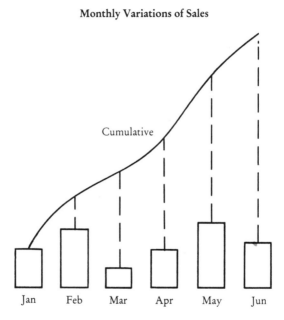

Figure 7.5 Combined bar and curve

7.3 Histogram

This is a specialised form of bar chart showing frequency distribution, where the peak is at the centre of the distribution.

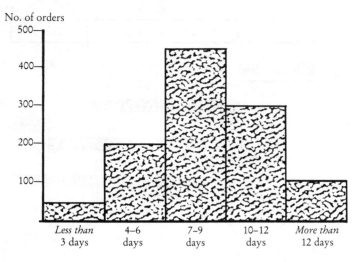

Figure 7.6   Histogram

7.4 Gantt chart

This is used to show the comparison between work which has been scheduled and work which has actually been accomplished in relation to time. In Figure 7.7 the work scheduled is shown by heavy lines and the work completed by the end of the second week by light lines.

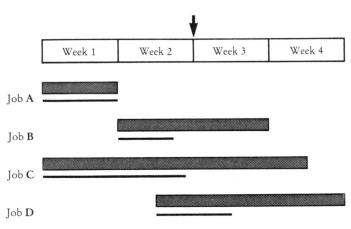

Figure 7.7   Gantt chart

7.5 Pictogram

This is a form of graph which is represented pictorially and is very useful for presentation to the general public. There are three important points to note:

the drawing must be clear and simple

each drawing must represent a stated amount

further amounts have to be shown by *further* pictures and not by larger pictures.

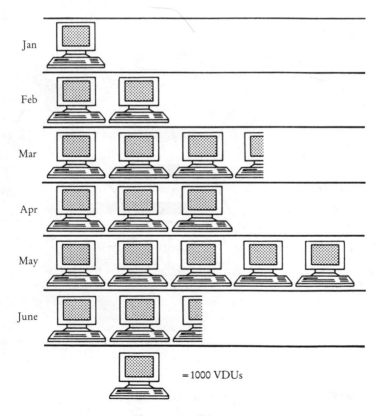

Figure 7.8   Pictogram

7.6 Pie chart

Pie charts are often used when it is necessary to show the relationship of parts to a whole. It is best to use as few component parts as possible and preferably not more than four or five.

There are two ways of focusing special attention on a single component:

    using a darker shading or colour
    separating the segment from the remainder of the pie.

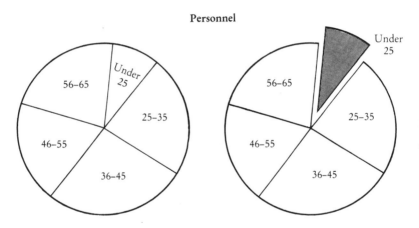

Figure 7.9   Pie charts

7.7 Visual planning control boards

Visual planning is quite simply a means of presenting the essential facts of a complex situation immediately and clearly. Properly used, visual planning ensures that the overall situation is grasped quickly, decisions can be taken faster and with greater confidence, problems can be more accurately defined and future trends and needs can be more effectively assessed.

The five stages for effective visual planning on control boards are:

defining the system and establishing the two axes
choosing an appropriate grid
displaying information to the best advantage, using chart pens, self-adhesive or magnetic shapes and tapes
selecting accessories for assembling and maintenance of the chart—uncomplicated in design, flexible in use and easy to assemble and re-assemble
providing suitable mountings for single charts, groups of charts and for transporting charts from one location to another—with provision for confidentiality where this is required.

The **perpetual year planner** (Fig. 7.10) is a popular form of visual planning control board. Printed on a metal board, this has magnetic moveable date strips and can be used year after year.

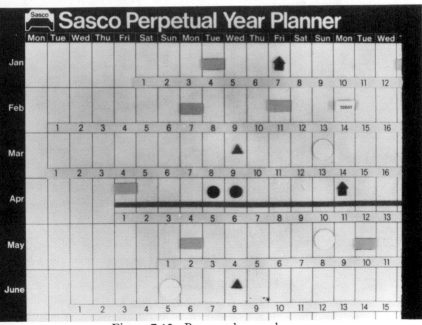

Figure 7.10 Perpetual year planner

A variant of this is the **fiscal planner** (Fig. 7.11) for use by accountants, local government officers and anybody who plans an April to March year.

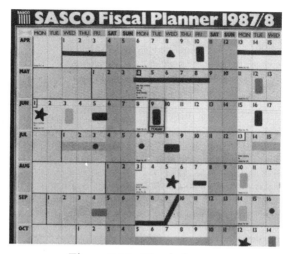

Figure 7.11   Fiscal planner

A wide range of matching visual planning components is available and more sophisticated equipment, such as executive chart cabinets which house up to nine grid charts in sliding tracks. These are ideal for housing information which requires a measure of security.

Part II
BUSINESS PROCEDURES

8 BUSINESS ENTERTAINING

Much goodwill can be derived from successful business entertaining; insufficient care and preparation may create a bad first impression and never lead to a good business relationship. Often the organisation of visits and the entertainment of visitors is the responsibility of a separate department which needs to be informed of the names of visitors, the purpose and length of the visit, dates and times of arrival and departure and any special requirements.

Those lacking expert assistance may find it helpful to create a 'Visitor Profile' with the following headings: Who?; Length of visit?; Purpose?; Where?; How much can we spend? Possible sub-headings are: Accommodation; Food and Drink; Transport; Excursions; Staff assistance; Outside agencies. The 'Who' section will cover not only name, designation and other background details but also whether the person to be entertained comes from the home country or abroad.

8.1 Home and overseas visitors

Whoever the visitors are, a warm welcome is essential, therefore:

confirm appointments in writing so that there is no confusion on either side

ensure that the visitors know how to reach the venue

supply the home visitor with a map accompanied by details of public transport and clear road and parking directions.

An overseas visitor may need to be met at an airport or station and must be told how to make contact and where to wait if necessary. Those meeting visitors should overestimate (rather than underestimate) the time allowed to reach the meeting point and both visitor and host need a mutual telephone number to contact in case of difficulty. The onus is on the host who has the advantage of local road/rail/air timetables and information services. If the guest has come straight from an intercontinental flight, allowances must be made for time differences and jet-lag, leaving an interval for rest and refreshment before the commencement of an important meeting or an exhausting tour.

The length of visit will dictate the type of hospitality to be offered.

8.2 Short term visits

Short term visits, such as half-day or full-day factory or office visits, invitations to drinks, lunch or dinner (possibly requiring overnight accommodation), need careful planning to ensure that the guest is suitably entertained and supplied with the maximum information without being rushed or made to feel part of a public relations exercise. To keep the personal touch:

> inform the receptionist of the expected time of arrival of the visitors

> make sure they are met at reception and personally escorted to the host's office or the meeting room

> appoint a member of staff to take care of the guests, arranging cloakroom facilities, providing refreshments and taking care of personal needs e.g. confirming travel times, checking appointments, making telephone calls

> if there is an interval between the arrival of visitors and the beginning of the meeting or tour, ensure that the callers are not allowed to wander about the premises unattended and that the waiting period is made as comfortable as possible.

If the visitor is to be shown round the factory or work site:

> obtain clearance from heads of departments

> arrange special safety equipment as needed, e.g. in 'hard hat' areas

> check with security services whether passes or identity tags are required

> organise transport to facilitate movement throughout the site

> give clear instructions on safety precautions and warnings of 'No smoking' zones.

An office visit may mean liaison between several departments with a carefully arranged timetable so that departmental heads, supervisors and other essential staff are available when required. In these circumstances:

> ensure that each department has a copy of the itinerary and that it is clear which member of staff is responsible for welcoming visitors and handing them on to the next department

> allocate departmental responsibility for provision of refreshments e.g. coffee/tea/lunch

arrange for the tour to end in plenty of time so that visitors can catch trains/planes or keep their next appointment

at the end of the tour make sure visitors are returned to the starting point so that questions can be answered, future action settled, belongings collected and the host can bid them farewell

occasionally it may be necessary for visitors to stay overnight and for accommodation to be provided; an invitation to dinner may be appropriate followed by some entertainment e.g. theatre, concert, cabaret—the host should make the necessary arrangements having regard to budget limits and the visitors' preferences.

8.3 Long term visits

Long term visits e.g. for a weekend or for several days, require more detailed planning, a careful choice of venue and a wider selection of leisure activities involving the considerations laid out below. The 'Visitor Profile' will show who is to be entertained and the length and purpose of the visit. Background details will give some clues as to the visitors' possible requirements and tastes. Authorities such as a national's embassy may be able to help with suggestions regarding entertainment, food and drink, particularly when there are restrictions on the grounds of religion or custom.

Budget

Before any arrangements can be made it is essential for the host to know how much can be spent. Most organisations have an annual allocation of funds for business entertaining and many have clear guidelines on the standard and extent of entertainment which can be provided. Towards the end of the financial year funds may be running low. Therefore whatever is available must be used to the best advantage.

Venue

Check what can be offered within the company e.g. meeting rooms, catering facilities (ranging from the supply of tea or coffee to providing informal drinks, lunches, formal and informal dinners), conference accommodation, printing (for invitations, publicity material, handouts).

If the required facilities are not available some research is necessary.

Never accept an estimate at face value; always visit, see the accommodation, take a check list of requirements and make sure the objectives can be met. Having selected a venue, establish a contact who will be responsible for seeing that the arrangements are carried out efficiently.

Menus

Ensure that the contact knows the limits of the budget and is able to provide a choice of menu to allow for special diets for vegetarians, diabetics, etc. Remember religious restrictions e.g. Jewish, Islamic. To such visitors some food and drink may be unacceptable e.g. meat (especially pork) and alcohol.

Staff

Involve as many staff as possible; inevitably there will be some who can relate to the visitors for various reasons; utilise their services; look to them for guidance e.g. on dietary and religious requirements; ask for assistance in interpreting, hosting and escorting; remember to thank them for any help they give.

Transport

If visitors have to be met or conveyed from one site to another, check available transport, company cars, public or private transport, referring to budget, time schedule and 'Visitor Profile'.

Social activities

If the visit is long term the 'Visitor Profile' needs to be expanded to highlight leisure activities and preferences, therefore:

> find out what leisure activities are available at the venue and within a convenient distance
>
> research local resources—theatres, concerts, sight-seeing excursions
>
> enlist the assistance of hotels, theatre/travel agents, visitors' centres and tourist boards.

Reservations

Confirm all reservations and requirements in writing. Keep to deadlines, particularly for catering when extra numbers and last minute orders for special meals can upset schedules. Check all arrangements by personal contact to avoid any misunderstandings thus ensuring the maximum comfort of guests.

Bibliography and useful sources of information:

Hotels and Restaurants in Great Britain. Pub. Automobile Association, annually.

Good Food Guide. Pub. Consumers' Association and Hodder & Stoughton, annually.

AA and *RAC Handbooks.*

Yellow Pages and *Thomson Local Directory* (for local catering services).

National and local newspapers; telephone information services (for entertainment and leisure activities).

The P.A.'s Handbook (Ch.17 Social and Business Entertaining), by Joan Moncrieff and Doreen Sharp. Pub. Macmillan Press, 3rd edn 1987.

9 MEETINGS

A meeting is a means by which a group of people with a common interest can share ideas, pool experiences and participate in decision-making. A properly conducted meeting is a method of two-way communication enabling information to be given and received, problems discussed, grievances aired, tactics explained and decisions taken.

9.1 Types of meeting

Formal meetings

A formal meeting is one which is closely controlled by regulations. The rules governing the conduct of meetings are set out in the Articles of Association of a company, a club's constitution or the standing orders of a local authority. A breach of these regulations may invalidate proceedings at a meeting. Examples of formal meetings:

Statutory Meetings required by law, e.g. the first meeting of the shareholders of a public limited company.

Ordinary general Often called **annual general** meetings, these are the regular yearly meetings of the members of an organisation. The Companies Acts require a public limited company to hold ordinary general meetings at intervals of not more than 15 months, and 21 clear days' notice must be given to all members who have the right to attend. Formal business only can be conducted at these meetings e.g. the presentation and adoption of the annual report and accounts and the appointment of officers and auditors. It is usual for the chairperson to review the past year, outline plans for the future and answer members' questions.

Extraordinary/special These are meetings called at the request of members or officers to discuss and vote upon urgent issues which are outside the scope of a general meeting. Such meetings are not held regularly but only when required to transact extraordinary or special business. Special regulations in the constitution or standing orders govern the convening and conduct of such meetings.

Shareholders Shareholders are members of a company and have the right to attend these meetings. A company may also call meetings of different classes of shareholders, e.g. preference shareholders and ordinary shareholders, when matters have to be discussed which affect one category of shareholders only.

Creditors The Companies Acts also provide for meetings of a company's creditors in the event of the company going into liquidation.

Board Those appointed by members to run the organisation on their behalf, e.g. directors, meet regularly to discuss strategy and make policy decisions. As the members of the board are accountable to the members of the company, provisions for the formal conduct of such meetings are made in the relevant legislation, e.g. the Companies Acts and the internal regulations of the organisations concerned.

Informal meetings

An informal meeting may be said to be one which is not closely constrained by legislation or internal regulations. Those attending the meeting are often well known to each other; the atmosphere is therefore more relaxed and the discussions less restrained. Such meetings may be called at short notice but any decisions taken may have to be confirmed by a higher authority. Examples of informal meetings:

Committee Meetings may be held at regular or irregular intervals depending upon the type of committee. The degree of formality depends upon the regulations governing the committee's formation.

Staff Staff meetings are generally informal, e.g. departmental meetings or meetings of certain categories of staff such as sales representatives. When a Staff Association is formed formal regulations are drawn up governing the appointment of representatives and the convening of meetings.

Working parties These may be formed by a parent committee for the purpose of discussing and reporting back on certain matters. Recommendations can be made but action cannot be taken without the approval of the parent committee.

Managers Intercommunication between departments and divisions is essential to good management. Managerial meetings, although informal, may have considerable influence upon the running of an organisation.

9.2 Preparation

Venue

The place in which a meeting is held can influence the effectiveness of the meeting. If the meeting place is too large communication between those attending may be limited; if it is too small discussion may be stifled. When making preparations for a meeting consideration must be given to:

> the size of the meeting room
> its availability and accessibility
> seating accommodation
> lighting and heating (or air conditioning)
> resources available, e.g. microphones, audio-visual aids, toilet facilities and cloakroom accommodation, availability of refreshments.

Notice

The notice of a meeting states the date, time and place of the meeting and the type of meeting to be held. The notice must be sent to all those entitled to attend; the length of notice required depends upon the type of meeting and the regulations governing it. Frequently the notice is sent out with the agenda and may appear on the same document as the agenda, e.g. as part of an internal memorandum calling an informal meeting.

Agenda

A list of items to be discussed at a meeting. It is the first step towards an effective meeting because it should:

> define the purpose of the meeting
> plan the content of the meeting
> give members the opportunity to prepare for the meeting.

A customary order for agenda items is:

> appointment of chairperson (if not already appointed)
> apologies for absence
> approval of the minutes of the previous meeting
> matters arising from the minutes
> correspondence
> reports of committees, working parties or officers

general business of the meeting
date of the next meeting
any other business.

The agenda for a meeting at which formal motions are to be discussed should contain the full wording of such motions.

9.3 Procedures

For a meeting to be effective and valid it is important that procedures and regulations are strictly followed. The chairperson, secretary and other officers are the persons most concerned with ensuring this.

Chairperson

The person appointed by members to take the chair is responsible for:

the correct conduct of the meeting, e.g. ensuring that the agenda is followed, that minutes are accurate, properly approved and signed, that regulations and procedures are observed
maintenance of order
deciding who shall speak; anyone addressing a meeting does so 'through the chair' and fair opportunity should be given for all aspects of an argument to be considered
ensuring that discussion keeps to the point of the business in hand
guiding the discussion and summing up when appropriate
formulating proposals and amendments
taking decisions on points of order
ascertaining the 'sense' of the meeting i.e. taking votes and declaring the results
closing or adjourning the meeting
ensuring that any necessary follow-up action is taken.

Secretary

The secretary must be thoroughly conversant with regulations and be prepared to assist the person in the chair with procedures before, during and after the meeting. The specific responsibilities of the secretary are:

to send out the notice convening the meeting in the required form and within the prescribed time
to draw up the agenda in consultation with the chairperson
to prepare the meeting room

to keep the attendance register

to make arrangements for recording votes

to draft the minutes and maintain the minute book

to remind members of any follow-up action required of them and ensure that reports and/or supporting documents are submitted in time for the next meeting.

The secretary may be a paid official or an honorary secretary. Sometimes a separate minutes secretary is appointed to be solely responsible for minuting the meeting.

Officers

Other officers may have specific duties to perform at a meeting. For example, the treasurer of a club or society may be required to report regularly upon the financial position of the organisation; chairpersons of sub-committees or working parties may be required to attend certain meetings to report back on the work of their groups.

9.4 Terminology

Some terms commonly used in connection with meetings are explained below:

ad hoc committee One appointed to deal with a particular job, on completion of which the committee is disbanded. (Sometimes called a *special purpose* committee.)

adjournment The postponement of completion of the business of a meeting. A meeting may be adjourned by the chairperson, with the consent of the meeting and subject to the regulations. Notice of an adjourned meeting must be given.

amendment A proposed alteration to a motion which adds, inserts, deletes or substitutes words.

ballot A secret vote by means of voting slips placed in a sealed ballot box.

casting vote A second vote which may be allowed to a chairperson to resolve a deadlock when an equal number of votes are cast for and against a motion.

closure A motion proposed with the object of ending discussion on a matter before the meeting.

co-option The power to invite other members to serve on a committee by majority vote of the elected members.

ex officio This term means 'by virtue of office'. A person who is not an elected member may be invited to attend a meeting by reason of his or her office, e.g. the official secretary to a committee.

in attendance Persons invited to attend a meeting to give expert advice, help or information.

in camera In private i.e. not open to the public.

intra vires Within the power of the person or organisation concerned.

lie on the table A motion or document (e.g. an application for membership of a club) on which no decision will be taken at present is said to 'lie on the table'.

majority The number of votes required to carry a motion. A *simple* majority is one vote more in favour of the motion than the number cast against. The regulations of an organisation define the number of votes required to pass a resolution.

motion A motion is a proposal, moved by a member, that certain action be taken. The motion must be seconded by another member before the chairperson puts the question to the vote. A motion passed by a majority vote becomes a resolution.

nem con No votes cast against a motion (although some members may have abstained from voting).

point of order A question raised by a member regarding procedure at a meeting or about a possible infringement of the regulations.

poll A method of voting which enables account to be taken of the number of votes each person holds. The way in which a poll is to be conducted is laid down in the regulations.

proxy One acting for another. A person may be appointed to vote on behalf of another who is unable to attend the meeting.

quorum The minimum number of persons required by the regulations to be in attendance to constitute a valid meeting.

show of hands A method of voting. The chairperson calls upon all those members in favour of a motion to raise one hand. When these have been counted by the tellers the chairperson asks for those against the motion and then those who wish to abstain, to raise their hands. The total number of votes cast for and against a motion, with the abstentions, should add up to the number of voters present at the meeting.

standing committee A permanent committee e.g. a local government housing committee.

sub-committee A small committee appointed by a main committee to deal with some specific part of the main committee's work.

teller One who is appointed to count votes at a meeting.

ultra vires Outside the power of the person or authority concerned.

unanimous A vote is unanimous when all members have voted in favour.

9.5 Minutes

The purpose of minutes is to keep a brief and accurate record of the business transacted at a meeting. Minutes need not be detailed but should be sufficiently clear to enable those absent from the meeting to follow the course of the meeting and to understand the reasons for the decisions taken.

Minutes should be in the third person and past tense. They must be approved by members, signed by the chairperson and should be kept in chronological order in a minute book for future reference.

All minutes should contain:

a description of the type of meeting
date, time and place of the meeting
names of those present with the chairperson's name first
a summary of the business discussed in the agenda order.

Minutes of a formal meeting such as an annual general meeting should include the full wording of motions put to the meeting with names of the proposer and seconder and a declaration by the chairperson of the result of the vote. If the result is not unanimous the minutes should record the number of votes cast for and against the motion and the number of abstentions. When a motion has been agreed by the correct majority according to the regulations governing the meeting, it becomes a resolution and the minutes should record 'It was resolved that . . .' followed by the full wording of the resolution.

When an amendment to a motion is proposed the amendment must be discussed and voted upon before the main motion. If the amendment is passed it is incorporated into the original motion, called the *substantive* motion, on which a vote is taken and recorded as above. If the amendment is not carried the chairperson will put the original motion to the vote. If the substantive motion is defeated the original motion cannot be voted upon.

An informal meeting, such as a staff meeting, may require more detailed minutes giving a summary of points made during discussion and including suggestions which were not accepted, as well as recording the decisions taken. These *minutes of narration* may also include the names of speakers for and against a proposal and the names of those from whom further action is required.

Copies of minutes of formal meetings are usually sent to members before the next meeting so that members can check their accuracy. The minutes of a company's annual general meeting may be approved at the next board meeting. Minutes of informal meetings are often read to members by the secretary at the next meeting.

If members agree to an alteration to the minutes the chairperson should make the alteration and initial it before signing the minutes as a correct record.

10 PLANNING A CONFERENCE/EXHIBITION

No two conferences or exhibitions can ever be alike; every business will have different aims and ideas and therefore guidelines can only be given in a very general way. The object of such occasions is to gather people together for a purpose and the first consideration is to define clearly what that purpose is. To set up a conference or exhibition is an expensive procedure, not to be undertaken lightly. Planning, strategy and timing are of vital importance if the occasion is to be sufficiently worthwhile and cost-effective. The following checklist will help prospective organisers to work out a campaign according to their own particular requirements and resources.

10.1 Aims and objectives

Conferences are held for one or a combination of the following reasons:

> to increase or renew business and professional contacts
> to exhibit and demonstrate goods and artefacts of all kinds
> to build up public relations
> to give or exchange information, including training sessions
> to explain future planning and policies
> to achieve and expand publicity
> to investigate and solve problems
> to build up morale.

10.2 Strategy and planning

Delegation

The principal Conference Organiser should make out a preliminary schedule of events, after which the operation becomes a group activity. Duties may be delegated to separate departments, although if the project is not over-ambitious a small group of two or three people may be able to organise the whole programme competently on their own. Delegation can of course be infinitely flexible, according to the firm's staff structure.

Naturally there should be a considerable amount of contact and co-operation between all the departments involved to ensure smooth progressive planning with the minimum amount of hold-ups and hiccups.

Chairperson

The ideal chairperson is someone willing to take on the job, who has a good platform presence, a quiet authority and a sense of humour. (There may be a different chairperson for different days if the conference is a lengthy one.)

The chairperson must be fully briefed on all matters concerning the conference, be firmly in control at all times, and amongst his or her general duties the following take priority:

to open the proceedings, welcome delegates and re-state the programme (announcing any changes that may have been necessary)

to be available to introduce speakers and be in control of 'question and answer' sessions

to keep the programme within its planned limits, keeping talks or demonstrations from running beyond their scheduled time

to close the conference formally and thank everyone concerned in its success.

Speakers and Guest of Honour

Speakers must be selected and approached early (months or even a year ahead) and asked if they will accept an invitation to lecture or give a talk and demonstration. The guest of honour will also need plenty of notice, allowing as much time as possible for the preparation of a speech. See that all acceptances are confirmed in writing and, in case of an unavoidable cancellation at a later stage, have one or two other names on a reserve list.

Write to or telephone the speakers to ascertain whether they need visual aids of any kind and take steps to see that these are provided; it may be necessary to hire microphones or other equipment. Make sure all electrical fittings are adequate and in good order, that acoustics and ventilation are good. The lecture room should be made quite ready beforehand, probably necessitating an early inspection with the caretaker and electrician.

Costs

Make a sensible forecast of possible costs and then add half as much again, since costs have a way of escalating. Many firms keep contingency funds for regular projects of this kind, but when arranging a first-time conference careful financial forecasting is vital. Costs are likely to go up during the period between the initial estimates and the presentation of final bills. As the project goes forward constant running checks should be made to ensure that expenses are kept as closely as possible within budget limits. A special extra fund should be kept available for unexpected emergencies.

Suitable dates

A conference may be contained in a single day, extend over a weekend or run for several days consecutively. Avoid clashing with bank and other public holidays or church festivals. If the conference is of interest to foreigners their holiday dates should also be considered (see Chapter 23.2). Peak working periods of the year should be avoided; these vary for different trades and professions. It is also as well to find out whether there are likely to be any rival conferences which could provide unwelcome competition.

Accommodation and venue

These depend entirely on the type of conference proposed, whether it is to be long or short term, residential or non-residential, held on the firm's own premises or away in another area. Probable requirements will be:

lecture hall (or halls) with platform, comfortable seating and good acoustics

exhibition halls with adequate display areas

rooms suitable for discussion groups and seminars

studios or workshops for training

lounge for coffee and bar facilities

dining room for lunches or formal dinners

adequate and suitable cloakrooms and toilet facilities

good kitchen accommodation if catering staff are involved

easy access and sufficient car-parking space for visitors.

When selecting accommodation attention must be given to cleanliness, heating and ventilation, possible draughty areas, pillars that could obstruct the view during lectures or demonstrations. If any handi-capped people are likely to attend, staff should be asked to stand by to give assistance if and where required. Remember that handicapped delegates may have difficulty with swing-doors and lifts.

If delegates are to stay overnight, hotel accommodation will be required with clean and comfortable bedrooms and other amenities. Any good hotel manager will be happy to show you the accommo-dation beforehand and discuss terms for single or block bookings.

The actual location of a conference or exhibition centre deserves attention. Quiet surroundings are best; avoid premises with adjacent building sites or goods yards at any time and school playgrounds during term-time.

The host's own business premises will probably be the most appropriate venue, but if they are not entirely suitable they may be made so with the help of an outside catering firm and local hotels to assist with overnight accommodation. Alternatively, another location may be more suitable, such as:

Purpose-built conference centre There are plenty of big modern conference centres that can be hired in many localities, providing every possible facility for large or small events of all kinds.

Hotels and guesthouses These can often provide excellent rooms specially adapted and equipped for conferences and exhibitions. Enquiries in the district via the local paper or *Yellow Pages* will provide a selection of possibilities.

Local authorities and other large organisations Many big con-cerns have their own colleges and training centres, often in converted country houses and mansions, with good accommo-dation and catering facilities. These are often available for booking during their holiday periods.

Universities Accommodation is available during the long vacation in many colleges in university towns and cities. Delegates and visitors usually appreciate the opportunity of using lecture rooms and halls of residence within interesting and historic settings of this kind.

Guest list and invitations

Invitations will be sent out according to the names on your guest list and it is as well to keep a record of acceptances and refusals so that, in the event of there not being as many acceptances as was hoped, a secondary reserve list can be made up to augment the numbers.

Invitation cards and a printed programme can be sent out separately, or an attractively printed brochure or leaflet may be produced with a separate or detachable tear-off reservation slip to be filled in and returned as an acceptance. The information printed on this reservation form should include the following:

announcement of the event, its aims and subject

the date or dates

the precise location and address

an introductory paragraph with any necessary explanatory notes

the programme for each day, setting out the various events and including the names of the speakers

administrative details, e.g. the fee to be paid, an address and telephone number for enquiries, a list of available hotels if the conference lasts more than a day

an acceptance slip to be returned with the fee, giving space for the delegate's name and address, the company represented, his or her status within that company and a telephone number for contact

a small sketch map of the district may be included, with directions as to how to find the conference buildings. The nearest railway station, airport, bus station and car-parking areas should be clearly indicated.

Programme construction

Naturally programmes will depend on the nature of the event and its duration. The following guidelines are very general and can be adapted as appropriate. Items to consider are:

a general assembly on the first day, when the Chairperson will welcome the delegates and formally open the conference

a series of related demonstrations and lectures

special seminars, discussions and practical workshops

films and illustrated talks

an exhibition (pictures, models, artefacts of all kinds)

excursions during 'leisure' time, perhaps on the last day, to a theatre or local place of interest

coffee and tea-breaks, formal or informal lunches, formal dinner on the last evening with a special guest-speaker.

Working events should not be timetabled to run too closely together; delegates will need a short break between talks and seminars. The printed programme might cover one specimen day as under:

Day I   (Chairperson's name)
  9.00   Arrival and coffee
  9.30   Welcoming address by the Chairperson
  9.35   Talk or lecture (subject, speaker's name and degrees or qualifications)
10.45   Coffee
11.00   Workshops of some kind, demonstrations, training sessions etc. (subject, instructor's name and qualifications)
12.00   Reports and assessment on previous session
–12.30
13.00   Lunch
14.30   Talk or lecture (subject, speaker's name, etc.)
15.30   Tea
15.50   Lecture or seminar (subject, speaker's name, etc.)
16.30   Open discussion
–17.00
17.00   Chairperson's winding up address
–17.05
19.30   Dinner

Catering

This may be carried out by your own company if the facilities are there, or left to outside caterers. If the former, consult the Catering Manager early so that he or she may order extra goods and equipment in plenty of time.

If outside caterers are to be engaged, write to several for specimen menus and estimates, stating your approximate requirements. It is not possible to give exact numbers before the acceptances come in or all tickets have been sold. The firm with the lowest charges may not necessarily be the best or most suitable. A personally recommended firm may be your best choice. Your reputation will be at stake, so do not make a snap decision but choose with care.

For a formal dinner ensure that flowers, printed menus, place-cards, etc., are not forgotten and put up a seating plan where the guests can see it before entering the dining-room.

Seating plans should be tactfully drawn up; the Chairperson and

Guest of Honour should be seated at the top table with any other principal after-dinner speakers and other important visitors.

Exhibits and reception area

Ways of exhibiting products are many and various since different articles require different display methods. Objects may be tastefully displayed in purpose-designed showcases, films specifically commissioned for information purposes and shown in a small cinema, video films shown on VDU screens, technical equipment demonstrated in working order by a trained operator, charts, graphs and diagrams put up for inspection on large display frames (see Chapter 7). Large exhibits, such as a building scheme, can be shown by means of scale models and photographs. Showcases and lighting, by today's sophisticated methods, can be skilfully and attractively combined.

By contrast some exhibits, pictures and prints for example, need only good wallspace and soft indirect lighting to be seen to the best advantage.

A reception area can provide a useful focal point for delegates on arrival, in addition to being a general meeting place and information centre. It is the ideal place to position the following:

Notice boards for plans of the area with directions to conference rooms, cloakrooms, etc., individual telephone messages, lists of names of the delegates attending.

Counter with attendant issuing leaflets and brochures such as those giving information about the firm (history, products, progress and development), details of training and career opportunities, extra printed programmes, information about local places of interest, travel facilities (train timetables, bus schedules and taxi services with telephone numbers), conference assessment forms for delegates to fill in and return when the conference is over, folders to hold papers conveniently and personal identification lapel badges (if these have not previously been sent out through the post).

General enquiry desk with a qualified and informed member of staff in attendance.

Display stands with posters and other exhibits concerning the theme of the conference.

Publicity and the press

Publicity for a conference is not always required, but, in cases where it is needed, the first thing to do is to contact the local or national press and send them the printed programme, with a covering letter saying that it would be appreciated if they would send a representative and a photographer to report on the event. When they arrive they should have all the assistance they require. Select a reliable member of staff to look after them and answer questions, but choose someone discreet and tactful enough to know that not *all* information is necessarily to be divulged.

The Public Relations Officer may also contact local or national radio and television stations if the occasion is of sufficient importance. (See Chapter 26 for useful addresses).

Safety and security

Insurance is of vital importance. Extra electrical equipment, temporary fittings and extensions, large groups of people, litter and cigarette ends all provide risks and nothing should be left to chance. Check carefully to see where there may be problems of safety and take steps to minimise the hazards and insure against them.

Fire exits must be clearly signposted, fire-doors *never* locked when people are on the premises, and fire-extinguishers should be placed at strategic points (all members of staff should be instructed in their use). Night watchmen or guard dogs may be employed for the hours when the buildings are virtually empty. The installation of a burglar-alarm system may be thought necessary. (See also Chapter 14).

Outside assistance and agencies

There are plenty of individuals and companies who would be happy to arrange everything for you, but the specialised conference agencies, though highly efficient, are expensive. However, smaller, single organisations may be employed separately, such as:

printers for brochures, programmes, posters, etc.
temporary clerical staff to assist with extra paperwork
security firms for overall safety planning
interpreter services if foreign delegates are to be present
bar staff and catering firms to help with meals and snacks
publicity agents to spread the news far and wide

display unit designers to set out your products in the most enticing way

video and photographic suppliers for display purposes.

The *Yellow pages* are an invaluable source of outside help, also the advertisements in the trade and technical papers concerned. You are not alone, help is at hand.

Winding up

A few last minute duties are important as soon as the conference is over. These include:

Tipping A tangible mark of appreciation for services rendered (caretaker, telephone operator, kitchen staff and so on) will be deserved and much appreciated.

Safety All electrical equipment should be checked and all rooms inspected and locked up before the building is finally vacated.

Acknowledgments Letters of thanks and appreciation to those concerned are a priority when the programme is safely completed. They should be sent off as promptly as possible.

An informal post-conference meeting of the various organisers and helpers should be held at a short time after the event, when delegates' assessments have come in and retrospective opinions can be formed as to how successful the conference proved to be. Good strategy will be worth repeating on future occasions; alternatively, much can be learnt from any miscalculations or mistakes.

All relevant records and copies of correspondence should be kept in a special 'Conferences' file for helpful reference on other similar occasions. Good contacts will be required again, others will need to be avoided.

Cuttings from press reports and photographs, when they appear, should also go into the 'Conferences' file, which will then form a valuable set of records on which to base future events.

10.3 Press conferences

A press conference has a different character and, because of its particular nature, requires special timing. The press are middlemen, passing on news to their own publications, and usually their information has to be up-to-the-minute and relayed swiftly. Early in the day, therefore, is the best time for a press conference. This allows reporters to contact their offices promptly and there should be a number of telephone booths and telex terminals within easy distance for their specific use.

A discussion period should be scheduled, after the information-giving session, so that the press can ask questions and fill out their facts as they wish before finally putting in their reports.

When a press conference is to be set up a suggested list of contacts for the organiser might be:

local newspapers

national daily and evening papers

chief news agencies

appropriate trade and technical or professional journals

radio and television networks

(see Chapter 26 for addresses).

Printed information may be given out at a press conference, confirming and augmenting any information given orally (—this should not be issued beforehand).

10.4 Confravision

If it is not practicable to bring delegates from various far-flung locations together conveniently, the British Telecom *Confravision* service may be the answer. Links between widely separated groups, using sound and vision lines of communication, make it possible to hold a 'meeting' even though the participants are not in the same room. Television screens at each terminal provide a visual and aural link each with the others. (See also Chapter 21.5)

Information about this service can be obtained from British Telecom Headquarters on 01-357 3982. *Confravision* studios are currently located in eight major cities, and international links have been developed between the UK and a number of foreign countries.

11 INTERVIEWING SKILLS

Training and experience are necessary if an interviewer is to become skilful enough to conduct an interview which is satisfactory to both sides. An interview should not be a one-sided affair; it should be a conversation of which the interviewer always has control. Its purpose is the exchange of information, both factual and behavioural, between interviewer and interviewee for a specific purpose. The responsibility for success rests with the interviewer who should always be fully prepared.

Before the interview the interviewer should consider:

the type of interview: its aim; the right approach to adopt

length of interview: allow sufficient time to achieve the objective and refer to a checklist of essential points to be covered

background information: documents to be read *before* the interview and to be available *during* the interview

location: size of room (too large becomes impersonal; too small, uncomfortable); adequate furniture and facilities (ashtrays, tea/coffee) to create a relaxed atmosphere; privacy, without noise and distractions.

During the interview the interviewer should:

establish confidence by putting the interviewee at ease

vary the types of questions asked in order to obtain the maximum information, avoiding questions which require only yes/no answers

listen and show interest in the interviewee noting the interviewee's voice tone and physical reactions, which will help the interviewer to understand better the answers to the questions

sum up from time to time to ensure that the interviewee understands the points made at each stage of the interview

take notes as the interview proceeds to avoid forgetting important points or repeating questions, but note-taking should be unobtrusive so that the interviewee is not distracted

be prepared to give information and clear up misunderstandings but encourage the interviewee to talk freely; the interviewer should not monopolise the conversation

clearly indicate when the interview has come to an end and make sure that the interviewee leaves in no doubt as to further action to be taken by both parties.

11.1 Recruitment interview

The aim of a recruitment interview is to select the best person to fill a staff vacancy either by internal or external recruitment. In terms of cost, public relations and future teamwork and achievement within the organisation, the outcome of such an interview is so important that the interviewer must prepare with care. A wrong decision can have lasting effects.

The approach should be to create a good impression of the organisation while being honest about the requirements of the job.

The interview cannot be hurried; it is necessary not only to assess the candidate's ability to do the job but also how he or she will fit into the working team.

Background material required includes:

> job description and specification of the person required
> candidate's application form or personal file (if internally recruited)
> company information which, in the case of an external recruit, needs to cover areas such as wage/salary structure, pensions, conditions of service, social amenities.

The location will probably be the interviewer's office. Whether across a desk or at a table the interview should be conducted so that both parties can see each other and neither is at a disadvantage, from misplaced light or inappropriate seating. There should be no interruptions, such as telephone calls, to stem the flow of the interview.

To put a candidate at ease the interviewer may start with open questions, i.e. those starting with *why, what, when* or *how*, or leading questions, i.e. those which indicate the required answer. As the interview progresses information can be extracted by specific questions and the interviewee's ability to deal with problem situations can be deduced from answers to hypothetical questions which have been already prepared by the interviewer.

Listening also involves watching to assess the candidate's reactions. Questions which are dodged or only partially answered may be re-stated in a different way. Eye-contact is important. Interviewers who keep their eyes on their notes miss a great deal of unspoken information.

A final summary of the interview should confirm the points covered; check that the interviewee has no further questions, ascertain whether or not the applicant is still interested if the job is offered and give a time within which the offer will be confirmed or withdrawn.

11.2 Counselling interview

Most people, at some time, seek expert advice to help them deal with problems which affect their personal or working lives. Sometimes the counsellor whose advice is sought is a member of an organisation which deals with specific problems, such as income tax queries or matrimonial difficulties; usually an appointment is made in such a case, and the interviewer has adequate time to prepare. Sometimes an interview is sought at short notice, however, and the interviewer has no advance warning of the problems to be discussed—a frequent occurrence when the person from whom advice is sought is a worker's manager or personnel officer.

The object of a counselling interview is to proffer advice, but the counsellor should remember that, at first, the interviewee may simply be seeking someone to whom the problem can be explained—perhaps an opportunity to voice a complaint which has never been put into words before.

The interviewer's attitude should be understanding and reassuring. A counselling interview must be unhurried, uninterrupted and private. Confidentiality must be assured.

Background material, such as a staff member's private file, may not be readily available at an unplanned interview but can be read and acted upon before the follow-up interview, which is essential when counselling.

An office environment is not suitable for a counselling interview unless telephone calls are re-routed and only those whose presence is requested are allowed to enter the office during the interview. The possibility of interruption can undermine confidence and so, when counselling interviews are frequent, a small room with comfortable furniture should be made available, where both parties can relax; this can create a more informal atmosphere and result in a more satisfactory outcome.

Counselling skills

All the interviewing skills are required when counselling, but tactics may differ from those used for other types of interview. These include:

   using 'open' questions to start the person talking (specific questions may be used to clarify)

   allowing the individual to talk freely, without interruption, until the problem has been determined, giving more than usual attention to listening and observing; remembering that it is important to be seen to be listening and that a pause in the narration may lead to further revelations if not interrupted; respecting silence but being prepared to re-start the flow of information by discreet questioning

   showing an understanding of the other person's position unemotionally, bearing in mind possible alternative interpretations of the problem

   advising: in other types of interview the interviewer is expected to give the interviewee information but in a counselling interview the individual is seeking advice; this must be given with discretion, since few people take advice easily and fewer act upon advice given.

The role of the counsellor is to:

   obtain the maximum information with the utmost care and the minimum interruption

   listen, understand and instil confidence

   help the interviewee to think through the problem and see possible solutions

   assist in the realisation of these solutions by providing names, addresses and telephone numbers of specialists in dealing with problems, e.g. Citizens' Advice Bureaux, Local Authorities' Social Services

   advise but not dictate; the decision must be made by the person concerned if he or she is to make future decisions without guidance and if the result of the present decision is not to be blamed upon the interviewer.

A follow-up interview is essential in order to:

   show the result of any action the interviewer has promised to take

   check developments and offer additional assistance if necessary

   encourage the interviewee to continue in a course of action or to take further action as required

discover whether or not the action advised has been followed and has proved successful; this will help the interviewer in subsequent cases.

11.3 Disciplinary interview

Mistakes, wrong attitudes or breaches of a company's code of discipline by an employee require a carefully handled interview, the object of which is to inform the person concerned of the errors made, suggest remedial action and take measures to prevent a recurrence of the fault.

The interviewer's approach should depend upon:

the seriousness of the offence

whether the employee has been called upon to attend a previous disciplinary interview

knowledge of the individual's temperament; some are easily upset by the mildest criticism, others become belligerent or defensive.

Before the interview the interviewer should:

get up to date with current employment legislation, particularly that concerning unfair dismissal

know all the facts about the current misdemeanour and what action can be taken e.g. a warning and/or further disciplinary proceedings

read previous reports on the employee's work

acquire background information about the person to be interviewed in order to understand behaviour and attitude

follow the company's guidelines and correct procedures e.g. liaise with union officials, inform the interviewee of entitlement to the presence of a representative and arrange for an interviewer's representative to attend if deemed necessary.

Written reports or complaints which have led to the employee being called for interview should be available for reference; also the company's handbook and appropriate guidelines e.g. safety rules.

During the interview the interviewer should:

adopt an informal approach initially, although the interview may become more formal as it progresses

be fair but firm

ensure that the person concerned understands the reason for the interview

listen to the interviewee's point of view

be prepared to explain company policy and the seriousness of the offence, particularly the effect on fellow workers

suggest remedies and improvements which can be made in attitudes and work; note reactions as these help the interviewer to determine whether to proceed further or whether a warning and another follow-up interview is sufficient action at this stage

leave the interviewee in no doubt as to what is expected of him/her and what further action is being taken by the interviewer.

After the interview the interviewer should:

write a full report immediately, recording action taken and warnings given

send a copy of the report to all concerned, including the individual and the union representative, and place a copy on file.

11.4 Appraisal interview

A successful appraisal interview requires careful preparation by both the interviewer and the interviewee, who must be given adequate notice of when and where the interview is to take place and with whom. The aim of an appraisal interview is frequently misunderstood. It is not a confrontation to highlight the worker's faults or to voice mutual complaints. It should be a discussion between a manager and a member of staff the purpose of which is to:

ensure that the scope of the job and its areas of responsibility are fully understood

define objectives and standards

assess performance, identify strengths and weaknesses and find means of improvement

determine training needs

consider potential for development.

Before the interview the interviewer should study:

the employee's job description

previous assessments, performance reviews and targets attained

the worker's self appraisal form if one has been completed (many companies use this method to help the interviewee prepare for the appraisal and, if copies are made available to interviewers, the information can be of considerable help to them).

During the interview the approach should be relaxed, considerate and friendly. As with all interviews uninterrupted privacy is essential and it is very important that the discussion should not be hurried. Unheeded grievances may impede progress in the coming year and lead to lack of co-operation and problems with other members of the staff. Difficulties may not be resolved immediately but, if the job-holder feels that they have been discussed and action will be taken, relations with management will be improved.

For the discussion to be of value both parties must listen carefully. The appraiser, particularly, should avoid talking too much, but should encourage the interviewee to present a point of view at the same time knowing when, tactfully, to halt the over-talkative.

Producing a summary of points made and actions decided upon at each stage of the interview can prevent repetitions and misunderstandings.

Finally, the manager's report or comments on the appraisal form should be seen by the employee who is then invited to make comments, the completed form being signed by both parties.

The interview should end on a positive note, with the interviewee clear about past performance, future prospects and action agreed. The interviewer must ensure that any action promised is undertaken without delay. A satisfactory appraisal interview can assist a manager's forward planning, boost staff morale and considerably improve staff/management relations.

Bibliography:
Interviewing in 26 Steps, John S. Gough. Pub. BACIE, 11th impr. March 1981.
A Guide to Interviewing Skills, Janis Grummit. Pub. The Industrial Society, repr. July 1985.
Selection Interviewing, Peter Whitaker. Pub. The Industrial Society, 1973, repr. May 1985.
Appraisal and Appraisal Interviewing, Brian Scott and Barry Edwards. Pub. The Industrial Society, 1972, repr. May 1986.

Part III
ORGANISATION AND FINANCE

12 BUSINESS STRUCTURES

12.1 Sole trader

Law

There is no legal formality required for setting up in business as a sole trader but every business has to comply with both local and state laws. For example, enquiry should be made with the local authority regarding the details of any bye-laws regarding fire regulations or whether planning permission is required for advertising on premises. Such local rules affect not only shops, offices and factory premises but also the use of private homes for business purposes.

Government statutes (Acts of Parliament) affect the conduct of business life in a wide variety of ways. Some of the areas and statutes are:

Goods Consumer Safety and Protection, Weights and Measures, Trade Descriptions

Employees Equal Pay, Race Relations

Premises Factories, Health and Safety, Control of Pollution

Finance Consumer Credit, Income Tax, PAYE, VAT.

Registration of business names

The Business Names Act 1985 stipulates that if the business is conducted under a name which is not the actual name of the proprietor then the following requirement must be met. At the place of business there must be prominently displayed: the business name, the activity of the business and the actual name of the owner. All business stationery must also carry the two names. The registration address varies according to the country in which the business is carried on, namely:

England and Wales Registrar of Companies, Companies Registration Office (CRO), Crown House, Crown Way, Maindy, Cardiff CF4 3UZ

Scotland 102 George Street, Edinburgh EH2 3DJ

Northern Ireland IDB House, 64 Chichester Street, Belfast BT1 4JX

Notification

Customs and Excise (VAT), the Inspector of Taxes and the DHSS must be told that trading has commenced, even if the sole trader's full-time employment is continuing.

Costs

Apart from the cost of any professional advice from a solicitor or accountant (prudence suggests this should be taken) there is no other legally required expense when starting a business. Profits will be taxed as personal income and liabilities will eventually be the responsibility of the person running the business.

12.2 Partnership

Partnerships are governed by the Partnership Act 1890 which specifies that persons carrying on business for profit constitute a partnership. Twenty is the maximum number of partners for all except special categories of business; at the present time these are: accountants, solicitors, members of the Stock Exchange, estate agents, auctioneers, surveyors and patent agents. Other businesses may be added at the discretion of the Secretary of State.

The legal requirements for setting up in business are basically the same for a partnership as for a sole trader (see p 113) with the addition of the points laid out below.

Deed of partnership

The Partnership Act 1890 sets out the consequences of partnership including financial arrangements, for example:

profits and losses shared equally

no entitlement to a salary or wage, nor to interest on capital invested in the business

interest at 5% will be paid to a partner who makes a loan, additional to capital; no interest will be charged on partnership withdrawals.

However, the partners can vary conduct within the partnership as decided between themselves when drawing up the deed of partnership. Professional advice should be sought for this.

Registration of business names

When the name of the business is not the names of the partners, then the same law applies as for the sole trader (see p 113).

If the partnership has more than twenty members the law stipulates that provided a list of all members is kept and is available at the main place of business the stationery does not have to contain these names.

Termination

Technically the partnership ends if a partner dies, becomes bankrupt, retires, becomes insane or if a new partner joins. The accounts should be finalised and creditors told of the change.

Management

All partners (unless they are limited partners) can participate in the management of the business and all have authority to bind the others and have access to the books of account.

Liability

Provided there is at least one general partner with unlimited liability, there can be partners who are specifically limited in their liability i.e. *sleeping partners*. Every limited partnership must be registered with the Registrar of Companies (see p 113). All general partners are jointly and severally liable for debts of the partnership. If for example they are equal partners and one cannot pay his or her portion of a partnership debt, the other(s) must shoulder it.

12.3 Limited companies

The limited company must be registered either as a *public* or a *private* company.

Public limited companies (plc)

Public limited companies are governed by the Companies Acts 1948-85. The 1985 Act is a consolidating Act which is expected to be fully implemented by the end of 1986. The Companies Acts are affected by the Insolvency Act 1985. All companies are required to register the following two documents with the Registrar of Companies (for address see p 113):

Memorandum of Association This must state that it is a public company, and gives:
the name of the company
domicile (it is usual to give the full address) of the company
a statement that the liability of its members is limited by shares or by guarantee, or a statement that members have unlimited liability
its share capital with details of number, value and category of share

the areas of activity in which the business will deal (known as the *objects clause*)

details of each subscriber and a witnessed signature to their undertaking to take up the shares stated to be their portion of the capital (there must be at least seven subscribers).

Articles of Association This governs the relationship between the members and the company e.g.

how alterations to the share capital have to be made

rules regarding notice of and proceedings at meetings

rules governing directors, etc.

There are model forms of the Memorandum and Articles which may be adopted or amended in 'Statutory Instrument 1985 No 805' for public and private companies with or without share capital, those with guaranteed liability, or unlimited liability.

When a company is formed, initial legal and accountancy fees and registration charges are incurred. There are then continuing costs in maintaining a register of shareholders and sending statutory returns to the Registrar of Companies (CRO) namely:

the annual return

the annual accounts

notices of change of directors of a limited company.

A company's shares can be bought and sold if they have been quoted on the Stock Exchange.

Private companies

The private company is governed by the rules and regulations of the public company with the following changes:

it does not have the statement in its Memorandum that it is a public company, but states that shares will not be offered to the public

there is a minimum of two subscribers to the Memorandum

its shares are not quoted on the Stock Exchange, but any changes of ownership need to be recorded.

12.4 Co-operatives

A co-operative is a business enterprise which is jointly owned by its members; as a rule these are the people who work in it although sometimes friends, relations or suppliers may also be members. Each member has one vote, but day-to-day business decisions come within the sphere of an appointed management often shared by rotation. Ownership may be:

proportional—when the members own a share in the assets in proportion to their investment

common—meaning that all members have an equal share in the assets regardless of the investment they have made.

Co-operatives registered under the Industrial and Provident Societies Acts must have at least seven members, all members of a co-operative may have limited liability if it has not registered as a limited company. The Act also lays down strict rules about interest paid on loans and the distribution of profit, and the business must be run for the mutual benefit of the members or of the community.

A co-operative may: (a) form as an original enterprise, e.g. Society for Worldwide Interbank Financial Telecommunications (SWIFT); (b) be a development of a partnership or (c) take over an ailing firm.

A co-operative must be registered with the Registrar of Friendly Societies (see address p 118), or if an incorporated limited company with the Registrar of Companies (see p 113).

Agencies

Co-operative Development Agency (CDA)

Broadmead House, 21 Panton Street, London SW1Y 4DR (Tel: 01-839 2987)

Holyoake House, Hanover Street, Manchester M60 0AS (Tel: 061-833 9379)

This is an organisation set up in 1978 by the Government to advise. Since 1984 it has made grants and loans to help establish, develop or provide training courses for co-operators and partnerships.

Highlands and Islands Development Board (HIDB)

Bridge House, Bank Street, Inverness IV1 1QR (Tel: 0463-234171)

Established in 1965 to provide finance and assistance for setting up and running community projects in the Highlands and Islands not only to co-operatives but also to manufacturing, service, agriculture, tourism and fisheries businesses.

Industrial Common Ownership Finance Co. (ICOF)
1st Floor, 4 Giles Street, Northampton NN1 1AA (Tel: 0604 37563)
Works closely with local authorities and offers advice, consultancy, and loan funds. Funds are available only to co-operatives which have registered with ICOM (see below).

Industrial Common Ownership Movement (ICOM)
7 The Corn Exchange, Leeds LS1 7BP (Tel: 0532-461737)
Advises on financial, management, legal and all aspects of common ownership. Provides model rules.

Job Ownership Ltd (JOL)
9 Poland Street, London W1V 3DG (Tel: 01-437 5511)
Sometimes known as the *Mondragon* system named after a town in the Basque region of Spain where a 1956 successful worker ownership has spread. A non-profit organisation which promotes conversion of existing firms to worker ownership. Advice free on first consultation. Provides model rules.

The Registry of Friendly Societies
England and Wales: 15 Great Marlborough Street, London W1V 2AX
(Tel: 01-437 9992)
Scotland: The Assistant Registrar for Scotland, 58 Frederick Street, Edinburgh EH2 1NB (Tel: 031-226 3224)
Northern Ireland: Department of Economic Development, IDB House, 64 Chichester Street, Belfast BT1 4JX (Tel: 0232 234488).
Information and advice about rules and registration is given for each separate part of the UK.

The Scottish Co-operative Development Committee
Templeton Business Centre, Templeton Street, Bridgeton, Glasgow G40 1DA (Tel: 041-554 3797)
Offers guidance similar to JOL but does not provide model rules.

12.5 Franchise

Franchise is a rapidly growing method of expanding or starting up in business with a proven product or service. It is not a business format but rather the taking on of an existing product or service which has a brand or product name. A franchisee may be a sole trader, partnership or limited company.

The franchisor is the organisation which is the innovator of the idea, has the rights in it and lays down the way in which the business is to be run. The franchisor ensures uniformity in such things as presentation, layout, format, recipes, premises, prices, stationery.

The person taking up and operating the business (the franchisee) pays a fee for the help and advice given during the starting up and initial launch period plus a continuing royalty and/or commission on goods supplied. The franchisee is assured of exclusive rights within an agreed area for a product range that has been successfully market tested and, often, advertised nationally. The franchisee and staff usually receive not only initial training but also subsequent updating when the franchisor introduces new lines or methods. To ensure a national standard of service and quality, the franchisor exercises control and supervision throughout the contract period.

From the end of the Second World War until about the early 1970s this type of business organisation was principally connected with major car manufacturers, oil companies and soft drink bottlers. There are now over 200 different franchise schemes in the UK. They include Holland and Barrett, the Body Shop, Prontaprint and Wimpy, as well as professional, rental, cleaning and educational services.

All of the high street banks offer special facilities to prospective franchisees and most franchisors will be able to suggest a bank which has been particularly helpful in the past. Personal investment is required and amounts start at around £3000.

The *British Franchise Association* publishes a guide and a list of its membership (see Bibliography p 122).

12.6 Starting a new small business

Definition
This concerns the person or persons considering starting a new

business (whether full or part-time) and having control of it (whether employing others or not). The business can be manufacturing, providing a service, or selling either retail or wholesale.

Skills

Apart from technical ability in the particular business the person (or persons) starting up in business will need a range of skills covering marketing, legal matters, accountancy principles and management techniques. They will need to possess:

> durability, in handling great demands on time and energy especially until established
>
> flexibility, in coping with changes in legislation, customer demand, materials supply, economic and political climate
>
> ability to update by keeping abreast of technical changes, improved methods, etc.
>
> ability to delegate when possible (and profitable to do so)
>
> decisiveness, in assessing the consequences of alternatives both in daily problem-solving and in forming a long-term objective
>
> enthusiasm to be conveyed to any employees and to customers.

Initial considerations

Market research

A new business must have established the market to whom its product/service is to be offered, from the following categories: male; female; employed; unemployed; home-based; teenagers; children; age-band e.g. 12-18, 18-30, 30-50, 50 upwards; social/economic group.

Premises

If the business is to be operated from home permission will be required. The local authority may stipulate that planning regulations must be observed. If the house is not personally owned the landlord, or mortgagor, must agree to the change of use. A household insurance policy for public liability, theft, fire and burglary may be invalidated unless the company has been told and agrees to continue indemnity.

Finance

Professional advice may be obtained from a solicitor, accountant or a bank manager. The Banking Information Service publishes a book, *The Banks and Small Firms*, which contains information on: eligibility

for aid and loans; capital investment appraisement; business systems; a list of some of the support that has been given to small firms by seven banks over the past five years (see Bibliography p 122).
Other useful addresses and contacts are:

Small Business Capital Fund	88 Baker Street, London W1M 1DC
Council for Small Industries in Rural Areas	35 Camp Road, Wimbledon Common, London SW19 4UP
Local council offices	
Manpower Services Commission	Ring Freefone and ask for *Enterprise.*
Government help and funding: small firms centres of the Department of Industry	

Type of business organisation

A small business may be: a sole trader; a partnership; a limited company or a co-operative (see 12.1, 12.2, 12.3, 12.4). *Note:* There is a legal requirement to notify Customs and Excise (VAT), Inspector of Taxes and the DHSS on commencement of business, even if full-time employment is continued.

Accounts

If financial help is needed from a bank or another source it will be necessary to submit at least the following forecasts when considering starting up in business:

- a forecasted **profit and loss account** stating the expected sales, cost of sales and all expenses likely to be incurred in making the target profit for the first year

- a forecasted **balance sheet** containing a list of all the assets, liabilities and capital at the end of the first year

- a **cash flow forecast** setting out how much money has to be spent and how much is actually received, month by month for the first year.

When the business is operating, the proprietor should compare the estimates with the actual results to ensure that any imbalance is corrected quickly. This is called *management accounting*.

Bibliography:

Starting Your Own Business. Pub. 'Which?' Magazine, 14 Buckingham Street, London WC2N 6DS, rev. edn 1986.

How to Start, Run and Succeed in Your Own Business, D Jones and W H Perry. Pub. Wheatsheaf Books Ltd, 1983, repr. 1984.

Working for Yourself, Godfrey Golzen. Pub. Kogan Page, 1986.

The Guardian Guide to Running a Small Business, Clive Woodcock. Pub. Kogan Page, 1986.

Accountants Digest No 162 (covering co-operatives). Produced and published by the Technical Services Dept of the Institute of Chartered Accountants in England and Wales, Autumn 1984.

Co-operating For Work (Booklet MS14). Pub. Manpower Services Commission Dept CW, 1983.

A Comprehensive Guide To Franchising. Pub. The British Franchise Association, Franchise Chambers, 75a Bell Street, Henley-upon-Thames, Oxon RG9 2BD.

The Banks and Small Firms. Pub. The Banking Information Service, 10 Lombard Street, London EC3V 9AR, 1985.

Advice and leaflets on all topics in this chapter are available from high street banks.

13 FINANCE AND BANKING

13.1 Banking services

Special services offered to business customers by high street banks

Home factoring
  The bank acts as the sales ledger accounts department for the client regarding the credit sales. To arrive at the discount rate to charge for this service, the bank considers the type of business, the average monthly sales and average value of each invoice and the average settlement date. The bank pays the monthly credit sales, less the discount, to the client. The client ceases to have the slow payer problem and can utilise the prompt cash payment to best advantage. The bank receives settlement from the debtors or suffers any eventual bad debt.

Foreign factoring
  Similar to the home scheme but the bank sends the invoices in the currency of the buyer and chances the fluctuations in rates of exchange.

Hire purchase facilities
  Through a subsidiary of the bank an arrangement is made by which the subsidiary company buys capital equipment and leases it to the client—this facility has possible tax benefits.

Bills—for export/import operations
  These may be for collection, negotiation or documentary credit. For example, where it is a British business making an export, the British bank makes contact with a foreign bank in the locality of the exporter. Documents of title are prepared by the British firm whose bank sends them to the foreign bank of the exporter in exchange for payment. If all is in order payment is made and the goods are despatched. The banks charge a commission for this service.

Forward exchange
  In circumstances where an importer needs to pay in the currency of the foreign supplier by a specified date, the amount can be predetermined by relating to the spot (today's) price. The currency is bought at a premium or discount which is quoted daily in the financial press.

Performance bond

In the building and construction industry it is usual for the tender to be accompanied by a performance bond. This is an assurance by a bank that their customer (the tenderer) is able to do the job to the standards and by the time limit specified.

Status enquiries

The bank can take up on behalf of a client a report from a prospective new customer's banker. The client then has an indication of the creditworthiness of the new customer.

Merchant banks

The bank can provide a specialist service for such situations as business mergers, registration services, management of pension or loan syndication.

Information and advisory services

The major banks offer a wide range of specialist knowledge to manufacturing and commercial businesses, thus ensuring that businesses consider the aid offered by the Government and other agencies. Some areas covered are:

   starting your own business
   financial control and planning for the small business
   financial incentives and assistance for industry.

Services offered to personal customers by high street banks

Borrowing

Bank loans are available to pay for furniture, holidays, car, caravan, boat, season ticket, improvements to the home or to buy a home on mortgage—provided that the borrower's bank manager is satisfied regarding repayment. The borrower should make comparisons to ascertain which bank offers the best rate of interest and terms. The law requires that annual percentage rate (APR) is clearly stated on all advertisements for loans.

Credit cards

Three credit cards—Access, Visa and Trustcard—have been issued by banks and it is estimated that 20 million have been issued in the UK. There is no charge to the cardholder who has one monthly account for all purchases with an option to pay in full, or over a period; the latter involves additional payment in the form of interest. These cards have almost worldwide acceptance.

Cash cards

In the UK over 17 million people have cash cards enabling them to obtain cash from over 14000 branches in the UK and over 8000 dispensing machines, many of which operate 24 hours a day.

Travel

Apart from the use of a credit card abroad, the banks provide other facilities for travellers. These include foreign currency, travellers' cheques in both sterling and foreign currencies which can be replaced if lost or stolen, and uniform Eurocheques which can be used in over five million shops, restaurants, garages, banks, etc. in the UK, Europe and Mediterranean countries. Most banks provide an emergency service to get cash to you quickly wherever you are, in case of need.

Insurance

The major banks have insurance subsidiaries which are staffed by specialists whose job is to get the best possible cover for customers at the most competitive price. The need may be simple, such as insuring holiday luggage, or complex, requiring a range of life policies or pension plans.

Investment

Not only will banks look after all aspects of any stock market investment(s), but they also offer unit trusts and a range of personal equity plans (PEPs) which were officially started on 1 January 1987.

Executor

Banks have long been operating the service of executorship at modest cost and they also give advice on minimising any possible Inheritance Tax, and help in the drawing up of a will.

Saving

This is the area covered by the bulk of the 200 different services provided by banks and where competition is greatest. A variety of schemes are aimed at children and regular savers, whilst investors are offered good terms for seven-day deposits, extra interest accounts and high interest cheque accounts.

13.2 Girobank

Girobank is the trading name of Girobank plc—an established clearing bank and wholly owned subsidiary of the Post Office Corporation.

The bank provides a comprehensive range of services using the national network of almost 20000 post offices for counter facilities.

Girobank is at the forefront of advanced computer technology which enables the bank to provide a fast and efficient service. The system is ideal for money movement between accounts, whether for rapid marshalling of funds, improved financial control or access to money markets. Money market dealings are handled from the bank's head office in the heart of London's financial sector.

A network of offices around the country, together with Girobank Scotland and Girobank Northern Ireland, provides close contact with business and personal customers and enables enquiries to be dealt with quickly and efficiently.

Services available to business customers

Services include:

full current account banking

nationwide service for the deposit of branch and agent takings at post offices, during long weekday business hours and Saturday mornings

withdrawal facilities and a change-giving service at local post offices

rapid marshalling of funds into central accounts to facilitate efficient cash management

full payment and collection services, including cheque, credit transfer, standing order and direct debit; Girobank is a sponsoring bank in the Bankers' Automated Clearing Services (BACS)

money market deposits for short, medium or long term investments

specialist investment services including wholesale deposits and certificates of deposit

cash transfer through Clearing House Automated Payments System (CHAPS) and Town Clearing

full international money transmission service for payments and receipts, foreign currency and travel finance facilities; rapid payments abroad can be arranged by a variety of methods from telex to SWIFT (Society for Worldwide Interbank Financial Telecommunications) credit facilities, including overdrafts, short and medium term loans, acceptance credits and leasing finance, advanced payment and deferred purchase schemes and financing for the purchase of local authority mortgages

direct credit of pay, allowances, expenses and occupational pensions; payment instructions can be in list form, on computer tape, or through another bank via BACS; cashcheques, encashable at post offices, can be used to make payment where the payee does not have a bank account

dividend payments

Transcash—whereby cash (and cheque by arrangement) may be paid in at post offices for credit to a Girobank account; ideal for paying accounts, mail order purchases and the collection of insurance premiums; the Transcash slips are forwarded to the payee after crediting by the bank

collection services enabling local authorities and housing associations to have rent, rates and mortgages paid by tenants and householders at convenient post offices

a facility for building societies allowing investors to make deposits to and withdrawals from their building society accounts at post offices.

Services available to personal customers

Services include:

full current account banking, without charges when in credit, withdrawal up to £50 every other day at either of two designated post offices, and a debit-only charging system on overdrawn accounts which operates only on the days an account is actually overdrawn

a free transfer service for payments to other Girobank account holders (this covers most household bills and many mail order payments)

a cheque card giving cheque cashing facilities at 20000 post offices and at branches of other banks, and guaranteeing cheques and transfer payments for up to £50; this card also allows you to draw up to £100 cash daily at a nominated post office

frequent statements of account (after every credit or ten debits)

high interest-bearing deposit account

personal loans and revolving credit, mortgage and bridging finance

travellers' cheques, foreign currency and postcheques which can be cashed at more than 90000 post offices in most European and several other countries automated banking, through the (LINK) network of automated teller machines (ATMs) for cash withdrawals, balance enquiries and statement ordering 24 hours a day, every day

a Visa credit card allowing instant credit and acceptable at nearly four million outlets worldwide, can also be used for cash withdrawals from Girobank ATMs in the UK and from Visa ATMs worldwide

a range of insurance services through leading UK insurance companies and specially designed for Girobank customers.

13.3 Building societies

Traditionally the purpose of a building society was to receive subscriptions from members to create a fund to make loans to them for the purchase of their residential homes. The loans were secured on the member's land. The first Act of Parliament governing building societies was passed in 1836 and the latest in 1986. The societies do not make a profit nor distribute a dividend. The scope and extent of the industry is shown in the following table:

Year	Number of societies	Value of assets	Owner-occupiers as % of all houses
1900	2286	£60 million	10 per cent
1984	190	£102 billion	61 per cent

In 1984 26 million building society subscribers created funds which enabled 6 million loans to be made to home owner-occupiers. In the same year between 15-20% of these loans were from insurance companies, local authorities and banks. The remaining 80-85% of home buyers were building society members. A person becomes a member whether lending or borrowing money from a building society.

Loans

Building society loans are of two kinds:

Annuity mortgages The borrower makes equal monthly repayments over 20 or 25 years to pay off the loan and interest. Charges in interest rates may vary the 'equal' monthly payments. In the early years of the loan the repayment covers mainly the interest charges, but in later years the capital sum borrowed takes the larger proportion of the repayments.

Endowment mortgages Monthly repayments cover the interest only but simultaneously premiums have to be paid for a life assurance policy which on maturity provides the means of repaying the capital sum. Such policies offer a 'with profits' option which may repay a larger amount at the end of the term.

Investment

Some of the schemes offered for investment are:

Ordinary shares About a third of all savers use this type of investment which allows a minimum deposit of £1, immediate withdrawal and competitive interest rates.

High interest share accounts These require a minimum deposit (e.g. £500 or £1000), allow withdrawal on demand and pay a higher rate of interest than ordinary shares.

Short notice accounts Similar to high interest share accounts but a specified number of days notice of withdrawal is required, or there is a loss of interest. The rate of interest paid is higher than for high interest share accounts.

Term shares A specified period of years is agreed (three to five years) for the deposit to remain untouched except for the death of the investor, otherwise a penalty is paid on the interest. A higher rate of interest is paid than on short notice accounts.

Regular savings A commitment is made that a regular amount will be saved each month which will attract a preferential rate of interest over the ordinary share savings rate. It is mainly used by prospective home-owners who are saving for the amount needed as a deposit.

Save as you earn (SAYE) This is another form of regular savings over a set period of time with a tax-free bonus at the end of the term.

New powers and services

The Building Society Act which came into force on 1 January 1987 gave societies wider powers in housing and banking services. Eighty per cent of a society's funds has to be raised from the investing public and mainly lent to home buyers. However, additional services may be offered to members, whilst for the first time in the history of the industry, non-members can be clients. The new services are as follows:

loans other than for home buying, possibly unsecured, may be granted to first time owner-occupiers to buy carpets and furniture for their house, and to other clients to buy e.g. cars, boats, caravans, or pay for holidays the insurance facilities previously enjoyed by members are now available to non-members whilst the range is increased by the addition of life, sickness, accident, home and contents cover

the range of savings described above is extended to include: stocks and shares dealings; unit trust management; management of personal equity plans (PEPs); financial and investment advice to the public and provide savings schemes through employers

foreign exchange services

surveys and valuations of land, estate agency and conveyancing services

loans on a second mortgage

land and property purchase

paying and collecting services for other organisations.

13.4 The Stock Exchange

The Stock Exchange was formed in 1773 to establish a market and code of conduct for the purchase and sale of securities. Historically companies were formed to finance exploration and trade and ended with the conclusion of the venture. The backers could withdraw their stake if successful in persuading someone else to buy their 'share'. The principle of shares originated in the late 17th century and has continued and developed through the industrial revolution to today's varied demands. The Stock Exchange has also progressed to meet the varying capital investment requirements of governments, industry and commerce through the same time scale.

Shares are bought and sold through stockbrokers who are also independent advisers on a wide range of financial subjects. The expertise thus required involves research by analysts to evaluate the prospects of industries, companies and their management to assess current and future share values. To buy or sell shares an approach can be made directly to a member of the Stock Exchange, to a local bank manager, solicitor or accountant, except for shares offered directly to the public. When a company offers shares to the public it must issue details (known as a *Prospectus*) of its assets and liabilities, and a summary of its history and trading results, etc. This enables the prospective purchaser to decide whether or not to buy shares.

On 27th October 1986 changes were made to consolidate the Stock

Exchange's position of pre-eminence in Europe and the international money market. Changes were also necessary to meet the government's budgeted increase in individual share ownership visualised by the Finance Act 1986. This Act outlined the personal equity plans (PEPs) which grant income tax relief on capital gains and investment income on shares within specified limits. The increasing interest of the individual investor was reflected in the response throughout the country to the British Telecom, Trustee Savings Bank and British Gas share issues.

Equities is the term given to 'ordinary' shares held by an investor. These shares are called *stock* when certain procedures have been taken to convert them from shares. If the business fails shareholders lose their investment, but usually a dividend is paid to them out of profits and there is the prospect of an increase in the value of the investment. A few companies offer shareholders a discount on their purchase of the company product or service e.g. travel, hotel bills, DIY or wine.

Securities is the term which includes not only equities but gilts, debentures, bonds, loans and stocks. See the glossary of Stock Exchange terms (Chapter 27.6) for a full list of terms.

When a deal is made on the Stock Exchange the parties receive a contract note which is an important legal document setting out the price and settlement date. This is the date when the seller transfers shares to the buyer who then pays for them.

The year is divided into two working week periods, labelled *accounts*. Settlement of all transactions during the account is usually made on the second Monday following the account and is called Account Day.

The stockbroker makes a charge for the service given in either selling or buying shares. After 27th October 1986 the fee ceased to be based on a fixed commission scale. There is also a stamp duty payable which can be varied by the Chancellor of the Exchequer's budget. Income from any of these investments is subject to income tax, and the sale of investments (other than gilts) is liable for Capital Gains Tax, again depending on the current budget ruling.

Some newspapers print details of the shares which are listed on the Stock Exchange in a form similar to that laid out on p 132.

1	2	3	4	5	6	7
High 224	**Low** 160	**Name of company** CBA 5p	**Price** 182-2	**Cover** 3.5	**Yield** 3.3	**P/E** 11.3

Columns 1 and 2 show the highest and lowest price paid (in pence) during the previous twelve months.

Column 3 gives the name of the company and in this example indicates that each share is a 5p share.

Column 4 quotes the current price in pence (182) and '−2' indicates that the price is 2p down on the previous trading day.

Column 5 means 'dividend cover' and indicates that had all profit been distributed instead of some being retained the dividend could have been 3.5 times higher than it was.

Column 6 makes an assumption that if a dividend is paid out at the previously declared rate, and that the price paid for the shares is at today's price (182p) then a £100 investment would give a return of £3.30.

Column 7 means 'price:earnings ratio' and relates the current price being paid for shares with the earnings the company is making. It is a reflection of the confidence which investors have in the company (which should be compared with other companies in the same line of business).

Note: Columns 6 and 7 are the opinions of the financial staff of the newspaper publisher.

14 SECURITY

Almost all large firms now have their own Safety Officer, someone who will deal with small routine matters as well as major security problems. If there is no Safety Officer, the General Manager or Head Caretaker should have the authority to maintain general conditions of safety on the firm's behalf.

Sensible basic vigilance is a vital part of any security system; the expense involved may well be much less than any possible consequent insurance claims against the company. Regular checking and renewal of worn fittings and furniture, careful inspection and care of electrical equipment, plumbing, locks, bolts and window catches, are all a matter of common sense in order to reduce the likelihood of painful and expensive accidents. All staff have a personal responsibility to notice, and to report to the proper quarter, any items of worn or otherwise faulty equipment (see Chapter 18.1).

14.1 Confidential information

Telephone conversations

If there are people within hearing when a confidential telephone call comes through, several courses of action are possible. One is to ask whether you may call back at a more convenient time, making sure that you know the caller's telephone number. Another is to ask the caller to hold while you move to a more privately situated extension, and a third is to ask the caller to ring back at a time when you know that you will be alone and able to take the call.

It should go without saying that anyone in possession of confidential information must guard at all times against being inadvertently drawn or tricked into divulging any part of it, whether on the telephone or in general conversation. 'I'm afraid I can't discuss that' or a flat 'I'm sorry, no comment' may be the only answer if a caller persists in being too inquisitive.

Documents

Confidential documents must be kept in their own private filing system, under lock and key, with only authorised staff having access to them. Letters, reports, minutes of meetings and company accounts which are only for restricted circulation must never be left about on desk tops or carried freely in folders that can be put down and forgotten or easily stolen. Outdated confidential documents to be destroyed should be burnt or put through a shredding machine.

Computerised data

Computerised information carries its own special risks, as the data can be tapped and read by anyone who knows how to retrieve it. Confidential computers should therefore be housed in their own separate, protected security room, or at least fitted with security locks and covers, a range of which is now on the market.

14.2 Financial responsibility

No single individual should be in charge of accounts. A second or even a third person should be available to check figures regularly, even in the case of something as minor as a petty cash box, to provide a safeguard against inaccuracies or any possible charge of pilfering. It is an accepted practice to double-check in this way and therefore no one should raise any objection. Larger accounts are of course dealt with by several members of staff and are eventually audited by a qualified firm of accountants. Continuous checking and cross-checking of all financial matters by a number of reliable people reduces the possibility of accounts being falsified.

Protection of cash

Banking and collection of money is frequently carried out too casually for safety. Various precautions should be taken when such journeys are made on a regular basis, e.g. the route taken to and from the bank should be varied; the day of the week, and the time of day when collection or delivery is made, should differ. It is always advisable for the person acting as courier to be accompanied, and at least one of the party should be male.

Firms such as *Securicor* undertake the protection of cash or other valuables in transit and the *Yellow Pages* directory provides a number of names of other security firms who can make suggestions and offer assistance for this and allied problems.

14.3 Outside organisations

Professional advice is always worth having. The Crime Prevention Officer at your local police station gives free help and advice on any aspect of security.

A wide choice of firms and agencies is to be found in *Yellow Pages* under 'Security Services'. There are companies providing equipment such as burglar alarm systems, grilles and gates, special safes and locks, as well as shredders and computer-locking devices. There are confidential enquiry agents, private detectives, personal guard services and dog patrols. Banks will guard special valuables in their safe-deposit vaults; safety-printers will produce documents or accounts and keep them confidential until their authorised disclosure date.

The *British Safety Council* issues publications advising on every aspect of business and industrial security. Helpful brochures and leaflets can also be obtained from the *Royal Society for the Prevention of Accidents* and from the *Fire Protection Association* (see Bibliography p 146 for addresses). The safety industry is extensive and constantly expanding to keep pace with present-day risks.

14.4 Office visitors

From a security aspect, and also as a matter of common courtesy, visitors should always be supervised. Expected callers with definite appointments pose no problem, but always consider the possibility that the man in overalls, wandering down a corridor, is not really an authorised workman. No stranger should ever be able to walk into a building and wander around it unsupervised.

A reliable and comfortable reception area is of vital importance, where callers can be received, checked in by internal telephone from reception to the person they are visiting, wait for an appointment if necessary, and then be personally escorted to the right destination.

When the visitor leaves the process should be reversed; a telephone call to the reception desk will ensure that the visitor is taken right to the door and is seen to leave the building.

Visitors can be issued with temporary badges or passes at the reception desk, when entry has been authorised, showing their name and the date. These temporary passes must be handed back by the visitors when they leave. In a big firm with a large number of personnel a system of entry passes for regular staff is a good one, although to work effectively this system must apply to the top management level as well as the general workforce.

Theft is an ever-present risk, especially in shops, stores and supermarkets, and any good security firm will advise on the precautionary measures to take. Closed-circuit television cameras may be of assistance, or a system of alarm tags to fix to portable goods which activate if the goods are taken away without being paid for.

14.5 Industrial safety

Safety in workshops, warehouses and factories is a specialised subject which depends on the nature of the premises and it is best to take the advice of specialists. Professional advice on all aspects of safe storage of goods can be obtained from the *British Safety Council*. Methods of storage vary enormously, according to the products concerned. For instance chemicals, paints, dry goods, special liquids, etc., all need special conditions consistent with complete safety. (See also 14.7.)

Machinery poses its own particular hazards. Moving parts are dangerous unless adequately screened; electricity, chemicals and molten metals can be highly dangerous unless properly protected and should be approached only by those who understand them.

The *British Safety Council* can offer invaluable advice on all risks of this kind and issues an extensive range of pamphlets which includes helpful information concerning the main causes of industrial accidents. (See Bibliography p 146.) It gives guidance on the conveying of heavy loads, safety measures affecting transport, different types of protective clothing and many other matters regarding prevention of accidents in business and industry.

14.6 Industrial espionage

Industrial spying is a flourishing and profitable industry as the acquisition of secret information can be worth a fortune. For instance, a new cost-cutting manufacturing process, the result of a long line of research, the likelihood of a takeover bid or an imaginative publicity project would be matters of very great interest to an industrial spy who could pass on information to a rival organisation.

Staff

It is vital for all employees always to be on guard against letting information escape inadvertently, whether written, verbal or on computer. Matters apparently trivial to one person can be of great importance to another. It is not possible to be too careful in conversation or with the transmission and storage of confidential data and documents.

Members of staff have been known to have been planted, sometimes for years, within a firm with the express purpose of becoming trusted and, at the same time, achieving a position where they can steal confidential information and pass it on. Many government departments have security staff to investigate prospective personnel thoroughly before taking them on, and again in considerable depth before promotion. All personnel managers, when engaging new employees for any kind of confidential or high security work, have a responsibility to make detailed enquiries into an applicant's previous contacts and work experience, in order to reduce the risk of infiltration into the firm by someone undesirable and dangerous.

Equipment

Competent industrial spies are patient and unobtrusive. They have access to various up-to-date specialised devices to help them and may be backed by an unscrupulous and efficient organisation willing to pay well for their services. They may use any of the following gadgets, singly or together:

> tiny transmitters to fit into a telephone, capable of relaying a conversation to a van or house several streets away
>
> suction microphones that can be attached almost invisibly to walls, windows or articles of furniture
>
> cameras that can photograph prints, plans or typescript from any distance up to 100 metres away
>
> short-wave recorders and receivers that can fit into a hat, a book or a briefcase
>
> tiny microphones, transmitters and recorders small enough to fit neatly into a matchbox, cigarette packet, wrist-watch, desk diary, etc., which can be placed casually on a desk or table or brought out during conversation.

There are confidential security agencies who will check office premises for hidden bugging devices, before important meetings.

14.7 Fire prevention

Foresight and planning are of vital importance in fire prevention and selected staff should be trained to undertake fire duties, as part of a set procedure under a designated Chief Fire Officer.

Setting up typical fire prevention scheme

The Chairman or Managing Director heads the campaign.

A Fire Prevention Committee is set up including, for example, a fire brigade representative, insurers, architects and a representative of HM Factory Inspectorate, to decide on a strategy to minimise fire risks. It is also useful to invite a risk assessor from an insurance company.

A Chief Fire Officer is appointed and a deputy to substitute for him/her when the Chief is away or otherwise unavailable. Both will have undergone training in fire prevention and precautions. He/she will work out a set procedure with full authority for setting off fire-alarms, calling out the fire brigade, calling up a private fire-fighting team and evacuating the building if necessary.

Selected personnel are trained to make regular checks at possible risk areas. Checks at night, when staff have left the premises, are quite as important as daytime inspections. Departmental managers or foremen with regular supervisory duties are suitable candidates for this task.

All employees are trained in the location of escape routes and fire exits and the positions and use of fire-fighting appliances, so that they know what to do when they hear a fire alarm, and where the nearest fire exit is to be found.

All exits should be clearly signposted and escape routes clearly marked. It must be possible to hear and recognise the sound of the alarm bell in all parts of the premises. Escape doors must *not* be locked when staff are on the premises and lifts should *not* be used in emergencies.

Fire-fighting equipment should be regularly and frequently checked to ensure that it is all in good working order; if it is not, replacements should be made immediately. The installation of smoke alarms or sprinkler systems may be worth consideration.

Occasional unscheduled fire-drills provide useful lessons in establishing how long it takes to evacuate a department or building. These exercises may be inconvenient and expensive in terms of business time lost, but if the result is that staff learn exactly how to take the quickest route out of the building with no panic, they prove well worthwhile.

Hazards

The following fire hazards merit special attention:

Smoking Cigarettes and matches are sometimes thrown aside carelessly.

Electricity Wiring and equipment can become worn, out-of-date or overloaded; trailing wires and flexes can be dangerous.

Portable heaters These should never be placed where there are draughts, nor put close to any flammable materials.

Rubbish Metal bins are the best containers for waste. Bonfires should be kept at a safe distance from buildings and sensibly supervised.

Dangerous goods Gas cylinders, chemicals, aerosols, paint, etc. require specialised storage.

Arson Regrettably these days precautions have to be taken against deliberate vandalism. All doors, windows and other means of access should be securely closed and locked when staff are away from the premises.

The local fire brigade can assist with suggestions for a fire prevention scheme for your particular business, and the *Fire Protection Association* exists to advise on planning, the provision of suitable equipment and training schemes for fire-safety personnel. Details of all these items are obtainable on request and useful leaflets, brochures and posters are also available. (See Bibliography p 146.)

14.8 Bomb scares

Dealing with a telephone warning

Any advance warning of an unexploded bomb usually comes over the telephone. When this happens the person receiving the warning call must keep calm and try to obtain as much information as possible. The following suggestions are recommended by the *Crime Prevention Section of New Scotland Yard*:

ask (1) *where* the bomb is located, (2) *when* it is timed to explode, (3) *what* it looks like, (4) *who* and *where* the caller is and (5) *why* the bomb has been planted

keep the caller talking, at the same time listening for an accent and trying to detect background noises; write down everything—the police will want as much information as possible when they arrive

inform the firm's Safety Officer at once, if there is one, or the most responsible person available; the police must be called immediately and the decision taken as to whether the building has to be evacuated.

Some firms like to have two different alarm systems, one for fire and one for bomb threats, as the procedure in each case may differ. A public address system may be used to give the alarm, providing that the person using it is absolutely calm and constructive in giving directions.

Staff should be asked to leave the building by routes leading *away* from the danger area if possible, and should *not* be sent past glass partitions or plate glass windows if this can be avoided. If personnel are already accustomed to fire-drills it ought to be possible to empty the building quickly and efficiently, with the minimum of confusion (see 14.7). There may, however, be good reasons for keeping staff inside the building, for instance if a car bomb has been planted in an outside car park.

The Safety Officer should arrange for the police to be met on arrival. There will then be a search. It is particularly important to remember that any place of shelter is checked before people are allowed to enter.

Letter bombs

Some innocent-looking objects can in fact be lethal. The *Crime Prevention Section of New Scotland Yard* recommends that any letter or packet which appears suspicious should be carefully inspected for any of the following:

> a tiny hole, as if made by a pin, in envelope or wrapping
> a foreign or otherwise strange style of writing
> no apparent airspace between the contents and the crease or fold of the envelope, the spare spaces being sealed down closely
> oil or grease marks
> visible wires
> a heavier weight than the size seems to merit
> a smell of almonds
> an unsolicited book
> something hard or stiff in a package or letter (about 2 oz or more in weight)
> an inner envelope with any of the above features, inside a normal outer envelope or wrapping.

Look for the postmark, the original source or the name of the sender; if in doubt, check with the sender. If you still feel you have something suspicious:

> put the letter or packet carefully on a flat surface, desk top or table, but *not* on the floor as it will later have to be inspected from all angles by the Crime Prevention Officer
> do not attempt to open it and do not allow anyone else to touch it

do not put it in water or any kind of container

leave it in an empty room with the door locked, keep the corridor outside clear and keep the key available for the police when they arrive.

It is worth noting that efficient mail bomb detector equipment is obtainable in a variety of types and sizes. A small desk model, for instance, can X-ray letters and small parcels, a conveyor-belt unit can feed a continuous stream of mail past the inspection area, and larger installations can screen suspect parcels and luggage. A typical all-purpose model is shown in Figure 14.1. An increasing number of major organisations are installing detector equipment in mail-rooms as part of their overall security systems, to provide reassurance and protection for staff.

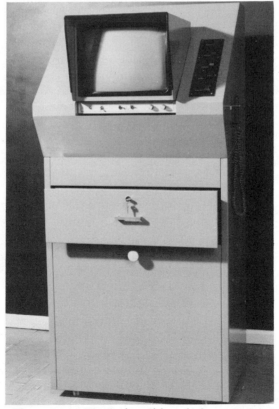

Figure 14.1 Typical mail-bomb detector unit

Car bombs

It is common sense always to leave a car with the windows closed, the bonnet internally fastened and the boot and doors securely locked whenever it has to be left unattended.

Places to check for explosive devices are under the car, along the exhaust pipe and under the engine, as well as under the wings and wheel arches. If you see unexplained wires or wooden switches, strange packages or anything else that arouses suspicion, *do not touch anything* but inform the police immediately.

14.9 Kidnapping and terrorist activities

Precautions

Everyone must now be aware that kidnapping is a common and recognised method of terrorism, undertaken for the purpose of obtaining money or bargaining power. Any person of wealth or influence, political or industrial, could be a prospective target in the violent world of today. It should not be necessary to state categorically that this is primarily and above all a matter for the police. *Department A7(3) of New Scotland Yard* are the people to contact. They offer comprehensive guidance on sensible precautions to be taken by anyone considered to be a possible target. The rest of this section lays out the main points contained in their advice.

Place of business

A security report should be made out on the building and grounds, location and surrounding areas of the business, and any overlooking vantage points.

Access to top-level offices and business suites should be controlled (special 'access control' schemes are obtainable from New Scotland Yard).

All reliable and responsible staff connected with VIPs should be trained in the action to take in the event of attack or violent intrusion.

A procedures plan should be worked out in advance, for use if the alarm system is activated.

Advance information on a VIP's movements should be restricted on a 'need to know' basis. This includes appointments in diaries, information in the press or special publicity notices, travel documents, etc., all of which should be kept concealed at all times.

Place of residence

A survey of the location, its position and surroundings should be made, including a check on neighbouring property and access routes. New Scotland Yard can advise on alarm systems and the prevention of unauthorised entry. Social visits and non-business appointments should be undertaken only with suitable precautions.

Travel

For **train journeys** made on a regular and therefore predictable basis, it is advisable to make a habit of choosing different places to sit, using a compartment already occupied, and not wearing or carrying anything distinctive such as an eye-catching buttonhole or conspicuous suitcase.

For **air travel** the booking should be made in a different name, and then changed at the last minute to the correct one. Again, plain inconspicuous luggage is advisable, which should always be kept locked and if possible within sight all the time, or checked immediately on return. Security arrangements needed abroad should be quietly planned and organised beforehand and should be confirmed before the journey is started.

It may be worth noting that a Hollywood firm, Trans World Entertainment, has produced a video guide to survival techniques in a hijack or kidnapping. In the video, a former Israeli army officer who lectures on terrorism in the United States gives much useful advice to travellers on personal conduct and behaviour in planes, airports and hotels to minimise the dangers of a terrorist attack. First distributed in America, the tape is scheduled to be released to British video outlets in 1987 and is entitled 'Travel without Terror'.

For **car travel** it is recommended that starting times be varied, that an inconspicuous car is used, with a plain-clothes chauffeur, and that the specially reserved VIP bay in the car park is not taken but an ordinary staff allocation used instead. The car should have a radio or telephone link with a base or headquarters, so that regular checks may be made during the journey.

The chauffeur should be qualified in defensive anti-terrorist driving techniques. Recognised courses of training along these lines are now available, intended to equip drivers and chauffeurs with the necessary expertise to get their passengers out of trouble. An advanced practical driving course of this kind, for training your chauffeur in anti-terrorist skills, may be worth very serious consideration.

The car should have sufficient petrol, be fully lockable, reliably roadworthy and with no distinguishing badges or stickers. The chauffeur should be wary of following cars and suspicious of unexpected diversions or roadblocks. In the event of trouble he or she will have to make a quick decision as to whether or not to make a detour.

Prior planning of journeys should always include taking note of alternative routes and places of safety, such as police stations, fire stations, ambulance depots, etc.

Prior precautions should include a telephone call, just before leaving, to a responsible contact at the destination point, to inform him or her of the time of departure and expected time of arrival. A special code-word should be chosen, to be used if confirmation is required later that any messages sent by the VIP are genuine. This code-word should only be known to the VIP, his or her family and the chauffeur.

Scotland Yard is very specific on one point. Its pamphlet, *Advice to persons considered vulnerable to kidnap*, states:

> 'It is understood that many small companies, in countries where this type of crime is prevalent, pay small ransoms and do not inform the police. IT IS VITAL THAT POLICE BE CALLED AND ASSUME RESPONSIBILITY IMMEDIATELY ON EVERY OCCASION, FOR ONCE A RANSOM HAS BEEN PAID ANOTHER DEMAND MAY BE MADE SOON AFTER.'

(The capital letters are theirs.)

Dealing with a kidnap call

If a kidnap has taken place there will be a telephone call some time later from the kidnappers. There are then several important things to remember and the person taking the call should *keep calm* and *keep the kidnapper talking*. They must try to remember everything that is said and to *write down* as much as possible so that an accurate report can be given later to the police. A foreign or regional accent, background noises and any other distinctive sounds are all significant. If you are ever in receipt of such a call:

   ask for as much information about the hostage as possible, whether they are well and if they may come to the telephone (if so, get the pre-arranged code-word from them) if you cannot speak directly to the hostage, ask for any of their special physical characteristics, which their family or friends could confirm

ask who and where the kidnapper is, what money is wanted and how and where delivery is to be made

ask how the person collecting it can be identified and how soon the hostage will be released after payment is made

try to judge whether the call is a hoax or a genuine threat

do anything you can to keep the caller talking (e.g. say that you cannot hear them, that the telephone line is faulty, ask them to repeat the information).

The results of such an attempted conversation may not be encouraging, but the main thing is to *keep talking, keep calm* and *inform the police* immediately afterwards.

The Crime Prevention Section of New Scotland Yard is located at Peel House, 105 Regency Street, London SW1P 4AN (Tel. 01-230 2367).

14.10 Insurance

In all matters of risk and security, insurance has a business priority that can hardly be overestimated. Policies must of course be updated regularly to keep pace with today's requirements, and premiums paid before their expiry date. Insurance premiums may seem expensive but, on the other hand, ignoring insurance cover can turn out to be an extremely costly mistake.

A risk assessor from an insurance company can give advice on ways of reducing the hazards in your firm as much as possible, perhaps by recommending minor alterations or rearrangements. When these risks have been minimised an adequate insurance scheme can be planned on the most sensible cost-effective basis.

Managements have a clear duty and responsibility to safeguard the interests of everyone concerned with their business activities. No firm operates in a vacuum; every company is part of a network and a major accident of any kind in one firm can have wide-ranging consequences of all kinds—physical, mental and financial—throughout the industry. An inadequate or lapsed policy or a carelessly unpaid premium can make all the difference between a minor nuisance and a major tragedy.

Bibliography:

Yellow Pages, for lists of security firms, safety equipment, etc.

British Safety Council Publications, lists obtainable from the BSC, National Safety Centre, Chancellor's Road, London W6 9RS.

Fire Protection Association Publications, lists obtainable from 140 Aldersgate Street, London EC1A 4HX.

Royal Society for the Prevention of Accidents (RoSPA) Publications, on all aspects of safety, available from the Industrial Safety Training Centre, 22 Summer Road, Acocks Green, Birmingham B27 7UT.

15 DISTRIBUTION OF GOODS

15.1 Regulations

There is a legal duty to report to HM Customs when goods are moved out of the country, to ensure that customs dues and tariffs are met. Unlike the law in many other countries, there is no statute in English law requiring the exporter (or importer) to employ a freight forwarder. However, the volume of regulations and rules and the consequent potential loss through error are a strong recommendation for utilising the services of a freight forwarder. All products have a tariff number which enables HM Customs and Excise officers to identify the declared contents of any export.

Varying regulations apply depending on the goods being exported and the country of destination. The British Overseas Trade Board (BOTB) publishes a free booklet *Help for Exporters* which includes a list of the telephone contact points where specialist market advice for an area can be obtained. The 48-page booklet provides a mine of information regarding the support available not only from the BOTB but from other organisations. Some examples are: Technical Help for Exporters (THE); Simplification of International Trade Procedures Board (SITPRO); local Chambers of Commerce; banks.

The import regulations of the destination country are of equal importance to the exporter. Items such as labelling, certification of origin, weights and measures, tariffs, vehicle regulations, etc., need to be observed scrupulously to ensure effective delivery to the customer. Delay at the port of entry will not impress the foreign customer and may involve storage charges until the documentation is clarified. Documentation varies according to category of goods, country of destination and method of transport. The following is an indication of the documentation likely to be involved with the export of goods:

HM Customs require the exporter (or agent) to 'make an entry' which provides a reference number which must be entered on the shipping documents

a commercial invoice setting out a description and the quantity of the consignment, with the requisite number of copies and, if required, a translation into the language of the consignee

a consular invoice is also required in some cases

certificate of origin

an air waybill *(if sent by air)*

CMR conditions of carriage *(if sent by road)*

CIM conditions of carriage *(if sent by rail)*

a bill of lading *(if sent by sea)*

insurance certificate.

The present nomenclature listing the codes for tariffs, Customs Co-operation Council Nomenclature (CCCN), is to be replaced on 1 January 1988 with a new worldwide system of coding and classifying goods. The new system is referred to as the **Harmonised System** (HS). At the same time the European Community's integrated tariff (TARIC) will be incorporated in the HS coding.

The two co-ordinating changes in the UK are named **Customs 88 Project.** More detailed information is available from: Customs 88 Project, HM Customs & Excise, Room 301, Dorset House, Stamford Street, London SE1 9PS.

Another move which will come into effect at that time to bring about more simplification is the **Single Administrative Document** (SAD).

15.2 Transportation

Air transport

There has been a dramatic increase in recent years in the volume of air freight. Some international airports have loading arrangements which enable a 747 jumbo jet freighter to dock straight into the warehouse building so that cargoes can be loaded quickly without being left out in the open. Some airports also have automated conveyor and storage systems. Loading is facilitated by the use of containers, pallets and the *igloo* (an air-consignment rigid box, sized for above-floor loading).

Because of the complex nature of the air freight industry it is advisable to seek the services of a member of the Institute of Freight Forwarders to obtain the most cost-effective service available. The range of this service can cover packages from one kilo in weight to a consignment requiring the chartering of a 747-200C aircraft which has a payload of 104 780 kgs. Freight forwarders can quickly arrange and assemble 'consolidated' consignments which achieve reduced charges for the consignor. 'Consolidated' means that several consignments are amalgamated into one so that, for air freight purposes, the combined packages are treated as a single consignment. Tariffs vary depending on:

whether the goods are from an industrial or a commercial user

the destination area (because different volume to weight ratios apply).

Leading international air freight forwarders, such as Trans Global Air Ltd, book regular cargo space and thus obtain concession rates which enable customers to save up to 60% off normal rates to many destinations. They also accumulate specialist knowledge of local rules and regulations regarding imports and exports which increases their ability to ensure efficient onward transhipment to outlying destinations. Trans Global have established an excellent reputation through their work with over 60 governments and government agencies around the world and have been employed as air freight specialists on building projects such as hotels, road construction and hydroelectrics. They have established a book division to cater for the special needs of British publishing houses regarding distribution and special cargo rates. Other services to customers are:

a fleet of vehicles providing a feeder link to seaports and airports

packing on the customer's premises

provision of all categories of insurance

granting permission to use a central warehouse as a receiving depot

a courier service for documents and time-sensitive items

a 'home move' service covering packing, collection, air transportation, customs clearance, delivery and unpacking at the new address.

Road transport

There are two major associations for the road transport industry:

Freight Transport Association Ltd (FTA)
St. John's Road, Tunbridge Wells, Kent TN4 9UZ

Road Haulage Association Ltd (RHA)
Roadway House, 104 New King's Road, London SW6 4LN.

Both associations keep members informed of legislation and other matters affecting the industry. They have a current list of members who offer specialist services ranging from 65 bhp vans for parcel services to 430 bhp tractors to haul trailers, or a combination of truck and draw-bar trailer for large lightweight goods. Bulk-load handling, tanker and refrigerated trucks cater for every business requirement. Manufacturers are offered a complete warehousing facility including a selection and packing operation.

The European Commission is committed to the removal of trade barriers by 1992, which means that continental hauliers will be seeking business throughout the UK. Eurotunnel have set a target date of 1993 for completion of the Channel Fixed Link. These two '90s projections will bring new factors into the haulage business in England and the RHA has begun preparations to meet the challenge.

When lorries operate in Europe and the Middle East additional requirements are:

> the appropriate 'T' form
>
> usually a TIR *(Transports Internationaux Routiers)* carnet to ensure free passage of containerised goods at intermediary customs point(s) en route
>
> vehicle registration document and driver's passport
>
> authority to drive the vehicle, rules of the road, speed, hours of driving and rest
>
> international driving licence (needed for some European countries)
>
> pre-arranged checkpoints for two-way relay of messages
>
> all documentary customs and tariff details, i.e. packing notes, value of each kind of goods carried, and the relevant customs codes for tariff purposes.

Rail transport

In his 1986 address, the President of the Chartered Institute of Transport said that rail's share of freight traffic had dropped in the previous twenty years from 21% to 9%. He explained that 70% of all goods were moved less than 30 miles and at least 90% of goods have an origin or destination away from a railway line, thus he acknowledged the economies and logistics which foster co-existence of the complementary transporters.

Railfreight International has specialist representatives located at Bristol, Glasgow, London and Manchester to cover the surrounding areas. It provides a service in refrigerated and insulated transport, as well as a list of freight forwarders and wagon operators. Charges are usually on a simple per-wagon basis but special contracts can be arranged. Uniform conditions of carriage with the various railways is assured through the CIM Convention. The EEC's Community Transit Procedure has eliminated the need for 'T' forms. Customs clearance, whether at ports or inland, is handled through British Rail or its accredited freight forwarders.

A useful publication is the *Documentation Handbook* available on request from: Railfreight International, Publicity Store, British Rail, Room 5, Melbury House, Melbury Terrace, London NW1 6JU.

Sea transport

The International Standards Organisation (ISO) has achieved a rationalisation of the sizes and range of containers to enable significant reductions in the time needed to load and unload vessels. Containerisation has resulted in a speedy turnaround of ships. Breakages and pilfering losses have also been reduced. Standardisation of facilities at ports of call, plus limiting the number of stops en route, has further reduced the voyage time for consignments. Containers can be loaded directly on to the large road haulage vehicles and trailers. The network of motorways linking European ports ensures fast road movement.

Businesses involved with shipping often use the services of freight forwarders to handle the documentation, viz: insurance, certificates of origin, customs licences, transportation to and/or from ports, and groupage (e.g. collecting sufficient freight to fill a container which is charged at a lower tariff than a part-loaded one). Cases have to be marked by a four-line code which has international acceptance, for example:

Code	Indicating
987	order number
HULL	destination
ICI	abbreviated name of consignee (Imperial Chemical Industries)
2/10	case identity (the second case in a consignment of ten to the same place, for the same consignee).

There are other standardised markings to indicate that a case has to be kept upright, that the goods are fragile or inflammable, and so on. Integrated shipment of goods by air/road/rail/sea has resulted in increased competition within the industry, resulting in transport becoming more cost-effective.

151

Courier service

See Chapter 20.2, 20.5.

Bibliography

Send It Anywhere Directory.   Pub. Kogan Page, 1983.

Croner's Reference Book for Exporters.   Pub. Croner Publications Ltd, November 1986.

Help for Exporters.   Pub. British Overseas Trade Board, January 1986.

Selling to Western Europe.   Pub. British Overseas Trade Board, 1986.

Railfreight International.   Pub. British Rail, 1984.

A Brief Introduction to Freight Forwarding.   Pub. Institute of Freight Forwarders Ltd, February 1985.

Part IV
GOVERNMENT AND LAW

John
O'Groats

All this extra distance and no extra cost

We can go near. Or we can go far.
Either way you'll have no extra to pay.

Just a simple single charge that
will guarantee delivery to any address
the length and breadth of Britain.

It's a service no other national
carrier could even begin to match.
And it's just one of an outstanding
range we can offer your business.

Call 01-200 0200 and ask for
Royal Mail Parcels.

You'll find no other carrier goes
quite so far to help you.

Royal Mail Parcels

Land's End

16 GOVERNMENT IN THE UNITED KINGDOM

16.1 The UK system of government

The United Kingdom is a unitary state with a constitutional Monarch, Queen Elizabeth II (*b* 1926), at its head. Legislative power resides in Parliament, which is a trinity of the Crown and two chambers, an upper house—the Lords, and a lower house—the Commons. The House of Commons, whose members alone are elected, is the dominant of these three branches of government. The majority party within this chamber forms the government of the day and from its ranks are drawn the Prime Minister and Cabinet, who assume day-to-day control of the nation's affairs. They work with the permanent government machine and frame new policies for passage through the Commons and the Lords. Outside Parliament, the judiciary ensures that these laws are adhered to, while local government and quangos (quasi-autonomous non-governmental organisations) carry out functions 'devolved' by Parliament.

16.2 Principal political institutions

Executive institutions

At the apex of the UK system of government stands an hereditary **Monarch**, whose powers are, in theory, extensive, including the right to appoint ministers, dissolve Parliament and give final approval (the Royal Assent) to all legislation. In practice, however, the Monarch's role is largely formal and ceremonial. She is constrained by the laws and conventions of the constitution and must act on the advice of the Prime Minister. The Queen is thus an apolitical figure who provides a stable and unifying focal point for the nation. Real executive power is wielded by her elected ministers within Parliament.

The political executive numbers around a hundred and is composed of members from the party or coalition which commands a majority in the House of Commons. It is chosen by the Prime Minister, who is the party's leader, with about 80% drawn from the Commons and the rest from the Lords. A quarter of this government team comprises 'whips', whose task is to ensure party discipline and loyalty in Parliament, and specialist law officers. The remainder of the team is primarily concerned with policy-making and overseeing the permanent executive machine, the Civil Service. They are assigned to different government departments, each usually having at its head a Secretary of State, with lower-ranking Ministers of State and junior Under-Secretaries of State below.

The top 20–25 members of the government meet together to co-ordinate policy making and executive actions in a **Cabinet**, which is selected by the Prime Minister. It convenes weekly in full session on Thursday mornings at the Prime Minister's offices at 10 Downing Street, while smaller specialised Cabinet committees and sub-committees meet more regularly, most of these enjoying independent decision-making powers. The Cabinet is the centrepiece of political authority in Britain, with its members being collectively responsible for decisions taken. Within the Cabinet, the **Prime Minister** is, in theory, 'first among equals', but is, in reality, the most important single member. Lacking detailed departmental responsibilities, the Prime Minister is able to concentrate on co-ordinating activities and determining priorities, as well as acting as the chief public spokesman for the government. The Prime Minister also enjoys extensive patronage powers, being able to award honours and appoint ministers, peers, ambassadors, senior civil servants, judges, Church of England bishops and the heads of Royal Commissions, quangos and nationalised industries.

Legislative institutions

The two chambers of Parliament—the Commons and the Lords—act as a vital check on the executive and form the links between the public and the government of the day.

The **House of Commons** is unquestionably the more important chamber, its support being essential to maintain the government in power. It also enjoys exclusive rights over financial bills and can override the Lords' vetos. The Commons comprises 650 members (MPs), who are elected on a 'first-past-the-post' basis in single member constituencies which, on average, comprise 65 000 electors. Elections are held at least every five years, with the Prime Minister exercising the right to ask the Monarch to dissolve Parliament and call fresh elections at an earlier date.

The Commons is concerned chiefly with three activities:

    the passage of legislation
    the debate of public issues
    the scrutiny of executive actions.

It meets in annual sessions beginning in November and ending in late October and sits for between 150 and 250 days per year. The timetable of the House is concerned overwhelmingly with government business, but time is also set aside for the opposition and for private members.

Legislation introduced in the House is almost exclusively framed by the government, although a few uncontroversial Private Members' Bills do find their way on to the statute book each year. This legislation needs to pass through a series of stages before it can become law. Firstly it is carefully scrutinised by government departments and lawyers and the views of interested bodies are sought, special Royal Commissions sometimes being set up for this purpose. It is then put before a Cabinet committee or full Cabinet, after which a **'Green Paper'** for discussion or **'White Paper'** for public and parliamentary notification is issued. The legislation is then presented to Parliament as a Bill and is given a general **First Reading** before the full House.

The principles behind the Bill are debated during its **Second Reading** and, if approved, it is sent to a legislative Standing Committee, composed of 20-50 members reflecting party strengths, or, if the Bill concerns important financial or constitutional matters, to a committee of the full House. During this **Committee Stage** each clause of the Bill is scrutinised and voted on in detail, with minor amendments improving the clarity of the measure frequently being made. The government can expedite discussion during the Committee Stage by applying the 'guillotine', setting a timetable for each clause.

The Bill with its amendments is subsequently put before the House again for the **Report Stage**. Last-minute changes can be made on this occasion and, if approved, it is sent to the full House for final approval after its **Third Reading**. For a Bill to become law, it needs to pass through a similar process in the House of Lords, after which it is given the **Royal Assent**. Between 50 and 70 such Bills gain approval each year. During this legislative procedure, backbench and opposition MPs are able to debate, scrutinise and propose amendments to government legislation. In addition, they keep a check on the work of the executive:

during the hour set aside for the questioning of government ministers at the start of each parliamentary day (between 2.30 and 3.30 pm, Tuesdays and Thursdays being set aside for questions to the Prime Minister)

during the 19 days allocated for debate on issues raised by the opposition through the new institutions of the 14 specialist Select Committees.

The **Select Committees**, twelve of which were set up in 1979, cover all departments except the Lord Chancellor's Law Office and comprise between nine and eleven MPs each, drawn from all parties, with chairmanships divided between the two major parties. They have the power to call witnesses and send for official papers.

The **House of Lords** forms a second chamber for scrutiny and debate. It is composed of 770 hereditary peers and 350 life peers, but its average daily attendance is only 300. Its membership is both elderly (many of the life peerages being awarded to those who have distinguished themselves in public service), and varied (including 24 Bishops of the Church of England, 2 Archbishops and 11 Law Lords). In party terms, almost 49% of its regular attenders support the Conservatives, 16% Labour, 10% the Liberal-SDP Alliance and 25% are independent crossbenchers. The Lords is of value in 'polishing up' Commons' legislation and as a forum for debate. It is also used for the introduction of non-controversial legislation, thus saving Commons' time. It lacks the power to veto Commons' legislation however, being able only to delay the implementation of non-financial Bills passed by the Commons in two successive sessions for a one-year period.

Judicial institutions

Outside Parliament, a vast judicial machine operates to ensure that parliamentary statutes and the common law are upheld. This judicial system is divided into functional branches and hierarchies. The major division is between **Civil** and **Criminal Law**, the former being concerned with damages against individuals and claims for compensation, the latter with offences against society in general which require exemplary punishment. Minor civil cases are dealt with by Circuit judges at the County Court level, more important cases being sent before the High Court. Minor (summary) criminal offences, for example driving misdeeds, are tried in Magistrates' Courts by Lay Magistrates (JPs).

More serious (indictable) criminal offences are sent to Crown Courts to be tried before a judge, and if the defendant pleads not guilty, a jury of twelve randomly selected lay people. Within each branch of the law, appeal to a higher court—the Crown Court, High Court, Court of Appeal and the House of Lords or, in certain instances, the European Court of Justice—is permissible. More than 2000 administrative tribunals also operate to hear disputes between the citizen and government agencies, dealing with issues such as rents, rates, pensions and social security benefits.

The judicial system deals with more than two million cases a year, at a cost to the State of more than £0.5 billion. Employed in its functioning are more than 44000 solicitors, 4800 barristers, 27000 JPs and 450 full-time judges.

JPs work part-time and are prominent members of the local community who have been recommended to the Lord Chancellor (a Cabinet member). They undergo a period of basic legal training, are advised by qualified clerks and are paid attendance allowances. **Solicitors and barristers** undergo specialised training and must pass examinations set by their professional bodies.

Judges are appointed from the ranks of barristers on the recommendation of the Lord Chancellor and, in the cases of the highest judges, the Prime Minister. Once appointed, they cannot be removed before their retirement at the age of 72 or 75. They thus enjoy considerable independence in decision-making, but are required to interpret the law on the basis of previous decisions ('judicial precedent') and in accordance with the strict wording of parliamentary statutes.

The Scottish judicial system differs somewhat, with the Sheriff Court taking the place of County Courts in civil cases, and with the Police, JP and Sheriff Courts replacing the Magistrates' Courts and Crown Courts in criminal offences. The Court of Sessions is the supreme civil court in Scotland and the High Court of Justiciary is the foremost criminal court.

16.3 Local government in the UK

Parliament enjoys sovereignty (supremacy) in the legislative sphere. No other body has law-making powers or can overrule an Act of Parliament. However, for convenience and to bring decision-making closer to the people, powers in specified areas have been delegated to lower tiers of government.

At the national level, there is a devolution of administrative and executive powers in the cases of Scotland, Wales and Northern Ireland, in recognition of their strong and specific identities. Both the Principality of Wales (population 3 million) and the Kingdom of Scotland (population 5.2 million), which were respectively united with England by Acts of Union in 1535 and 1707, have their own Secretaries of State in the Cabinet (usually a fellow national), junior ministers and 'offices', which take over many of the administrative and executive functions carried out by central government departments in England (population 46.5 million).

The **Welsh Office**, which is based primarily in Cardiff (although an additional small ministerial office exists in London), has full responsibility in Wales for health, housing, local government, primary and secondary education, town and country planning, water and sewerage, roads, forestry, tourism, national parks and historic buildings. The **Scottish Office**, based in Edinburgh, has even greater powers, being concerned additionally with economic planning (running the Scottish Development Agency), agriculture, fisheries, the police and fire services. It employs 9000 civil servants in five functionally divided departments. These offices are dependent upon central government for funding, but are often able to frame independent and innovative policies of their own.

Arrangements for Northern Ireland (population 1.7 million) have traditionally differed. The Province, while also sending MPs to the House of Commons, was unique in possessing its own two-chambered Parliament at Stormont between 1921 and 1972, to which Westminster devolved extensive powers, as well as its own prime minister and civil service. Direct rule from Westminster had, however, to be imposed following sectarian violence between 1968 and 1972. The Stormont Parliament was suspended in March 1972 and a **Northern Ireland Office** was set up instead, based in Belfast and London. It has responsibilities for health and social services, finance, manpower services, education, the environment, commerce and agriculture. It is functionally divided into departments, with its public servants drawn largely from the old Northern Ireland Civil Service, but its Secretary of State and junior ministers are, of necessity, of English descent. Attempts to resurrect a locally elected national assembly in Northern Ireland in the years since 1972 have so far failed.

Throughout the UK there are also subnational tiers of local government to which Westminster has devolved policy-making and administrative powers in specific fields. Its political members are elected and raise a portion of their income locally through the imposition of rates. In broad terms, local government is responsible for the provision of primary and secondary education, public housing, local buses, refuse collection, the personal social and health services, the police and fire services, roads (excluding motorways), environmental health, as well as regulating standards and local activities. They also provide leisure and cultural amenities and often promote local tourism and industries. Taken together, the local government machine is vast, its spending amounting to almost 10% of gross domestic product (GDP), or a quarter of total public spending, and it employs almost three million people. It is under the political direction of more than 100 000 locally elected 'amateur' councillors, elected for four-year terms, who are paid attendance allowances and are served by professional local government officers.

The local government system in the UK today follows a three-tier structure. The top and most important tier is that of the **County Council** (or **Regional Council** in Scotland) which is responsible for overall planning, transport, the police and fire services, education, personal social services and waste disposal facilities. Below these councils, but not subservient to them, are the **District and Metropolitan District Councils** which are concerned with housing, local planning, environmental health, leisure activities and waste collection. At the bottommost rung are the **Parish, Town or Community Councils** with responsibility for local parish amenities.

In England's seven major cities, London, Birmingham (West Midlands), Liverpool (Merseyside), Greater Manchester, Leeds (West Yorkshire), Sheffield (South Yorkshire) and Newcastle (Tyne and Wear), Metropolitan Councils used to exist, but were abolished in 1986, their functions being transferred to Metropolitan District and Borough Councils and, in a number of cases, to new **Joint Boards** composed of members nominated by the District and Borough Councils. In Northern Ireland, the democratic element is far weaker because of Direct Rule and sectarian problems. The distribution of local councils in England, Scotland, Wales and Northern Ireland is as follows:

England: 39 'Shire' County Councils; 36 Metropolitan District Councils; 296 Non-Metropolitan District Councils; 32 London Borough Councils; over 8000 Parish/Town Councils.

Scotland: 9 Regional Councils; 53 District Councils; over 1200 Community Councils; 3 Island Councils for the Western Isles, Orkneys and Shetlands (with the powers of Regional and District Councils).

Wales: 8 County Councils; 37 District Councils; over 500 Community Councils.

N Ireland: Area Boards (appointed directly by the Secretary of State); 26 District Councils (concerned with local environmental and recreational services).

The funds for local government are partly obtained from rates imposed on local householders and businesses, from council house rents and from leisure amenity charges. More than 60% of local government's income is, however, provided by central government in the form of the Rate Support Grant and specific grants for services such as the police and transport. In recent years, central government's control over local government spending and revenue raising has been tightened, with penalties being set for councils which raise rates above specified limits.

16.4 The permanent government machine

Government today is involved in a wide range of regulative, promotional and service activities. State spending accounts for more than 45% of GDP and almost 30% of the national workforce is employed in the public sector. In charge of this labyrinth of activities are more than 100000 elected officials, who are served in turn by 1.6 million full-time, professional public servants.

The central government's **Civil Service** numbers 620000 and is divided on departmental and functional rank lines. There are currently 15 major Departments of State and 16 more minor or sub-departments.

Major departments

Ministry of Agriculture, Fisheries and Food (MAFF); Ministry of Defence (MOD); Dept of Education and Science (DES); Dept of Employment (DE); Dept of Energy; Dept of the Environment (DOE); Foreign and Commonwealth Office (FCO); Dept of Health and Social Security (DHSS); Home Office; Northern Ireland Office; Scottish Office; Dept of Trade and Industry (DTI); Dept of Transport; HM Treasury; Welsh Office.

Minor Departments

Lord Chancellor's Dept; Office of Arts and Libraries; HM Customs and Excise; Export Credits Guarantee Dept; Central Office of Information (COI); Board of Inland Revenue; Law Officers' Dept; Management and Personnel Office (MPO); Ordnance Survey Dept;

Overseas Development Administration (ODA); Parliamentary Counsel's Office; Paymaster General's Office; Office of Population Censuses and Surveys; Procurator General and Treasury Solicitor's Dept; HM Stationery Office (HMSO); Office of Telecommunications (Oftel).

The largest departments are Defence (which, including the Royal Ordnance Factories, employs 98 000), Health and Social Security (90 000), Employment (55 000), the Home Office (33 000), Environment (21 000), Transport (13 000) and Trade and Industry (12 000). Within these departments, civil servants are divided functionally into grades, namely Administrative Officers, concerned with policy, and Executive and Clerical Officers, with its implementation. There are also specialist technical personnel. A number of departments, such as the DOE, DTI, DHSS and the Department of Employment, have a regional structure; the latter two also boast a large network of local offices.

The remainder of white-collar public servants work at the local government level, in public corporations (nationalised industries) and **quangos**. The latter are government agencies which have been set up by statute to carry out executive actions or to operate in an advisory, regulatory or promotional capacity. There are more than 1000, prominent examples being the Regional Health and Water Authorities, the Manpower Services Commission, the University Grants Committee, the Housing Corporation, the Milk Marketing Board, the National Consumer Council, the Equal Opportunities Commission and the Atomic Energy Authority. Quango heads are appointed by government, but are given considerable freedom of action, within financial limits, and are expected to manage their enterprises in an efficient, non-political manner.

16.5 Political parties and organised interest groups

Political power is exercised in the UK by **parties** organised at the national and local levels. These parties are based on broad ideologies and philosophies of government and appeal to different social groups and areas. They present detailed policy programmes and manifestos to the public at election-time and, once elected, serve as their representatives and form a vital bridge in the political system.

In England, Scotland and Wales four parties dominate: on the right of the political spectrum the Conservatives (membership 1.2 million, leader Mrs Margaret Thatcher), on the left, the Labour Party (membership 270 000, leader Mr Neil Kinnock). In between stand two parties, the Liberals (membership 105 000, leader Mr David Steel) and the Social Democratic Party (SDP) (membership 55 000, leader Dr David Owen), which temporarily combine as the Liberal-Social Democratic Alliance for election contests. In Scotland and Wales nationalist parties, Plaid Cymru (PC) and the Scottish National Party (SNP), are also significant entities and have seats inside the Commons. The most important minor party in Britain is the ecologist Green Party, although it enjoys no parliamentary representation.

Party politics in Northern Ireland differ substantially from that on the British mainland. The Conservative, Labour and Liberal-SDP Alliance parties do not contest elections in the Province. Instead sectarian-based Protestant and Catholic parties vie for power in local and parliamentary elections. On the Protestant side, two major Unionist parties dominate, the Official Unionist Party (OUP) (leader Mr James Molyneaux) and the hardline Democratic Unionist Party (DUP) (leader Rev. Ian Paisley), with the smaller Ulster Popular Unionist Party (UPUP) also being of importance. On the Catholic Nationalist side stand the moderate Social Democratic and Labour Party (SDLP) (leader Mr John Hume) and the extreme nationalist Provisional Sinn Fein (PSF) (leader Mr Gerry Adams), the political offshoot of the Irish Republican Army (IRA). In addition to these parties, there are a large number of minor parties, the most important of which is the non-sectarian Alliance Party of Northern Ireland.

SEATS WON BY PARTIES IN THE JUNE 1983 GENERAL ELECTION

	England	*Scotland*	*Wales*	*N Ireland*	*Total*
Conservative	362	21	14	—	397
Labour	148	41	20	—	209
Liberal	10	5	2	—	17
Social Democratic	3	3	0	—	6
Scottish Nationalist	—	2	—	—	2
Plaid Cymru	—	—	2	—	2
Official Unionist	—	—	—	11	11
Democratic Unionist	—	—	—	3	3
Social Democratic and Labour	—	—	—	1	1
Provisional Sinn Fein	—	—	—	1	1
Ulster Popular Unionist	—	—	—	1	1
Total	523	72	38	17	650

The **franchise** in elections is granted to all UK subjects over the age of 18 with the exception of peers, those certified as mentally ill and persons serving more than twelve months' imprisonment. Voting is by the simple majority system in single member constituencies, except in the case of local elections in Northern Ireland, where a proportional representation system applies. Candidates in parliamentary elections must be over the age of 21, be nominated by ten electors and provide a deposit of £500, which is reimbursed if 5% or more of the vote is achieved. Civil servants, judges, members of the armed forces, peers, Church of England and Roman Catholic clergymen, undischarged bankrupts, the certified insane and prisoners serving more than twelve months are debarred from standing for the Commons. Candidates in local elections must be over the age of 21 and must, in addition, have employment or residency connections with the area for which they stand, but cannot be an employee of the local authority in question.

While political parties seek to exercise power directly over the full range of government affairs, numerous smaller **interest groups** and **pressure groups** work outside Parliament and local government chambers, attempting to influence policy decisions in more narrowly specific spheres. These groups seek variously to promote or to defend their interest in the face of government legislation and are concerned with a wide variety of matters, economic, professional and political. Prominent economic interest groups include the Trades Union Congress (membership 9 million) and its constituent trade unions, the Confederation of British Industry, the British Road Federation and the National Farmers' Union.

Prominent professional interest groups include the British Medical Association, the Law Society and the Police Federation. Examples of political interest groups are Greenpeace and the Campaign for Nuclear Disarmament. These groups use a variety of tactics in an effort to influence public opinion and political decision makers.

Political interest groups concentrate, in particular, upon demonstrations and other forms of public action. Economic and professional interest groups involve themselves most prominently in consultation with and in the lobbying of politicians and civil service and quango leaders at Westminster, Whitehall and in the provinces. A number of the groups sponsor MPs, either directly or indirectly, the Labour and Conservative parties being significantly dependent upon trade union and business funding. Many pressure groups are quasi-permanent, others are temporarily formed to oppose specific decisions of local or national government.

163

17 LEGISLATION IN THE EIGHTIES

Since 1 January 1980 over 400 new public general Acts of Parliament have appeared on the statute books. Some of them have yet to come fully into force and some have very limited relevance to the general public. There remain, however, a large number of statutes which have come into force in the present decade which have considerable importance to a large number of people. It is clearly beyond the scope of this work to deal with all of these and this section focuses, therefore, on certain features of recent legislation which have an impact on commercial life. The matters discussed below arise from complex legislation and contain many pitfalls for the unwary. Specialist advice from a solicitor or other professional adviser is highly recommended for anyone affected by this legislation.

17.1 The Business Expansion Scheme

As part of a general government policy to encourage the formation of new businesses financed by private capital, the Business Start-Up Scheme was introduced by the Finance Act 1981. The basic idea of this scheme was to allow individuals relief from income tax on the amount of money paid for shares in new unquoted companies, provided that various conditions were met—including a requirement that the company in question should carry on a 'new' trade. The problem which the scheme was designed to help alleviate was the difficulty experienced by entrepreneurs in finding risk capital for new ventures. Inevitably, a significant proportion of new ventures do not succeed, and a private individual risks losing his or her investment. However, if tax relief is given on the investment, the net effect is that the government pays a proportion of the investment, reducing the risk of the individual by a proportion equivalent to that person's highest rate of tax.

The Business Start-Up Scheme attracted a great deal of interest but it was soon found to be too restrictive in its operation, and the **Finance Act 1983** replaced it with the Business Expansion Scheme, often referred to by its initials BES. The BES is not confined to new companies or new trades and although, as explained below, it is subject to a number of conditions, it can provide a considerable incentive for investment in unquoted companies.

The relief

Briefly, the BES allows an individual who is UK resident and who subscribes up to £40 000 in any tax year for 'eligible shares' in one or more 'qualifying' companies, to set the cost of that investment against his or her total taxable income for the year in question. An additional benefit introduced by the Finance Act 1986 is that shares issued under the BES after 18 March 1986 will be exempt from capital gains tax on their first disposal, provided that the BES relief applying to those shares has not been withdrawn.

Conditions

BES relief can only be claimed by a qualifying individual who subscribes for new eligible shares in a qualifying unquoted company. Those shares must have been issued for the purpose of raising money for a qualifying trade which is being carried on or will be carried on within two years by the company or by a qualifying subsidiary. Eligible shares are ordinary shares which carry no preferential rights. The concepts of 'qualifying individual', 'qualifying company' and 'qualifying trade' are explained below.

Indirect investment

The subscription may be made either directly or through an approved investment fund. In the case of direct investment, relief is not available for investments of less than £500 in any one company in any tax year. This lower limit does not apply to indirect investments through a fund, however, and this enables investors to spread risk in comparatively small investments over a number of companies in which a fund invests on their behalf.

Qualifying individuals

In order to qualify for relief, an individual must be resident and ordinarily resident in the UK within the meaning of the tax legislation at the time of the investment. Also, the individual must not be connected with the company which issues the shares or become so connected within the five years after making the investment.
The main rules relating to connection with a company are:

> the individual or his/her associate must not be an employee, partner or paid director of the company
> the individual and his/her associates must not control the

company or possess more than 30% of the ordinary share capital, or loan capital and issued share capital or voting power in the company.

For this purpose, an associate includes a husband or wife, lineal ancestor or descendant, a partner and certain persons with whom the individual has connections through a trust. A director is not regarded as a paid director when they are only repaid travelling and other expenses, but he or she must not be paid any remuneration.

Qualifying companies

For a company to be 'qualifying':

- it must have been incorporated in the UK and must be resident only in the UK
- it must not be quoted on the Stock Exchange and its shares must not be dealt in on the Unlisted Securities Market
- it must not be a subsidiary of or be controlled by any other company and any subsidiaries it has must be at least 90% owned by it
- all of its share capital must be fully paid up
- it must either carry on a qualifying trade or exist for the purpose of holding shares in its subsidiaries, which must all carry on qualifying trades.

Qualifying trades

The purpose of the BES is to encourage investment in risky ventures which might otherwise have difficulty raising capital. Because of this, the **Finance Act 1983** excluded from the definition of 'qualifying trade' certain activities, principally in the financial sector, which the scheme was not designed to encourage. These included commodity and securities dealing, banking, insurance and the provision of legal and accountancy services. After the introduction of the BES, there was some concern that too much BES money was being channelled into low-risk, asset-backed ventures such as property development, investment in fine wines, etc. To combat this, recent Finance Acts have placed considerable restrictions on the applicability of the BES to activities such as these and the Government has powers to bring in further restrictions by statutory instrument if further action is necessary.

Claiming relief

Claims for relief can be made when the qualifying trade has been carried on for at least four months and must be made within two years of that date, or (if later) two years from the end of the tax year in which the investment is made. The procedure for claiming relief firstly involves the company applying to the Inland Revenue for approval of the company and its trade for the purposes of the BES. Once approval has been obtained, the company may issue forms to its BES shareholders containing a certificate which the shareholders must pass on to the Inland Revenue when claiming relief in their personal taxation.

Limitation and withdrawal of relief

Relief cannot be claimed on more than £40000 invested by an individual investor (and his/her spouse) in any one tax year.

If the conditions of relief relating to the company cease to be satisfied within three years after the date of the investment or (if later) three years after the company began to carry on a qualifying trade, the relief is withdrawn. Relief is also wholly or partly withdrawn if the individual receives value from the company or disposes of his or her shares within five years. Value is received from the company if, for example, it redeems the shares or provides a loan or some other benefit to the individual.

Relief is not available unless the shares are subscribed for and issued for a bona fide commercial purpose and not as a scheme or arrangement one of the main purposes of which is the avoidance of tax.

Seeking BES finance

The BES has proved to be a considerable success and, because of this, it has been extended indefinitely by the **Finance Act 1986**. It still remains difficult, however, for companies seeking BES investment to make contact with individuals wishing to take advantage of the scheme, owing to the very considerable restrictions which the law places on the ability of companies to offer shares to individuals. These restrictions are contained in the Companies Act 1985 and the Prevention of Fraud (Investments) Act 1958, replaced by the **Financial Services Act 1986**. Contravention of these provisions is a very serious matter and companies seeking BES investment from members of the public should always seek professional advice. However, contacting an approved investment fund would not amount to an offer to the public and might provide a company with more straightforward access to BES funds.

17.2 Share incentive schemes

There has been a trend in several industrial countries, over the last two or three decades, to encourage employees to acquire shares in the companies for which they work. In this way, the employees receive an additional incentive to work hard and this benefits both the company and, more indirectly, the economy of the country in question.

The incentive can be provided to the employee in a number of different ways, but the two main methods involve either the acquisition of shares by the employer (or a trust on his or her behalf) wholly or partly paid for by the company itself or the acquisition by the employee of options to buy shares at a later date. An option is simply a right to call upon the company to issue shares to the option holder at a particular price. The advantage to employees arises if, say, they have an option to buy shares at £1 each and the share price has moved up to £5 each. They can realise a profit by buying at the lower price and selling at the higher.

In the UK, the basic taxing provisions are structured so as to tax as income any benefits obtained from employment, including shares and share options. In ordinary cases, the disposal of shares or options by an individual gives rise to a charge to capital gains tax rather than income tax. In the case of shares or options acquired by employees in their employment, however, income tax is in many instances payable on any gain on disposal or deemed gain where shares are acquired on special terms and held for a specified period. The treatment of capital gains as income is particularly unattractive for higher rate tax payers, who find themselves paying tax at rates higher than the uniform rate for capital gains tax. It may also be disadvantageous for many basic rate tax payers, however, if their gain would otherwise fall within the annual allowance for capital gains tax, bearing no tax at all.

To encourage employee share ownership, specific exemptions from the basic taxing provisions have been enacted in various Finance Acts. Each of these involves the establishment of a scheme which must be approved by the Inland Revenue before relief is given. Details of the schemes are given below. It is important to appreciate that these schemes provide exceptions to the basic taxing provisions and that relief from income tax will not be available unless the schemes are properly set up and operated.

Approved Profit-Sharing Schemes

Approved Profit-Sharing Schemes were introduced by the **Finance Act 1978** and involve an employing company paying a part of its profits to trustees, who use these funds to buy shares in the company (or its parent company) for the benefit of eligible employees. The shares are appropriated to the individual employees but must normally be retained by the trustees for a two-year retention period. After this period, the employees may instruct the trustees to dispose of the shares, but the disposal is only exempt from income tax in normal circumstances if it takes place after a further three years. The company is allowed relief from corporation tax on the amount of profits which it applies towards the acquisition of shares for employees by the trustees of the scheme.

Participants

The scheme must be open to all individuals who are full-time directors and employees of the company concerned and have been such for the qualifying period (not exceeding five years) laid down by the rules of the particular scheme. A participant must be someone who pays tax under Schedule E and must not have had shares appropriated to him or her under another approved scheme run by the same or a connected company. No relief is available to an individual if the employing company is a close company and the individual or his/her associates hold more than 25% of the ordinary shares.

Shares

The scheme shares must be shares of the employing company or its parent company. They must be fully paid up and must be part of the ordinary share capital of the company. Except in the case of workers' co-operatives, the shares cannot be redeemable and must not be subject to any special restrictions which do not apply to all shares of the class. It is permissible for companies to include a provision in their Articles of Association which obliges employees or directors to sell their shares when they cease to hold their office or employment with the company, but this will only be allowed if it applies to all shares of the class—not only to scheme shares—and if the compulsory sale is for a cash consideration. Except in the case of employee-controlled companies, the company concerned must only have one class of ordinary share or, if it has more than one, the majority of the class of shares used in the scheme must not be held by employees.

Approval

Relief from income tax will not be given unless the scheme is set up in accordance with the provisions of the Finance Act 1978 and is approved by the Inland Revenue. Relief will not be available if the conditions of the scheme are not observed. The scheme must provide for shares, acquired by the trustees, to be appropriated to eligible employees or directors within 18 months of purchase by the trustees. In general, the shares must be retained by the Trustees for two years after appropriation (the *retention period*) although there are special provisions to deal with takeover bids, mergers, etc. which may occur during this period. The retention period comes to an end before two years in the event of the death of the participant, if he or she reaches pensionable age or if he or she ceases to be employed by reason of disability or redundancy. In the case of a workers' co-operative where the scheme shares are redeemable, the retention period comes to an end when the employee ceases to be employed by the co-operative, for any reason.

At the end of the retention period, the participant can instruct the trustees to sell his or her shares, but if the disposal takes place before the fifth anniversary of the date when the shares were appropriated to that person (the *release date*), they will be subject to income tax on the value of the shares at the date of appropriation. This provision does not apply in the case of the death of a participant before the release date and if the participant reaches pensionable age or loses his or her job through disability or redundancy, the income tax charge is levied only on 50% of the relevant value. If the participant instructed disposal of his or her shares in the year prior to the release date, the appropriate percentage will be 75%.

The value of shares which may be apportioned to any participant in any one tax year must not exceed 10% of his or her salary for the year in question or £1250, whichever is greater, subject to an overall limit of £5000.

Savings-Related Share Option Schemes

Savings-Related Share Option Schemes were introduced by the **Finance Act 1980** and provided an opportunity for employees to benefit from the increase in the share price in their employer company or its parent by exercising an option to acquire shares at the end of a prescribed period. Such a scheme operates by the relevant company granting to a participant an option to acquire shares at a price not less than 90% of the market value of those shares at the time of the grant of the option. The participant must enter into an approved Save As You Earn (SAYE) contract at the same time as he or she receives his or her option and the acquisition of shares by the exercise of the option must be paid for out of the proceeds of the SAYE contract—i.e. the savings which he or she makes and the tax free bonus paid at the end of the contract period (the *bonus date*). The SAYE contract must provide for a monthly payment into a building society or other approved savings body not exceeding £100 and must last for between five and seven years.

Participants are not obliged to use the savings from the SAYE contract to buy shares, but if they decide to do so, they must exercise their option within the six months after the bonus date. If the participant dies within this six month period, his or her executors have twelve months from the bonus date to exercise the option.

Participant and shares

The qualifications for participants in Savings-Related Share Option Schemes are similar to those which apply to participants in Approved Profit Sharing Schemes, and the shares must satisfy similar criteria.

There are no special provisions relating to workers' co-operatives.

Approval

A scheme requires to be approved by the Inland Revenue before relief is given. The scheme must allow participants to exercise options prior to the bonus date on the attainment of pensionable age, on termination of employment through injury, disability or redundancy or (after three years from the grant of the option) on termination of employment for any other reason. In each of these circumstances, the option must be exercised within six months after the relevant event and will be eligible for the taxation relief provided by the scheme. The scheme must also provide the executors of a deceased participant with the opportunity to exercise the option within the twelve months following the participant's death even if this occurs before the bonus date. Again, this exercise will be eligible for relief. The scheme may provide for the exercise of options prior to the bonus date in the event of a takeover bid and in other similar circumstances, but in this case, if the option is exercised pursuant to such a provision within three years of the grant of the option, no relief will be available.

Approved Share Option Schemes

The Share Incentive Schemes introduced by the 1978 and 1980 Finance Acts were generally welcomed but met with criticism in some quarters on two main grounds—(1) they were both relatively limited in their extent, the 1978 Scheme being limited to £5000 per annum and the 1980 Scheme being limited to £1200 per annum plus bonuses; (2) in order to obtain approval, they had to be open to all employees and directors who met the relevant criteria. In response to these points, the **Finance Act 1984** introduced a new Approved Share Option Scheme, which could relate to considerably larger sums and could be offered to employees or directors selected, largely, at the discretion of the board of directors of the relevant company.

Under the scheme, a company may award options to selected employees or directors. The aggregate value of unexercised options held by a participant must not exceed, at any time, the greater of £100 000 or four times that person's current or preceding year's salary, provided that the salary is subject to PAYE. The value of shares covered by an option must normally be the market value of the shares assessed in the period of 30 days prior to the grant of the option.

Participants

Participants must be either full-time directors (normally 25 hours per week) or qualifying employees, who are required to work at least 20 hours per week. As in other schemes, a person will not be eligible to be a participant if the employing company or its parent is a close company and he or she has a material interest in it.

Shares

The shares which may be the subject of an Approved Share Option Scheme are subject to criteria similar to those which apply to Approved Profit Sharing Schemes and Savings-Related Share Option Schemes.

Approval

A scheme requires to be approved by the Inland Revenue before any options may be granted under it. The scheme may allow a participant to exercise an option at various times, but relief from income tax will only be obtained if the time of exercise of an option is not less than three years nor more than ten years after the date of the grant of the option. In addition, an option may not be exercised less than three years after the participant last exercised an option under an Approved Share Option Scheme. If the participant dies, his or her executors may exercise any options which he or she had and obtain tax relief without being subject to the 'three year' rules provided that they exercise the options not later than one year after the participant's death and not later than ten years after the grant of the options in question.

17.3 Purchase by a company of its own shares

It has been an established rule of UK company law for nearly 100 years that a limited company may not purchase its own shares and this basic prohibition is now contained in the **Companies Act 1985**. The rule was created to avoid a company reducing its capital without the authority of the court and to prevent a company from artificially manipulating its share price by 'trafficking' in its own shares.

There are some instances, however, particularly in the case of private companies, when the capacity of a company to buy its own shares may be of considerable benefit. In family-owned companies, for example, one shareholder may die or may wish to have no further active involvement in the business. In these circumstances, there may be a need to release capital represented by that shareholder's holding in the company while at the same time a desire on the part of the other shareholders not to allow the sale of the shares to any outsiders. If the other shareholders do not have or cannot raise sufficient funds to purchase the shares for themselves, the options open to them were often liquidation or a complicated petition to the court for authority to reduce the company's capital. The Companies Act 1981 introduced provisions allowing for the purchase by limited companies of their own shares in certain circumstances. These provisions are now contained in the Companies Act 1985 and operate by way of an exception to the general prohibition referred to above. They apply both to public and private limited companies but only the provisions which relate to the latter will be considered below.

Procedure

In order to purchase its own shares, a company must have power to do so contained in its Articles of Association. Shares may not be purchased unless, after the purchase, there are at least two shareholders in the company and there remains in issue at least one share which is not redeemable. All purchases by a company of its own shares must be approved by a special resolution of the company in general meeting. A copy of the contract for the purchase (or, if there is no written contract, a memorandum of its terms) must be available at the meeting at which the resolution is passed and must also be available for inspection at the registered office of the company for at least 15 days prior to the meeting. The special resolution would be ineffective if it had not been passed, had it not been for the fact that the votes attached to the shares which were to be purchased by the company were cast in favour of the resolution.

Shares may be purchased out of distributable profits, the proceeds of a fresh issue of shares and, subject to certain conditions, out of capital. Payment for shares out of capital is only permitted if, and to the extent that, the available profits of the company together with the proceeds from any fresh issue of shares, are insufficient to make the required purchase. 'Available profits' are determined by reference to accounts prepared as at a date within three months prior to the date of the statutory declaration of the company's directors referred to below.

It is illegal for a company to purchase shares out of capital unless the directors make a statutory declaration to the effect that the company will, during the twelve months after the payment for shares out of capital, be able to pay its debts as they fall due. This statutory declaration must be supported by a report from the company's auditors. No later than one week after the statutory declaration the company must pass a special resolution approving the purchase, and the special resolution will be ineffective unless the statutory declaration and auditors' report are available for inspection at the meeting at which the resolution is passed. The purchase must take place no earlier than five weeks and no later than seven weeks after the date of the special resolution.

In the week following the special resolution, the company must publish, in the *London Gazette* and in an appropriate national newspaper, a notice with details of the resolution and the proposed purchase, informing any creditor of the company of their right, within five weeks of the resolution, to apply to the court for an order prohibiting the purchase. The court may, on the application of such a creditor or a shareholder of the company who did not vote in favour of the special resolution, either confirm or cancel the purchase or make such other order as it thinks fit. The Act also makes provision for notification to be given in the prescribed manner to the Registrar of Companies at appropriate stages in the procedure.

Taxation

In ordinary circumstances, the purchase by a company of its own shares for more than the subscription price originally paid for those shares would be treated as a distribution by the company equal to the amount of the excess. This would give rise to an advance corporation tax liability on the part of the company and the distribution would be investment income in the hands of the shareholder, with the appropriate tax credit. However, the Finance Act 1982 introduced provisions which prevented such treatment in two cases, both of which involve unquoted companies.

The first case concerns the purchase of shares by a company to raise money for the payment of capital transfer tax, provided that substantially all of the purchase price is used for such a payment, that the payment is made within two years of death and that the capital transfer tax liability could not otherwise have been paid without undue hardship.

The second case arises where the whole or main purpose of the purchase is to benefit a trade carried on by the company or by any of its 75% subsidiaries, provided that certain conditions are satisfied and provided also that the purchase is not mainly aimed at avoiding tax or enabling the seller of the shares to participate in the company's profits without receiving a dividend. In order to satisfy the conditions contained in the Finance Act, the selling shareholder must be resident and ordinarily resident in the UK in the tax year when the purchase is made and must have held the shares for at least five years. Special provisions apply where the seller has acquired the shares from his or her spouse or under a will or intestacy or where the seller holds the shares as an executor.

After the transaction, the selling shareholder and his or her associates must have reduced the nominal value of their shareholding in the company and their entitlement to a share in the company's profits by at least one quarter. The selling shareholder (and his or her associates) must also have no control over the company after the transaction and there must be no arrangements in place which would result in such control being regained after a period of time. A procedure exists for obtaining prior clearance from the Inland Revenue. Stamp duty is payable on the transfer of shares from the seller to the company at the normal rates.

17.4 Personal liability and disqualification of directors

Personal liability of directors

It has always been a fundamental feature of a limited liability company that its directors are not personally liable for the debts and obligations of the company. There have always been some exceptions to this general rule, but it has only been in rare cases, normally involving conduct which is clearly fraudulent, that ordinary creditors of a company have had any recourse against directors themselves. This position has been altered by the introduction of the concept of 'wrongful trading' in the Insolvency Act 1985, now replaced by the **Insolvency Act 1986**.

If a company has gone into insolvent liquidation, it is now possible for a liquidator to apply to the court for an order declaring that a director should contribute, from his or her own funds, to the company's assets. The court will not make such an order, however, if it is satisfied that the person concerned took every step which he or she should have taken to minimise potential loss to the company's creditors when they knew, or ought to have known, that the company had no reasonable prospect of avoiding insolvent liquidation.

Disqualification of directors

The Insolvency Act 1985 also introduced provisions, now contained in the **Company Directors Disqualification Act 1986**, giving the court wider powers to disqualify directors. In every liquidation, receivership or administration, the relevant officer now has a duty to report to the Department of Trade on the conduct of directors. On the basis of this report, the Secretary of State may apply to the court for a disqualification order if it appears expedient in the public interest. If such an application is made in the case of directors of an insolvent company, the court has a duty to make an order if it is satisfied that their conduct makes them unfit to be concerned in the management of a company.

17.5 The Data Protection Act 1984

The Data Protection Act 1984 introduced important new controls on the use of computers for holding information on living individuals. The Act uses a number of new expressions, the meanings of which are explained below.

A new Register has been established, under the control of the Data Protection Registrar, and with effect from 11 May 1986 data users who hold personal data on computers have been obliged to register details of the data they hold, the purposes for which the data is held, the sources of the data, the categories of person to whom the data may be disclosed and the foreign countries to which the data may be transferred. Failure to register will constitute an offence. There is also an obligation on computer bureaux to register particulars of their names and addresses.

The Act also imposes a duty on data users to adhere to certain principles regarding the collection, holding and disclosure of personal data. A further feature of the Act is that data subjects are now given the right to obtain access to personal data concerning them, the right to have that information rectified if it is inaccurate and the right to seek compensation for damage and distress caused by the loss, destruction or unauthorised disclosure of personal data.

There are a number of exceptions from the effects of the Act, including an exception for personal data held by an individual and 'concerned only with the management of his personal, family and household affairs or held by him only for recreational purposes'. The Act is, therefore, unlikely to affect the ordinary domestic use of home computers for Christmas card lists, etc. Anyone contemplating more extensive use of a computer in connection with personal data, however, should obtain further information (see p 178).

Terminology

The following are key expressions used in the Data Protection Act 1984:

computer bureau   A person (including a company or firm) who processes personal data for data users or allows data users to process personal data on his or her equipment.

data   Information recorded in a form in which it can be processed by equipment operating automatically in response to instructions given for that purpose.

data subject   An individual who is the subject of personal data.

data user   A person (including a company or firm) who controls the contents and use of a collection of personal data which is, or is to be, processed automatically.

personal data   Information about a living individual (not a company or corporation), including expressions of opinion but excluding indications of the intentions of the data user relating to that individual.

Further information

Booklets containing guidance on the Act are available from the Office of the Data Protection Registrar, Springfield House, Water Lane, Wilmslow, Cheshire SK9 5AX (Tel. 0625 535777). Application packs for registration containing the Registrar's notes on procedure may be obtained from post offices.

Part V
OFFICE SAFETY, EQUIPMENT
AND SERVICES

NOW CUSTOMERS IN ALL THESE COUNTRIES CAN CONTACT YOU POSTAGE-FREE!

You already know the value of the Business Reply service. It means customers don't have to pay for a stamp when they reply. So they're more likely to answer direct mail – which encourages sales. And they're likely to pay bills more quickly – which improves cash flow.

Now the Royal Mail has introduced a NEW Business Reply service – for British companies who export and advertise to twelve countries in Europe.

Business Reply envelopes and cards can now be included in your mailings to the following countries: Belgium, Denmark, Finland, France, Holland, Iceland, Luxembourg, Monaco, Norway, Portugal, Spain, Sweden.

The new service could mean a lot to your company's profits – and it costs surprisingly little. What's more, your own postage for letters up to 20g to all EEC member countries is now down to 18p . . .

You need the details of International Business Reply.

Please write to:

Sally Bennett, FREEPOST (no stamp required), Royal Mail International Letters, Room 320, 52 Grosvenor Gardens, LONDON SW1W 0YA

ROYAL MAIL
INTERNATIONAL LETTERS

18 HEALTH AND SAFETY

18.1 Health and safety at work: checklist

First aid

Is first aid kit regularly inspected and replenished? ☐ ☐
Are there trained first aiders always available? ☐ ☐
Are the names and the location of first aiders
prominently displayed? ☐ ☐
Has any provision been made for a permanent/
temporary first aid room? ☐ ☐

Accidents

Is there a standard procedure for reporting
accidents? ☐ ☐

Fire

Are fire notices prominently displayed? ☐ ☐
Are fire doors closed but never locked? ☐ ☐
Are flammable liquids handled with caution and
stored safely? ☐ ☐
Is the fire alarm in good working order? ☐ ☐
Is a regular fire drill carried out? ☐ ☐
Is adequate fire-fighting equipment installed and is
it checked at regular intervals? ☐ ☐

Radiators

Are these kept completely free? ☐ ☐

Electrical equipment

Are there any unguarded electric fires? ☐ ☐
Are there any trailing flexes? ☐ ☐
Are machines switched off/unplugged when not in
use? ☐ ☐
Are any electric points overloaded? ☐ ☐
Are all electrical appliances regularly serviced? ☐ ☐

Machinery

Are guards fitted to any dangerous machinery? ☐ ☐

Protective clothing

If special clothing has been issued against a
particular hazard is it being used correctly? ☐ ☐

Passages

Are these free from obstructions of any kind? ☐ ☐

Stairs

Is there a handrail?
Are the stair treads at all worn?

☐ ☐
☐ ☐

Flooring

Are any floor coverings badly worn?
Are floors clean but not highly polished?

☐ ☐
☐ ☐

Ventilation

Is there a flow of fresh air without draughts?

☐ ☐

Lighting

Is the lighting completely adequate in all parts of
the rooms and corridors?

☐ ☐

Temperature

Is the minimum standard 16°C?

☐ ☐

Space

Is there 400 cubic feet of working space per person?

☐ ☐

Toilets

Are the sanitary provisions and supply of
wash-basins adequate?

☐ ☐

Drinking water

Is there a constant supply of fresh drinking water?

☐ ☐

Filing

Are files kept at the right height?
Are cabinets placed so that there is ample room
when any drawer is fully extended?
Are drawers ever left open to trip up the unwary?

☐ ☐
☐ ☐
☐ ☐

Waste paper

Are there sufficient waste paper baskets?

☐ ☐

Noise

Is the level of noise acceptable?

☐ ☐

Safety Officer

Is there a Safety Officer or Representative on the
staff?

☐ ☐

Safety policy

Is there a written policy statement on safety and
are staff aware of it?

☐ ☐

18.2 Emergency first aid in the office

Serious emergencies

Cardiac arrest

This is the most serious medical emergency likely to be encountered in the office. Although it is likely to be an extremely rare occurrence, it is important to know what action to take. The patient will certainly die if nothing is done, but if resuscitation is attempted there may be as much as a 50% chance of saving his life. Resuscitation must be begun urgently—within three to four minutes—or permanent brain damage may occur.

The main signs of cardiac arrest are:

    unconsciousness

    absent pulses

    absent respiration

    dilated pupils (after a few minutes).

The most likely sufferers are males aged 45-64. The loss of consciousness is sudden and the patient will look pale. You will not be able to feel a pulse at the wrist (below the thumb) or below the chin (at the angle of the jaw). Most cardiac arrests are due to heart attacks and the patient may have complained of chest pain before collapsing.

Action to be taken:

    summon others to help you; one person should immediately dial 999 and call an ambulance

    strike the lower half of the sternum (breast bone) with a hard blow of the fist. If this fails to work within ten seconds and there is still no pulse, external cardiac massage should be attempted

    working together, one person should perform external cardiac massage (Fig. 18.1) while another should apply artificial respiration (Fig. 18.2). Lay the patient on the floor on his back. The neck should be arched and the chin braced to establish a clear air passage (Fig. 18.3). Loosen clothing around the neck, waist and chest and remove dentures.

The first person places the heel of one hand over the lower third of the patient's sternum (breast bone) with the heel of the other hand on top of the first hand. With arms straight, the rescuer rocks forward, pressing on the lower half of the sternum, depressing it 3-5 cms. This is done at the rate of approximately one depression per second.

Fig. 18.1 Cardiac massage

The second person performs mouth to nose or mouth to mouth respiration. He takes a deep breath through the mouth, sealing his lips round the patient's mouth (in which case the nostrils should be pinched shut) or round the nose, blowing into the patient's lungs until the chest rises. The rescuer then takes away his mouth and watches the chest fall. This is repeated 12-15 times per minute—about once for every five times the sternum is depressed as above. The first person should stop depressing the sternum while air is being blown into the patient's lungs by the second person. Both should continue until medical help arrives.

Fig. 18.2 Artificial respiration

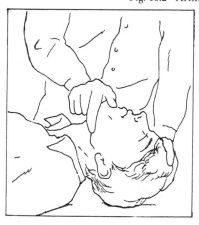 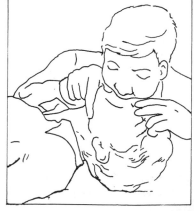

Fig. 18.3   Making a clear air passage

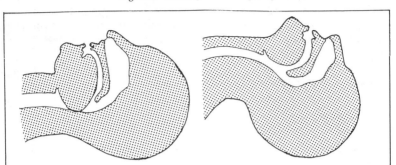

Unconsciousness

(The patient is still breathing, the heart is beating, and the pulse is present). Possible causes:

  stroke
  drug or alcohol overdose
  diabetes
  epileptic fit
  simple faint.

Lay the patient on the floor on his side. This is the easiest position for the patient to breathe in without choking. Loosen tight clothing around the neck and waist and remove dentures.

In the case of a simple faint the patient will rapidly recover when lying down. If consciousness is not regained within a few minutes, call an ambulance. If the patient is frothing at the mouth and making odd noises, if his limbs are jerking or if he is very stiff rather than limp, he is likely to be having an epileptic fit. He will be unconscious and will not hear what is being said to him. Clear a space so that he cannot injure himself by knocking against furniture. If possible, remove dentures, which may obstruct breathing. It is not necessary to put anything in the mouth; even if the patient does bite his tongue it will heal rapidly.

Wait two to three minutes. Recovery will probably occur quite quickly and consciousness will be regained. The patient will probably be sleepy and may complain of aches and pains. At this stage it may be helpful to seek advice from the patient's general practitioner if he or she can be contacted by telephone. If the fit does not stop in the space of two or three minutes help should be summoned urgently.

Electric shock
Action to be taken:

switch off the current

if necessary, pull the patient away from the electricity source by his clothes

if cardiac arrest has occurred, proceed as in the previous section.

Major fall
(A fall from a height where serious injury to spine or legs could have occurred)
Action to be taken:

do not move the patient if serious injury is suspected

call an ambulance

give nothing to eat or drink.

Minor emergencies

It is useful to have a **first aid kit** to deal with minor emergencies. The suggested contents of such a kit are:

soluble aspirin and paracetamol tablets for headaches and minor aches and pains

adhesive dressings such as Elastoplast in various shapes and sizes for cuts and bruises

non-sticky dressings such as Melolin to cover temporarily more serious wounds which will require stitches or other treatment in a doctor's surgery or a casualty department (also crêpe bandages to hold these dressings in place)

cotton wool and antiseptic solution to clean grazes and small cuts (a small bowl is useful for this purpose)

gauze swabs (several layers of these may be applied to a cut which is bleeding heavily; pressure is then applied with hands or by bandaging the swabs in place to stop the bleeding)

triangular bandage to make a sling to support an injured arm, wrist or hand (this may be done before treatment is sought from a doctor)

scissors, safety pins and tweezers.

Nose bleeds

The patient should sit or lie down quietly. An assistant, or the patient himself, should then press over the bleeding nostril for ten minutes without moving. This is almost certain to stop the bleeding. Afterwards the patient should avoid blowing or cleaning his nose and thus disturbing the newly-formed blood clot.

Eye accidents

It is possible to remove an eyelash or small dust particle from the corner of the eye using a rolled-up tissue. It is best to seek medical help with other foreign bodies. If anything is sprayed or splashed in the eye, wash the eye immediately with plenty of water.

Burns

Run the burned part under a cold tap. If skin is broken or blistered, cover with a clean, dry, non-stick dressing. If it is extensive, cover in the same way and seek medical help.

18.3 Disablement

In order to register as disabled, a person must have injuries, disease or congenital deformities which have lasted for more than twelve months and which cause substantial difficulty in finding suitable employment. A registered disabled person then becomes the holder of a **green card**. This system is entirely voluntary and many people with disabilities are not registered, either because they do not wish to be or because they are not eligible. They and their employers, however, may need advice and practical help to enable them to find work.

The Manpower Services Commissions Disablement Advisory Service, which can be contacted through local job centres (listed in the telephone directory under *Manpower Services Commission*) provides a comprehensive service of advice and practical and financial help to allow people with all sorts of disabilities to work. They provide many information booklets, including those covering specific medical conditions. They may finance necessary adaptation of work premises or equipment, or may loan (permanently) expensive equipment to help a disabled individual to work. They can also arrange for assessment of capability at an employment rehabilitation centre.

Types of disability

Arthritis

This is the most common cause of long-standing disability and affects both sexes and all ages. The extent of disability depends on which joint or joints are involved. The usual problems are pain and restriction of movement. Pain can often be controlled with drugs but, if inadequately controlled, can affect concentration and work performance. Restriction of movement leads to many problems, but it is often possible to get round these. An occupational therapist can visit the office and assess the problems of the disabled individual, and then any adaptation required may be financed by the Manpower Services Commission.

A 'Fares to Work' scheme organised by the same body will help meet the cost of a taxi or pay a fee to a colleague for transporting a disabled person who is unable to use public transport. Even when a person is severely disabled and, for example, confined to a wheelchair (also through conditions other than arthritis) work may be feasible with alterations to the office and to the facilities.

Epilepsy

There is no reason why an epileptic should not work normally in an office. Most epileptics are normal in every way, except during fits. The majority of epileptics are on drugs which are very effective in preventing fits; this is certainly the aim of treatment. If a fit does occur, it may be very alarming to an observer who has not previously seen one, and it is desirable that colleagues should have some idea of what to expect should a fit occur and of how to deal with it. Anticonvulsant drugs used in epilepsy may cause drowsiness and impaired concentration and co-ordination, and therefore affect work performance. Epileptics who have had a daytime fit during the last three years may not drive a motor vehicle.

Diabetes

This condition should normally present no problems at work. Diabetics should eat regularly and should not miss meals. They should carry a supply of glucose in case of hypoglycaemia or low blood sugar, which may be caused by insufficient food or too much exercise. Colleagues should know about the person's diabetic condition. Drowsiness, faintness and uncharacteristically irritable, difficult or confused behaviour may be an indication that the blood sugar is too high or too low.

Many diabetics must test their urine for sugar before meals in order to keep their blood sugar well-controlled. They may also need to give themselves insulin injections: toilet facilities should therefore be adequate.

Heart problems

These may arise when a person convalescing from a heart attack or heart surgery returns to work. The return should be gradual. Initially it would be preferable for the person to work part-time and at a slower pace, but there is no reason why both the hours and the pace should not be increased gradually to the previous level over the course of a few weeks. It is very important for the affected individual not to smoke.

Psychiatric problems

Psychiatric illness is one of the most difficult disabilities to deal with for both the sufferer and for colleagues. A person who is mentally ill is likely to be unable to cope with work and either may not realise that he is ill, or may realise it but be unable to do anything about it. As a result, extra pressure is put on colleagues and goodwill may be exhausted. It may then be very difficult for an individual who has already suffered considerable loss of confidence to get back to work. What is required in dealing with such a person is great patience and understanding, together with an ability to disregard events leading up to the breakdown, which may have caused a fair degree of disruption. Communication with the individual's general practitioner, with his permission, may be helpful in dealing with him.

Eye problems

In an office it may be difficult for a person who develops a visual handicap to work normally. It is important to make things as easy as possible by ensuring that light is good. In the case of blindness or partial blindness, the Royal National Institute for the Blind can give advice on aids and financial assistance may be provided for the blind person to engage a part-time reader.

Severe kidney disease

A person suffering from severe kidney disease, chronic renal failure, will feel permanently tired and below par, and as a result will function below his or her optimum. Shorter working hours and perhaps longer breaks may help, and part-time work may be needed if dialysis is required. The Manpower Services Commission may provide a grant to allow for job-splitting or job-sharing in this situation. Following a kidney transplant, a person should be able to get back to working at full capacity.

Respiratory diseases

People disabled by respiratory diseases such as asthma, bronchitis and emphysema, will be mainly limited by how much moving round, climbing stairs, etc. is required. As in other conditions, the Manpower Services Commission may be able to fund modifications to premises, such as lift installation. Affected individuals will benefit from a clean, smoke-free atmosphere.

Ileostomy and colostomy

Even teenagers may require ileostomy and colostomy for serious bowel disease and once convalescence is complete there is no reason why colleagues should even know about the disability. The colostomy or ileostomy, which is an opening of the bowel on the abdomen over which a bag is worn for the collection of excrement, should not smell or cause any risk to others as far as hygiene is concerned, and the person should lead a normal life with it. Adequate toilet facilities should be provided.

Multiple sclerosis

This is the most common neurological disease affecting young adults. It is difficult to deal with because its symptoms and time course are so variable. Modification of duties and responsibilities should take this variability into account. This disease may cause problems with mobility and eyesight, or possibly psychiatric symptoms. Dealing with these difficulties should be as discussed in previous sections.

AIDS

This disease has only been described recently; people are inexperienced in dealing with it and therefore it causes a great deal of fear, panic and hysteria. A person who is known to have been infected with the AIDS virus should work normally. A proportion of these people, perhaps 10%, will later become ill with AIDS and when ill will probably be unable to work. Spread of the disease is by sexual intercourse or by contact with the blood of an infected person through broken skin. If someone with the AIDS virus has a bleeding cut or abrasion, it should be dealt with by someone with medical knowledge. Spilled blood should be cleaned with diluted household bleach by someone wearing rubber gloves. Sharing a room, chair, coffee cup or toilet will *not* cause another to catch AIDS from an individual who is infected with the virus.

18.4 The use of drugs

The drugs considered here are those prescribed to individuals under medical supervision, those purchased over the counter for minor illnesses, and drugs of abuse which may be legally prescribed but misused or which are illegally obtained. Alcohol and nicotine also fall into the category of drugs which, though legal and freely available, may nonetheless be abused.

Prescribed drugs

The majority of these are unlikely to affect an individual's work performance or have any effect noticeable to colleagues or workmates. The category of drugs which may cause difficulties are those which act on the nervous system such as sedatives, tranquillisers and anti-depressants. Tranquillisers and antidepressants are prescribed for moderately severe psychological disturbances such as anxiety or depression. These drugs may very well cause drowsiness or slowing up of mental faculties, but as the underlying illness may also cause slowing up and difficulty with concentration it may be difficult to distinguish between the effect of drugs and the effect of the illness. If the problem is severe, it would be better for the affected individual to remain off work until recovery.

Over-the-counter drugs

Antihistamines are an example of a commonly used group of drugs which although bought for allergies and hay fever may also affect the central nervous system. These drugs can cause drowsiness and impaired work performance.

Illegal drug use

This is not likely to be a very common problem in the office as the individuals who are users of illegal drugs, such as heroin, usually have great difficulty holding down a job and are rarely in regular employment for any length of time. This problem would therefore be more likely to be found in the case of a new or temporary employee who is relatively unknown to other staff.

Signs to look for in someone who is using illegal drugs:

    drowsy, slowed up, or dreamy behaviour

    appearing 'high' in a manner not appropriate to situation or surroundings

    loss of judgement

    irritability

    shakiness

    unexplained sudden absence from work

    spending long periods in toilet

    intravenous injection needle marks on hands, forearms at the elbow, or on the neck

    very small pupils

    thin, pale, unhealthy appearance.

If there is a suspicion that illegal drugs are being used, the police should be notified.

Alcohol

This is the 'drug' problem which is most likely to arise in the office. Alcohol abuse is all too frequent nowadays and in times of stress moderate drinking may very well get out of control.

Signs to look for:

    unreliable time-keeping, particularly in the mornings, and absenteeism, particularly on Mondays

    shakiness, particularly in the mornings

    smell of alcohol on the breath in the mornings

    reddish/purplish complexion with bloodshot eyes

    obvious drunkenness at work with slurred speech, drowsiness and poor co-ordination

    frequent lunch-time or afternoon drinking with consumption habitually greater than others

    domestic, marital, social or relationship problems.

Alcohol misuse is a very difficult problem to deal with and sometimes it seems easier to overlook it and to cover up for the individual concerned. Affected individuals often deny the problem to family, friends, colleagues and even to themselves. To cover up for and overlook the problem is in fact more likely to harm than help the unfortunate victim; it usually delays the person from seeking medical help or making any attempt to deal personally with the problem. Therefore, although it may seem brutal, it is preferable to confront the individual, suggest appropriate help, and issue warnings if work is suffering.

Smoking

Nowadays there is evidence that cigarette smoke can harm the health not only of the smoker but also of people in the vicinity who inhale the smoke passively. It would be preferable for smoking to be banned from any office where there are non-smokers present and allowed only in a specially designated area.

19 OFFICE MACHINERY AND EQUIPMENT

19.1 Binding machines

Binding units enable loose sheets of paper to be bound together into booklets.

Comb binding A two-stage operation in which the papers are first punched and then spiral bound, either with metal or plastic.

Thermal binding The papers are placed inside pre-glued covers which are then put into the machine. When the sheets are firmly bonded into the covers a timer activates a buzzer and a warning light.

19.2 Communications equipment

Telephone answering machine

A telephone answering machine is switched on when a telephone is unmanned. It plays a pre-recorded message inviting the caller to leave a message which is then recorded and can be played back later. If the machine is linked to a computer the number of messages recorded can be visually displayed. Some machines allow a remote playback to be activated which means that the user can phone in and have the messages played back over the telephone.

Radiopaging system

Members of staff who are not based in an office can be contacted by means of a radiopaging system. A high frequency signal or bleep alerts the user of a call. Several messages can be stored on the pocket-sized receiver and messages can be received from more than one source by using different bleeps for different callers.

Qwertyphone

A qwertyphone is a compact 'memory-phone-cum-computer-terminal' with a typewriter keyboard and liquid crystal display. It can be used as a 'memotyper' as well as providing access to on-line databases and electronic mailbox systems. Numbers can be stored, then amended and searched by name, address, occupation or number.

Interactive video

Communication takes place by means of a video display. The system can be used for sales promotions and training purposes. Information is stored on a laser disk controlled by a microcomputer with suitable software. Video disks can also be used to store archive material.

Electronic mail

Messages are sent and received using a microcomputer linked to a telephone system by means of a modem. A modem is a telecommunications device which enables microcomputer users to transmit and receive data over a communications system. Messages can be filed electronically and retrieved later.

Telex, fax and videotex

See Chapter 21.8.

19.3 Calculators and computers

Calculators

Electronic calculators vary in size from wafer-thin pocket calculators to desk-top models with print-out facilities. The size of a calculator does not reflect its power. Some models are programmable and may have extra features such as time and date display, electronic diary and notepad facilities.

Computers

Networks

Integrated computer systems capable of handling text, data, image, graph and voice are now available providing the business user with a complete information processing facility. Work stations situated at different locations can be linked to the computer network to provide distributed data processing facilities. An open system network allows different makes and standards of system to be interconnected.

Microcomputers

It is very difficult to define a typical microcomputer. There are many makes and models available, ranging from powerful desk-top business microcomputers, with as much processing power as small minicomputers, to portable home computers. Off-the-shelf applications software is readily available for the business user including database management systems, accounts, word processing and spreadsheet packages. Many systems now feature the use of a *mouse*, a small hand-held device connected to a microcomputer. When the mouse is rolled across the desk surface a pointer is moved across the screen and when the pointer is positioned on a word or pictorial image (*icon*) a button can be pressed on the mouse initiating an activity, e.g. loading a file from disk or editing text.

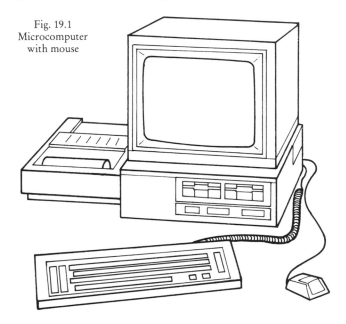

Fig. 19.1
Microcomputer
with mouse

Minicomputer

Minicomputers are usually smaller than mainframes but may in fact be more powerful than small, old mainframe equipment. A minicomputer can support several programming languages and multiprogramming as well as offering more processing power and storage capacity than a micro.

Mainframe computer

A large, fast, powerful general-purpose mainframe computer provides centralised computing facilities for an organisation and is capable of supporting a large number of terminals.

Mainframe and minicomputers are used to carry out traditional data processing functions such as payroll, customer accounts and stock control. The type of equipment used depends upon the needs of the user.

19.4 Copiers

Office copiers are used to produce exact copies from an original document. Copying falls into three main categories; low, medium and high volume.

Low and medium volume

Low and medium volume copiers use a dry toner process and feature the latest technology. Different types of paper can be used and the print enlarged or reduced in size. The number of copies required is selected from a touch-sensitive console and a self-diagnostic panel displays symbols visually to indicate when the paper is getting low or if more toner should be added.

High volume

High volume copiers are usually faster and more robust, with the option to print on both sides of the paper. Other facilities include automatic collating and stapling of documents and automatic reset so that a long-run job may be interrupted to make a single copy. Offset machines can be used for high speed, high volume printing in black and white or colour. Sophisticated technology allows all functions to be done at the touch of a button.

Copier control

It is possible to monitor the use of copiers using a management information system which can give a precise account of photocopier use. Identity codes and account numbers are allocated to departments.

19.5 Dictating machines

Pocket dictating machines

A dictating machine is used either in or out of the office to record speech. The recording is stored on magnetic tape and transcribed later.

New machines are slimline in shape, with electronic touch control and a digital display in minutes and seconds. They are often advertised as electronic notebooks.

Centralised dictating

A centralised dictating system provides audio-typing facilities for all departments. Documents are dictated using a remote control microphone. Transcriptions are carried out in a typing pool under the direction of a supervisor.

19.6 Mailing equipment

The type of mailing equipment used depends upon the volume and nature of mail that needs to be handled.

Mobile sorting trolley

A mobile sorting trolley can be used to sort and distribute incoming mail after it has been time and date stamped.

Electronic postal scales

Electronic postal scales feature a digital display of weight and postage rates with touch selection for different classes of mail, e.g. first class, second class or recorded delivery.

Franking machine

Envelopes or adhesive labels are fed into the franking machine and endorsed with the pre-selected date and postage rate. A logo or advertising slogan can be printed on the envelopes at the same time. On some models envelopes are automatically fed in, sealed and franked.

Users of franking machines must conform to the following conditions:

(1) Authority must be obtained from the local head post office before starting to use a machine.

(2) Payments in advance for postage or value cards must be made at a specified post office.

(3) Franked correspondence must be faced, bundled (as detailed in the poster 'How to post franked mail', or as required by the local Head

Postmaster) and either handed in at a specified post office or posted within special envelopes in posting boxes agreed by the Head Postmaster. Enquiries about these conditions should be addressed to the local Head Postmaster.

(4) The Royal Mail needs to have a completed control card at the close of business each working week, whether or not the machine has been used, to check that the machine is working properly.

(5) Only the supplying company may repair or modify machines. Users must have the machine inspected and maintained by the supplying company not less than twice in each six-month period, or as specified by the Royal Mail, in order to ensure clear impressions and complete accuracy in recording.

(6) Machines are available from supplying companies authorised by the Royal Mail. Enquiries about the supply of franking machines and the types available should be addressed to these firms:

Envopak Ltd
Powerscroft Road, Sidcup, Kent   DA14 5EF   01-302 2500

Hasler (Great Britain) Ltd
Hasler Works, Commerce Way, Croydon   CR0 4XA   01-680 6050

Pitney Bowes Ltd
The Pinnacles, Harlow, Essex   CM19 5BD   (0279) 26731

Roneo Alcatel Ltd
Mailroom Division
PO Box 66, South Street, Romford   RM1 2AR   (0708) 46000

Scriptomatic Ltd
Scriptomatic House, Torrington Park, London   N12 9SU   01-445 0163

Addressing machines

Addressing machines can be used to select, sort and print addresses from a mailing list, although computerised systems linked to word processors are being used increasingly to deal with high volume direct mail.

Computerised mailing machines

A computerised system enables forms to be separated, folded, inserted, sealed and franked. Computerised mailing machines are efficient when dealing with large amounts of outgoing mail.

Miscellaneous mailing equipment

Other items of equipment used in the mailing room include joggers and collators to sort papers into order, perforators to punch holes and automatic folding, inserting, tying and sealing machines.

Shredding machines are generally housed in the mailing room; they are used for disposing of used envelopes, unwanted papers and confidential waste.

19.7 Storage of information

Indexing

Strip indexing Information is entered on a strip which is then inserted into a holder. All the strips are visible and the system can be updated by simply adding or removing the strips.

Visible indexing Visible index cards overlap displaying the bottom section of the card so that it is visible when the card is filed.

Blind indexing Index cards are stored one behind the other in a box, tray or cabinet.

Rotary indexing Rotary index cards are secured to a central spindle which rotates when cards are being searched. There are both horizontal and vertical systems.

Filing

Vertical filing In a vertical filing cabinet documents are filed one behind another in drawers. The files may be suspended from rails and subdivided according to the indexing system in use.

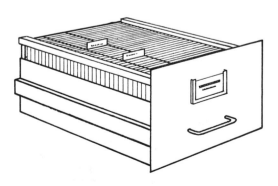

Lateral filing In a lateral filing cabinet documents are stored side by side, like books on a shelf. The files may be suspended from rails. Lateral filing systems hold more files and take up less space than vertical systems.

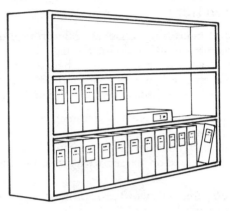

Horizontal filing Paper records are stored flat one on top of another in drawers. This method is suitable for filing large plans and drawings.

Microfiling Papers are photographed and reduced in size then stored as microfilm in rolls, on sheets, in transparent jackets or aperture cards. Microfilm can be processed directly from a computer.

The documents are read by inserting the film into a microfilm reader. This method of filing is useful for storing archival materials, parts manuals, bank records and for library work.

Computerised filing

Computer aided microfilm retrieval Microfilmed documents, and relevant information about them, are fed into a computer along with film and frame references. Frames have an image which can be detected by a photocell which enables the frames to be counted. Documents can be searched, sorted, indexed and retrieved.

Database management systems Customer records, personnel files and other records can be stored on a computer then searched, sorted and retrieved electronically using a database management system. Records can be printed or merged with other documents to produce a report.

Documents prepared on a word processor can be stored on disks and retrieved electronically.

19.8 Text handling equipment

Electronic lettering systems

An electronic lettering system is used to produce type on an adhesive-backed tape to be inserted into text and used for headlines or subheadings.

Electronic typewriters

Electronic typewriters are replacing manual and electric models. Electronic machines have fewer moving parts and usually have at least a single line visual display and an internal memory. The display allows editing to take place before a document is printed. Text can be stored and if amendments are needed the whole document does not have to be re-typed.

Video typewriters

A screen and external disk storage drive can be added to some electronic typewriters. These machines do not have full word processing facilities but are popular with typists who feel comfortable using a familiar keyboard.

Word processors

A word processor consists of a *keyboard* to enter text, a *screen* to view what has been typed, a *disk drive* to store the documents, and a *printer*. Once a document has been typed it can be stored and retrieved. Text can be inserted and deleted, sections can be moved within the document or transferred to another document. The layout can be altered and pages numbered automatically without any re-typing. Standard letters can be produced and automatically merged with a mailing list. Spelling can be checked against a dictionary.

Phototypesetters

Publication-quality print can be prepared for printing using a small computer-assisted typesetting system. Reports, accounts, price lists, etc., prepared on a word processor, can be input into phototypesetters. The type, in digital form, can then be slanted to form italics, compressed, enlarged, reduced or expanded before being printed. Type takes up less space than typewritten text.

Printers

The quality of the printed document depends upon the type of printer used.

Dot matrix printers Dot matrix printers operate at high speeds and offer a choice of type sizes and styles. They are comparatively cheap to purchase but the quality of the print may be poorer than that produced by a daisy wheel or laser printer. Models are available which can be switched to near letter quality print mode.

Daisy wheel printers A daisy wheel printer with a carbon ribbon will produce high quality print. The print wheel must be changed if different type sizes or type fonts are required.

Ink jet printers Ink jet printers are fast and quiet. The ink is sprayed onto the paper.

Laser printers A laser printer is an intelligent copier. Printing takes place at high speed producing superb quality documents. Many types and styles of text can be printed as well as graphics and the machine is virtually silent.

20 THE ROYAL MAIL

20.1 Business economy services

Mailsort 1

If a company can pre-sort a first class mailing of 4000 or more items, it could qualify for a discount of up to 14% on the postage and still get the normal first class delivery. This high level of discount has a number of conditions:

at least 90% of the addresses to be correctly postcoded

pre-sortation down to delivery offices in bundles of at least 25 letters.

(*Note:* Assistance may be available on sortation software changes for pre-sort services users.)

An extra 2% discount is available to those companies who are able to post Mailsort items early in the day (i.e. before 1.00 pm). As the postcode is the key to efficient pre-sortation, the Royal Mail can provide assistance in the postcoding of address lists.

Volume	Delivery Office Sortation Discount	County/Post Town Residue
4000—25000	11%	For early
25000—50000	12%	posting or
50000—300000	13%	OCR readable
over 300000	14%	only

This service replaces the first class letter contract service.

Mailsort 2

If a company can pre-sort a second class mailing of 4000 or more letters it could qualify for a discount of up to 14% on the postage and still get the normal second class delivery. Similarly the high level of discount involves conditions which have to be met:

at least 90% of the addresses to be correctly postcoded

pre-sortation down to delivery offices in bundles of at least 25 letters

(County or Post Town residues qualify for a reduced discount—see below).

Volume	Delivery Office Sortation Discount	County/Post Town Sortation Discount
4000—25000	11%	7%
25000—50000	12%	7%
50000—300000	13%	7%
over 300000	14%	7%

Plus an extra 2% discount on all OCR readable residues.
This service replaces the second class discount service.

Mailsort 3

For scheduled advertising or less time-sensitive mailsorts, i.e. with a delivery span of seven working days, mailings of over 4000 letters which can be pre-sorted to delivery offices, a company could qualify for a discount of up to 32% off the standard price. The conditions of postcoding and pre-sortation common through Mailsort 1 and Mailsort 2 apply. This facility can save money for companies who send large quantities of non-urgent mail-circulars, price lists, reports and direct mail, etc. Because postage costs are significantly reduced, Mailsort 3 allows more frequent mailings and/or the mailings of more items.

Volume	Delivery Office Sortation Discount	County/Post Town Sortation Discount
4000—10000	18%	15%
10000—25000	22%	15%
25000—50000	25%	15%
50000—300000	26%	15%
300000—1 million	29%	15%
over 1 million	32%	15%

Plus an extra 2% discount on all OCR readable residues.
This service replaces the bulk rebate service.

Response services

Business Reply, Freepost and *Admail* are designed to stimulate customer response by simplifying the response process—whether answering advertising messages or paying bills.

Business Reply

A company can make it easier and quicker for customers to pay bills by enclosing a pre-printed *Business Reply* card, envelope or label (first or second class). It is ideal for:

obtaining immediate orders from direct mail shots

offering follow-up literature

facilitating communications between agents and head offices

enhancing a company's image in terms of efficiency, enthusiasm and customer service

improving cash flow.

Freepost

Freepost offers three services:

First class pre-printed
Second class pre-printed
Second class non-pre-printed.

Freepost is ideal for:

press advertising

television and radio advertising

direct mail or door-to-door

special on-pack offers.

Admail

This is a redirection service which enables direct response advertisers to quote a local or prestigious address but to have replies re-routed direct to their fulfilment house anywhere in the UK. Postage can be paid by the respondents or the service can be used in conjunction with *Freepost*.

Incentive discount for growth (IDG)

This facility is designed for companies who spend over £20 000 a year on postage—and whose volume of postage increases year by year. Such companies can qualify for up to 20% discount on the real value of the year's increase. If the amount of business mail sent out by a company is increasing, with an IDG contract it may be possible to save money on the extra real postage costs.

A company involved in direct mail, direct marketing, or with large customer lists, can benefit in particular—with savings on spin-off mailings, statements, or reminders—because IDG allows more mail to be despatched without a proportionately increased postage cost.

The Postcode Project

To help postcode firms' mailing lists, the Royal Mail has introduced *The Postcode Project*. This project offers advice, assistance and under certain conditions a financial contribution that may help substantially with the cost of postcoding a company's computer-based address list.

Any company which frequently uses computerised mailing lists of at least 20 000 addresses held in a format that the bureaux, with whom the Royal Mail has contacts, can handle may be eligible for financial aid to assist with the computerised postcoding of the list. This process may leave some manual postcoding left to be done for which no assistance is given.

A number of computer agencies have devised programs for adding postcodes to addresses, using the Royal Mail's *Postcode Address File* as the database. The Royal Mail has contracts with such agencies and has used independent research to confirm the agencies' high standards.

Printed postage impression

Printed postage impressions (PPI) are a pre-printed alternative to traditional stamps and franking machines. If large quantities of identical letters, packets or parcels are despatched a PPI simplifies the handling and accountancy procedures. It is only necessary to stock the pre-printed envelopes in readiness for use. This time-saving facility is particularly valuable when used in conjunction with Royal Mail discounts.

There are separate designs which cover Mailsort 1, 2 and 3 service indicators.

Making the most of postal weight allowances

When a company sends out a business letter—or an invoice statement or receipt—it is usually lightweight (probably less than 15g), but the initial weight allowance is 60g before any extra postage is incurred. So it would surely make sense to enclose a sales leaflet, a price list, a special message, for no extra postage. Regular POP or similar sized envelopes normally have sufficient strength and flexibility to carry additional leaflets.

Intelpost

Intelpost is one of the largest electronic messaging services in the world. It transmits clear facsimiles of any document up to A4 size—letters, reports, contracts, quotations, drawings, plans, graphs. It is fast, reliable and confidential. It is also widespread—there are over 100 *Intelpost* centres in Britain and 2000 overseas; no other electronic mail service can offer anything approaching this vast level of coverage.

Intelpost can speed communication for every type and size of business. Companies with fax machines, telex or computers can use it from their own premises; companies without these facilities can use it from Intelpost centres throughout Britain. Fast collection and delivery services mean Intelpost works well even if the recipient has no equivalent technology.

Intelpost is not expensive. There are no fees, subscriptions or electronic mailbox costs; prices are very competitive and are based entirely on the number of pages, the destination and the method of delivery.

Household Delivery Service

The Household Delivery Service enables a company to advertise its services or products through the mail without needing to address an envelope. The advertising material is delivered by professionals—the regular postman with the normal mail and it is therefore more likely to be read.

Household Delivery can be particularly useful when linked to a press, TV or radio campaign and it can include a reply-paid card to encourage potential customers to respond—also a useful way to build up a customer list.

Household Delivery is therefore an exceptionally valuable way to advertise a product or service to a specific area or areas—which can range from one postcode sector to the whole country (by *Acorn* if you wish), including Northern Ireland. Any enquiries should be addressed to:

Royal Mail Services for Business Economy
Freepost (no stamp required)
33 Grosvenor Place
London
SW1X 1EE

20.2 Datapost services

Sameday

Facilities: a same-day door-to-door service by radio controlled motorcycles and vans. Ideal for goods and documents needing rapid pickup and high speed delivery. The service gives a money-back same-day guarantee within 80 UK cities and towns and between centres directly linked by rail.

Advantages: high security, extremely competitive prices, and locally based service.

Overnight

Facilities: guaranteed next-day delivery of goods up to 27·5 kg to any point in Britain. Separate, fast-stream handling and supervision, signatures against transfer en route. An exclusive air network supplements Inter-City rail and the biggest delivery fleet in the country. Special staff are employed as necessary to reach remote destinations.

Advantages: a service for parcels that have to be there tomorrow— both regular consignments and one-off packages. Delivery by 10.00 am or noon and backed by the *Datapost Double Guarantee*—money-back promise and free insurance against loss, damage or delay. Security guaranteed by Royal Mail's unmatched experience and resources.

International

Facilities: fast delivery to key commercial centres worldwide. Backed by the *Datapost Double Guarantee* (see above).

Sample times	
London to Bahrain	24 hours
Aberdeen to Zürich	48 hours
Birmingham to Tokyo	72 hours
Manchester to The Hague	24 hours

Advantages: competitive pricing with no hidden extras. Datapost packs available for still further economy. Minimal paperwork and a variety of contract options. Datapost is available through 2500 post offices, or contract pickup, or same-day collection via Freefone Datapost.

Any enquiries should be addressed to:

Datapost Marketing Department
Freepost (no stamp required)
33 Grosvenor Place
London
SW1X 1EE

20.3 Special services

Special Delivery

Extra assurance for first class letter mail.

This service provides delivery by a Royal Mail messenger for letters and packets arriving at a delivery office centre on the next working day after posting but too late for normal delivery on that day.

In addition to first class postage a Royal Mail Special Delivery fee of £1.50 must be paid. A *Certificate of Posting* will be issued. Items must be posted at post office counters by the *Latest Recommended Posting Times* for next working day delivery. The special delivery fee will be refunded automatically to the sender if an item posted by the latest recommended posting time does not receive delivery on the next working day after posting.

This service is *not* available to the Isle of Man, the Channel Islands or the Irish Republic.

Express Delivery

The Express Delivery Service is available for letter packets addressed to places in the Channel Islands or the Isle of Man and for both letters and parcels to the Irish Republic. It is not available for second class letters.

This service allows for delivery of a postal packet by special messenger after arrival which will ensure earlier delivery than by normal handling. Express Delivery items are sent from the office of posting to the office of delivery in ordinary mails. The fee is £1·50 in addition to full ordinary postage. In the Irish Republic additional charges are collected from the addressee when delivery is made by messenger more than one mile from the delivery office.

Express Delivery items arriving at the office of delivery after the first ordinary delivery of letters may sometimes be included in a normal delivery. In such cases a refund of the Express Delivery fee will be made on application.

Any enquiries should be addressed to:

Royal Mail Special Services
Freepost (no stamp required)
33 Grosvenor Place
London
SW1X 1EE

20.4 Parcels services

National goods distribution

Packages up to 25 kg can be delivered anywhere in the country, normally within three days. A contract service is available which saves having to weigh and stamp each individual parcel. Any company sending over 20 parcels weekly is eligible and can obtain a printed postage impression (PPI). Royal Mail Parcels can bill the customer at regular intervals and collect from their premises. Large consignments (usually 200 or more a week) qualify for flat rates when collection is free.

Lightweight parcels can be posted at letter post rates. Recorded delivery is possible and there is additional compensation for loss or damage if items are sent by registered post. Worthwhile rebates are available for bulk (over 4250) mailings of identical packets.

Zonal distribution
County parcels

This service offers a reduced rate for parcels posted and delivered within a specified area, usually a group of counties (see map opposite). It is especially attractive for firms with a sizeable proportion of their customers fairly close at hand.

(See *Rider* services p 212 for details of overnight parcel delivery within the London Postal Area and within the North East, Northern Ireland and Thames Valley.)

Reduced-rate county parcels

County areas
1. Avon/Gloucestershire/Somerset/
   Wiltshire
2. Staffordshire/Warwickshire/West
   Midlands/Worcestershire
3. Bedfordshire/Leicestershire/
   Northamptonshire
4. Derbyshire/Nottinghamshire
5. Cambridgeshire/Lincolnshire/
   Norfolk/South Humberside/
   Suffolk
6. Dyfed/Gwent/Herefordshire/
   Mid-Glamorgan/South
   Glamorgan/West Glamorgan
7. Cheshire/Lancashire
8. Cumbria/Dumfriesshire/
   Kirkcudbrightshire/Wigtownshire

9. Northern Ireland
10. Berwickshire/East Lothian/Fife/
    Kinross-shire/Midlothian/
    Peeblesshire/Roxburghshire/
    Selkirkshire/West Lothian
11. Aberdeenshire/Banffshire/
    Kincardineshire
12. Argyll/Arran/Ayrshire/Bute/
    Clackmannanshire/Coll/Colonsay/
    Dunbartonshire/Gigha/Iona/
    Islay/Jura/Lanarkshire/Mull/
    Renfrewshire/Stirlingshire/Tiree
13. Angus/Caithness/Canna/Eigg/
    Inverness-shire/Moray/
    Nairnshire/Perthshire/Rhum/
    Ross-shire/Skye/Sutherland
14. North Humberside/North
    Yorkshire/South Yorkshire/West
    Yorkshire
15. Berkshire/Buckinghamshire/
    Oxfordshire

16. Dorset/Hampshire/Isle of Wight
17. East Sussex/Kent/West Sussex
18. Clwyd/Gwynedd
19. Powys/Shropshire
20. Cornwall/Devon
21. Barra/Benbecula/Harris/Lewis/
    North Uist/South Uist
22. Orkney
23. Shetland Islands

In these areas, delivery is within a single county:
24. Surrey
25. Middlesex
26. Hertfordshire
27. Essex
28. Merseyside (including South Wirral)

211

'Rider' services

A new range of services is being developed specifically for local business. *Rider* services operate in areas where a particular need for local overnight collection and delivery service exists. There are four *Rider* services in operation:

Nightrider (serving the London Postal Area)

Parcel Rider (serving Northern Ireland)

Tyne Rider (serving the North East)

Thames Rider (serving Berks, Bucks, Oxon and adjacent areas of the Thames Valley).

Watch out for further introductions of *Rider* Services.

Trakback

This new signed delivery service, available to parcel contract holders only, gives verbal confirmation of delivery normally five days after posting and a copy of the recipient's signature as an optional extra. Royal Mail Parcels will supply a *Trakback* bar-coded label which must be attached to each parcel—which is then sent in the normal way. The recipient signs for the parcel on delivery, the bar-code being read and entered into a computer. To confirm delivery a free call is made to the *Trakback Response Centre*.

For further information telephone 01-200 0200 and ask for Royal Mail Parcels.

Royal Mail Parcels
Signed Delivery Service

20.5 International services

Airstream

A new Royal Mail International letter service for customers sending more than 2 kg of international letters per collection. It is available worldwide and offers substantial financial savings for large users. It is an ideal service for correspondence, financial mail, travel schedules, reports and personalised mailshots.

Contract facilities (printed papers)
Bulk airmail (BAM)
This is a fast service—3 to 4 days delivery—specifically geared to large quantity despatches of printed papers to **Europe**. It is ideal for books, magazines, direct mailshots or any type of printed paper traffic with a European destination.

Accelerated surface post (ASP)
This covers destinations **outside Europe** and uses air transport for speed compared with surface transport for economy.

ASP takes a fraction of the time of ordinary surface mail, yet often costs very little more. This means that you can get all sorts of printed paper/material direct to people overseas in a matter of days—instead of several weeks or months. In fact ASP is the perfect 'happy medium'; it provides for a service intermediate in price and speed between existing air and surface mail services.

Contract facilities (parcels)
Air and surface parcel services; anyone sending in excess of 30 parcels per week may qualify for special tariffs. Payment is on account using postage paid impressions.

Direct agents bag service
A special service for customers wishing to send books, periodicals or other printed matter by a surface route to a single addressee (e.g. a retail outlet or agent abroad). The service is available **worldwide**; delivery 4–8 weeks.

Worldwide high speed courier
Datapost International (see p 208).

Swiftair
This is a high-speed letter post service available to all countries. Items must be handed over a post office counter, or included in firms' collections (but kept separate from other correspondence to ensure proper handling). Each item must bear a *Swiftair* label and this should

be affixed at the top left hand corner of the address side—in the case of items going outside Europe, immediately below the blue airmail label.

A Royal Mail Service

The Royal Mail aims for *Swiftair* items to be flown to the country of destination on the day after posting (subject to availability of flights) and delivered at least one day earlier than the ordinary airmail services. Any enquiries should be addressed to:

Royal Mail International Marketing Department
Freepost (no stamp required)
33 Grosvenor Place
London
SW1X 1EE

International Business Reply Service

This service enables businesses who wish to obtain replies from their clients overseas, without putting those clients to the expense of paying the return postage, to enclose in their communication unstamped reply cards or envelopes bearing the special International Business Reply Service design. Their clients can then post the reply cards or envelopes back to the UK in the normal way but without having to buy and affix postage stamps. Instead, the addressee in the UK will pay the charges on all the replies that he or she receives.

Completed *International Business Reply* cards and envelopes will be returned as European All-Up mail.

The service is currently available to twelve major European countries and there are plans to extend it to other countries in the near future. Any enquiries should be addressed to:

Sally Bennett
Freepost (no stamp required)
Royal Mail International Letters
Room 320
52 Grosvenor Gardens
London
SW1W 0YA

21 TELECOMMUNICATIONS

21.1 Business telephone systems

This is a highly technical and rapidly changing area because of the development of new technologies and the convergence of micro-processor based computing and telecommunication facilities.

Public telephone network (PTN)

Telecommunications apparatus must be approved and must undergo stringent tests for safety and operational performance. It is possible to choose from a variety of sources whether to buy, rent or lease the telephone apparatus to be connected to the line. Equipment is covered by a *Branch Systems General Licence* and users must abide by its terms.

The Government has laid down marking orders which require all apparatus to be clearly marked to show whether or not it has been approved for connection to the British Telecom network.

 Green circle APPROVED for connection

 Red Triangle NOT approved for connection

Private branch exchange (PBX)

A private branch exchange is a customers' switching apparatus which routes calls between extensions and the public telephone network, and internally between extensions.

Private automatic branch exchange (PABX)

PABX is an automatic version of PBX which permits calls to be dialled direct from extensions. If it is desirable to control the number of outgoing calls then some extensions can have restricted external dialling. Incoming calls are usually routed through the switchboard but the system may incorporate a direct dialling-in facility which enables callers to dial extensions directly without going via the operator.

Key telephone systems

A key telephone system allows groups of incoming lines to be associated with a number of telephone stations; any extension user can then take an incoming call and transfer it, if necessary, to the wanted section. An operator is not required. For economy this system can be used with simple approved plug-in telephones.

Call connect systems

Advances in microelectronics have resulted in sophisticated PBX systems which now offer the following additional facilities to business users:

    long numbers can be coded

    the telephone system can re-direct calls to other extensions when the first one is engaged, or automatically re-dial when the number called is engaged

    internal and external calls can be initiated from each extension

    the user can put a bar on incoming calls or alternatively put a bar on outgoing calls

    all incoming calls can be directed to another telephone

    calls can be diverted to another extension if the call remains unanswered or if the called telephone is engaged

    loudspeaker telephones leave the user's hands free and can be used when several people need to be involved in a call

    a call waiting facility provides a means of answering an incoming call when the user is already engaged upon another call

    the three party service enables the customer to set up a three-way conversation on his or her telephone.

Call cost indicators

The cost of calls can be monitored either as they are being made or over a period of time. A print-out records the time, date, number called, duration and cost of each call.

Cordless telephones

Cordless telephones allow staff who work in small businesses, such as garages, hairdressers or on building sites, easy access to a telephone so that business is not lost.

Payphones

Traditional pay-on-answer coinphones are being replaced by micro-processor-controlled public and rented payphones with credit display and follow-on call facilities.

21.2 Cashless calling

Account call
For account calls a special code is entered instead of money and the cost is charged to the phone bill.

Credit call
This is a credit call payment system for national and international calls. Calls are charged to the customer's credit card.

Freefone
Freefone calls are available through the operator and are good for business since they encourage people to communicate. A business may use a Freefone number which enables customers to make a call without charge and the Freefone subscriber pays the bill.

Linkline
The Linkline service is designed for advertisers of a wide variety of goods and services. Customers can call Linkline 0800 free or Linkline 0345 at a local charge, wherever they may be on British Telecom's network in the UK. The rest of the charge will be met by the renter.

Phonecard
Phonecard allows payment for calls in advance. Phonecards which entitle the user to a specific number of units can be purchased at post offices, tobacconists and newsagents displaying the Phonecard logo.

21.3 Operator services

Advice of duration and charge (ADC)
ADC calls are available through the operator who will ring back at the end of a call to advise the caller of the charge and duration.

Alarm call
The alarm call service is available through the operator who will ring a given number at the time requested.

Transferred charge call

The operator speaks to the called number and, if the incoming call is accepted, the charge is transferred to that number.

21.4 Information services

CityDirect

A service for frequent callers to North America.

CityCall

A SuperCall financial information service providing nine bulletins of continually updated financial information.

Guidelines

This is the general term given to British Telecom recorded information services which are obtained by dialling the appropriate number (see your local phone book). Guidelines include:

FT Cityline   Information provided through the Financial Times industrial ordinary share index to keep customers in touch with the Stock Market. The information is updated seven times a day.

Traveline   Information on rail, road, sea and air provided by the BBC and available to the public.

Timeline   Timeline gives the caller the correct time.

Weatherline   Local weather forecasts provided by the Meteorological Office.

Other Guideline information services include: Albumline, Cricketline, Discline, Leisureline, Carebear Bedtime Storyline, Raceline, Radioline, Skiline and Sportsline.

Touch screen

Touch screen systems can be used to eliminate the use of a keyboard. Examples of users include:

city currency dealers (City Business System)
airport control (Touchdown)
police communications (Touchline).

21.5 Conferencing

Audio conferencing

National and International Conference Call Services permit several users at various locations to conduct a business meeting using the telephone as a link. It is possible to connect calls between several countries.

Video conferencing

Videostream is a service which links participants in sound and vision. The system is available in the UK and internationally. It enables groups of people to see and speak to each other, making it possible to hold board meetings, sales meetings and seminars without the expense of long distance travel. Special studios are not required.

Confravision is a public videoconferencing service. Studios which can accommodate up to six people are located in eight major cities (see p 105).

21.6 Mobile communications

Cellular radio network

Radiophone   Office staff who have to spend a lot of time away from the office but who need to keep in touch with the office or with customers will find the radiophone useful. Models are available that work from the car battery, other models work in or out of the car and some are small enough to fit in a handbag or briefcase.

Radiopaging

Radiopaging is available nationwide; the latest radiopagers have the facility to receive and display written messages. Messages can be sent to the pager via telex, datel or through an answering bureau. Some pagers have the option to vibrate rather than bleep; this facility is particularly useful when the wearer is in a meeting or working in a noisy environment such as in an airport or on a building site.

Pinpoint

Using radio technology this service enables fleet operators and security firms to keep track of vehicles. It provides a considerable defence against crime.

Voicebank

A computerised voice storage and forward system. Voicebank mailboxes store a total of 48 messages each up to one minute long. The Voicebank service provides the businessman with an efficient and cost-effective method of keeping in touch 24 hours a day.

Voicemail

Telephone system users are provided with a voice message facility. Voicemail is a modular minicomputer system with disk message store.

Mobile radiopayphones

Trainphone Mobile radiopayphones are available on several mainline rail routes.

Ferryphone Trials involving the use of radiopayphones are being carried out on selected ferry routes.

Mobile radiopayphones are also being used on certain long distance coach routes.

21.7 Data transmission systems

Integrated digital exchanges

An integrated digital network such as *System X* can connect voice and data to a customer concurrently or change from one to the other midway through a call. With integrated digital access customers can be connected to advance network services including telex, fast facsimile, electronic mail, picture videotex, graphics, electronic fund transfer and slow scan TV.

Public switched telephone network (PSTN)

Wide area networks offer immediate access to a computer regardless of distance. A visual display unit at one location is linked to a computer at another location, e.g. airline reservations terminals. Remote offices can be linked to a central computer saving overheads on payroll, personnel and other business functions. Scientists, engineers and designers can benefit from on-line access to stored information and the problem-solving capability of computers.

Packet Switchstream (PSS)
Packet Switchstream is a switched data network providing a public computer data transmission service.

Multistream
Multistream is an enhanced version of Packet Switchstream currently offering videotex access and an error protection facility. The range of facilities will soon be extended in readiness for the 'cashless society'.

An electronic funds transfer at point-of-sale service will link shops with banks and credit card companies allowing anyone with a bank account to pay electronically for goods and service with an encoded plastic card.

It will also be a message-handling service for Packet Switchstream allowing electronic mail, telex and teletex all to interconnect.

Private circuits
A line can be leased to connect two sites. Private circuits may be connected through switching apparatus, data terminals or other apparatus.

Kilostream
Kilostream supplies fast links between customers' premises and can carry voice, data or vision.

Megastream
Megastream circuits of even greater speed and capacity are being used by large businesses in the design of their corporate networks.

Satstream
Satstream offers private satellite links for business communication. Voice and data communications are aimed at the satellite by dish aerials. The signal is carried to the satellite where it is bounced back and re-transmitted around the world to a receiving aerial. Satstream is a service primarily for large organisations. It is used for international

telecommunication transmission, telephone, computer traffic, videoconferencing, fax and electronic distribution of mail.

21.8 Data transmission services

Imtran

A system which links telephone conversation with still television pictures and enables graphic designers, architects and engineers to see and advise on drawings and plans at remote locations. X-ray and body-scan pictures can be sent over the telephone network which enables surgeons away from hospitals to examine records or pictures seconds after they are available.

Photo videotex

Photo videotex enables full colour photographic images to be displayed with text and graphics. This can be used in many service areas including travel, mail order shopping and by estate agencies.

Teleshopping

This is a grocery delivery service linked to *Prestel* for Central London customers.

Telemessages

Specifications, quotations or other messages may be sent by telephone, telex, *Prestel*, *Dialcom* or through a customer's computer terminal. The telemessages are delivered by post on the next working day. For a small extra charge an exact copy of the telemessage can be delivered to the sender.

Telex

For legal and security reasons many messages have to be in writing. Telex provides a fast, clear textual communication facility between national and international subscribers. Proof of sending and receiving is made possible by the use of answerback codes which are printed at the top and bottom of all telex messages. Subscribers are issued with a Telex Directory which lists telex numbers and answerback codes.

The *TextDirect* service enables registered users to send and receive telexes through electronic typewriters, word processors or personal computers.

Telex plus

Network facilities now include short-code number selection, call re-direction and broadcast calls. Telex equipment may be connected to computer-controlled exchanges. Telex with electronic terminals can interconnect with Packet Switchstream into other services such as teletex.

Teletex

Teletex is a fully automatic international telecommunications service for sending messages between terminals. Business correspondence, statistics and simple messages can be sent to users around the world at thirty times the speed of telex. Messages are sent memory to memory which means that messages can be prepared, stored and sent when appropriate. Repeated attempts are automatically made to get a message through and all attempts are recorded on a log. Each terminal has a unique identity to provide secure communications. Each message is headed by a call identification line which includes the date and time sent, the identification of the sender and the called teletex number.

The service conforms to international standards but is also flexible. Teletex terminals may be electronic typewriters with a teletex adapter, modern electronic telephone exchanges, multi-purpose computers or small business microcomputers.

Electronic mail

BT Gold has over 200 000 electronic mailboxes compatible with the Dialcom worldwide electronic mail system. The mailboxes operate through a computer linked to the telephone network. A user must have an identity number and a password. Documents can be prepared 'off-line' and then sent at high speed to one mailbox or to a number of different mailboxes simultaneously. Using a small microcomputer text can be sent and received from any location as long as there is a telephone line.

Facsimile transmission (Fax)

Facsimile systems allow companies to keep pace with modern business communication needs. Fax machines linked to the telephone system are similar in appearance to desk-top copiers. Many paper communications are drawings, diagrams or pictures and these can be sent electronically by using facsimile machines. Equipment compatible with defined international standards can connect with a national and international fax network making it possible to exchange information with businesses all over the world.

Delayed transmission features allow documents to be sent automatically at any time of day or night. The original is exactly reproduced at its destination, normally in black and white, although some equipment can reproduce in full colour. Both parties must have compatible equipment. Delegates travelling to conferences or business meetings do not need to carry all the necessary documentation with them but can use delayed-timer polling facilities to collect their documents from other machines.

Bureaufax

Bureaufax is used to transmit documents overseas and does away with compatibility problems. A business does not even need to have its own fax machine to use the service, neither does the addressee. The customer in the country of origin can send a document by hand, post or fax to a Bureaufax Counter Office; it is then transmitted to a similar office in the destination country. From there the copy can be transmitted by fax to the final destination if that business has a fax machine. Alternatively the copy could be delivered by post or collected by the addressee.

Videotex

Videotex is a generic term for teletext and viewdata.

Teletext uses television channels to transmit information over the air via broadcast signals e.g. *Ceefax* and *Oracle*.

Viewdata falls into two categories: public and private. *Prestel* is the registered trademark for public viewdata in the United Kingdom. It is a generally available mass service and can be used by businesses, by private individuals at home or in public places such as libraries. Each user is given a number and a password and can use either a *Prestel* set or a microcomputer linked to the telephone line with a modem, to access pages of information. *Prestel* offers a variety of services including news and information. Export information, investment statistics, company information and tax guides are a few examples. *Prestel* is a two-way system; users can receive information and send messages to other users or to the information providers. Response pages allow users to order goods, book a hotel or theatre seat or purchase services such as insurance.

Private viewdata systems can be set up to disseminate information within an organisation.

21.9 International communications

International Direct Dialling (IDD)

It is possible to dial direct to hundreds of countries in the world.

International Linkline

Customers abroad can call companies in the UK free of charge. The cost of the call is met by the renter.

International Packet Switchstream (IPSS)

International Packet Switchstream offers data transmission connections to networks in 40 countries.

International Kilostream

International Kilostream is a private digital circuit service currently available to the USA, Hong Kong, Japan, South Africa, Singapore and Bahrain.

International business services

International telex, telemessage and telegram services transmit data abroad via the telephone or packet switching networks. Electronic mail and conferencing facilities are available internationally.

International telemessages This service is available only to the USA.

International telegrams International telegrams are available worldwide and are charged according to length of message and distance sent.

Data Direct This is an international high speed public data service linking the UK and the USA.

International travel

INMARSAT (Maritime satellite) On the seas worldwide, vessels and rigs which are equipped for satellite services can use the direct-dial satellite services. A ship's number can be obtained by dialling International Directory Enquiries. Services provided include telephone, telex, telegrams, data transmission, fax, access to Prestel, International Packet Switchstream and electronic mail.

MAR (Maritime and aeronautical radio) Public air-to-ground telephone and telex services are provided through MAR. An earth station is being commissioned that will allow airlines to provide an automatic telephone service via satellite to aircraft passengers.

Part VI
USEFUL INFORMATION

22 GEOGRAPHICAL AND TRAVEL INFORMATION

22.1 Countries of the world

Country	Capital	Official language(s)	Currency
Afghanistan	Kabul	Pushtu, Dari	Afghani (Af) = 100 puls
Albania	Tirana/Tiranë	Albanian	Lek (L) = 100 quintars
Algeria	El Djazair/ Algiers	Arabic	Dinar (AD) = 100 centimes
Andorra	Andorra la Vella	Catalan	French Franc and Spanish Peseta
Angola	Luanda	Portuguese	Kwanza (Kz) = 100 lweis
Antigua and Barbuda	St John's	English	East Caribbean Dollar (EC$) = 100 cents
Argentina	Buenos Aires	Spanish	Austral (Arg$) = 100 centavos
Australia	Canberra	English	Dollar (A$) = 100 cents
Austria	Vienna	German	Schilling (Sch) = 100 groschen
Bahamas	Nassau	English	Dollar (BA$) = 100 cents
Bahrain	Manama	Arabic	Dinar (BD) = 1000 fils
Bangladesh	Dhaka	Bangla (Bengali)	Taka (Tk) = 100 poisha
Barbados	Bridgetown	English	Dollar (Bds$) = 100 cents
Belgium	Brussels	Flemish, French	Franc (BFr) = 100 centimes
Belize	Belmopan	English	Dollar (Bz$) = 100 cents
Benin	Porto Novo	French, English	CFA Franc (CFAFr) = 100 centimes
Bhutan	Thimphu	Dzongkha (Tibetan/ Burmese)	Ngultrum (N) = 100 chetrums
Bolivia	La Paz	Spanish	Peso (B$) = 100 centavos

Country	Capital	Official language(s)	Currency
Botswana	Gaborone	English	Pula (Pu) = 100 thebe
Brazil	Brasilia	Portuguese	Cruzado/Cruziero (Cr) = 100 centavos
Brunei	Bandar Seri Begawan	Malay	Dollar (Br$) = 100 cents
Bulgaria	Sofia	Bulgarian	Lev (Lv) = 100 stotinki
Burkina Faso	Ouagadougou	French	CFA Franc (CFAFr) = 100 centimes
Burma	Rangoon	Burmese	Kyat (K) = 100 pyas
Burundi	Bujumbura	Kirundi, French	Franc (BuFr) = 100 centimes
Cameroon	Yaoundé	French, English	CFA Franc (CFAFr) = 100 centimes
Canada	Ottawa	English, French	Dollar (C$) = 100 cents
Cape Verde Islands	Praia	Creole Portuguese	Escudo (CVEsc) = 100 centavos
Central African Republic	Bangui	French	CFA Franc (CFAFr) = 100 centimes
Chad	N' Djamena	French	CFA Franc (CFAFr) = 100 centimes
Chile	Santiago	Spanish	Peso (Ch$) = 100 centesimos
China	Beijing (Peking)	Puronghua (Mandarin Chinese)	Renminbi Yuan (RMBY or $) = 100 fen
Colombia	Bogotá	Spanish	Peso (Col$) = 100 centavos
The Comoros	Moroni	French, Arabic	CFA Franc (CFAFr) = 100 centimes
Congo	Brazzaville	French	CFA Franc (CFAFr) = 100 centimes
Cook Islands	Avarua	English, Polynesian dialects	New Zealand Dollar (NZ$) = 100 cents
Costa Rica	San José	Spanish	Colon (CR₡) = 100 centimos
Cuba	Havana	Spanish	Peso (Cub$) = 100 centavos

Country	Capital	Official language(s)	Currency
Cyprus	Nicosia	Greek, Turkish	Pound (C£) = 1000 mills
Czechoslovakia	Prague	Czech, Slovak	Koruna (Kčs) = 100 heller
Denmark	Copenhagen	Danish	Krone (DKr) = 100 øre
Djibouti	Djibouti-Ville	French, Arabic	Franc (DjFr) = 100 centimes
Dominica	Roseau	English	East Caribbean Dollar (EC$) = 100 cents
Dominican Republic	Santo Domingo	Spanish	Peso (DR$) = 100 centavos
Ecuador	Quito	Spanish	Sucre (Su) = 100 centavos
Egypt	Cairo	Arabic	Pound (E£) = 100 piastres
El Salvador	San Salvador	Spanish	Colón (ES₡) = 100 centavos
Equatorial Guinea	Malabo	Spanish	Ekuele (E) = 100 centimes
Ethiopia	Addis Ababa	Amharic	Birr (Br) = 100 cents
Fiji	Suva	English, Fijian, Hindi	Dollar (F$) = 100 cents
Finland	Helsinki	Finnish	Markka (FMk) = 100 penniä
France	Paris	French	Franc (Fr) = 100 centimes
Gabon	Libreville	French	CFP Franc (CFPFr) = 100 centimes
The Gambia	Banjul	English	Dalasi (Di) = 100 butut
German Democratic Republic (E Germany)	East Berlin	German	GDR Mark/ Ostmark (M) = 100 pfennig
Germany, Federal Republic of (W Germany)	Bonn	German	Deutsche Mark (DM) = 100 pfennig
Ghana	Accra	English	Cedi (₡) = 100 pesawas

Country	Capital	Official language(s)	Currency
Greece	Athens	Greek	Drachma (Dr) = 100 lepta
Grenada	St George's	English	East Caribbean dollar (EC$) = 100 cents
Guatemala	Guatemala City	Spanish	Quetzal (Q) = 100 centavos
Guinea	Conakry	French	Syli (Sy) = 100 cauris
Guinea-Bissau	Bissau	Portuguese	Peso (GBP) = 100 centavos
Guyana	Georgetown	English	Dollar (G$) = 100 cents
Haiti	Port-au-Prince	French	Gourde (Gde) = 100 centimes
Honduras	Tegucigalpa	Spanish	Lempira (La) = 100 centavos
Hong Kong	Victoria	English, Chinese	Dollar (HK$) = 100 cents
Hungary	Budapest	Hungarian	Forint (Ft) = 100 fillér
Iceland	Reykjavik	Icelandic	Króna (IKr) = 100 aurar
India	New Delhi	Hindi	Rupee (Re) = 100 paisa
Indonesia	Jakarta	Bahasa Indonesian	Rupiah (Rp) = 100 sen
Iran	Tehran	Farsi	Rial (RI) = 100 dinar
Iraq	Baghdad	Arabic	Dinar (ID) = 1000 fils
Ireland, Republic of	Dublin	Irish, English	Pound/punt (IR£) = 100 pence/pighne
Israel	Jerusalem	Hebrew	Shekel (IS) = 100 agorot
Italy	Rome	Italian	Lira (L) = 100 centesimi
Ivory Coast	Abidjan (commercial) Yamoussoukro (political and administrative)	French	CFA Franc (CFAFr) = 100 centimes
Jamaica	Kingston	English	Dollar (J$) = 100 cents

Country	Capital	Official language(s)	Currency
Japan	Tokyo	Japanese	Yen (Y) = 100 sen
Jordan	Amman	Arabic	Dinar (JD) = 1000 fils
Kampuchea (Cambodia)	Phnom Penh	Khmer	Riel (CRI) = 100 sen
Kenya	Nairobi	Kiswahili	Shilling (KSh) = 100 cents
Kiribati	Tarawa	I-Kiribati, English	Australian Dollar (A$) = 100 cents
Korea, Democratic People's Republic of (N Korea)	Pyongyang	Korean	Won (NKW) = 100 chon
Korea, Republic of (S Korea)	Seoul	Korean	Won (W) = 100 chun
Kuwait	Kuwait City	Arabic	Dinar (KD) = 1000 fils
Laos	Vientiane	Lao	Kip (Kp) = 100 at
Lebanon	Beirut	Arabic	Livre/Pound (L£) = 100 piastres
Lesotho	Maseru	Sesotho, English	Malote (LSM) = 100 licente
Liberia	Monrovia	English	Dollar (L$) = 100 cents
Libya	Tripoli	Arabic	Dinar (LD) = 1000 dirhams
Liechtenstein	Vaduz	German	Swiss Franc (SFr) = 100 centimes
Luxembourg	Luxembourg-Ville	German	Franc (LFr) = 100 centimes
Macao	Macao City	Portuguese	Pataca (Pat) = 100 avos
Madagascar	Antananarivo	French, Malagasy	Franc (MgFr) = 100 centimes
Malawi	Lilongwe	Chichewa, English	Kwacha (MK) = 100 tambala
Malaysia	Kuala Lumpur	Bahasa Malaysia (Malay)	Dollar (M$) = 100 cents

Country	Capital	Official language(s)	Currency
Maldives	Malé	Dhivehi	Rufiyaa (MRf) = 100 laris
Mali	Bamako	French	CFA Franc (CFAFr) = 100 centimes
Malta	Valletta	English, Maltese	Pound (M£) = 100 cents
Mauritania	Nouakchott	French, Arabic	Ouguiya (U) = 5 khoums
Mauritius	Port Louis	English, French	Rupee (MR) = 100 cents
Mexico	Mexico City	Spanish	Peso (Mex$) = 100 centavos
Monaco	Monaco	French	Franc (MnFr) = 100 centimes
Mongolia	Ulan Bator	Mongolian	Tugrik (Tug) = 100 möngö
Morocco	Rabat	Arabic	Dirham (DH) = 100 centimes
Mozambique	Maputo	Portuguese	Metical (MZM) = 100 centavos
Namibia	Windhoek	Afrikaans, English	Rand (R) = 100 cents
Nauru	Yaren District	English, Nauruan	Australian Dollar (A$) = 100 cents
Nepal	Kathmandu	Nepali	Rupee (NRp) = 100 pice
Netherlands	Amsterdam (The Hague— seat of government)	Dutch	Guilder (Gld) or Florin = 100 cents
New Zealand	Wellington	English	Dollar (NZ$) = 100 cents
Nicaragua	Managua	Spanish	Córdoba (C) = 100 centavos
Niger	Niamey	French	CFA Franc (CFAFr) = 100 centimes
Nigeria	Lagos	English	Naira (N) = 100 kobo
Norway	Oslo	Norwegian	Krone (NKr) = 100 ore
Oman	Muscat	Arabic	Rial Omani (RO) = 1000 baizas

Country	Capital	Official language(s)	Currency
Pakistan	Islamabad	Urdu	Rupee (Rp) = 100 paisa
Panama	Panama City	Spanish	Balboa (Ba) = 100 centesimos
Papua New Guinea	Port Moresby	English, Hiri Motu, Melanesian Pidgin	Kina (K) = 100 toca
Paraguay	Asunción	Spanish	Guarani (G) = 100 centimos
Peru	Lima	Spanish	Sol (S) or Inti = 100 centavos
Philippines	Manila	Tagalog, Cebuano	Peso (PP) = 100 centavos
Poland	Warsaw	Polish	Zloty (Zl) = 100 groszy
Portugal	Lisbon	Portuguese	Escudo (ESc) = 100 centavos
Puerto Rico	San Juan	Spanish	Dollar ($) = 100 cents
Qatar	Doha	Arabic	Riyal (QR) = 100 dirhams
Romania	Bucharest	Romanian	Leu (pl. Lei) = 100 bani
Rwanda	Kigali	French, Kinyarwanda	Franc (RWFr) = 100 centimes
St Kitts-Nevis	Basseterre	English	East Caribbean Dollar (EC$) = 100 cents
St Lucia	Castries	English	East Caribbean Dollar (EC$) = 100 cents
St Vincent	Kingstown	English	East Caribbean Dollar (EC$) = 100 cents
San Marino	San Marino	Italian	Lira (SML) = 100 centesimi
São Tomé and Principe	São Tomé	Portuguese	Dobra or Escudo (ESP) = 100 centavos
Saudi Arabia	Riyadh	Arabic	Riyal (SAR) = 100 halalas
Senegal	Dakar	French	CFA Franc (CFAFr) = 100 centimes

Country	Capital	Official language(s)	Currency
Seychelles	Victoria	English, Creole	Rupee (SR) = 100 cents
Sierra Leone	Freetown	English	Leone (Le) = 100 cents
Singapore	Singapore City	Chinese, English, Malay, Tamil	Ringgit or Dollar (S$) = 100 cents
Solomon Islands	Honiara	English	Dollar (SI$) = 100 cents
Somalia	Mogadishu	Somali, Arabic	Shilling (SoSh) = 100 centesimi
South Africa	Pretoria (administrative) Cape Town (legislative)	Afrikaans English	Rand (R) = 100 cents
Spain	Madrid	Spanish	Peseta (Pa) = 100 centimos
Sri Lanka	Colombo	Sinhala, Tamil	Rupee (SLR) = 100 cents
Sudan	Khartoum	Arabic	Pound (S£) = 100 piastres
Surinam	Paramaribo	Dutch	Guilder (SGld) or Florin = 100 cents
Swaziland	Mbabane	English, SiSwati	Lilangeni (Li) = 100 cents
Sweden	Stockholm	Swedish	Krona (SKr) = 100 øre
Switzerland	Berne	German, French, Italian, Romansch	Swiss Franc (SFr) = 100 centimes
Syria	Damascus	Arabic	Pound (Syr£) = 100 piastres
Taiwan	Taipei	Mandarin Chinese	New Dollar (NT$) = 100 cents
Tanzania	Dar es Salaam	Swahili, English	Shilling (TSh) = 100 cents
Thailand	Bangkok	Thai	Baht (Bt) = 100 satang
Togo	Lomé	French, Kabiye, Ewe	CFA Franc (CFAFr) = 100 centimes
Tonga	Nuku'alofa	Tongan	Pa'anga or Tongan Dollar (T$) = 100 seniti

Country	Capital	Official language(s)	Currency
Trinidad and Tobago	Port of Spain	English	Dollar (TT$) = 100 cents
Tunisia	Tunis	Arabic	Dinar (TD) = 1000 millemes
Turkey	Ankara	Turkish	Lira (TL) = 100 kuros
Tuvalu	Funafuti	Tuvaluan (Samoan)	Australian Dollar (A$) = 100 cents
Uganda	Kampala	English	Shilling (USh) = 100 cents
Union of Soviet Socialist Republics	Moscow	Russian	Rouble (Rub) = 100 kopeks
United Arab Emirates	Abu Dhabi	Arabic	Dirham (DH) = 100 fils
United Kingdom	London	English	Pound sterling (£) = 100 pence
United States of America	Washington DC	English	Dollar ($) = 100 cents
Uruguay	Montevideo	Spanish	New Peso (UrugN$) = 100 centesimos
Vanuatu	Port Vila	Bislama, English, French	Vatu (V) = 100 centimes
Venezuela	Caracas	Spanish	Bolivar (B) = 100 centimos
Vietnam	Hanoi	Vietnamese	Dồng (D) = 100 hào
Western Samoa	Apia	English, Samoan	Tala or Western Samoan Dollar (WS$) = 100 sene
Yemen Arab Republic (N Yemen)	Sana'a	Arabic	Riyal (YR) = 100 fils
Yemen People's Democratic Republic (S Yemen)	Aden	Arabic	Dinar (YD) = 1000 fils
Yugoslavia	Belgrade	Serbo-Croat, Slovene, Macedonian	Dinar (D) = 100 paras
Zaire	Kinshasa	French	Zaire (Z) = 100 makuta

Country	Capital	Official language(s)	Currency
Zambia	Lusaka	English	Kwacha (K) = 100 ngwee
Zimbabwe	Harare	English	Dollar (Z$) = 100 cents

22.2 World time zones

World standard times

Since the end of the 19th century a system of World Standard Time by zones has been used. By this system the world is divided into 24 time zones, each comprising of approximately 15° of longitude and representing one hour of time. Individual countries adopt a convenient standard time, although some large countries, e.g. USA, Canada, USSR, are divided into several time zones.

The measurement of the time follows the East-West progress of the sun across the world's surface, using the **Greenwich Meridian** as the starting point and **Greenwich Mean Time** (GMT) as the base time. All countries East of the Greenwich Meridian are ahead of GMT and those to the West are behind GMT. The date changes on the **International Date Line** (an imaginary division, approximately 180° from the Greenwich Meridian, passing through the Pacific Ocean). *(For map see Chapter 24.4).*

Hours ahead of or behind GMT

Abu Dhabi +4	Brisbane +10	Djakarta +7	Kuwait +3
Accra 0	Brussels +1	Doha +3	Lagos +1
Adelaide +9½	Bucharest +2	Dubai +4	Lima −5
Algiers 0	Budapest +1	Dublin 0	Lisbon 0
Amman +2	Buenos Aires −3	Frankfurt +1	London 0
Amsterdam +1	Cairo +2	Geneva +1	Luxembourg +1
Ankara +2	Calcutta +5½	Gibraltar +1	Madeira −1
Athens +2	Canberra +10	Hanoi +7	Madras +5½
Auckland +12	Cape Town +2	Helsinki +2	Madrid +1
Baghdad +3	Caracas −4	Hobart +10	Malta +1
Beijing +8	Chicago −6	Hong Kong +8	Manila +8
Beirut +2	Copenhagen +1	Islamabad +5	Mauritius +4
Belgrade +1	Dallas −6½	Istanbul +3	Melbourne +10
Berlin +1	Damascus +3	Jakarta +8	Mexico City −6
Berne +1	Darwin +9½	Jerusalem +2	Milan +1
Bombay +5½	Delhi +5½	Johannesburg +2	Montevideo −3
Bonn +1	Detroit −5	Karachi +5½	Montreal −5
Brindisi +1	Dhaka +6½	Kuala Lumpur +7½	Moscow +3

Munich +1	Perth +8	Rotterdam +1	Tokyo +9
Muscat +4	Prague +1	Sana'a +3	Toronto −5
Nairobi +3	Pretoria +2	San Francisco −8	Tripoli +2
Naples +1	Quebec −5	Santiago −4	Tunis +1
New York −5	Rabat 0	Seoul +9	Vancouver −8
Nice +1	Rangoon +6½	Singapore +7½	Vienna +1
Nicosia +2	Rawalpindi +5	Sofia +2	Warsaw +1
Oslo +1	Reykjavik 0	Stockholm +1	Washington −5
Ottawa −5	Rio de Janiero −3	Suez +2	Wellington +12
Panama −5	Riyadh +3	Sydney +10	Winnipeg −6
Paris +1	Rome +1	Tehran +3½	Zurich +1

Note: In some countries Summer Time or **Daylight Saving Time** operates during part of the year. These variations from Standard Time are decided annually.

22.3 International airports and airlines

Airports

Airport	Telephone
Abu Dhabi (Abu Dhabi International)	77277/77335
Accra (Kotoka International)	76171
Amsterdam (Schipol)	(020) 5179111
Athens (Athinai)	(01) 97991
Auckland (Auckland International)	275 3899
Baghdad (Baghdad International)	5518888/5519999
Bahrain (Bahrain International)	32133/321640
Bangkok (Don Muang)	511 0121
Basel (Basel-Mulhousen)	(061) 57-31-11
Benghazi (Benina)	97147/86329
Berlin (Tempelhof)	(030) 690 9601
Bombay (Santa Cruz International)	535491
Boston (Logan)	(617) 482 2930
Brunei (Bandar Seri Bagawan)	6531
Buenos Aires (Ezeiza)	6200043
Cairo (Cairo International)	968866
Chicago (O'Hare International)	(312) 686 2200
Copenhagen (Kastrup)	(01) 41-1-31
Damascus (Damascus International)	555601
Dar es Salaam (Dar es Salaam International)	42211
Delhi (Palam)	392719
Durban (Louis Botha International)	(031) 42-6184
East Berlin (Schonefeld)	672 4068
Frankfurt (Frankfurt/Main)	(0611) 69-01
Freetown (Lungi International)	025 215
Gaborone (Gaborone International)	53731/53732
Geneva (Geneva Intercontinental)	(022) 98-11-22
Harare (Harare International)	50422
Helsinki (Vantaa International)	82921
Hong Kong (Kai Tak International)	(3) 8297531
Houston (Houston Intercontinental)	(713) 443 4364
Jeddah (Jeddah International)	27211
Johannesburg (Jan Smuts)	(011) 975 1185
Kingston (Norman Manley International)	928 6057
Kuala Lumpur (Subang International)	03-760717/760723/760833
Kuwait (Kuwait International)	740296
Lagos (Murtala Muhammed)	31631
Lima (Jorge Chavet International)	529570
Lisbon (Lisbonne)	882591/881101/885011
London (see UK Airports: 22.4)	

Los Angeles (Los Angeles International)	(213) 646 5252
Lusaka (Lusaka International)	(011) 74331/74213
Madrid (Barajas)	(1) 222-11-65
Manila (Luzon International)	828 1784
Mexico City (Benito Juárez International)	571-36-00/571-30-07/571-34-32
Montreal (Dorval)	(514) 636 3223
Moscow (Sheremetyevo)	294-18-31/158-79-35
Nairobi (Jomo Kenyatta International)	822111
Nassau (Nassau International)	(809) 77281
New York (J F Kennedy International)	(212) 471 7594
Oman (Seeb International)	619210
Osaka (Itami International)	(06) 863 1121
Oslo (Furnebu)	(02) 12-13-40
Ottawa (Ottawa International)	(613) 998 3151
Paris (Charles de Gaulle International)	(1) 862-12-12/862-19-14
Peking (Beijing Capital)	555531
Prague (Ruzyně)	334
Puerto Rico (Puerto Rico International)	(809) 791-0030/791-0054
Rangoon (Mingaladon)	40111/40221/40231
Reykjavik (Reykjavik)	(91) 17430
Rio de Janeiro (Galeao)	398 6060
Rome (Leonardo da Vinci International)	(4867) 601541
Rotterdam (Zestienhoven)	(010) 371144
Santiago (Arturo Merino Benitez)	719152/733968
Shanghai (Hung-Chaio)	536530
Singapore (Changi International)	5421122
Sofia (Sofia International)	451121/26
Stockholm (Arlanda)	(08) 24-40-00
Sydney (Kingsford Smith)	(02) 667-0544
Taipei (Chiang Kai Chek International)	(033) 832001/832004
Tehran (Mehrabad)	641171
Tel Aviv (Ben Gurion International)	(03) 972610/972615
Tokyo (Haneda International)	(03) 747 0511
Tokyo (Narita International)	(0476) 32-2102/32-6417
Toronto (Toronto International)	(416) 676 3000
Vancouver (Vancouver International)	(604) 273-2311
Vienna (Schwechat)	(0222) 77700
Warsaw (Okecie)	46-11-82/46-99-56
Washington DC (Dulles International)	(301) 787 7079
Wellington (Wellington International)	888 500
Zurich (Zurich Intercontinental)	(01) 816-22-11

Airlines

Airline	Reservations	Flight enquiries
Aer Lingus	01-734 1212	01-734 1212
Aeroflot	01-493 7436	01-759 2529
Air Canada	01-759 2636	01-897 1331
Air France	01-499 9511	01-759 2311
Air India	01-491 7979	01-897 6311
Air Jamaica	01-734 1782	01-759 2595
Air Lanka	01-439 0291/3	01-439 0291
Air New Zealand	01-930 3434	(0293) 518033
Alia (Royal Jordanian Airlines)	01-734 2557	01-745 7031
Alitalia (Italian Airlines)	01-602 7111	01-759 1198
Austrian Airlines	01-439 0741	01-745 7191
British Airways	01-897 4000	01-759 2525
British Caledonian	01-668 4222	(0293) 25555
BWIA International	01-734 3796	01-839 7155
Caribbean Airways	01-636 2151/4	(0293) 28822
Cathay Pacific	01-930 7878	(0293) 502087
Cyprus Airways	01-388 5411	01-388 5425
Egyptair	01-734 2395/6	01-759 1520
El Al (Israel Airlines)	01-437 9255	01-759 9771
Finnair	01-408 1222	01-759 1258
Gulf Air	01-408 1717	01-897 0402
Iberia (International Airlines of Spain)	01-437 5622	01-759 4321
Icelandair	01-499 9971	01-745 7051
JAL (Japan Air Lines)	01-408 1000	01-759 9880

Airline	Reservations	Flight enquiries
KLM (Royal Dutch Airlines)	01-568 9144	01-750 9820
Kuwait Airways	01-935 8795	01-745 7772
Lufthansa (German Airlines)	01-408 0442	01-759 5642
MAS (Malaysian Airline System)	01-491 4542	01-759 2595
Middle East Airlines	01-493 5681	01-759 9211
Olympic Airways	01-846 9080	01-846 9080
Pakistan International Airlines	01-734 5544	01-759 2544
Pan Am (Pan American World Airways)	01-409 0688	01-409 0688
Qantas	(0345) 747767	(0345) 747767
SAA (South African Airways)	01-734 9841	01-897 3645
Sabena (Belgian World Airlines)	01-437 6950	01-437 6950
SAS (Scandinavian Airlines)	01-734 4020	01-734 4020
Singapore Airlines	01-747 0007	01-745 4151
Swissair	01-439 4144	01-745 7191
TAP (Air Portugal)	01-828 0262	01-828 0262
Thai Airways International	01-499 9113	01-897 1331
TWA (Trans World Airlines)	01-636 4090	01-636 4090
Virgin Atlantic	(0293) 38222	(0293) 38222
World Airways	01-434 3252	(0293) 502073

For UK airlines see p 241.

22.4 UK travel information

Air commuter services

British Airways Super Shuttle	01-897 4000
London Heathrow *to* Belfast/Edinburgh/Glasgow/Manchester	
British Caledonian	01-668 4222
London Gatwick *to* Aberdeen/Glasgow/Edinburgh/Manchester	
British Midland Diamond Service	01-581 0864
London Heathrow *to* Edinburgh/Glasgow	
Edinburgh *to* Amsterdam	
Glasgow *to* Amsterdam/East Midlands/Jersey/Guernsey	

UK airlines

Air Atlantique	(0203) 307566	Channel Express Air Services	(0202) 570701
Air Europe	01-651 3611		
Air UK	01-551 4988	Dan-Air	01-680 1011
Airways International Cymru	(0446) 711811	Guernsey Airlines	(0481) 35727
		Highland Express Airways	(0292) 79822
Anglo Airlines	(0293) 510131	Jersey European Airways	(0392) 64440
Aurigny Air Services	(0481) 822886		
		Loganair	041-889 3181
Britannia Airways	01-568 9144	Manx Airlines	01-493 0803
British Airways	01-897 4000	Monarch Airlines	(0582) 424211
British Caledonian	01-668 4222	Orion Airways	(0332) 812469
British Midland	01-581 0864	Virgin Atlantic Airways	(0293) 38222
Brymon Airways	01-549 6535		
Cal Air International	01-409 0814		

UK airports

(For map see p 279)

Aberdeen (Dyce)	(0224) 722331	Birmingham International	021-767 5511
Alderney (The Blaye)	(0481) 822711	Blackpool (Squire's Gate)	(0253) 43061
Barra (North Bay)	041-889 1311	Bournemouth (Hurn)	(0202) 579751
Belfast International (Aldergrove)	(0232) 229271	Bristol (Lulsgate)	(0275) 874441
Belfast Harbour (Sydenham)	(0232) 57745	Cardiff—Wales (Rhoose)	(0446) 711211
Benbecula (Balivanich)	(0870) 2051	Carlisle (Crosby)	(0228) 73641
		Cork	965388

Coventry (Baginton)	(0203) 301717
Dublin	(0001) 379900
Dundee (Riverside Park)	(0382) 643242
East Midlands (Derby)	(0332) 810621
Edinburgh (Turnhouse)	031-333 1000
Exeter (Clyst Honiton)	(0392) 67433
Fetlar	095783 267
Fort William Heliport	(0397) 4182
Galway (Carnmore)	(0009) 84300/ 84392
Glasgow/(Paisley)	041-887 1111
Gloucester/ Cheltenham (Staverton)	(0452) 856681
Guernsey	(0481) 37766
Humberside (Ulceby)	(0652) 688456
Inverness (Dalcross)	(0463) 232471
Islay (Glenegadale/ Port Ellen)	(0496) 2361
Isle of Man (Ronaldsway)	(0624) 823311
Isle of Skye (Ashaig/Broadford)	(04712) 202
Isles of Scilly (St Mary's)	(0720) 22677
Jersey (States)	(0534) 46111
Kirkwall (Orkney)	(0856) 2421
Leeds/Bradford	(0532) 509696
Lerwick (Sumburgh)	(0950) 60645
(Tingwall)	(059) 584 306
Liverpool (Speke)	051-486 8877
London-Battersea Heliport	01-228 0181

London City (Stolport)	01-568 9111 (opening late 1987)
London (Gatwick)	(0293) 28822
London (Heathrow)	01-759 4321
Londonderry (Eglinton)	(0504) 810784
Luton	(0582) 36061
Manchester International	061-489 3000
Newcastle (Woolsington)	091-286 0966
Newquay (RAF St Mawgan)	(0637) 860551
Norwich	(0603) 411923
Papa Westray	(0856) 3535
Penzance Heliport	(07366) 4296
Plymouth (Roborough)	(0752) 705151
Prestwick	(0292) 79822
Rothesay Heliport	(0292) 79822
Shannon	61444
Shoreham (Brighton/Hove/Worthing)	(0273) 452304
Southampton (Eastleigh)	(0703) 612341
Southend	(0702) 340201
Stansted	(0279) 502380
Stornoway (Lewis)	(0851) 2256
Teesside	(0325) 332811
Tiree (Reef)	(08792) 456
Tresco Heliport (Scilly)	(0720) 22083
Unst (Baltasound)	(095781) 404/5/6/7
Waterford (Portlaw)	(0005) 75580
Weston-super-Mare Heliport	(0934) 28726
Wick	(0955) 2215

British Rail

Services from London:
(*to* East Anglia and Essex)	01-283 7171
(*to* Midlands, N Wales, North West, W Coast to Scotland)	01-387 7070
(*to* Southern England)	01-928 5100
(*to* W of England, W Midlands, S Wales)	01-262 6767
(*to* W Yorkshire, North East, E Coast to Scotland)	01-287 2477

Services from Birmingham (New Street):	021-643 2711
from Bristol (Temple Meads):	(0272) 294255
from Cardiff (Central):	(0222) 28000
from Edinburgh (Waverley):	031-556 2451
from Glasgow (Central):	041-204 2844
from Leeds (City):	(0532) 448133
from Liverpool (Lime Street):	051-709 9696
from Manchester (Piccadilly):	061-832 8353
from Newcastle (Central):	(0632) 326262
from Sheffield:	(0742) 26411

Eastern Region:
(York)	(0904) 53022

London:
(Charing Cross)	01-928 5100
(Euston and St Pancras)	01-387 7070
(Fenchurch Street)	01-283 7171
(King's Cross)	01-278 2477
(Liverpool Street)	01-283 7171

London Midland Region:
(Birmingham)	021-643 2711

Scottish Region:
(Glasgow)	041-204 2844
(Edinburgh)	031-556 2451

Southern Region:
(Waterloo and Victoria)	01-928 5100

Western Region:
(Paddington)	01-262 6767

Motorail Services:	01-387 8541

Sleeper Services:
(Euston)	01-388 6061
(King's Cross)	01-278 2411
(Paddington)	01-723 781

Hoverspeed City Link:
(London *to* Paris)	(0304) 216205
	01-554 7061

Car ferry services

B & I Line
(Liverpool *to* Dublin)	051-227 3131
(Holyhead *to* Dublin and Dun Laoghaire)	(0407) 50222
(Fishguard *to* Rosslare)	(0348) 872881

Brittany Ferries
(Portsmouth *to* St Malo)	(0705) 827701
(Plymouth *to* Roscoff and Santander)	(07527) 21321
(Cork *to* Roscoff)	021-507 666

DFDS Seaways
(Harwich *to* Esbjerg, Hamburg and Gothenburg)	(0255) 554681
(Newcastle *to* Esbjerg, Bergen and Gothenburg)	(0632) 575655

Hoverspeed Ltd
(Dover *to* Boulogne and Calais)	(0843) 595555/594881
	01-554 7061

North Sea Ferries Ltd
(Hull *to* Zeebrugge; Ipswich *to* Rotterdam)	(0482) 795141

P & O Ferries
(Dover *to* Boulogne)	(0304) 203399
(Southampton *to* Le Havre)	(0703) 32131

Sealink British Ferries
01-834 8122

(Dover *to* Boulogne, Calais, Dunkirk and Ostend; Fishguard *to* Rosslare; Folkestone *to* Boulogne; Harwich *to* Hook of Holland; Heysham *to* Douglas (Isle of Man); Holyhead *to* Dun Laoghaire; Newhaven *to* Dieppe; Portsmouth *to* Channel Islands and Cherbourg; Stranraer *to* Larne; Weymouth *to* Channel Islands and Portsmouth)

Sealink Isle of Wight Services
(0705) 827744

(Portsmouth and Lymington *to* Isle of Wight)

Townsend Thoresen
(0304) 203388

(Dover *to* Boulogne, Calais and Zeebrugge; Felixstowe *to* Zeebrugge; Portsmouth *to* Cherbourg and Le Havre; Larne *to* Cairnryan)

Car hire services
Alamo Rent A Car	01-897 0536	Telex 261863
Avis	01-848 8733	Telex 933936
Avis Chauffeur Drive	01-897 2621	Telex 905016
Budget	(0800) 181181	Telex 877994
Godfrey Davis Chauffeur Drive	01-834 6701	Telex 22819
Godfrey Davis Europcar	01-950 5050	Telex 25468

Guy Salmon	01-408 1255	Telex 21213
Hertz	01-679 1777	Telex 8812947
Key Rent-a-Car	01-897 7777	Telex 917061
Swan	01-995 4665	Telex 935102
Travelwise	01-582 1769	Telex 21120

Consult *Yellow Pages* for your local branches.

Passport offices

Belfast
Hampton House, 47–53 High Street, Belfast BT1 2AB   (0232) 232371

Glasgow
Empire House, 131 West Nile Street, Glasgow G1 2RY   041-332 0271

Liverpool
5th Floor, India Building, Water Street, Liverpool L2 0QZ   051-237 3010

London
Clive House, 70–78 Petty France, London SW1H 9HD   01-213 3000

(A–D)	01-213 3261	(E–K)	01-213 7272
(L–Q)	01-213 6098	(R–Z)	01-213 6915

Newport
Olympia House, Upper Dock Street, Newport NPT 1XA   (0633) 56292

Peterborough
55 Westfield Road, Westwood PE3 6TG   (0733) 895555

Travel associations and bodies

Air Transport Operators Association   (0428) 4804
Clembro House, Weydown Road, Haslemere, Surrey GU27 2QE

Air Transport Users Committee   01-242 3882
129 Kingsway, London WC2B 6NN

Association of British Travel Agents   01-637 2444
55/57 Newman Street, London W1P 4AH

British Airports Authority   (0293) 517755
Gatwick Airport, Gatwick, W Sussex RH6 0HZ

British Vehicle Rental Leasing Association   (0243) 786782
13 St John's Street, Chichester, W Sussex PO19 1UU

Civil Aviation Authority   01-379 7311
CAA House, 45/59 Kingsway, London WC2B 6TE

Guild of British Travel Agents   01-930 2278
60/61 Trafalgar Square, London WC2N 5DS

22.5 UK counties and regions

Common written abbreviations of the English counties preferred by the Royal Mail are given in brackets after each county. The form *Salop* (for Shropshire) is also used in speech. There are no commonly used abbreviations for Welsh and Northern Irish counties or Scottish regions. *(For map see p 276.)*

England

Avon
Bedfordshire
 (Beds)
Berkshire
 (Berks)
Buckinghamshire
 (Bucks)
Cambridgeshire
 (Cambs)
Cheshire
Cleveland
Cornwall
Cumbria
Derbyshire
Devon
Dorset
Durham
East Sussex
Essex
Gloucestershire
 (Glos)
Greater London
Greater Manchester

Hampshire
 (Hants)
Hereford and
 Worcester
Hertfordshire
 (Herts)
Humberside
Isle of Wight (IOW)
Kent
Lancashire
 (Lancs)
Leicestershire
 (Leics)
Lincolnshire
 (Lincs)
Merseyside
Middlesex
 (Middx)
Norfolk
Northamptonshire
 (Northants)
Northumberland
 (Northd)
North Yorkshire
 (N Yorks)

Nottinghamshire
 (Notts)
Oxfordshire
 (Oxon)
Shropshire
 (Salop)
Somerset
South Yorkshire
 (S Yorkshire)
Staffordshire
 (Staffs)
Suffolk
Surrey
Tyne and Wear
Warwickshire
 (Warwicks)
West Midlands
West Sussex
West Yorkshire
 (W Yorkshire)
Wiltshire
 (Wilts)

Wales

Clwyd
Dyfed
Gwent

Gwynedd
Mid Glamorgan
Powys

South Glamorgan
West Glamorgan

Northern Ireland

Antrim
Armagh
Down

Fermanagh
Londonderry
 (Co. Derry)

Tyrone

Scotland

Borders
Central
Dumfries and
  Galloway
Fife

Grampian
Highland
Lothian
Orkney

Shetland
Strathclyde
Tayside
Western Isles

23 CALENDARS

23.1 Calendars 1987-2000

1987

	January	February	March	April	May	June
M	5 12 19 26	2 9 16 23	2 9 16 23 30	6 13 20 27	4 11 18 25	1 8 15 22 29
T	6 13 20 27	3 10 17 24	3 10 17 24 31	7 14 21 28	5 12 19 26	2 9 16 23 30
W	7 14 21 28	4 11 18 25	4 11 18 25	1 8 15 22 29	6 13 20 27	3 10 17 24
T	1 8 15 22 29	5 12 19 26	5 12 19 26	2 9 16 23 30	7 14 21 28	4 11 18 25
F	2 9 16 23 30	6 13 20 27	6 13 20 27	3 10 17 24	1 8 15 22 29	5 12 19 26
S	3 10 17 24 31	7 14 21 28	7 14 21 28	4 11 18 25	2 9 16 23 30	6 13 20 27
S	4 11 18 25	1 8 15 22	1 8 15 22 29	5 12 19 26	3 10 17 24 31	7 14 21 28

	July	August	September	October	November	December
M	6 13 20 27	3 10 17 24 31	7 14 21 28	5 12 19 26	2 9 16 23 30	7 14 21 28
T	7 14 21 28	4 11 18 25	1 8 15 22 29	6 13 20 27	3 10 17 24	1 8 15 22 29
W	1 8 15 22 29	5 12 19 26	2 9 16 23 30	7 14 21 28	4 11 18 25	2 9 16 23 30
T	2 9 16 23 30	6 13 20 27	3 10 17 24	1 8 15 22 29	5 12 19 26	3 10 17 24 31
F	3 10 17 24 31	7 14 21 28	4 11 18 25	2 9 16 23 30	6 13 20 27	4 11 18 25
S	4 11 18 25	1 8 15 22 29	5 12 19 26	3 10 17 24 31	7 14 21 28	5 12 19 26
S	5 12 19 26	2 9 16 23 30	6 13 20 27	4 11 18 25	1 8 15 22 29	6 13 20 27

1988

	January	February	March	April	May	June
M	4 11 18 25	1 8 15 22 29	7 14 21 28	4 11 18 25	2 9 16 23 30	6 13 20 27
T	5 12 19 26	2 9 16 23	1 8 15 22 29	5 12 19 26	3 10 17 24 31	7 14 21 28
W	6 13 20 27	3 10 17 24	2 9 16 23 30	6 13 20 27	4 11 18 25	1 8 15 22 29
T	7 14 21 28	4 11 18 25	3 10 17 24 31	7 14 21 28	5 12 19 26	2 9 16 23 30
F	1 8 15 22 29	5 12 19 26	4 11 18 25	1 8 15 22 29	6 13 20 27	3 10 17 24
S	2 9 16 23 30	6 13 20 27	5 12 19 26	2 9 16 23 30	7 14 21 28	4 11 18 25
S	3 10 17 24 31	7 14 21 28	6 13 20 27	3 10 17 24	1 8 15 22 29	5 12 19 26

	July	August	September	October	November	December
M	4 11 18 25	1 8 15 22 29	5 12 19 26	3 10 17 24 31	7 14 21 28	5 12 19 26
T	5 12 19 26	2 9 16 23 30	6 13 20 27	4 11 18 25	1 8 15 22 29	6 13 20 27
W	6 13 20 27	3 10 17 24 31	7 14 21 28	5 12 19 26	2 9 16 23 30	7 14 21 28
T	7 14 21 28	4 11 18 25	1 8 15 22 29	6 13 20 27	3 10 17 24	1 8 15 22 29
F	1 8 15 22 29	5 12 19 26	2 9 16 23 30	7 14 21 28	4 11 18 25	2 9 16 23 30
S	2 9 16 23 30	6 13 20 27	3 10 17 24	1 8 15 22 29	5 12 19 26	3 10 17 24 31
S	3 10 17 24 31	7 14 21 28	4 11 18 25	2 9 16 23 30	6 13 20 27	4 11 18 25

1989

	January	February	March	April	May	June
M	2 9 16 23 30	6 13 20 27	6 13 20 27	3 10 17 24	1 8 15 22 29	5 12 19 26
T	3 10 17 24 31	7 14 21 28	7 14 21 28	4 11 18 25	2 9 16 23 30	6 13 20 27
W	4 11 18 25	1 8 15 22	1 8 15 22 29	5 12 19 26	3 10 17 24 31	7 14 21 28
T	5 12 19 26	2 9 16 23	2 9 16 23 30	6 13 20 27	4 11 18 25	1 8 15 22 29
F	6 13 20 27	3 10 17 24	3 10 17 24 31	7 14 21 28	5 12 19 26	2 9 16 23 30
S	7 14 21 28	4 11 18 25	4 11 18 25	1 8 15 22 29	6 13 20 27	3 10 17 24
S	1 8 15 22 29	5 12 19 26	5 12 19 26	2 9 16 23 30	7 14 21 28	4 11 18 25

	July	August	September	October	November	December
M	3 10 17 24 31	7 14 21 28	4 11 18 25	2 9 16 23 30	6 13 20 27	4 11 18 25
T	4 11 18 25	1 8 15 22 29	5 12 19 26	3 10 17 24 31	7 14 21 28	5 12 19 26
W	5 12 19 26	2 9 16 23 30	6 13 20 27	4 11 18 25	1 8 15 22 29	6 13 20 27
T	6 13 20 27	3 10 17 24 31	7 14 21 28	5 12 19 26	2 9 16 23 30	7 14 21 28
F	7 14 21 28	4 11 18 25	1 8 15 22 29	6 13 20 27	3 10 17 24	1 8 15 22 29
S	1 8 15 22 29	5 12 19 26	2 9 16 23 30	7 14 21 28	4 11 18 25	2 9 16 23 30
S	2 9 16 23 30	6 13 20 27	3 10 17 24	1 8 15 22 29	5 12 19 26	3 10 17 24 31

1990

	January	February	March	April	May	June
M	1 8 15 22 29	5 12 19 26	5 12 19 26	2 9 16 23 30	7 14 21 28	4 11 18 25
T	2 9 16 23 30	6 13 20 27	6 13 20 27	3 10 17 24	1 8 15 22 29	5 12 19 26
W	3 10 17 24 31	7 14 21 28	7 14 21 28	4 11 18 25	2 9 16 23 30	6 13 20 27
T	4 11 18 25	1 8 15 22	1 8 15 22 29	5 12 19 26	3 10 17 24 31	7 14 21 28
F	5 12 19 26	2 9 16 23	2 9 16 23 30	6 13 20 27	4 11 18 25	1 8 15 22 29
S	6 13 20 27	3 10 17 24	3 10 17 24 31	7 14 21 28	5 12 19 26	2 9 16 23 30
S	7 14 21 28	4 11 18 25	4 11 18 25	1 8 15 22 29	6 13 20 27	3 10 17 24

	July	August	September	October	November	December
M	2 9 16 23 30	6 13 20 27	3 10 17 24	1 8 15 22 29	5 12 19 26	3 10 17 24 31
T	3 10 17 24 31	7 14 21 28	4 11 18 25	2 9 16 23 30	6 13 20 27	4 11 18 25
W	4 11 18 25	1 8 15 22 29	5 12 19 26	3 10 17 24 31	7 14 21 28	5 12 19 26
T	5 12 19 26	2 9 16 23 30	6 13 20 27	4 11 18 25	1 8 15 22 29	6 13 20 27
F	6 13 20 27	3 10 17 24 31	7 14 21 28	5 12 19 26	2 9 16 23 30	7 14 21 28
S	7 14 21 28	4 11 18 25	1 8 15 22 29	6 13 20 27	3 10 17 24	1 8 15 22 29
S	1 8 15 22 29	5 12 19 26	2 9 16 23 30	7 14 21 28	4 11 18 25	2 9 16 23 30

1991

	January	February	March	April	May	June
M	7 14 21 28	4 11 18 25	4 11 18 25	1 8 15 22 29	6 13 20 27	3 10 17 24
T	1 8 15 22 29	5 12 19 26	5 12 19 26	2 9 16 23 30	7 14 21 28	4 11 18 25
W	2 9 16 23 30	6 13 20 27	6 13 20 27	3 10 17 24	1 8 15 22 29	5 12 19 26
T	3 10 17 24 31	7 14 21 28	7 14 21 28	4 11 18 25	2 9 16 23 30	6 13 20 27
F	4 11 18 25	1 8 15 22	1 8 15 22 29	5 12 19 26	3 10 17 24 31	7 14 21 28
S	5 12 19 26	2 9 16 23	2 9 16 23 30	6 13 20 27	4 11 18 25	1 8 15 22 29
S	6 13 20 27	3 10 17 24	3 10 17 24 31	7 14 21 28	5 12 19 26	2 9 16 23 30

	July	August	September	October	November	December
M	1 8 15 22 29	5 12 19 26	2 9 16 23 30	7 14 21 28	4 11 18 25	2 9 16 23 30
T	2 9 16 23 30	6 13 20 27	3 10 17 24	1 8 15 22 29	5 12 19 26	3 10 17 24 31
W	3 10 17 24 31	7 14 21 28	4 11 18 25	2 9 16 23 30	6 13 20 27	4 11 18 25
T	4 11 18 25	1 8 15 22 29	5 12 19 26	3 10 17 24 31	7 14 21 28	5 12 19 26
F	5 12 19 26	2 9 16 23 30	6 13 20 27	4 11 18 25	1 8 15 22 29	6 13 20 27
S	6 13 20 27	3 10 17 24 31	7 14 21 28	5 12 19 26	2 9 16 23 30	7 14 21 28
S	7 14 21 28	4 11 18 25	1 8 15 22 29	6 13 20 27	3 10 17 24	1 8 15 22 29

1992

	January	February	March	April	May	June
M	6 13 20 27	3 10 17 24	2 9 16 23 30	6 13 20 27	4 11 18 25	1 8 15 22 29
T	7 14 21 28	4 11 18 25	3 10 17 24 31	7 14 21 28	5 12 19 26	2 9 16 23 30
W	1 8 15 22 29	5 12 19 26	4 11 18 25	1 8 15 22 29	6 13 20 27	3 10 17 24
T	2 9 16 23 30	6 13 20 27	5 12 19 26	2 9 16 23 30	7 14 21 28	4 11 18 25
F	3 10 17 24 31	7 14 21 28	6 13 20 27	3 10 17 24	1 8 15 22 29	5 12 19 26
S	4 11 18 25	1 8 15 22 29	7 14 21 28	4 11 18 25	2 9 16 23 30	6 13 20 27
S	5 12 19 26	2 9 16 23	1 8 15 22 29	5 12 19 26	3 10 17 24 31	7 14 21 28

	July	August	September	October	November	December
M	6 13 20 27	3 10 17 24 31	7 14 21 28	5 12 19 26	2 9 16 23 30	7 14 21 28
T	7 14 21 28	4 11 18 25	1 8 15 22 29	6 13 20 27	3 10 17 24	1 8 15 22 29
W	1 8 15 22 29	5 12 19 26	2 9 16 23 30	7 14 21 28	4 11 18 25	2 9 16 23 30
T	2 9 16 23 30	6 13 20 27	3 10 17 24	1 8 15 22 29	5 12 19 26	3 10 17 24 31
F	3 10 17 24 31	7 14 21 28	4 11 18 25	2 9 16 23 30	6 13 20 27	4 11 18 25
S	4 11 18 25	1 8 15 22 29	5 12 19 26	3 10 17 24 31	7 14 21 28	5 12 19 26
S	5 12 19 26	2 9 16 23 30	6 13 20 27	4 11 18 25	1 8 15 22 29	6 13 20 27

1993

	January	February	March	April	May	June
M	4 11 18 25	1 8 15 22	1 8 15 22 29	5 12 19 26	3 10 17 24 31	7 14 21 28
T	5 12 19 26	2 9 16 23	2 9 16 23 30	6 13 20 27	4 11 18 25	1 8 15 22 29
W	6 13 20 27	3 10 17 24	3 10 17 24 31	7 14 21 28	5 12 19 26	2 9 16 23 30
T	7 14 21 28	4 11 18 25	4 11 18 25	1 8 15 22 29	6 13 20 27	3 10 17 24
F	1 8 15 22 29	5 12 19 26	5 12 19 26	2 9 16 23 30	7 14 21 28	4 11 18 25
S	2 9 16 23 30	6 13 20 27	6 13 20 27	3 10 17 24	1 8 15 22 29	5 12 19 26
S	3 10 17 24 31	7 14 21 28	7 14 21 28	4 11 18 25	2 9 16 23 30	6 13 20 27

	July	August	September	October	November	December
M	5 12 19 26	2 9 16 23 30	6 13 20 27	4 11 18 25	1 8 15 22 29	6 13 20 27
T	6 13 20 27	3 10 17 24 31	7 14 21 28	5 12 19 26	2 9 16 23 30	7 14 21 28
W	7 14 21 28	4 11 18 25	1 8 15 22 29	6 13 20 27	3 10 17 24	1 8 15 22 29
T	1 8 15 22 29	5 12 19 26	2 9 16 23 30	7 14 21 28	4 11 18 25	2 9 16 23 30
F	2 9 16 23 30	6 13 20 27	3 10 17 24	1 8 15 22 29	5 12 19 26	3 10 17 24 31
S	3 10 17 24 31	7 14 21 28	4 11 18 25	2 9 16 23 30	6 13 20 27	4 11 18 25
S	4 11 18 25	1 8 15 22 29	5 12 19 26	3 10 17 24 31	7 14 21 28	5 12 19 26

1994

	January	February	March	April	May	June
M	3 10 17 24 31	7 14 21 28	7 14 21 28	4 11 18 25	2 9 16 23 30	6 13 20 27
T	4 11 18 25	1 8 15 22	1 8 15 22 29	5 12 19 26	3 10 17 24 31	7 14 21 28
W	5 12 19 26	2 9 16 23	2 9 16 23 30	6 13 20 27	4 11 18 25	1 8 15 22 29
T	6 13 20 27	3 10 17 24	3 10 17 24 31	7 14 21 28	5 12 19 26	2 9 16 23 30
F	7 14 21 28	4 11 18 25	4 11 18 25	1 8 15 22 29	6 13 20 27	3 10 17 24
S	1 8 15 22 29	5 12 19 26	5 12 19 26	2 9 16 23 30	7 14 21 28	4 11 18 25
S	2 9 16 23 30	6 13 20 27	6 13 20 27	3 10 17 24	1 8 15 22 29	5 12 19 26

	July	August	September	October	November	December
M	4 11 18 25	1 8 15 22 29	5 12 19 26	3 10 17 24 31	7 14 21 28	5 12 19 26
T	5 12 19 26	2 9 16 23 30	6 13 20 27	4 11 18 25	1 8 15 22 29	6 13 20 27
W	6 13 20 27	3 10 17 24 31	7 14 21 28	5 12 19 26	2 9 16 23 30	7 14 21 28
T	7 14 21 28	4 11 18 25	1 8 15 22 29	6 13 20 27	3 10 17 24	1 8 15 22 29
F	1 8 15 22 29	5 12 19 26	2 9 16 23 30	7 14 21 28	4 11 18 25	2 9 16 23 30
S	2 9 16 23 30	6 13 20 27	3 10 17 24	1 8 15 22 29	5 12 19 26	3 10 17 24 31
S	3 10 17 24 31	7 14 21 28	4 11 18 25	2 9 16 23 30	6 13 20 27	4 11 18 25

1995

	January	February	March	April	May	June
M	2 9 16 23 30	6 13 20 27	6 13 20 27	3 10 17 24	1 8 15 22 29	5 12 19 26
T	3 10 17 24 31	7 14 21 28	7 14 21 28	4 11 18 25	2 9 16 23 30	6 13 20 27
W	4 11 18 25	1 8 15 22	1 8 15 22 29	5 12 19 26	3 10 17 24 31	7 14 21 28
T	5 12 19 26	2 9 16 23	2 9 16 23 30	6 13 20 27	4 11 18 25	1 8 15 22 29
F	6 13 20 27	3 10 17 24	3 10 17 24 31	7 14 21 28	5 12 19 26	2 9 16 23 30
S	7 14 21 28	4 11 18 25	4 11 18 25	1 8 15 22 29	6 13 20 27	3 10 17 24
S	1 8 15 22 29	5 12 19 26	5 12 19 26	2 9 16 23 30	7 14 21 28	4 11 18 25

	July	August	September	October	November	December
M	3 10 17 24 31	7 14 21 28	4 11 18 25	2 9 16 23 30	6 13 20 27	4 11 18 25
T	4 11 18 25	1 8 15 22 29	5 12 19 26	3 10 17 24 31	7 14 21 28	5 12 19 26
W	5 12 19 26	2 9 16 23 30	6 13 20 27	4 11 18 25	1 8 15 22 29	6 13 20 27
T	6 13 20 27	3 10 17 24 31	7 14 21 28	5 12 19 26	2 9 16 23 30	7 14 21 28
F	7 14 21 28	4 11 18 25	1 8 15 22 29	6 13 20 27	3 10 17 24	1 8 15 22 29
S	1 8 15 22 29	5 12 19 26	2 9 16 23 30	7 14 21 28	4 11 18 25	2 9 16 23 30
S	2 9 16 23 30	6 13 20 27	3 10 17 24	1 8 15 22 29	5 12 19 26	3 10 17 24 31

1996

	January	February	March	April	May	June
M	1 8 15 22 29	5 12 19 26	4 11 18 25	1 8 15 22 29	6 13 20 27	3 10 17 24
T	2 9 16 23 30	6 13 20 27	5 12 19 26	2 9 16 23 30	7 14 21 28	4 11 18 25
W	3 10 17 24 31	7 14 21 28	6 13 20 27	3 10 17 24	1 8 15 22 29	5 12 19 26
T	4 11 18 25	1 8 15 22 29	7 14 21 28	4 11 18 25	2 9 16 23 30	6 13 20 27
F	5 12 19 26	2 9 16 23	1 8 15 22 29	5 12 19 26	3 10 17 24 31	7 14 21 28
S	6 13 20 27	3 10 17 24	2 9 16 23 30	6 13 20 27	4 11 18 25	1 8 15 22 29
S	7 14 21 28	4 11 18 25	3 10 17 24 31	7 14 21 28	5 12 19 26	2 9 16 23 30

	July	August	September	October	November	December
M	1 8 15 22 29	5 12 19 26	2 9 16 23 30	7 14 21 28	4 11 18 25	2 9 16 23 30
T	2 9 16 23 30	6 13 20 27	3 10 17 24	1 8 15 22 29	5 12 19 26	3 10 17 24 31
W	3 10 17 24 31	7 14 21 28	4 11 18 25	2 9 16 23 30	6 13 20 27	4 11 18 25
T	4 11 18 25	1 8 15 22 29	5 12 19 26	3 10 17 24 31	7 14 21 28	5 12 19 26
F	5 12 19 26	2 9 16 23 30	6 13 20 27	4 11 18 25	1 8 15 22 29	6 13 20 27
S	6 13 20 27	3 10 17 24 31	7 14 21 28	5 12 19 26	2 9 16 23 30	7 14 21 28
S	7 14 21 28	4 11 18 25	1 8 15 22 29	6 13 20 27	3 10 17 24	1 8 15 22 29

1997

	January	February	March	April	May	June
M	6 13 20 27	3 10 17 24	3 10 17 24 31	7 14 21 28	5 12 19 26	2 9 16 23 30
T	7 14 21 28	4 11 18 25	4 11 18 25	1 8 15 22 29	6 13 20 27	3 10 17 24
W	1 8 15 22 29	5 12 19 26	5 12 19 26	2 9 16 23 30	7 14 21 28	4 11 18 25
T	2 9 16 23 30	6 13 20 27	6 13 20 27	3 10 17 24	1 8 15 22 29	5 12 19 26
F	3 10 17 24 31	7 14 21 28	7 14 21 28	4 11 18 25	2 9 16 23 30	6 13 20 27
S	4 11 18 25	1 8 15 22	1 8 15 22 29	5 12 19 26	3 10 17 24 31	7 14 21 28
S	5 12 19 26	2 9 16 23	2 9 16 23 30	6 13 20 27	4 11 18 25	1 8 15 22 29

	July	August	September	October	November	December
M	7 14 21 28	4 11 18 25	1 8 15 22 29	6 13 20 27	3 10 17 24	1 8 15 22 29
T	1 8 15 22 29	5 12 19 26	2 9 16 23 30	7 14 21 28	4 11 18 25	2 9 16 23 30
W	2 9 16 23 30	6 13 20 27	3 10 17 24	1 8 15 22 29	5 12 19 26	3 10 17 24 31
T	3 10 17 24 31	7 14 21 28	4 11 18 25	2 9 16 23 30	6 13 20 27	4 11 18 25
F	4 11 18 25	1 8 15 22 29	5 12 19 26	3 10 17 24 31	7 14 21 28	5 12 19 26
S	5 12 19 26	2 9 16 23 30	6 13 20 27	4 11 18 25	1 8 15 22 29	6 13 20 27
S	6 13 20 27	3 10 17 24 31	7 14 21 28	5 12 19 26	2 9 16 23 30	7 14 21 28

1998

	January	February	March	April	May	June
M	5 12 19 26	2 9 16 23	2 9 16 23 30	6 13 20 27	4 11 18 25	1 8 15 22 29
T	6 13 20 27	3 10 17 24	3 10 17 24 31	7 14 21 28	5 12 19 26	2 9 16 23 30
W	7 14 21 28	4 11 18 25	4 11 18 25	1 8 15 22 29	6 13 20 27	3 10 17 24
T	1 8 15 22 29	5 12 19 26	5 12 19 26	2 9 16 23 30	7 14 21 28	4 11 18 25
F	2 9 16 23 30	6 13 20 27	6 13 20 27	3 10 17 24	1 8 15 22 29	5 12 19 26
S	3 10 17 24 31	7 14 21 28	7 14 21 28	4 11 18 25	2 9 16 23 30	6 13 20 27
S	4 11 18 25	1 8 15 22	1 8 15 22 29	5 12 19 26	3 10 17 24 31	7 14 21 28

	July	August	September	October	November	December
M	6 13 20 27	3 10 17 24 31	7 14 21 28	5 12 19 26	2 9 16 23 30	7 14 21 28
T	7 14 21 28	4 11 18 25	1 8 15 22 29	6 13 20 27	3 10 17 24	1 8 15 22 29
W	1 8 15 22 29	5 12 19 26	2 9 16 23 30	7 14 21 28	4 11 18 25	2 9 16 23 30
T	2 9 16 23 30	6 13 20 27	3 10 17 24	1 8 15 22 29	5 12 19 26	3 10 17 24 31
F	3 10 17 24 31	7 14 21 28	4 11 18 25	2 9 16 23 30	6 13 20 27	4 11 18 25
S	4 11 18 25	1 8 15 22 29	5 12 19 26	3 10 17 24 31	7 14 21 28	5 12 19 26
S	5 12 19 26	2 9 16 23 30	6 13 20 27	4 11 18 25	1 8 15 22 29	6 13 20 27

1999

	January	February	March	April	May	June
M	4 11 18 25	1 8 15 22	1 8 15 22 29	5 12 19 26	3 10 17 24 31	7 14 21 28
T	5 12 19 26	2 9 16 23	2 9 16 23 30	6 13 20 27	4 11 18 25	1 8 15 22 29
W	6 13 20 27	3 10 17 24	3 10 17 24 31	7 14 21 28	5 12 19 26	2 9 16 23 30
T	7 14 21 28	4 11 18 25	4 11 18 25	1 8 15 22 29	6 13 20 27	3 10 17 24
F	1 8 15 22 29	5 12 19 26	5 12 19 26	2 9 16 23 30	7 14 21 28	4 11 18 25
S	2 9 16 23 30	6 13 20 27	6 13 20 27	3 10 17 24	1 8 15 22 29	5 12 19 26
S	3 10 17 24 31	7 14 21 28	7 14 21 28	4 11 18 25	2 9 16 23 30	6 13 20 27

	July	August	September	October	November	December
M	5 12 19 26	2 9 16 23 30	6 13 20 27	4 11 18 25	1 8 15 22 29	6 13 20 27
T	6 13 20 27	3 10 17 24 31	7 14 21 28	5 12 19 26	2 9 16 23 30	7 14 21 28
W	7 14 21 28	4 11 18 25	1 8 15 22 29	6 13 20 27	3 10 17 24	1 8 15 22 29
T	1 8 15 22 29	5 12 19 26	2 9 16 23 30	7 14 21 28	4 11 18 25	2 9 16 23 30
F	2 9 16 23 30	6 13 20 27	3 10 17 24	1 8 15 22 29	5 12 19 26	3 10 17 24 31
S	3 10 17 24 31	7 14 21 28	4 11 18 25	2 9 16 23 30	6 13 20 27	4 11 18 25
S	4 11 18 25	1 8 15 22 29	5 12 19 26	3 10 17 24 31	7 14 21 28	5 12 19 26

2000

	January	February	March	April	May	June
M	3 10 17 24 31	7 14 21 28	6 13 20 27	3 10 17 24	1 8 15 22 29	5 12 19 26
T	4 11 18 25	1 8 15 22 29	7 14 21 28	4 11 18 25	2 9 16 23 30	6 13 20 27
W	5 12 19 26	2 9 16 23	1 8 15 22 29	5 12 19 26	3 10 17 24 31	7 14 21 28
T	6 13 20 27	3 10 17 24	2 9 16 23 30	6 13 20 27	4 11 18 25	1 8 15 22 29
F	7 14 21 28	4 11 18 25	3 10 17 24 31	7 14 21 28	5 12 19 26	2 9 16 23 30
S	1 8 15 22 29	5 12 19 26	4 11 18 25	1 8 15 22 29	6 13 20 27	3 10 17 24
S	2 9 16 23 30	6 13 20 27	5 12 19 26	2 9 16 23 30	7 14 21 28	4 11 18 25

	July	August	September	October	November	December
M	3 10 17 24 31	7 14 21 28	4 11 18 25	2 9 16 23 30	6 13 20 27	4 11 18 25
T	4 11 18 25	1 8 15 22 29	5 12 19 26	3 10 17 24 31	7 14 21 28	5 12 19 26
W	5 12 19 26	2 9 16 23 30	6 13 20 27	4 11 18 25	1 8 15 22 29	6 13 20 27
T	6 13 20 27	3 10 17 24 31	7 14 21 28	5 12 19 26	2 9 16 23 30	7 14 21 28
F	7 14 21 28	4 11 18 25	1 8 15 22 29	6 13 20 27	3 10 17 24	1 8 15 22 29
S	1 8 15 22 29	5 12 19 26	2 9 16 23 30	7 14 21 28	4 11 18 25	2 9 16 23 30
S	2 9 16 23 30	6 13 20 27	3 10 17 24	1 8 15 22 29	5 12 19 26	3 10 17 24 31

23.2 World holidays

Since the dates of holidays vary each year according to the day of the week upon which they fall and other considerations, all dates should be regarded as **approximate**. When a date given refers specifically to the **1987** observance of a holiday it is marked *. The following list shows only **all-day** holidays and does not include regional and local holidays within countries.

Note: Certain countries do not observe Sunday as a general holiday; these include Afghanistan, Algeria, Bahrain, Bangladesh, Djibouti, Egypt, Iran, Iraq, Israel, Jordan, Kuwait, Libya, Maldives, Mauritania, Nepal, Oman, Pakistan, Qatar, Saudi Arabia, Somali, Sudan, Syria, United Arab Emirates, Yemen Arab Republic and Yemen People's Democratic Republic.

	JANUARY	
1	New Year's Day	all countries EXCEPT: Afghanistan, Bangladesh, Bhutan, Burma, Egypt, Ethiopia, Iran, Libya, Nepal, Oman, Pakistan, Qatar, Saudi Arabia, Sri Lanka, Tanzania, Yemen Arab Republic
	Day of Liberation	Cuba
	National Day	Haiti, Sudan
2	Ancestry Day	Haiti
	Bank Holiday	(1 day) New Zealand, Scotland; (2 days) Japan
	Public Holiday	(1 day) Botswana, Czechoslovakia, Grenada, Mauritius, Mongolia, Romania, St Lucia, Seychelles, Taiwan, Western Samoa, Yugoslavia; (2 days) South Korea
	Bank Holiday	Taiwan
3	Revolution Anniversary	Burkina Faso
4	Independence Day	Burma
	Martyrs of Independence	Zaire
5	*Epiphany	Venezuela
6	Epiphany	Andorra, Austria, Cyprus, Dominican Republic, Greece, Italy, Liechtenstein, Puerto Rico, San Marino, Spain, Sweden
	Army Day	Iraq
7	Christmas (Eastern Orthodox)	Egypt, Ethiopia

9	Day of National Mourning	Panama
10	*Twelfthtide	Finland
11	Hostos' Birthday	Puerto Rico
	King Prithvi Memorial Day	Nepal
	Republic Proclamation Day	Albania
13	Liberation Day	Togo
15	Adults' Day	Japan
16	Martyrs' Day	Benin
18	Revolution Day	Tunisia
19	Epiphany	Ethiopia
	*Martin Luther King's Birthday	Puerto Rico, USA (34 States and DC)
20	Army Day	Lesotho, Mali
	National Heroes' Day	Cape Verde Islands, Guinea-Bissau
21	Feast of Our Lady of Altagracia	Dominican Republic
22	Discovery Day	St Vincent
24	Economic Liberation Day	Togo
26	*Australia Day	Australia
	Duarte's Day	Dominican Republic
	Republic Day	India
27	St Devote's Day	Monaco
28	Democracy Day	Rwanda
29	*Chinese New Year	(1 day) Brunei, South Korea, Malaysia; (2 days) Singapore; (3 days) Hong Kong, Taiwan
	*Spring Festival	(3 days) Macao
30	*Spring Festival	(4 days) China
31	Independence Day	Nauru

FEBRUARY

1	Senegambia Day	Gambia, Senegal
2	Candlemas Day	Liechtenstein
3	Basanta Panchami	Nepal
	Heroes' Day	Mozambique, São Tome and Principe
	St Blás' Day	Paraguay

4	Commencement of the Armed Struggle	Angola
	Independence Day	Sri Lanka
5	Arusha Declaration Anniversary	Tanzania
	Constitution Day	Mexico
	St Agatha's Day	San Marino
6	Waitangi Day/ National Day	New Zealand
7	Independence Day	Grenada
8	8th February Revolution	Iraq
9	St Maron's Day	Lebanon
11	Armed Forces Day	Liberia
	National Foundation Day	Japan
	Youth Day	Cameroon
12	Lincoln's Birthday	USA (many States)
	*Macha Bucha Day	Thailand
	Union Day	Burma
16	*Washington's Birthday	Puerto Rico, USA
18	Independence Day	Gambia
19	Late King Tribhuvan Memorial and Democracy Day	Nepal
21	Shaheed Day	Bangladesh
22	Independence Day	St Lucia
23	National Day	Brunei
	Republic Day	Guyana
25	National Day	(3 days) Kuwait
	Revolution Day	Surinam
26	*Maha Shivarata	Nepal
	*Maha Sivarathri	Sri Lanka
27	Independence Day	Dominican Republic

MARCH

1	Heroes' Day	Paraguay
	Independence Movement Day	South Korea

2	*Carnival	(1 day) Andorra, St Lucia; (2 days) Bolivia, Brazil, Dominica, Ecuador, Panama, Uruguay, Venezuela
	Declaration of Establishment of Authority of People	Libya
	*Discovery Day	Guam
	Peasants' Day	Burma
	*Shrove Monday	Greece, Luxembourg
	Victory of Adwa Day	Ethiopia
3	*Carnival	Liechtenstein, Portugal
	*Mardi Gras	Haiti
	Martyrs' Day	Malawi
	*Shrove Tuesday	Monaco
	Throne Day	Morocco
	Unity Day	Sudan
4	*Ash Wednesday	Jamaica
5	Chiefs' Day	Vanuatu
6	Independence Day	Ghana
8	International Women's Day	Mongolia, USSR
	National Day	Libya
	Revolution Day	Syria
	Women's Day	Cape Verde Islands, Guinea-Bissau, Yemen PDR
9	Baron Bliss Day	Belize
	*Commonwealth Day	Swaziland
10	Labour Day	South Korea
11	*Decoration Day	Liberia
12	Anniversary of Renewal	Gabon
	Independence Day	Mauritius
	Moshoeshoe's Day	Lesotho
15	J J Roberts' Day	Liberia
17	St Patrick's Day	Irish Republic, Northern Ireland
18	Day of the Supreme Sacrifice	Congo
19	St Joseph's Day	Andorra, Costa Rica, Liechtenstein, San Marino, Venezuela

20	Independence Day	Tunisia
	Oil Day	Iran
21	Juárez' Birthday	Mexico
	New Year's Day	Afghanistan
	Now Rooz	(4 days) Iran
	Spring Day	Iraq
	Vernal Equinox	Japan
	*Youth Day	Zambia
23	Pakistan Day	Pakistan
	*Emancipation Day	Puerto Rico
	*St Joseph's Day Holiday	Colombia
25	Greek Independence Day	Cyprus, Greece
	Universal Vote	San Marino
26	Independence Day	Bangladesh
27	*Ascension of the Prophet Muhammad	Indonesia
	Resistance Day	Burma
28	Liberation Day (British Troops)	Libya
29	Anniversary of President Boganda's Death	Central African Republic
	Memorial Day	Madagascar
30	*Youth Day/Chinese Martyrs' Day	Taiwan
31	*Icaka New Year	Indonesia
	National Day	Malta

APRIL

1	Bank Holiday	Burma
	Captain Regent's Day	San Marino
	Islamic Republic Day	Iran
	*Liberation Day	Uganda
	Youth Day	Benin
2	13th of Farvardin	Iran
3	Proclamation of 2nd Republic	Guinea
4	National Day	Hungary, Senegal
5	Arbor Day	South Korea

6	Chakri Memorial Day	Thailand
	Ching Ming Festival	Hong Kong, Macao, Taiwan
	Founder's Day	South Africa
	Patriots' Day	Ethiopia
	Revolution Day	Sudan
7	Mozambican Women's Day	Mozambique
9	Martyrs' Day	Tunisia
10	*National Fast and Prayer Day	Liberia
11	National Heroes' Day	Costa Rica
12	*Palm Sunday (Eastern Orthodox)	Egypt
	*Redemption Day	Liberia
13	*Monday of Holy Week	Uruguay
	Songkran Festival Day	Thailand
14	Americas' Day	Haiti, Honduras
	Sinhala and Tamil New Year	Nepal, Sri Lanka
	*First Day of Passover	Israel
	*Thingyan Holiday	(3 days) Burma
	*Tuesday of Holy Week	Uruguay
15	Assumption of Power by Supreme Military Council	Niger
	*Bengali New Year	Bangladesh
	*Holy Wednesday	El Salvador, Uruguay
16	De Diego's Birthday	Puerto Rico
	*Holy Thursday	Argentina, Brazil, Colombia, Costa Rica, Denmark, Ecuador, El Salvador, Guatemala, Honduras, Iceland, Mexico, Nicaragua, Norway, Paraguay, Philippines, Spain, Uruguay, Venezuela
17	Burmese New Year	Burma
	Evacuation Day	Syria
	*Good Friday	most Western countries
18	*Easter/Holy Saturday	Australia, Belize, Botswana, Brazil, Chile, Costa Rica, Cyprus, Fiji, France, Ghana, Guatemala, Hong Kong, Macao, Malawi, Mexico, Papua New Guinea, Seychelles, Solomon Islands, Spain, Uganda, Western Samoa, Zambia
	Independence Day	Zimbabwe

19	Constitution Day	Venezuela
	*Easter Day	most Western countries
	Landing of the 33 Orientales	Uruguay
	Defence Forces Day	Zimbabwe
	Republic Day	Sierra Leone
20	*Easter Monday	most Western countries
	*Last Day of Passover	Israel
	*Sham Al-Naseem/El-Nassim	Egypt, Sudan
21	*Easter Tuesday	Nauru
	Independence Hero Tiradentes	Brazil
23	*First Day of Summer	Iceland
	National Sovereignty and Children's Day	Turkey
24	Victory Day	Togo
25	Anzac Day	Australia, New Zealand, Tonga, Western Samoa
	Liberation Day	Italy, Portugal, Macao
	National Flag Day	Swaziland
	Sinai Liberation Day	Egypt
26	*Day of Remembrance	Israel
	Union Day	Tanzania
27	Sawr Revolution Day	Afghanistan
	National Day	Togo
29	Emperor's Birthday	Japan
30	Queen's Birthday	Netherlands

	MAY	
1	International Labour Day/ May Day	(1 day) many countries; (2 days) Bulgaria, Yemen Arab Republic, USSR, Yugoslavia; (3 days) Romania
2	Birthday of HM Jigme Dorji Wangchuck	Bhutan
	King's Birthday	Lesotho
3	Constitution Day	Japan

4	*Bank Holiday	UK
	*Labour Day/May Day Holiday	Barbados, St Kitts-Nevis, St Vincent
5	Birthday of Crown Prince Tupouto'a	Tonga
	Children's Day	Japan, South Korea
	Coronation Day	Thailand
	Liberation Day	Netherlands
	Puebla Battle	Mexico
6	Martyrs' Day	Syria
8	*Armistice Day 1945	France, Monaco
9	National Day	Czechoslovakia
	Victory Day	USSR
11	*Visakha Bucha Day	Thailand
12	*Full Moon of Kason	Burma
	*Vesak Day	Malaysia, Singapore
13	*Waisak/Vesak Full Moon	Indonesia; (2 days) Sri Lanka
14	Independence Day	Israel
	Kamuzu Day	Malawi
	National Day	Paraguay
	National Unification Day	Liberia
15	*Revelation of the Koran	Brunei
	*General Prayer Day	Denmark
	Independence Day	Paraguay
17	Constitution Day	Nauru, Norway
18	Las Piedras Battle	Uruguay
	*Victoria Day	Canada
19	Youth and Sports Day	Turkey
20	Mouvement Populaire de la Revolution (MPR) Day	Zaire
	National Day	Cameroon
21	Battle of Iquique	Chile
22	National Heroes' Day	Sri Lanka
23	Fête Nationale	Morocco
	Labour Day	Jamaica

24	Day of Slav Literature, Bulgarian Education and Culture	Bulgaria
	Independence Battle	Ecuador
25	Africa Day	Chad, Mali, Mauritania, Zambia, Zimbabwe
	*Spring Bank Holiday	Gibraltar, UK
	Bermuda Day	Bermuda
	*Commonwealth Day Holiday	Belize
	Independence Day	Argentina, Jordan
	*Memorial Day	Puerto Rico, USA
27	*Ascension Eve	France, Ivory Coast, Madagascar
28	*Ascension	Andorra, Austria, Belgium, Botswana, Burkina Faso, Burundi, Cameroon, Central African Republic, Denmark, France, FRG, Haiti, Iceland, Indonesia, Ivory Coast, Lesotho, Liechtenstein, Luxembourg, Madagascar, Monaco, Namibia, Netherlands, Norway, Rwanda, Senegal, South Africa, Swaziland, Switzerland
	*Eid-al-Fitr	Jordan
29	*Bank Holiday	Belgium
	*Hari Raya Puasa	(1 day) Singapore; (2 days) Brunei
	*Feast of Fitr	(1 day) Ethiopia; (2 days) Algeria, Indonesia
	*Ramazan Bayram	Cyprus
30	*Feast of Fitr	Sri Lanka
31	Republic Day	Namibia, South Africa

JUNE

1	*Ascension Holiday	Colombia, Venezuela
	Children's Day	Cape Verde Islands
	Independence Holiday	(3 days) Western Samoa
	*June Holiday	Irish Republic
	Madaraka Day	Kenya
	Mother's Day	Central African Republic
	*Queen's Birthday Observance	New Zealand
	*Tuen Ng/Dragon Boat Festival	Hong Kong, Macao, Taiwan
	Victory Day	Tunisia

2	Coronation of the Fourth Hereditary King	Bhutan
	National Day	Italy
	Youth Day	Tunisia
3	*Pentecost	Israel
	The Supreme Head of State's Birthday	Malaysia
4	Emancipation Day	Tonga
	June 4th Revolution Day	Ghana
5	Constitution Day	Denmark
	15th Khordad Uprising	Iran
	*Labour Day Holiday	Bahamas
	Liberation Day	Seychelles
	President's Birthday	Equatorial Guinea
6	Flag Day	Sweden
	Memorial Day	South Korea
	*Whitsuntide	Finland, France
7	Liberation Day	Chad
8	*Whit Monday	Andorra, Austria, Bahamas, Barbados, Belgium, Burkina Faso, Central African Republic, Denmark, Dominica, France, FRG, Gabon, GDR, Greece, Grenada, Iceland, Ivory Coast, Liechtenstein, Luxembourg, Madagascar, Monaco, Netherlands, Norway, Rwanda, St Kitts-Nevis, St Lucia, St Vincent, Senegal, Solomon Islands, Sweden, Switzerland, Trinidad and Tobago
	*Queen's Birthday Observance	Australia (except Western Australia)
10	Camões and Portuguese Communities/Portugal Day	Macao, Portugal
	Great Arab Revolt and Army Day	Jordan
	Malvinas Islands Memorial	Argentina
11	Evacuation Day (US Troops)	Libya
12	Independence Day	Philippines
	Peace with Bolivia	Paraguay
	*Queen's Birthday Observance	Solomon Islands

13	*Queen's Birthday	Hong Kong, St Kitts-Nevis
15	*Bank Holiday	Macao
	*Queen's Birthday Observance	Bermuda, Fiji, Hong Kong
17	Independence Day	Iceland
	National Day	FRG
18	*Corpus Christi	Andorra, Austria, Bolivia, Brazil, Costa Rica, Dominican Republic, Equatorial Guinea, Grenada, Haiti, Liechtenstein, Macao, Paraguay, Poland, Portugal, St Lucia, Seychelles, Spain, Trinidad and Tobago
	Evacuation Day	Egypt
	Fête Dieu	Monaco
19	Artigas Day	Uruguay
	Labour Day	Trinidad and Tobago
	*Midsummer Eve	Finland, Sweden
	Righting Day	Algeria
20	Flag Day	Argentina
	*Midsummer Day	Finland, Sweden
22	Corrective Move	Yemen PDR
	*Corpus Christi Holiday	Colombia, Venezuela
23	National Day	Luxembourg
24	Anniversary of Currency, Promulgation, Constitution and Day of Fishers	Zaire
	Battle of Carabobo	Venezuela
	City of Macao Day	Macao
	St John's Day	Andorra
25	Independence Day	Mozambique
26	Independence Day	Madagascar, Somali
	*Independence Feast	(2 days) Djibouti
29	*Bank Holiday	El Salvador
	Independence Day	Seychelles
	Sts Peter and Paul	Chile, Colombia, Costa Rica, Peru, San Marino, Venezuela
30	Army Day	Guatemala
	Bank Holiday	Ecuador, El Salvador, India, Peru, Sri Lanka
	Independence Day	Zaire

JULY

1	Bank Holiday	Bangladesh, Egypt, Guatemala, Pakistan, Taiwan
	Canada Day	Canada (except Newfoundland)
	*Caricom Day	St Vincent
	Day of Freedom	Surinam
	Independence Day	Burundi, Rwanda
	Mid-Year Holiday	Thailand
	Republic Day	Ghana
	Takeover Day	Nauru
	Union Day	Somali
2	*Carnival	St Vincent
3	*Independence Day Holiday	USA (many States)
4	Fighters' Day	Yugoslavia
	Independence Day	Puerto Rico, USA
	Philippine-American Friendship Day	Philippines
5	Independence Day	Algeria, Venezuela
	National Day	Rwanda
6	*Caribbean Day	Guyana
	*Family Day	Lesotho
	*Heroes' Day	Zambia
	*Republic Day	Malawi
7	Independence Day	Solomon Islands
	Saba Saba Peasants' Day	Tanzania
	*Unity Day	Zambia
9	Independence Day	Argentina
	Youth Day	Morocco
10	Armed Forces Day	Mauritania
	Full Moon of Waso	Burma
	Independence Day	Bahamas
11	National Day	(3 days) Mongolia
12	Independence Day	São Tome and Principe
13	*Buddhist Lent	Thailand
	*National Holiday	(2 days) Monaco
	*Law of 20 Dec. 1906	France
	*Orangeman's Day Holiday	Northern Ireland

14	Bastille Day	France
	14th July Revolution	Iraq
15	The Sultan of Brunei's Birthday	Brunei
17	Constitution Day	South Korea
	Munoz-Rivera's Birthday	Puerto Rico
	17th July Revolution	Iraq
18	Constitution Day	Uruguay
19	Anniversary of the Sandinista Revolution	Nicaragua
	Martyrs' Day	Burma
20	Independence Day	Colombia
	*President's Day	Botswana
21	First Sermon of Lord Buddha and Death of Jigme Dorji Wangchuck	Bhutan
	National Day	Belgium
	*Public Holiday	Botswana
22	King's Birthday	Swaziland
	National Day	Poland
23	Egyptian National Day	Egypt, Libya, Syria
24	Bolivar's Day	Ecuador, Venezuela
25	Annexation of Guanacaste	Costa Rica
	Constitution Day	Puerto Rico
	National Holiday	Cuba
	Republic Day	Tunisia
	St James' Day/Santiago Day	Spain
26	Independence Celebrations	Liberia; (2 days) Maldives
	National Rebellion Day	Cuba
27	Barbosa's Birthday	Puerto Rico
	*National Holiday	Cuba
28	Independence Celebrations	(2 days) Peru
	People's Holiday	San Marino
30	Independence Day	Vanuatu
	*Cup Match Holiday	Bermuda

31	Revolution Day	Congo
	*Somers Day	Bermuda

AUGUST

1	Discovery Day	Trinidad and Tobago
	Freedom Day	Guyana
	Harvest Day	Rwanda
	National Day	Switzerland
	Parents' Day	Zaire
	*Santa Domingo Day	Nicaragua
2	Our Lady of the Angels	Costa Rica
3	Armed Forces Day	Equatorial Guinea
	*August Holiday Monday	Dominica, Fiji, Iceland, Irish Republic, St Kitts-Nevis, Scotland
	Emancipation Day	Bahamas, Grenada, St Lucia, St Vincent
	Farmers' Day	Zambia
	*Independence Day	Jamaica, Niger
	*Kadooment Day	Barbados
	Martyrs of Colonialism	Guinea-Bissau
	President's Birthday	Tunisia
	*San Salvador Feast	(4 days) El Salvador
4	Arafa	Afghanistan
	*Fast of Av	Israel
	*Id-al-Adha	(3 days) Lebanon
	National Holiday	Burkina Faso
	Public Holiday	Grenada
	*Wakfet Arafet	Egypt
5	*Courban Bairam/ Kurban Bayram	(1 day) Cyprus; (2 days) Egypt; (4 days) Turkey
	*Eid Adha	(3 days) Afghanistan
	*Hari Raya Haji	Singapore
	*Id-al-Adha	Algeria, Ethiopia, Indonesia
6	*Id-ul-Azha	Sri Lanka
	Independence Day	Bolivia
7	National Holiday	Colombia

9	National Day	Singapore
10	Independence Day	Ecuador
	*Public Holiday	Singapore
11	Accession of King Hussein	Jordan
	Heroes' Day	(2 days) Zimbabwe
	Independence Day	Chad
12	Queen's Birthday	Thailand
13	Independence Day	Central African Republic
	The Three Glorious Days	(3 days) Congo
	Women's Day	Tunisia
14	Independence Day	Pakistan
	Mid-August Holiday	(2 days) Italy
	Oued-Ed-Dahab	Morocco
15	Assumption	most Roman Catholic countries
	Constitution Day	Equatorial Guinea
	Independence Day	India
	Liberation Day	South Korea
	Mothers' Day	Costa Rica
	National Constitution Day	Papua New Guinea
	St Mary's Day	Gambia
16	Restoration of the Republic	Dominican Republic
17	Anniversary of General San Martin's Death	Argentina
	*Assumption Holiday	Colombia, Luxembourg
	*Bank Holiday	Belgium
	Independence Day	Gabon, Indonesia
19	Independence Day	Afghanistan
20	Constitution Day	Hungary
23	National Day	Romania
24	*National Holiday	Liberia, Romania
25	Constitution Day	Paraguay
	Independence Day	Uruguay
26	*Muslim New Year	Algeria, Djibouti, Egypt, Indonesia, Malaysia
29	*Public Holiday	Hong Kong
30	St Rose of Lima Day	Peru

31	*Bank Holiday	Macao
	Independence Day	Trinidad and Tobago
	*Liberation Day	Hong Kong
	National Day	Malaysia
	*Summer Bank Holiday	UK (except Scotland)

SEPTEMBER

1	Anniversary of the Arrival of the Military Committee for National Recovery	Central African Republic
	Libya Unity Day	Libya, Syria
	President's Report	Mexico
2	Independence Day	Vietnam
3	*Ashora/Achoura	Afghanistan, Algeria
	Independence Day	Qatar
	Liberation Day	Monaco
	St Marinus Day	San Marino
	3 Sept. 1934 Commemoration	Tunisia
6	Armed Forces Day	São Tome and Principe
	Defence of Pakistan Day	Pakistan
	Independence Day	Swaziland
7	Independence Day	Brazil
	*Labour Day	Bermuda, Canada, Puerto Rico, USA
	*Settlers' Day	Namibia
	Victory Day	Mozambique
8	*Cultural Festival	Rwanda
	Our Lady of Meritxell	Andorra
9	National Day	(2 days) Bulgaria
10	National Day	Belize
11	Anniversary of the Death of Quaid-e-Azam	Pakistan
	Ethiopian New Year and Reunion of Eritrea with Ethiopia	Ethiopia
	National Liberation	Chile

12	Revolution Day	Ethiopia
	National Day	Cape Verde Islands, Guinea-Bissau
14	Battle of San Jacinto	Nicaragua
15	Independence Day	Costa Rica, El Salvador, Guatemala, Honduras, Nicaragua
	Respect for the Aged Day	Japan
16	Independence Day	Mexico, Papua New Guinea
17	Day of the National Hero	Angola
18	National Anniversary	Chile
	Victory of Uprona	Burundi
19	Armed Forces Day	Chile
	Independence Day	St Kitts-Nevis
21	Independence Day	Belize
22	National Day	Mali
23	Autumn Equinox	Japan
	National Day	Saudi Arabia
24	Establishment of the Republic	Guinea-Bissau
	Feast of Our Lady of Mercy	Dominican Republic
	*Jewish New Year 5748	(2 days) Israel
	Republic Day	Trinidad and Tobago
25	Armed Forces Day	Mozambique
	Referendum Day	Rwanda
26	YAR National Day	Yemen Arab Republic; Yemen People's Democratic Republic
27	Feast of the Finding of the True Cross	Ethiopia
28	Birthday of Confucius	Taiwan
	*Queen's Birthday Observance	Western Australia
29	Battle of Boqueron Day	Paraguay
30	Agricultural Reform Day	São Tome and Principe
	National Day	Botswana

OCTOBER

1	Armed Forces Day	South Korea
	Bank Holiday	Burma
	Captain Regent's Day	San Marino
	National Day	(1 day) Macao, Nigeria; (2 days) China
	Public Holiday	Botswana
2	Independence Day	Guinea
	Mahatma Gandhi's Birthday	India
3	*Day of Atonement	Israel
	Francisco Morazán's Birthday	Honduras
	National Foundation Day	South Korea
4	Independence Day	Lesotho
5	Constitution Day	Vanuatu
	*National Sports Day	Lesotho
	Portugal Republic Day	Macao, Portugal
	Thanksgiving Day	St Lucia
	*United Nations Day	Barbados
6	Armed Forces Day	Egypt
	Liberation Day	Syria
7	Constitution Day	USSR
	*End of Buddhist Lent	Burma
	Evacuation Day	Libya
	Foundation Day	GDR
	*Moon Festival	South Korea, Taiwan
8	*Chinese Mid-Autumn Festival	Hong Kong, Macao
	Combat of Angamos	Peru
	*Feast of Tabernacles (First Day)	Israel
9	Independence Day	Uganda
	Independence of Guayaquil	Ecuador
	Korean Alphabet Day	South Korea
10	Beginning of the Independence Wars	Cuba
	Health-Sports Day	Japan
	Kruger Day	Namibia, South Africa
	National Day	Fiji, Taiwan

12	*Columbus Day	Argentina, Belize, Colombia, Ecuador, El Salvador, Mexico, Puerto Rico, USA (most States), Uruguay, Venezuela
	Day of the Race	Chile, Costa Rica, Guatemala, Paraguay
	Discovery Day	Bahamas, Honduras
	Lotu-o-Tamai	Western Samoa
	National Day	Equatorial Guinea, Spain
	*Revolution Anniversary Observance	Panama
	*Thanksgiving	Canada
14	Founder's Day/Youth Day	Zaire
	Revolution Day	Yemen PDR
15	Evacuation Day	Tunisia
	*Feast of Tabernacles (Last Day)	Israel
17	Dessaline's Day	Haiti
	Mothers' Day	Malawi
19	*National Heroes' Day	Jamaica
20	Kenyatta Day	Kenya
	1944 Revolution Anniversary	Guatemala
21	Armed Forces Day	Honduras
	*Deepavali	Malaysia, Singapore, Sri Lanka
	Revolution Anniversary	(2 days) Somali
22	*Diwali	Fiji
23	Chulalongkorn Day	Thailand
24	Independence Day	Zambia
	United Nations Day	Haiti, Swaziland
25	Restoration Day	Taiwan
26	Armed Forces Day	Benin, Rwanda
	*Labour Day	New Zealand
	National Day	Austria
	*October Holiday	Irish Republic
	*Restoration Day Observance	Taiwan
27	Angam Day	Nauru
	Anniversary of the country's name change	Zaire
	Independence Day	St Vincent

28	Greek National Day	Cyprus, Greece
29	Turkish National Day	Cyprus, Turkey
31	*All Saints' Observance	Finland, Sweden
	Birthday of Chiang Kai-Shek	Taiwan
	Chung Yeung Festival	Hong Kong
	*Festival of Ancestors	Macao

NOVEMBER

1	All Saints' Day	most Roman Catholic countries
	Anniversary of the Revolution	Algeria
2	*All Saints' Observance	most Roman Catholic countries
	All Souls' Day	Ecuador, El Salvador, Haiti, Macao, Mexico, Uruguay
	*Arbor Day Observance	Western Samoa
	*Bank Holiday	Belgium
	Commemoration of the Dead	San Marino
	*Law of 23 Dec. 1904	France
	Memorial Day	Brazil
	*Prophet Mohammed's Birthday	Fiji
3	Culture Day	Japan
	Independence Day	Dominica
	Independence from Colombia	Panama
	Independence of Cuenca	Ecuador
	*Mouloud Al-Nabi	Djibouti
4	*Birthday of the Prophet	Cyprus, Indonesia, Malaysia
	Constitution Day	Tonga
	Flag Day	Panama
	St Charles' Day	Andorra
5	Anniversary of the First Cry of Independence	El Salvador
	*Full Moon of Tazaungdaing	Burma
	*Milad-Un-Nabi	Sri Lanka
	*Thanksgiving Day	Liberia
6	Al-Massira Day	Morocco

7	Anniversary of the October Socialist Revolution	Bulgaria, Hungary, Mongolia; (2 days) USSR
	National Revolution Day	Bangladesh
8	Queen's Birthday	Nepal
9	Iqbal Day	Pakistan
11	Armistice/Remembrance/ Veterans' Day	Belgium, Bermuda, Canada, France, Monaco Puerto Rico, USA
	Birthday of HM Jigme Singye Wangchuck	(3 days) Bhutan
	Independence Day	Angola
	Republic Day	(2 days) Maldives
12	Birthday of Dr Sun Yat Sen	Taiwan
14	King Hussein's Birthday	Jordan
	Maulid	Ethiopia
	Readjustment Day	Guinea-Bissau
	Proclamation of the Republic	Brazil
16	*Independence of Cartagena	Colombia
	*Prince Charles' Birthday	Fiji
17	Armed Forces Day	Zaire
18	*Day of Penance	FRG
	National Day	Morocco; (2 days) Oman
	Vertières Day	Haiti
19	Discovery Day	Puerto Rico
	Garifuna Day	Belize
	Liberation Day	Mali
	Prince of Monaco Holiday	Monaco
20	Mexican Revolution	Mexico
22	Independence Day	Lebanon
23	Labour Thanksgiving Day	Japan
24	National Day	Zaire
25	Independence Day	Surinam
26	*Thanksgiving	Puerto Rico, USA

28	Independence Day	Albania, Mauritania
	Independence from Spain	Panama
	Proclamation of the Republic	Chad
29	Liberation Day	Albania
	President Tubman's Birthday	Liberia
	Republic Day	(2 days) Yugoslavia
30	Independence Day	Barbados, Yemen PDR
	National Day	Benin
	National Heroes' Day	Philippines
	*Unity Day	Vanuatu

DECEMBER

1	Proclamation of the Republic	Central African Republic
	Restoration of Independence	Macao, Portugal
2	National Day	Laos; (2 days) United Arab Emirates
4	King Tupou I Day	Tonga
5	Discovery Day	Haití
	King's Birthday	Thailand
6	Independence Day	Finland
7	Independence Day	Ivory Coast
	*King's Birthday Observance	Thailand
8	Immaculate Conception	most Roman Catholic countries
	Mothers' Day	Panama
9	Independence Day	Tanzania
10	Constitution Day	Thailand
	Human Rights Day	Equatorial Guinea
	Foundation of the Popular Movement for the Liberation of Angola (MPLA)	Angola
12	*National Holiday	Mauritania
	Independence Day	Kenya
	Our Lady of Guadalupe	Mexico

13	Republic Day	Malta
	St Lucia Day	St Lucia
16	Day of the Covenant	Namibia, South Africa
	King Mahendra Memorial Day and Constitution Day	Nepal
	National Day	Bahrain
	Victory Day	Bangladesh
17	National Day	Bhutan
18	National Day	Niger
21	Power of the People Day	São Tome and Principe
22	Tree Planting Day	Malawi
24	Christmas Eve	Austria, Cape Verde Islands, Denmark, Finland, Liechtenstein, Macao, Portugal, San Marino, Sweden, (and a half-holiday in most other countries)
25	Christmas Day	all countries EXCEPT: Afghanistan, Albania, Algeria, Bahrain, Bhutan, Bulgaria, China, Cuba, Egypt, Ethiopia, Iran, Iraq, Israel, Japan, Kuwait, Libya, Maldives, Mauritania, Mongolia, Morocco, Nepal, Oman, Qatar, Romania, Saudi Arabia, Somali, Thailand, Tunisia, Turkey, USSR, United Arab Emirates, Yemen Arab Republic, Yemen PDR, Yugoslavia
26	Boxing Day/Christmas Holiday/St Stephen's Day	most countries
28	*Boxing Day Observance/ Christmas Holiday/ St Stephen's Holiday	Irish Republic, Luxembourg, New Zealand, Nigeria, Papua New Guinea, UK, Vanuatu
29	Christmas Holiday	Irish Republic, Northern Ireland
	King's Birthday	Nepal
30	Bank Holiday	Colombia, El Salvador
	National Day	Madagascar
	Rizal Day	Philippines
31	Bank Holiday/New Year's Eve/St Sylvester's Day	many countries
	Feed Yourself Day	Benin
	Foundation of the Party and People's Republic of Congo	Congo
	Revolution Day	Ghana

24 MAPS

24.1 Europe and EEC

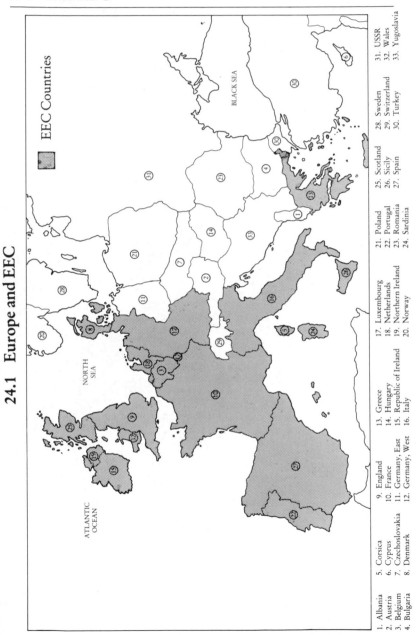

■ EEC Countries

1. Albania
2. Austria
3. Belgium
4. Bulgaria
5. Corsica
6. Cyprus
7. Czechoslovakia
8. Denmark
9. England
10. France
11. Germany, East
12. Germany, West
13. Greece
14. Hungary
15. Republic of Ireland
16. Italy
17. Luxembourg
18. Netherlands
19. Northern Ireland
20. Norway
21. Poland
22. Portugal
23. Romania
24. Sardinia
25. Scotland
26. Sicily
27. Spain
28. Sweden
29. Switzerland
30. Turkey
31. USSR
32. Wales
33. Yugoslavia

24.2   Counties and Regions of the UK and Ireland

SCOTLAND
48. Borders
49. Central
50. Dumfries and
    Galloway
51. Fife
52. Grampian
53. Highland
54. Lothian
55. Orkney
56. Shetland
57. Strathclyde
58. Tayside
59. Western Isles

NORTHERN
IRELAND
60. Antrim
61. Armagh
62. County Down
63. Fermanagh
64. Londonderry
65. Tyrone

REPUBLIC OF
IRELAND
74. Carlow
75. Cavan
76. Clare
77. Cork
78. Donegal
79. Dublin
80. Galway
81. Kerry
82. Kildare
83. Kilkenny
84. Laoighis
85. Leitrim
86. Limerick
87. Longford
88. Louth
89. Mayo
90. Meath
91. Monaghan
92. Offaly
93. Roscommon
94. Sligo
95. Tipperary
96. Waterford
97. Westmeath
98. Wexford
99. Wicklow

ENGLAND
1. Avon
2. Bedfordshire
3. Berkshire
4. Buckinghamshire
5. Cambridgeshire
6. Cheshire
7. Cleveland
8. Cornwall
9. Cumbria
10. Derbyshire
11. Devon
12. Dorset
13. Durham
14. East Sussex
15. Essex
16. Gloucestershire
17. Greater London
18. Greater Manchester
19. Hampshire
20. Hereford and
    Worcester
21. Hertfordshire
22. Humberside
23. Isle of Man (NB
    Crown Dependency
    not UK county)
24. Isle of Wight
25. Kent
26. Lancashire
27. Leicestershire
28. Lincolnshire
29. Merseyside
30. Norfolk
31. Northamptonshire
32. Northumberland
33. North Yorkshire
34. Nottinghamshire
35. Oxfordshire
36. Shropshire
37. Somerset
38. South Yorkshire
39. Staffordshire
40. Suffolk
41. Surrey
42. Tyne and Wear
43. Warwickshire
44. West Midlands
45. West Sussex
46. West Yorkshire
47. Wiltshire

WALES
66. Clwyd
67. Dyfed
68. Gwent
69. Gwynedd
70. Mid Glamorgan
71. Powys
72. South Glamorgan
73. West Glamorgan

24.3   UK Travel Networks

24.3A   Motorways of UK and Ireland

24.3B British Rail InterCity Routes

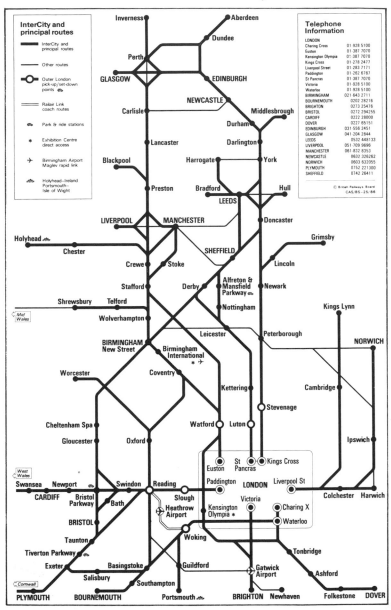

InterCity and principal routes

▬▬▬ InterCity and principal routes

— Other routes

⊶O⊶ Outer London pick-up/set-down points 🅿

═══ Railair Link coach routes

🅿 Park & ride stations

✳ Exhibition Centre direct access

✈ Birmingham Airport Maglev rapid link

⚓ Holyhead–Ireland Portsmouth– Isle of Wight

Telephone Information

LONDON
Charing Cross	01-928 5100
Euston	01-387 7070
Kensington Olympia	01-387 7070
Kings Cross	01-278 2477
Liverpool Street	01-283 7171
Paddington	01-262 6767
St Pancras	01-387 7070
Victoria	01-928 5100
Waterloo	01-928 5100
BIRMINGHAM	021-643 2711
BOURNEMOUTH	0202 28216
BRIGHTON	0273 25476
BRISTOL	0272 294255
CARDIFF	0222 28000
DOVER	0227 85151
EDINBURGH	031-556 2451
GLASGOW	041-204 2844
LEEDS	0532 448133
LIVERPOOL	051-709 9696
MANCHESTER	061-832 8353
NEWCASTLE	0632 326262
NORWICH	0603 632055
PLYMOUTH	0752 221300
SHEFFIELD	0742 26411

© British Railways Board
CAS/BS-25/86

24.3C Airports of UK and Ireland

1. Aberdeen	14. Coventry	26. Humberside	39. London City
2. Alderney	15. Dublin	27. Inverness	(Stolport)
3. Barra	16. Dundee	28. Islay	40. London (Gatwick)
4. Belfast International	17. East Midlands	29. Isle of Man	41. London (Heathrow)
5. Belfast Harbour	18. Edinburgh	30. Isle of Skye	42. Londonderry
6. Benbecula	19. Exeter	31. Isles of Scilly	43. Luton
7. Birmingham	20. Fetlar	32. Jersey	44. Manchester
International	21. Fort William,	33. Kirkwall	International
8. Blackpool	Heliport	34. Leeds/Bradford	45. Newcastle
9. Bournemouth	22. Galway	35. Lerwick (Sumburgh)	46. Newquay
10. Bristol	23. Glasgow	36. Lerwick (Tingwall)	47. Norwich
11. Cardiff-Wales	24. Gloucester/	37. Liverpool	48. Papa Westray
12. Carlisle	Cheltenham	38. London, Battersea	49. Penzance Heliport
13. Cork	25. Guernsey	Heliport	50. Plymouth

51. Prestwick
52. Rothesay Heliport
53. Shannon
54. Shoreham
55. Southampton
56. Southend
57. Stansted
58. Stornoway
59. Teesside
60. Tiree
61. Tresco Heliport
62. Unst
63. Waterford
64. Weston-super-Mare Heliport
65. Wick

Note: this map shows CAA licensed airports which have at least one resident airline, and CAA licensed heliports. *(See also Chapter 22.4)*

24.4 Time Zones

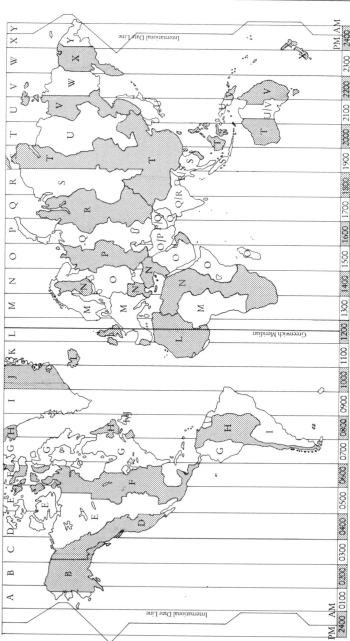

WORLD TIMES AT 12 NOON GMT

Note: some countries have adopted half-hour time zones which are indicated on the map as a combination of two coded zones. For example, it is 1730 hours in India at 1200 GMT. The standard times shown above are subject to variation in certain countries where Daylight Saving/Summer Time operates for part of the year. *(See also Chapter 22.2.)*

25 WEIGHTS AND MEASURES

25.1 Metric and imperial

Quick equivalents

Often it is only necessary to make approximate conversions between metric and imperial measurements and the following rough equivalents are useful. (For *precise* conversion figures consult the tables on p 282).

Length

1 in	2·5 cm	1 cm	0·4 in
1 ft	0·3 m	1 m	1·1 yd
1 yd	0·9 m	1 km	0·6 mile
1 fathom	1·8 m		
1 mile	1·6 km		
1 nautical mile	1·8 km		

Weight

1 oz	28 gm	1 g	0·03 oz
1 lb	0·4 kg	1 kg	2·2 lb
1 stone	6·3 kg	1 quintal	2 cwt
1 cwt	51 kg	1 tonne	0·9 ton
1 ton	1·02 tonnes		

Capacity

1 cu in	16 cm^3	1 cm^3	0·06 cu in
1 cu ft	0·03 m^3	1 m^3	1·3 cu yd
1 cu yd	0·75 m^3	1 litre	1·75 pints
1 pint	0·5 litres	1 hectolitre	2·75 bushels
1 quart	1·1 litres		
1 gallon	4·5 litres		
1 bushel	36·3 litres		

Area

1 sq in	6·5 cm^2	1 cm^2	0·15 sq in
1 sq ft	0·1 m^2	1 m^3	1·2 sq yd
1 sq yd	0·8 m^2	1 acre	120 sq yd
1 sq mile	259 hectares	1 hectare	2·5 acres
1 acre	4047 m^2	1 km^2	0·4 sq miles

Conversion tables

The following tables may be used to convert imperial units to metric units, and vice versa.

cm		in	m		ft	km		miles
2·54	1	0·3937	0·3048	1	3·28084	1·60934	1	0·62137
5·08	2	0·7874	0·6096	2	6·562	3·219	2	1·243
7·62	3	1·1811	0·9144	3	9·843	4·828	3	1·864
10·16	4	1·5748	1·2192	4	13·123	6·437	4	2·485
12·70	5	1·9685	1·5240	5	16·404	8·047	5	3·107
15·24	6	2·3622	1·8288	6	19·685	9·656	6	3·728
17·78	7	2·7559	2·1336	7	22·966	11·265	7	4·350
20·32	8	3·1496	2·4384	8	26·247	12·875	8	4·971
22·86	9	3·5433	2·7432	9	29·528	14·484	9	5·592

cm^2		sq in	m^2		sq ft	km^2		sq miles
6·4516	1	0·155	0·0929	1	10·764	2·58999	1	0·3861
12·903	2	0·310	0·1858	2	21·528	5·18	2	0·772
19·355	3	0·465	0·2787	3	32·292	7·77	3	1·158
25·806	4	0·620	0·3716	4	43·056	10·36	4	1·544
32·258	5	0·775	0·4645	5	53·820	12·95	5	1·931
38·710	6	0·930	0·5574	6	64·583	15·54	6	2·317
45·161	7	1·085	0·6503	7	75·347	18·13	7	2·703
51·613	8	1·240	0·7432	8	86·111	20·72	8	3·089
58·064	9	1·395	0·8361	9	96·875	23·31	9	3·475

cm^3		fl oz	litre		imp gal	g		oz
28·4131	1	0·0352	4·5456	1	0·21997	28·3495	1	0·03527
56·826	2	0·0704	9·092	2	0·4399	56·6990	2	0·07054
85·239	3	0·1056	13·638	3	0·6599	85·0485	3	0·10581
113·652	4	0·1408	18·184	4	0·8799	113·3980	4	0·14108
142·065	5	0·1760	22·730	5	1·0998	141·7475	5	0·17635
170·478	6	0·2112	27·277	6	1·3198	170·0970	6	0·21162
198·891	7	0·2464	31·823	7	1·5398	198·4465	7	0·24689
227·305	8	0·2816	36·369	8	1·7598	226·7960	8	0·28216
255·718	9	0·3168	40·915	9	1·9797	255·1455	9	0·31743

kg		lb	tonne		ton	newton		lbf
0·45359	1	2·20462	1·0160	1	0·984205	4·4482	1	0·2248
0·907	2	4·409	2·032	2	1·9684	8·896	2	0·4496
1·361	3	6·614	3·048	3	2·9526	13·345	3	0·6744
1·814	4	8·818	4·064	4	3·9368	17·793	4	0·8992
2·268	5	11·023	5·080	5	4·9210	22·241	5	1·1240
2·722	6	13·228	6·096	6	5·9052	26·689	6	1·3489
3·175	7	15·432	7·112	7	6·8894	31·138	7	1·5737
3·629	8	17·637	8·128	8	7·8736	35·586	8	1·7985
4·082	9	19·842	9·144	9	9·8578	40·034	9	2·0233

How to use the tables

The central figures can be read as either metric or imperial, e.g. on line 7 of the first table:

$$7 \text{ in} = 17.78 \text{ cm} \qquad 7 \text{ cm} = 2.7559 \text{ in.}$$

Values above 9 may be obtained by decimal point adjustment and addition, e.g. in the third table:

To convert 573 miles to km

$$
\begin{aligned}
500 \text{ miles} &= 804.7 \text{km} \\
70 \text{ miles} &= 112.65 \text{km} \\
3 \text{ miles} &= 4.828 \text{km} \\
\hline
573 \text{ miles} &= 922.178 \text{km}
\end{aligned}
$$

Such results should be treated as approximations. In the example given the conversion of 500 miles is correct only to the nearest 0·1 km, therefore the final sum can be correct only to the same degree; hence the conversion of 573 miles from the table is correctly stated as '922·2 km to the nearest 0·1 km'. The precise figure for 573 miles is 922·154 112 km.

25.2 International system of units

The Système International d'Unités has been internationally adopted as a coherent system of units (SI units of measurement) for the measurement of all physical quantities.

Base units

Seven independent quantities have been chosen which are measured in the *base units* of the system (Table 25.2   p 285).

Derived units

To measure any other quantity, a *derived unit* is formed by multiplying or dividing any two or more base units, or powers of them, together; e.g. speed is measured in metres per second, where the metre and the second are base units. The more frequently used derived units have been given names of their own for convenience, e.g. power is measured in watts, where one watt is derived from one kilogram multiplied by one metre squared divided by one second cubed.

Abbreviations

Each unit name has an agreed abbreviation (column 3 in Table 25.2). To abbreviate a unit compounded from more than one unit name, the abbreviations of the constituent units are written with a small space between them, e.g. a newton metre is abbreviated N m. Where a unit is raised to a power, the conventional algebraic indices are used, e.g. a metre squared, or square metre, is abbreviated m^2.

Division of units

The word *per* indicates division by all succeeding units. To abbreviate units which are to be divided, negative indices are preferred, but a solidus (/) may be used, e.g. metre per second is abbreviated $m\ s^{-1}$ or m/s, kilogram per metre cubed is $kg\ m^{-3}$ or kg/m^3.

Multiples and submultiples

To avoid the use of many zeros in either very large or very small numbers, prefixes indicating multiplication or division by some power of a thousand (Table 25.1) can be added to a unit, e.g. mega-: multiply by a million, so a megawatt (1 MW) is a million watts; milli-: divide by a thousand, so a milliwatt (1 mW) is a thousandth of a watt.

TABLE 25.1

prefix	abbrev.	factor	
exa-	E	10^{18}	= million million million
peta-	P	10^{15}	= thousand million million
tera-	T	10^{12}	= million million
giga-	G	10^{9}	= thousand million
mega-	M	10^{6}	= million
kilo-	k	10^{3}	= thousand
*hecto-	h	10^{2}	= hundred
*deca- *deka-	da	10	= ten
*deci-	d	10^{-1}	= tenth
*centi-	c	10^{-2}	= hundredth
milli-	m	10^{-3}	= thousandth
micro-	μ	10^{-6}	= millionth
nano-	n	10^{-9}	= thousand millionth
pico-	p	10^{-12}	= million millionth
femto-	f	10^{-15}	= thousand million millionth
atto-	a	10^{-18}	= million million millionth

*These prefixes are used only exceptionally where kilo- or milli- would be impractical; thus a centimetre ($\frac{1}{100}$ metre) is accepted as an everyday unit of convenient size, but it is not a preferred SI unit.

TABLE 25.2

Equivalents are given to four significant figures' accuracy, except where they are exact as indicated by bold figures.

Quantity	SI unit	abbreviation and derivation	equivalent in British units	SI equivalent of one British unit
Base units				
Length	**metre**	m	3·281 feet	0·3048 m
Mass*	**kilogram**	kg	2·205 pounds	**0·453 592 37** kg
Time	**second**	s	—	—
Temperature interval	**kelvin**	K	$\frac{9}{5}$ °Fahrenheit	$\frac{5}{9}$ K
Current, electric	**ampere**	A	—	—
Amount of substance	**mole**	mol	—	—
Luminous intensity	**candela**	cd	0·9833 candle	1·017 cd
Some derived and additional units				
Length	kilometre	km	0·6214 mile	1·609 km
	centimetre	cm	0·3937 inch	**2·54** cm
*Mass	tonne, metric ton	t = Mg	0·9842 ton	1·016 t
Area	metre squared	m²	10·76 ft²	0·092 90 m²
	hectare	ha = 10 000 m²	2·471 acres	0·4047 ha
Volume	metre cubed	m³	1·308 yd³	0·7646 m³
	litre	1 = dm³	0·2200 gal (UK)	4·546 litres
*Weight; Force	newton	N = kg m s⁻²	0·2248 lbf	4·448 N
Energy; Work; Heat	joule	J = m N = kg m² s⁻²	0·2388 calorie 0·7376 ft lbf 1 kJ = 0·9478 Btu	**4·1868** J 1·356 J 1·055 kJ
Power	watt	W = J s⁻² = kg m² s⁻³	0·001 341 hp	745·7 W
Velocity; Speed	metre per second	m s⁻¹	3·281 ft/s	0·3048 m s⁻¹
	kilometre per hour	km h⁻¹	0·6214 mile/h	1·609 km h⁻¹
Pressure; Stress	pascal	Pa = N m⁻²	1 kPa = 0·1450 lbf/in²	6·895 k Pa
	bar	bar = 10⁵ Pa	14·50 lbf/in²	0·068 95 bar
Frequency	hertz	Hz = s⁻¹	1 c/s	1 Hz
Angle	radian	rad	57° 18′	$\frac{\pi}{180}$ rad
Solid angle	steradian	sr	—	—
Temperature, absolute	degree Celsius or Centigrade	°C	$\left(\frac{9}{5} t°C + 32\right)$ °F	$\frac{5}{9}$ (t °F − 32) °C
	kelvin	K	$\frac{9}{5}$ degree Rankine	$\frac{5}{9}$ K
Potential difference; Electromotive force	volt	V = kg m² s⁻³ A⁻¹ = W A⁻¹		
Resistance electrical Reactance Impedance	ohm	Ω = kg m² s⁻³ A⁻² = V A⁻¹		
Capacitance, electrical	farad	F = kg⁻¹ m⁻² s⁴ A² = A s V⁻¹		
Inductance, magnetic	henry	H = kg m² s⁻² A⁻² = V s A⁻¹		

*The mass of a body is the quantity of matter in it; its weight is the force with which the earth attracts it, and is directly proportional to its mass. The use of the term "weight", where "mass" is strictly intended, is acceptable in non-technical usage when referring to objects within the earth's atmosphere.

25.3 Mathematical symbols

+	plus	⊂	is a subset of
−	minus	∃	there exists
±	plus or minus	∀	for all values of
×	multiply by	*	denotes an operation
÷	divide by	⇔	is equivalent to; if and only if
=	is equal to	⇒	implies
≡	is identically equal to	{} ∅	empty set
≈ ≑	is approximately equal to	{x, y}	the set whose members are x and y
≠	is not equal to	E	universal set
>	is greater than	N	the set of natural numbers
≫	is much greater than	W	the set of whole numbers
≯	is not greater than	Z	the set of integers
<	is less than	Q	the set of rational numbers
≪	is much less than	R	the set of real numbers
≮	is not less than	C	the set of complex numbers
≥	is greater than or equal to	→	maps to
≤	is less than or equal to	∴	therefore
∩	intersection	∵	because
∪	union	∠	angle
∈	is member of set	∣	parallel
		L	perpendicular

25.4 Miscellaneous

Temperature conversion

°Celsius		°Fahrenheit
−17·78	0	32·0
−12·22	10	50·0
−6·67	20	68·0
−1·11	30	86·0
4·44	40	104·0
10·00	50	122·0
15·56	60	140·0
21·11	70	158·0
26·68	80	176·0
32·24	90	194·0
37·80	100	212·0

Boiling point of water 100°C/212°F **Freezing point of water** 0°C/32°F

Clothing and shoe sizes

The following tables show equivalent sizes of clothes and shoes according to the British, American, and continental European measurement systems. The equivalents are only approximate.

Shoes

British		3		3½	4	4½	5	5½	6	6½	7
American		4½		5	5½	6	6½	7	7½	8	8½
Continental		36		36	37	38	38	39	39	40	41
British				7½	8	8½	9	9½	10	10½	11
American				8½	9½	9½	10½	10½	11½	11½	12
Continental				42	42	43	43	44	44	45	46

Men's shirts

British	14	14½	15	15½	16	16½	17	17½
American	14	14½	15	15½	16	16½	17	17½
Continental	35/36	37	38	39/40	41	42	43	44

Women's dresses

British	8	10	12	14	16	18	20	22
American	6	8	10	12	14	16	18	20
Continental	36	38	40	42	44	46	48	50

Women's sweaters

British	34	36	38	40	42	44
American	34	36	38	40	42	44

Men's sweaters

British	34	36	38	40	42	44
American	small	medium		large	extra	large

Inch/centimetre equivalents

inch	12	13	14	15	16	17	18	19	20	21
cm	30	33	35	38	41	43	45	48	51	53
inch	22	23	24	25	26	27	28	29	30	32
cm	55	58	61	63	66	69	71	74	76	81
inch	34	36	38	40	42	44	46	48	50	52
cm	85	91	97	102	107	112	117	122	127	132

Roman numerals

I	=	1	L	=	50
II	=	2	LI	=	51
III	=	3	LII, etc.	=	52, etc.
IV	=	4	LX	=	60
V	=	5	LXI	=	61
VI	=	6	LXII, etc.	=	62, etc.
VII	=	7	LXX	=	70
VIII	=	8	LXXI	=	71
IX	=	9	LXXII, etc.	=	72, etc.
X	=	10	LXXX	=	80
XI	=	11	LXXXI	=	81
XII	=	12	LXXXII, etc.	=	82, etc.
XIII	=	13	XC	=	90
XIV	=	14	XCI	=	91
XV	=	15	XCII, etc.	=	92, etc.
XVI	=	16			
XVII	=	17	C	=	100
XVIII	=	18	CC	=	200
XIX	=	19	CCC	=	300
XX	=	20	CD	=	400
XXI	=	21	D	=	500
XXII, etc.	=	22, etc.	DC	=	600
XXX	=	30	DCC	=	700
XXXI	=	31	DCCC	=	800
XXXII, etc.	=	32, etc.	CM	=	900
XL	=	40			
XLI	=	41	M	= 1000
XLII, etc.	=	42, etc.	MM	= 2000

The Greek alphabet

A	α	alpha	=a	N	ν	nū	=n
B	β	bēta	=b	Ξ	ξ	xī	=x *(ks)*
Γ	γ	gamma	=g	O	o	omīcron	=o
Δ	δ	delta	=d	Π	π	pī	=p
E	ϵ	epsīlon	=e	P	ϱ	rhō	=r
Z	ζ	zēta	=z	Σ	$s\sigma$	sigma	=s
H	η	ēta	=ē	T	τ	tau	=t
Θ	$\theta\ \vartheta$	thēta	=th *(th)*	Υ	υ	ūpsīlon	=u *(yōo, oŏ, ü)*

(often transcribed *y*)

I	ι	iōta	=i	Φ	ϕ	phī	=ph *(f)*
K	$\varkappa$	kappa	=k	X	χ	chī	=kh *(hh)*

(often transcribed *ch*, as in Latin)

Λ	λ	lambda	=l	Ψ	ψ	psī	=ps
M	μ	mū	=m	Ω	ω	ōmega	=ō

The Greek alphabet, apart from its use as the official script in Greek-speaking areas, is of worldwide importance as a source of symbols used in all branches of science and mathematics. The equivalents in our alphabet given above are intended as a guide to transliteration and as an indication of the anglicised pronunciation of ancient Greek. We have not attempted to describe modern Greek pronunciation.

26 MEDIA

This chapter lists a selection of useful UK media addresses. The addresses and telephone numbers listed were correct at the time of going to press. For additional information on the media market consult:

Benn's Media Directory	PO Box 20, Sovereign Way, Tonbridge, Kent TN9 1RQ
Brad (British Rate & Data)	76 Oxford Street, London W1N 9FD

For local companies and contacts consult *Yellow Pages*. (See also Chapter 6: Advertising and Publicity.)

26.1 Magazines and journals

Business

The Banker	102-8 Clerkenwell Road, London EC1M 5SA
British Business	Millbank Tower, Millbank, London SW1P 4QU
Business	234 King's Road, London SW3 5UA
Business Bulletin	The Guildhall, Dartmouth, Devon TQ6 9RY
The Business Economist	11 Bay Tree Walk, Watford, Herts WD1 3RX
Business Graduate	John Wiley & Sons Ltd, Baffins Lane, Chichester, Sussex PO19 1UD
Business Traveller	49 Old Bond Street, London W1X 3AF
COMLON	LCCI Examinations Board, Marlowe House, Station Road, Sidcup, Kent DA15 7BJ
Economic Affairs	2 Lord North Street, London SW1P 3LB
Investors Chronicle	Greystoke Place, Fetter Lane, London EC4A 1ND
Link-Up	Mark Allen Publishing Ltd, Battersea Business Centre, 103-9 Lavender Hill, London SW11 5QL
Money Observer	The Observer Ltd, 8 St Andrew's Hill, London EC4V 5JA
Multinational Business	Economist Publications, 40 Duke Street, London W1A 1DW
Small Business	Small Business Bureau, 32 Smith Square, London SW1P 3HH
Stockmarket Confidential	57-61 Mortimer Street, London W1N 7TP
Venture UK	Cover Publications Ltd, PO Box 381, Mill Harbour, London E14 9TW

Business equipment

Buckley's Guide to Office Automation	IT Publishing Ltd, 6 Hanover Square, London W1R 9HH
Business Computing & Communications	Morgan-Grampian House, 30 Calderwood Street, London SE18 6QH
Business Equipment Digest	BED Business Journals Ltd, 44 Wallington Square, Wallington, Surrey SM6 8RG
Business Systems & Equipment	Maclean Hunter Ltd, 76 Oxford Street, London W1N 9FD
Communication Technology Impact	Elsevier International Bulletins, Mayfield House, 256 Banbury Road, Oxford OX2 7DH
Microinfo	Microinfo Ltd, PO Box 3, Alton, Hants GU34 2PG
Office Equipment Index	Maclaren Publishers Ltd, PO Box 109, Maclaren House, 19 Scarbrook Road, Croydon CR9 1QH
Office Equipment News	AGB Business Publications, Audit House, Field End Road, Eastcote, Ruislip, Middx HA4 9LT
Office Magazine	Patey Doyle (Publishing) Ltd, Wilmington House, Church Hill, Wilmington, Dartford, Kent DA2 7EF
Office Trade News	(address as above)
Office Weekly	Good Times Publishing, 4a Duke Street, Manchester Square, London W1M 6EA
Televisual	Centaur Ltd, 60 Kingly Street, London W1R 5LH
Wharton's Complete Office Automation Guide	Wharton Publishing Ltd, Regal House, London Road, Twickenham, Middx TW1 3QS
What to Buy for Business	What to Buy Ltd, 11 King's Road, Chelsea, London SW3 4RP

Current affairs

Contemporary Review	61 Carey Street, London WC2 2JG
The Economist	25 St James's Street, London SW1A 1HG
Encounter	44 Great Windmill Street, London W1V 7PA
New Internationalist	42 Hythe Bridge Street, Oxford OX1 2EP
New Socialist	150 Walworth Road, London SE17 1JT
New Society	5 Sherwood Street, London W1V 7RA
New Statesman	14-16 Farringdon Lane, London EC1R 3AU
Newsweek	25 Upper Brook Street, London W1Y 1PD
Parliamentary Affairs	Oxford University Press, Walton Street, Oxford OX2 6DP

The Spectator	56 Doughty Street, London WC1N 2LL
Time Magazine	Time & Life Building, New Bond Street, London W1Y 0AA
Tribune	308 Gray's Inn Road, London WC1X 8DY

Management and administration

Better Your Business	Causton Hall, Cross Road, Croydon, Surrey CR0 6TB
The British Journal of Administrative Management	40 Chatsworth Parade, Petts Wood, Orpington, Kent BR5 1RW
Business Express	22 Vineyard Road, Wellington, Telford, Shropshire TF1 1HB
Chief Executive	Morgan-Grampian House, 30 Calderwood Street, London SE18 6QH
Co-operative Marketing & Management	418 Chester Road, Manchester M16 9HP
The Director	10 Belgrave Square, London SW1X 8PH
First Voice	Yorkshire Communications Group, 17A Monckton Road, Wakefield, W Yorks WF2 7AL
Futures	PO Box 63, Bury Street, Guildford, Surrey GU2 5BH
Government Executive	342/362 Corn Exchange Buildings, Manchester M4 3BU
In Business Life	1 High Street, Christchurch, Dorset BH23 1AE
In Business Now	Millbank Tower, Millbank, London SW1P 4QU
Industrial Management & Data Systems	62 Toller Lane, Bradford, W Yorks BD8 9BY
International Management	McGraw Hill House, Shoppenhangers Road, Maidenhead, Berks SL6 2QL
Journal of General Management	Henley Management College, Greenlands, Henley-on-Thames, Oxon RG9 3AU
Long Range Planning	Headington Hill Hall, Oxford OX3 0BW
Management & Marketing Abstracts	(address as above)
Management News	British Institute of Management, Management House, Parker Street, London WC2B 5PT
Management Today	30 Lancaster Gate, London W2 3LP
Managerial & Decision Economics	Baffins Lane, Chichester, Sussex PO19 1UD
Mind Your Own Business	106 Church Road, London SE19 2UB

| Western Management | The Studio, Hinton Lane, Clifton, Bristol BS8 4NS |
| Works Management | Franks Hall, Horton Kirby, Kent DA4 9LL |

Personnel management

Employment Gazette	HMSO, PO Box 276, London SW8 5DT
IPM Digest	8 Lichfield Road, Kew, Surrey TW9 3JR
Journal of Management Development	62 Toller Lane, Bradford, W Yorks BD8 9BY
Manpower	Manpower House, 270-2 High Street, Slough SL1 1LJ
Personnel Management	1 Hills Place, London W1R 1AG
Personnel Resource Management	PO Box 45, Dorking, Surrey RH5 5YZ
Personnel Review	62 Toller Lane, Bradford, W Yorks BD8 9BY

26.2 Newspapers

Daily

Daily Express	121-8 Fleet Street, London EC4P 4JT 01-353 8000
Daily Mail	Northcliffe House, Tudor Street, London EC4Y 0JA 01-353 6000
Daily Mirror	33 Holborn, London EC1P 1DQ 01-353 0246
Daily Record	40 Anderston Quay, Glasgow G3 8DA 041-248 7000
Daily Telegraph	135 Fleet Street, London EC4P 4BL 01-353 4242
Financial Times	10 Cannon Street, London EC4P 4BY 01-248 8000
Glasgow Herald	195 Albion Street, Glasgow G1 1QP 041-552 6255
The Guardian	119 Farringdon Road, London EC1R 3ER 01-278 2332
The Independent	40 City Road, London EC1Y 2DB 01-253 1222
Irish News & Belfast Morning News	113-7 Donegall Street, Belfast BT1 2GE (0232) 24164
Morning Star	75 Farringdon Road, London EC1M 3JX 01-405 9542

The Scotsman	20 North Bridge, Edinburgh EH1 1YT
	031-225 2468
The Star	Great Ancoats Street, Manchester M60 4HB
	061-236 2112
The Sun	1 Pennington Street, London E1 9XP
	01-481 4100
The Times	1 Pennington Street, London E1 9XN
	01-481 4100
Today	70 Vauxhall Bridge Road, London SW1V 2RP
	01-630 1333
Western Mail	Thomson House, Havelock Street, Cardiff CF1 1WR
	(0222) 33022

Sunday newspapers

The Mail on Sunday	Northcliffe House, London EC4Y 0JA
	01-353 6000
News of the World	1 Pennington Street, London EC1 9BH
	01-481 4100
News on Sunday	Caxton House, 13-16 Borough Road, London SE1 0AL
	01-928 4902/4898
The Observer	8 St Andrew's Hill, London EC4V 5JA
	01-236 0202
Press & Journal	PO Box 43, Lang Stracht, Mastrick, Aberdeen AB9 8AF
	(0224) 690222
Sunday Express	121-8 Fleet Street, London EC4P 4JT
	01-353 8000
Sunday Mail	40 Anderston Quay, Glasgow G3 8DA
	041-248 7000
Sunday Mirror	33 Holborn, London EC1P 1DQ
	01-353 0246
Sunday News	51-9 Donegall Street, Belfast BT1 2GB
	(0232) 244441
Sunday People	9 New Fetter Lane, London EC4A 1AR
	01-353 0246
Sunday Post	2 Albert Square, Dundee DD1 9QJ
	(0382) 23131
Sunday Telegraph	135 Fleet Street, London EC4P 4BL
	01-353 4242
Sunday Times	1 Pennington Street, London E1 9XW
	01-481 4100
Sunday Today	70 Vauxhall Bridge Road, London SW1V 2RP
	01-630-1333

Evening newspapers

Belfast Telegraph	124 Royal Avenue, Belfast BT1 1EB
	(0232) 221242
The Evening Express	PO Box 43, Lang Stracht, Mastrick, Aberdeen
	AB9 8AF
	(0224) 690222
The Evening News	20 North Bridge, Edinburgh EH1 1YT
	031-225 2468
The Evening Times	195 Albion Street, Glasgow G1 1QP
	041-552 6255
The London Daily News	33 Holborn Circus, London EC4 1AR
	01-822 2323
The London Standard	121 Fleet Street, London WC1N 2QB
	01-353 8000
South Wales Echo	Thomson House, Havelock Street, Cardiff
	CF1 1WR
	(0222) 33022

National newspaper groups

Newspaper Publishing PLC	40 City Road, London EC1 2DB
	01-253 1222
Northcliffe Newspapers Group Ltd	Tudor Street, London EC4Y 0JA
	01-353 4000
Thomson Regional Newspapers Ltd	Pemberton House, East Harding Street, London EC4A 3AS
	01-353 9131

26.3 News agencies

Agence France Press (AFP)	Chronicle House, Fleet Street, London EC4Y 8BB
	01-353 7461
Anglo Danish Press (ADP)	Grosvenor Works, Mount Pleasant Hill, London E5 9NL
	01-806 3232
Associated Press (AP)	12 Norwich Street, London EC4A 1BP
	01-353 1515
Canadian Press (CP)	23 Norwich Street, London EC4A 1EJ
	01-353 6355
Deutsche Press-Agentur (DPA)	85 Fleet Street, London EC4P 1BE
	01-353 8594
Gemini News Service	40-43 Fleet Street, London EC4Y 1BT
	01-353 2567
Inter Press Service (IPS)	86-100 St Pancras Way, London NW1 9ES
	01-482 4951

Jewish Chronicle News & Feature Service	25 Furnival Street, London EC4A 1JT 01-405 9252
Jiji Press	IPC, 76 Shoe Lane, London EC4A 3JB 01-353 5417
Middle East News Agency (MENA)	Communications House, Gough Square, London EC4A 3DE 01-353 5455
Newslink Africa	IPC, Suite 441, 76 Shoe Lane, London EC4A 3JB 01-353 0186
New Zealand Associated Press (NZAP)	107 Fleet Street, London EC4A 2AN 01-353 2686
New Zealand Press Association (NZPA)	85 Fleet Street, London EC4Y 1DY 01-353 5430
Reuters	85 Fleet Street, London EC4P 4AJ 01-250 1122
Tass News Agency	Communications House, 12-16 Gough Square, London EC4A 3JH 01-353 9831
United Press International (UPI)	8 Bouverie Street, London EC4Y 8BB 01-353 2282

26.4 Radio

National radio

BBC Radio	Broadcasting House, London W1A 1AA 01-580 4468
BBC Radio North	Broadcasting Centre, 146/146a Woodhouse Lane, Leeds LS2 9PX (0532) 441188
BBC Radio North East	Broadcasting House, New Bridge Street, Newcastle upon Tyne NE1 8AA (0632) 320961
BBC Radio North West	Oxford Road, Manchester M60 1SJ 061-236 8444
BBC Radio Scotland	Queen Street, Edinburgh EH2 1JF 031-225 3131
BBC Radio Ulster	Ormeau Avenue, Belfast BT2 8HQ (0232) 244400
BBC Radio Wales	Llantrisant Road, Llandaff, Cardiff CF5 3YQ (0222) 564888

BBC local radio

BBC Radio Aberdeen	Broadcasting House, Beech Grove Terrace, Aberdeen AB9 2ZT (0224) 635233
BBC Radio Bedfordshire	PO Box 476, Luton LU1 5BA (0582) 459111
BBC Radio Bristol	PO Box 194, 3 Tyndalls Park Road, Bristol BS8 1PP (0272) 741111
BBC Radio Cambridgeshire	PO Box 96, Broadcasting House, Hills Road, Cambridge CB2 1LD (0223) 315970
BBC Radio Cleveland	PO Box 1548, Broadcasting House, Newport Road, Middlesbrough TS1 5DG (0642) 225211
BBC Radio Clwyd	The Old Schoolhouse, Glanrafon Road, Mold, Clwyd CH7 1PA (0352) 56821
BBC Radio Cornwall	Phoenix Wharf, Truro, Cornwall TR1 1UA (0872) 75421
BBC Radio Cumbria	Hilltop Heights, London Road, Carlisle CA1 2NA (0228) 31661
BBC Radio Derby	PO Box 269, Derby DE1 3HL (0332) 361111
BBC Radio Devon	PO Box 100, Exeter EX4 4DB (0392) 215651 PO Box 5, Seymour Road, Plymouth PL3 5BD (0752) 260323
BBC Radio Essex	198 New London Road, Chelmsford CM2 9AB (0245) 262393
BBC Radio Foyle	PO Box 927, Rock Road, Londonderry BT48 7NE (0504) 69101
BBC Radio Furness	Hartington Street, Barrow-in-Furness, Cumbria LA14 5FH
BBC Radio Guernsey	Commerce House, Les Banques, St Peter Port, Guernsey (0481) 28977
BBC Radio Gwent	Powys House, Cwmbran, Gwent NP44 1YF (06333) 72727
BBC Radio Highland	7 Culduthel Road, Inverness IV2 4AD (0463) 221711

BBC Radio Humberside	63 Jameson Street, Hull HU1 3NU
	(0482) 23232
BBC Radio Jersey	Broadcasting House, Rouge Bouillon, St Helier, Jersey
	(0534) 70000
BBC Radio Kent	Sun Pier, Chatham, Kent ME4 4EZ
	(0634) 46284
BBC Radio Lancashire	King Street, Blackburn BB2 2EA
	(0254) 62411
BBC Radio Leeds	Broadcasting House, Woodhouse Lane, Leeds LS2 9PN
	(0532) 442131
BBC Radio Leicester	Epic House, Charles Street, Leicester LE1 3SH
	(0533) 27113
BBC Radio Lincolnshire	PO Box 219, Newport, Lincoln LN1 3DF
	(0522) 40011
BBC Radio London	35a Marylebone High Street, London W1A 4LG
	01-486 7611
BBC Radio Manchester	PO Box 90, New Broadcasting House, Oxford Road, Manchester M60 1SJ
	061-228 3434
BBC Radio Merseyside	55 Paradise Street, Liverpool L1 3BP
	051-708 5500
BBC Radio Nan Eilean	BBC Rosebank, Church Street, Stornoway, Isle of Lewis PA87 2LS
	(0851) 5000
BBC Radio Newcastle	Broadcasting Centre, Barrack Road, Newcastle upon Tyne NE99 1RN
	091-232 4141
BBC Radio Norfolk	Norfolk Tower, Surrey Street, Norwich NR1 3PA
	(0603) 617411
BBC Radio Northampton	PO Box 1107, Northampton NN1 2BE
	(0604) 20621
BBC Radio Nottingham	York House, Mansfield Road, Nottingham NG1 3JB
	(0602) 415161
BBC Radio Orkney	Castle Street, Kirkwall, Orkney KW15 1HD
	(0856) 3939
BBC Radio Oxford	242 Banbury Road, Oxford OX2 7DW
	(0865) 53411
BBC Radio Sheffield	Ashdell Grove, 60 Westbourne Road, Sheffield S10 2QU
	(0742) 686185

BBC Radio Shetland	Brentham House, Lerwick, Shetland ZE1 0LR (0595) 4747
BBC Radio Shropshire	2/4 Boscobel Drive, Shrewsbury SY1 3TT (0743) 248484
BBC Radio Solent	South Western House, Canute Road, Southampton SO9 4PJ (0703) 631311
BBC Radio Solway	Elmbank, Lover's Walk, Dumfries DG7 1NZ (0387) 68008
BBC Radio Stoke-on-Trent	Conway House, Cheapside, Hanley, Stoke-on-Trent ST1 1JJ (0782) 24827
BBC Radio Sussex	1 Marlborough Place, Brighton BN1 1TU (0273) 680231
BBC Radio Tweed	Municipal Buildings, High Street, Selkirk TD7 4BU (0750) 21884
BBC Radio WM (West Midlands)	PO Box 206, Birmingham B5 7SD 021-472 5141
BBC Radio York	20 Bootham Row, York YO3 7BR (0904) 641351

Independent local radio

Beacon Radio **(Wolverhampton)**	PO Box 303, 267 Tettenhall Road, Wolverhampton WV6 0DQ (0902) 757211
BRMB **(Birmingham)**	PO Box 555, Radio House, Aston Road North, Birmingham B6 4BX 021-359 4481/9
Capital Radio **(London)**	Euston Tower, Euston Road, London NW1 3DR 01-388 1288
Chiltern Radio **(Luton/Bedford)**	Chiltern Road, Dunstable LU6 1HQ (0582) 666001
County Sound **(Guildford)**	The Friary, Guildford, Surrey GU1 4YX (0483) 505566
Devonair Radio **(Exeter/Torbay)**	The Studio Centre, 35/37 St David's Hill, Exeter EX4 4DA (0392) 30703
Downtown Radio **(Belfast)**	Newtownards, Co. Down BT23 4ES (0247) 815555
Essex Radio **(Southend/Chelmsford)**	Radio House, Clifftown Road, Southend-on-Sea SS1 1SX (0702) 333711

GWR Radio **(Swindon/ Bristol/West Wilts)**	PO Box 2000, Swindon SN4 7EX (0793) 853222
Hereward Radio **(Peterborough/ Northampton)**	PO Box 225, 114 Bridge Street, Peterborough PE1 1XJ (0733) 46225
Invicta Radio **(Maidstone/ Medway/Kent)**	15 Station Road East, Canterbury CT1 2RB (0227) 67661
Leicester Sound **(Leicester)**	Granville House, Granville Road, Leicester LE1 7RW (0533) 551616
LBC **(London)**	PO Box 261, Communications House, Gough Square, London EC4P 4LP 01-353 1010
Manx Radio **(IOM)**	PO Box 219, Broadcasting House, Douglas Head, Douglas, IOM (0624) 73589
Marcher Sound **(Wrexham/Deeside)**	PO Box 238, Mold Road, Gwersyllt, Wrexham LL11 1BT (0978) 752202
Mercia Sound **(Coventry)**	Hertford Place, Coventry CV1 3TT (0203) 28451
Metro Radio **(Tyne & Wear)**	Radio House, Longrigg, Swalwell, Newcastle upon Tyne NE99 1BB 091-488 3131
Moray Firth Radio **(Inverness)**	PO Box 271, Inverness IV1 1UJ (0463) 224433
NorthSound Radio **(Aberdeen)**	45 King's Gate, Aberdeen AB2 6BL (0224) 632234
Pennine Radio **(Bradford/ Huddersfield/Halifax)**	PO Box 235, Pennine House, Forster Square, Bradford BD1 5NP (0274) 731521
Piccadilly Radio **(Manchester)**	127/131 The Piazza, Piccadilly Plaza, Manchester M1 4AW 061-236 9913
Plymouth Sound **(Plymouth)**	Earl's Acre, Alma Road, Plymouth PL3 4HX (0752) 27272
Radio Aire **(Leeds)**	PO Box 362, 51 Burley Road, Leeds LS3 1LR (0532) 452299
Radio Broadland **(Norwich/ Gt Yarmouth)**	St George's Plain, Colgate, Norwich NR3 1DD (0603) 630621
Radio City **(Liverpool)**	PO Box 194, 8–10 Stanley Street, Liverpool L69 1LD 051-227 5100
Radio Clyde **(Glasgow)**	Clydebank Business Park, Clydebank G81 2RX 041-941 1111

Radio Forth **(Edinburgh)**	Forth House, Forth Street, Edinburgh EH1 3LF 031-556 9255
Radio Hallam **(Sheffield/ Barnsley/Doncaster/ Rotherham)**	PO Box 194, Hartshead, Sheffield S1 1GP (0742) 71188
Radio Luxembourg	38 Hertford Street, London W1Y 8BA 01-493 5961
Radio Mercury **(Reigate/Crawley)**	Broadfield House, Brighton Road, Crawley RH11 9TJ (0293) 519161
Radio Orwell	Electric House, Lloyds Avenue, Ipswich IP1 3HZ (0473) 216971
Radio Tay **(Dundee/Perth)**	PO Box 123, Dundee DD1 9UF (0382) 29551
Radio Tees **(Teesside)**	74 Dovecot Street, Stockton-on-Trent TS18 1HB (0642) 615111
Radio Trent **(Nottingham)**	29/31 Castle Gate, Nottingham NG1 7AP (0602) 581731
Radio 210 **(Thames Valley/ Reading)**	PO Box 210, Reading RG3 5RZ (0734) 413131
Radio Victory **(Portsmouth)**	PO Box 257, Portsmouth PO1 5RT (0705) 827799
Radio West **(Bristol)**	PO Box 963, Watershed, Canons Road, Bristol (0272) 279900
Radio Wyvern **(Hereford/Worcester)**	5/6 Barbourne Terrace, Worcester WR1 3JM (0905) 612212
Red Dragon Radio **(Cardiff)**	Radio House, West Canal Wharf, Cardiff CF1 5XJ (0222) 384041
Red Rose Radio **(Preston/Blackpool)**	St Paul's Square, Preston PR1 1YE (0772) 556301
Saxon Radio **(Bury St Edmunds)**	Long Brackland, Bury St Edmunds (0284) 701511
Severn Sound **(Gloucester/Cheltenham)**	Old Talbot House, 67 Southgate Street, Gloucester GL1 1TX (0452) 423791
Signal Radio **(Stoke-on-Trent)**	Stoke Road, Stoke-on-Trent ST4 2SR (0782) 417111
Southern Sound **(Brighton)**	Radio House, Franklin Road, Portslade BN4 2SS (0273) 422288

Suffolk Group Radio **(Ipswich/Bury St Edmunds)**	Electric House, Lloyds Avenue, Ipswich IP1 3HZ (0473) 216971
Swansea Sound **(Swansea)**	Victoria Road, Gowerton, Swansea SA3 3AB (0792) 893751
Two Counties Radio **(Bournemouth)**	5/7 Southcote Road, Bournemouth BH1 3LR (0202) 294881
Viking Radio **(Humberside)**	Commercial Road, Hull HU1 2SG (0482) 25141
West Sound **(Ayr)**	54 Holmston Road, Ayr KA7 3BD (0292) 283662
Wiltshire Radio	Old Lime Kiln, High Street, Wootton Bassett, Swindon (0793) 853222

26.5 Television

BBC television

BBC Television	Television Centre, Wood Lane, London W12 7RJ 01-743 8000
BBC Breakfast Time	Television Centre, Lime Grove Studios, London W12 7RJ 01-743 8000
BBC TV East	St Catherine's Close, All Saints Green, Norwich NR1 3ND (0603) 619331
BBC TV Midlands	BBC Broadcasting Centre, Pebble Mill Road, Birmingham B5 7QQ 021-472 5353
BBC TV North	Broadcasting Centre, Woodhouse Lane, Leeds LS2 9PX (0532) 441188
BBC TV North East and Cumbria	Broadcasting House, 54 New Bridges Street, Newcastle upon Tyne NE1 8AA (0632) 321313
BBC North West	New Broadcasting House, Oxford Road, Manchester M60 1SJ 061-236 8444
BBC TV Northern Ireland	Ormeau Avenue, Belfast BT2 8HQ (0232) 244400

BBC TV Scotland	BBC Broadcasting House, Queen Margaret Drive, Glasgow G12 8DG 041-339 8844
BBC TV South	South Western House, Canute Road, Southampton SO9 1PF (0703) 26201
BBC TV South West	Broadcasting House, Seymour Road, Plymouth PL3 5BD (0752) 29201
BBC TV Wales	Llantrisant Road, Llandaff, Cardiff CF5 2YQ (0222) 654888
BBC TV West	Broadcasting House, Whiteladies Road, Bristol BS8 2LR (0272) 732211
BBC World Service	Bush House, Strand, London WC2B 4PH 01-257 2090

Independent television

Anglia TV	Anglia House, Norwich NR1 3JG (0603) 615151
Border TV	TV Centre, Carlisle CA1 3NT (0228) 25101
Central Independent TV	Central House, Broad Street, Birmingham B1 2JP 021-643 9898 East Midlands TV Centre, Lenton Lane, Nottingham NG7 2NA (0602) 863322
Channel TV	TV Centre, Rouge Bouillon, St Helier, Jersey, CI (0534) 73999
Channel 4	60 Charlotte Street, London W1P 2AX 01-631 4444
Grampian TV	Queen's Cross, Aberdeen AB9 2XJ (0224) 646464
Granada TV	TV Centre, Manchester M60 9EA 061-832 7211
HTV (Wales)	TV Centre, Cardiff CF5 6XJ (0222) 590590
HTV (West)	TV Centre, Bath Road, Bristol BS4 3HG (0272) 778366
Independent Television News (ITN)	48 Wells Street, London W1P 4DE 01-637 2424

London Weekend TV	South Bank TV Centre, Kent House, Upper Ground, London SE1 9LT 01-261 3434
Scottish TV	Cowcaddens, Glasgow G2 3PR 041-332 9999
Sianel Pedwar Cymru (S4C)	Sophia Close, Cardiff CF1 9XY (0222) 43421
Television South (TVS)	TV Centre, Northam Road, Southampton SO9 5HZ (0703) 34211 TV Centre, Vinters Park, Maidstone ME14 5NZ (0622) 54945
Television South West (TSW)	Derry's Cross, Plymouth PL1 2SP (0752) 663322
Thames Television	Thames Television House, 303-316 Euston Road, London NW1 3BB 01-387 9494
TV-AM	Breakfast TV Centre, Hawley Crescent, London NW1 8EF 01-267 4300/4377
Tyne Tees Television	TV Centre, City Road, Newcastle upon Tyne NE1 2AL 091-261 0181
Ulster Television	Havelock House, Ormeau Road, Belfast BT7 1EB (0232) 228122
Yorkshire Television	TV Centre, Leeds LS3 1JS (0532) 438283

26.6 Direct mail

(See also Chapters 6.4: Advertising and Publicity and 20.1: Royal Mail)

Advice and assistance on direct mail can be obtained from the following organisations:

Direct Mail Producers Association	34 Grand Avenue, London N10 3BP 01-883 7229
Direct Mail Sales Bureau	12-13 Henrietta Street, London WC2E 8JJ 01-836 4081
Direct Mail Services Standards Board	92 New Cavendish Street, London W1M 7FA 01-636 7581

Some companies offering direct mail services

(See also *Yellow Pages* for local companies)

ADS (Marketing Resources)	72 Sackville Street, Manchester M1 3NJ 061-236 6564
Amherst Direct Mail Ltd	Amherst House, Ferring Street, Ferring, Worthing BN12 5JR (0903) 502251
Astro Mailing	3 Elmdon Road, Marston Green, Birmingham B37 7BS 021-779 6771
Avon Direct Mail Services Ltd	Unit 7, Harbour Road Estate, Portishead, Bristol BS20 9EG (0272) 842487
Bowker Mailing Services	Erasmus House, Epping CM16 4BU (0378) 77333
Britannica Mailing Service	Mappin House, 156-162 Oxford Street, London W1N 0HJ 01-637 3371
CCN Communications	70 Sackville Street, Manchester M1 3NJ 061-236 1862
Contract Mail Ltd	97 Kilburn Square, Kilburn High Road, London NW6 6PS 01-328 4447
Datamail Ltd	10 South Bank Business Centre, 140 Battersea Park Road, London SW1 4NB 01-720 1202
Distribution and Media Sales (UK) Ltd	30 Bridge Road, Haywards Heath RH16 1TU (0444) 414041
Halligan Advertising Services Ltd	66 Addison Road, Bromley BR2 9TT 01-646 6917
Hardings Mail Services Ltd	Unit 6, Elms Industrial Estate, St Martin's Way, London SW17 0JH 01-947 8477/8/9
Holborn Direct Mail Co.	Capacity House, 2-6 Rothsay Street, Tower Bridge Road, London SE1 4UD 01-407 6444
Ibis Information Services Ltd	Waterside, Lowbell Lane, London Colney, St Albans AL2 1DX (0727) 25209
Industrial Direct Mail Service	Windsor Court, East Grinstead House, East Grinstead RH19 1XA (0342) 26972
List Management Services Ltd	Nassau House, 122 Shaftesbury Avenue, London W1V 7DJ 01-439 3844

Marketforce Ltd	Advance House, Brent Crescent, London NW10 7XR 01-961 1880
Pauline Marks Ltd	Postmark House, Cross Lane, London N8 7SD 01-348 4294
Mastermail Direct Advertising Ltd	Mastermail House, 8 Morocco Street, London SE1 3HB 01-403 2373
O E McIntyre Ltd	McIntyre House, Canning Place, Liverpool L1 8HY 01-209 1566
Parade Direct Marketing Ltd	PO Box 145, 127 Hagley Road, Birmingham B16 8XT 021-455 0223
Response Analysis & Mailing Ltd (RAM)	22 Stephenson Way, London NW1 2HD 01-387 0832
Simmonds Direct Mail Group	82-84 Peckham Rye, London SE15 4HB 01-639 0331
Streets Ahead Mailing Services	8 The Quadrant, Hoylake, Merseyside L47 2EE 051-632 3162
Waterhouse Direct Mail Services	10 Peterborough Mews, New Kings Road, London SW6 3BL 01-731 6900

27 GLOSSARIES

27.1 Business

acceptance (1) Agreement to enter into a contract. (2) Agreement to pay a bill of exchange, usually by signing it.

accepting house A financial institution which accepts bills of exchange as well as carrying out other financial activities.

annual accounts A company's financial statements, including the profit and loss account and the balance sheet. Public limited companies are required by law to publish annual accounts.

annual percentage rate (APR) A method of calculating the interest rates on hire-purchase agreements. The 1974 Consumer Credit Act prevented sellers from quoting misleading interest rates by requiring them to quote only the APR.

annual report The report which a company sends to its shareholders each year. It may include the annual accounts.

appreciation An increase in the value of an asset or commodity.

assessment (1) The valuation of property in order to calculate the amount to be paid in rates. (2) The examination of income and profit in order to calculate the amount to be paid in tax.

assurance A type of insurance which does not depend on a possible future occurrence. Regular premiums are paid, and a lump sum is paid out by the assurers, either on the death of the assured person or on a stated date.

audit A systematic examination of the financial records of a business, to check that transactions have been accurately recorded and to make sure that the company's statements and reports give a true and fair view of its financial position.

balance sheet A statement of a company's financial position at a specified time. It shows what the company *owns* (i.e. assets) and what it *owes* (i.e. liabilities).

bill of lading An official receipt for goods to be shipped stating the terms and conditions under which the goods will be transported.

black economy Ordinary economic activities carried on in such a way as to avoid the payment of taxes. No invoices or official documents are issued for work done, and payment is in cash or in kind.

black market A situation in which there is an illegal trade in certain goods or services. Shortages, rationing and strict price controls all tend to produce a black market, where prices are usually high.

bonded goods Imported goods on which duty is payable. They must be stored in a bonded warehouse ('in bond') until the duty is paid or until they are re-exported.

break-even point The stage in business activity where production and sales are such that total income equals total costs, and neither profit nor loss is made.

British Standards Institution (BSI) An organisation which lays down minimum standards of quality for a wide range of manufactured goods. A product carrying the BSI 'Kite mark' is one that conforms to BSI quality specifications.

capital expenditure The buying of machinery and other long-lasting assets which will be used in the production process over a long period of time.

capital gains Profit obtained by selling an asset. It may be liable to tax.

capital-intensive A production process or industry which requires a comparatively large amount of capital (money and equipment) in relation to the amount of labour required is called capital-intensive (e.g. oil-refining and car-manufacturing).

cartel An association between two or more independent organisations producing the same product, arranged to pursue a common policy on controlling prices and production in order to reduce or eliminate competition between cartel members.

collateral security Documents such as shares or the title deeds to property, given by a borrower to a lender as a safeguard for a loan and returned to the borrower when the loan is repaid.

compound interest Interest which is calculated on the original amount *plus* any interest which has already accumulated.

cost-benefit analysis A type of study which compares the cost of a particular course of action with the resulting benefits. It takes into account the 'social' costs and benefits as well as the strictly financial ones.

costing The process of measuring and analysing the cost of a business activity, product, department, etc. Accurate costing is essential to business control and planning.

critical path analysis A planning technique showing all the separate jobs within a project, and the time each job should take. The 'critical path' is the order of doing the jobs which will ensure the fewest delays and the minimum cost of the project.

current assets Assets such as stock, cash in hand and debts owed, which change rapidly in the course of normal business.

current liabilities Debts or amounts owing to others expected to be paid within twelve months from the date of the balance sheet (e.g. creditors and tax payable).

cybernetics A science which studies communication and control functions in humans and machines. The knowledge gained can be applied to the management of large groups of people or complex systems of machinery.

deed of covenant A legal agreement in which a person promises to pay a fixed sum for an agreed period of time. It enables the payer to deduct tax from the total payment.

deficit (1) The amount by which a company's liabilities are greater in value than its assets or its spending greater than its income. (2) A situation in which the balance of payments shows that imports exceed exports.

deflation A decrease in demand, production and prices, which can be achieved by restricting the amount of money available in the economy.

depreciation (1) A reduction in the value of an asset. (2) This reduction as reflected in a company's accounts. A set percentage of the asset's value is converted into an expense at the end of each accounting period.

devaluation A reduction in the value of a currency as compared with other currencies. It is achieved by lowering the exchange rate, and usually has the effect of reducing a country's imports.

diminishing returns The law of diminishing returns states that, beyond a certain point, *increased* use of a production facility will result in *decreased* output (because of break-downs, etc.).

dumping Selling goods in a foreign market at a price which is below the cost of production, or below the competitive price level in that market.

endowment assurance A combination of life assurance and long-term saving. In return for the payment of regular premiums, the assurance company agrees to pay a fixed sum on a specified future date or on the death of the assured person.

ergonomics The scientific study of man in relation to his working environment. The results obtained are used to make changes in equipment design, working routines and working environment in order to improve efficiency.

exchange control Government regulations concerning foreign currency transactions, designed to protect the stability of the national currency. Britain abolished exchange control in 1979.

exchange rate The ratio at which one currency can be exchanged for another (e.g. 1·50 US dollars to £1). Exchange rates affect the relative cheapness or expensiveness of imports and exports and therefore influence the economy in general.

ex gratia payment A payment which is a favour or goodwill gesture and not the result of any legal obligation or contract.

feasibility study A systematic investigation of a particular project to find out if it is technically possible and if it is desirable from a financial point of view.

fixed assets Assets which will be of use to a business over a long period of time (e.g. land, buildings, equipment and trademarks).

fixed capital Items such as premises and equipment, or the money used to buy them.

fixed costs Any costs which are not affected by the level of production (e.g. rent, rates and interest repayments).

float (1) To launch a company, by drawing up various documents and sending them to the Registrar of Companies for official clearance to proceed with selling shares in the company. (2) A reserve of cash for small expenses, giving change, etc.

flow chart A diagram showing all the stages in a process and the order in which they are performed. (See also under Computing p 320).

franchise An agreement allowing someone to sell someone else's product or service, subject to certain conditions. Franchise-buyers usually have to restrict their operations to a specific area.

freeze (1) A government order that prices and/or wages are to remain at a certain level. (2) A general restriction or ban placed on some activity (e.g. the giving of bank loans or the manufacturing of weapons).

frozen asset Any asset which cannot easily be sold or converted into cash.

gearing The ratio between a company's permanent capital and the total value of loans made to it. The higher the gearing, the greater the proportion of borrowed money to 'own' money.

goodwill (1) The part of the value of a business which results from its popularity and reputation, as opposed to its capital, stock, etc. (2) The difference between the actual price paid for a business and the total value of its assets.

green pound The agreed value of the pound used to express EEC agricultural prices in sterling and to measure the level of Britain's contribution under the Common Agricultural Policy. Its value differs from that of the pound sterling.

gross national product (GNP) The total value of the goods and services produced within a country (i.e. the gross domestic product) plus the income from property held in foreign countries.

group trading When a number of traders join together (e.g. in order to improve distribution) to make bulk buying possible or to cut administration costs, this is called group trading.

hidden price increase A reduction in the quality or quantity of a product or service without any change in price.

holding company A company whose main purpose is to exercise financial control over one or more other companies by acquiring a majority shareholding in it (or them).

hyperinflation A serious economic situation in which the rate of inflation rises very rapidly and the value of money falls steeply.

inflation An economic situation in which the general level of prices increases progressively. This causes the real value of money to fall since a certain amount of money can buy fewer goods and services.

inflationary spiral A situation in which inflation diminishes the real value of money, causing employees to demand higher wages: higher wages result in increased production costs, causing higher prices and raising inflation further.

information technology (IT) Electronic, telecommunications and computer technology as applied to the gathering, recording and communicating of information.

infrastructure Things such as transport systems, power, education, etc. which are essential to the functioning of an economy or the well-being of a nation.

intangible assets Assets such as trademarks and goodwill which have no physical existence but which are of financial benefit to a company.

interim accounts Financial information about a company relating to a period which is shorter than the financial year.

invisible exports and imports The export and import of services. Foreigners holidaying in Britain, or making use of British banking, insurance, shipping services, etc. are providing the country with invisible exports. British people holidaying abroad represent invisible imports.

J-curve A small initial deterioration or decrease followed by a larger improvement or increase. This appears as a J-shaped curve on a graph.

joint and several liability The responsibility of any one member of a group for the actions or debts of any or all of the others, and the responsibility of the group as a whole for the actions or debts of any one member.

Keynesian economics J. M. Keynes was an influential British economist of the 1930s. He argued that governments should spend money to counteract business recessions, and that greater investment in industry was necessary to achieve higher levels of national income.

labour-intensive Any business activity which requires a large amount of labour relative to capital is said to be labour-intensive (e.g. hand-tailoring and repair services).

limited company A company whose shareholders enjoy limited liability. This means that if the company has debts an individual shareholder is personally liable for those debts only up to the value of his or her shareholding.

limited liability See **limited company**.

liquid assets Cash and other assets that can quickly and easily be converted into cash (e.g. shares, bank deposits).

liquidation (1) The winding-up of a company which can no longer pay its debts. (2) The paying of a debt.

liquidator The official receiver appointed by the bankrupt company or by its creditors to make a list of the company's assets and liabilities, sell the assets, pay the debts and distribute any money left over to the shareholders.

liquidity (1) The amount of cash or liquid assets a company has, which can be used to pay debts. In general, a high liquidity is a good thing. (2) A measure of the ease with which an asset can be turned into cash.

loss leader A product in a shop sold at a very low price to attract customers, in the expectation that they will also buy other products and so provide an overall profit for the retailer.

M1 A term used in describing or measuring the UK money supply. M1 equals all notes and coins in current general circulation plus all instantly-withdrawable bank deposits.

M3 M3 equals M1 plus all privately-held bank deposits plus all privately-held foreign currency bank deposits.

macroeconomics The study of economics on a large scale, for example national income, international trade, etc.

microeconomics The study of economics on a small scale, for example, the prices of individual products or the performances of individual companies or industries.

minimum lending rate The minimum rate of interest at which the Bank of England agrees to lend money to discount houses. This in turn influences the rate at which banks and building societies lend money to individuals.

minority shareholding The holding of less than 50% of a company's shares (by an individual or group). Minority shareholders have little influence on the company's policy, but they are legally protected from 'unfair' actions of the majority.

mixed economy An economy in which the ownership of the means of production is partly public (nationalised industries) and partly private (individuals and companies).

monetarism An economic policy based chiefly on the control of a country's money supply, in the belief that this is the main factor influencing the rate of inflation and economic activity.

mutual insurance company A type of insurance company in which the policy-holders are also the shareholders, profits being distributed among them by means of either cash payments or reduced premiums.

net assets The total value of assets (both fixed and current) minus the current liabilities. This figure is usually shown on balance sheets and is an important indication of the value of the company.

net price The price to be paid after taking into account any discounts or deductions.

net profit The gross profit minus all operating and selling costs.

nominal partner A person who allows his or her name to be used in association with a business (e.g. to maintain goodwill) although he or she has no financial interest in it or other connection with it.

operational research Scientific techniques (such as critical path analysis) used to study and improve problem-solving and decision-making in an organisation.

overcapacity The state of having more workers, machinery, factory space, etc. than is needed to meet the existing demand for one's product.

public limited company A company having at least two members and shares which are available to the general public (but not necessarily quoted on the Stock Exchange). It must publish its accounts and must include the words 'public limited company' (or PLC) in its name.

per pro Short for *per procurationem*, a Latin phrase meaning 'by the agency of another'. It is written (in the form **pp**) next to a signature to show that the person is signing on behalf of (and with the full authority of) another.

personal allowance The sum of money a person is allowed to earn which is not subject to income tax. The actual amount is different for married and unmarried people.

price discrimination Pricing a product at different levels for different markets. This can be made possible by the markets being far apart geographically, or by the markets being divided into separate classes of consumer.

price-fixing (1) The setting of prices by the government. (2) An agreement between two or more producers, sellers, etc. to fix the price of a product at a level which is favourable to themselves. This is usually illegal.

prices and incomes policy Government measures to restrict (or ban) wage/salary increases and price increases, in an attempt to reduce inflation and unemployment.

profit and loss account A financial statement of a company's income and spending over an accounting period. A simple profit and loss account shows total sales value minus labour, raw materials, rent and rates costs, etc. to give the trading profit.

profit-sharing An agreement under which employees receive a share of the company's profits.

profit-taking The selling-off of shares in order to profit from the original rise in price.

quango The acronym for 'quasi-autonomous non-governmental (or national government) organisation'—a body set up and funded by the government to supervise or develop activity in areas of public interest.

quid pro quo A Latin phrase meaning 'something for something'. It is used to describe a favour or concession made by one party to a business transaction in return for a previous favour or concession made by the other party.

rationalisation The reorganising of a business activity or industry in order to achieve greater efficiency and savings.

real wages The value of wages expressed not in money but in terms of the goods and services that can be bought with them.

recession A period of decline in overall economic activity, usually accompanied by an increase in unemployment.

reflation An increase in overall economic activity, brought about by the government increasing the supply of currency, reducing interest rates, etc.

registered office The official address of a company, where legal documents, etc. should be sent and where certain records are kept for public inspection.

restrictive practice (1) Any activity which is designed to prevent or curtail competition, and which is therefore against the public interest e.g. price-fixing and agreements to sell only in certain areas. (2) Used to describe certain trade-union-related practices which are felt to be against the public interest.

revaluation (1) The setting of a new value on an asset, e.g. to reflect current market prices more accurately. (2) An increase in the value of a currency as compared with other currencies.

running costs The cost of materials and labour, and anything else required for the normal operation of a machine, a company department or the company as a whole.

secured creditor A creditor who has the right to take and dispose of the assets of a debtor if the debtor fails to pay.

sequestration The removal of an organisation's assets, e.g. to protect its creditors, or while a legal dispute is being settled.

simple interest Interest which is calculated on the original amount only (ignoring any interest which has already accumulated).

sinking-fund A fund formed by regularly setting aside sums of money (which accumulate interest) in order to pay off some future debt, e.g. the replacement of assets.

sole trader A person who owns and controls his or her own business. (See also Chapter 12.1).

standard costing A system in which actual costs are compared with a series of predetermined standard costs. Any major differences between the two sets of figures can then be investigated.

statutory income The estimate of income received during a financial year, which is used to calculate the amount of tax due.

statutory returns The annual return which must be sent to the Registrar of Companies after each annual general meeting. It includes copies of accounts, lists of shareholders, details of directors, etc.

takeover Gaining control of a company by buying the majority of its shares, usually achieved by offering shareholders a figure well above the existing market price for their shares.

tangible assets Assets which have a physical existence, such as equipment and buildings.

tax loss A loss that can be set against taxable profits in order to reduce the amount of tax which has to be paid.

tender An offer to do a job, supply goods, etc. for a certain price. Contracts involving the supply of large numbers of items or the carrying-out of major pieces of work are 'put out to tender' so that various firms compete for the contract.

throughput The amount of material handled by a process or the amount of production achieved, in a specified time.

tolerance The allowable range of variation in the size of a product. It is sometimes expressed as a percentage of the 'ideal' size.

trade cycle The pattern of alternating increase and decrease in general levels of business activity. Many factors affect trade cycles and both the 'slump' and the 'boom' parts of a cycle may vary in extent and in length of time.

trading account A document giving financial information about a company's operation during a specified accounting period.

trading certificate A document issued by the Registrar of Companies which allows a company to start its business activities.

undercapitalised If a company has not enough capital and reserves for it to continue trading at the desired level, it is said to be undercapitalised.

undersubscription The situation that exists when a company wishing to issue share capital seeks applications for shares and fewer shares are applied for than are available.

undistributed profits Profits that have not been paid to shareholders but have been retained in the company (all profits made are owed to shareholders, but directors do not have to pay all the profits to them).

unearned income Income gained from investments, etc. not from working. It is sometimes taxed at a different rate from earned income.

unpresented cheques Cheques written out by an account holder and sent to suppliers or paid for services received, but not yet passed to the account holder's bank for payment.

valuation Estimating the value (in money terms) of something, especially an official estimate made for insurance purposes, etc.

valuation of investment The realisable value of investments held.

value added The difference between the cost of the materials required for some manufacturing process and the money received from the sale of the finished goods.

value-added tax (VAT) A government indirect tax on goods and services, based on the 'value added' as a result of manufacturing and marketing, etc.

variable cost A cost which varies in direct proportion to the output or activity of a business.

vertical integration A situation in which a company merges with (or takes over) another company which is involved in a different stage of producing the same product.

wage differentials The differences in the wages paid to different classes or groups of workers, e.g. to skilled and unskilled workers or to workers doing similar jobs in different industries.

warranty (1) An undertaking in a contract of sale, the breach of which might give rise to a claim for damages. (2) An undertaking, generally written, guaranteeing that goods sold are fit for use, etc., and stating the manufacturer's responsibility to repair or replace the goods should they prove faulty. (3) A declaration by an insured person that statements made by him or her to the insurers are true and that stipulated conditions have been fulfilled.

wasting asset   Any asset, especially a natural resource, whose value decreases as it is used up, and which cannot be replaced or renewed.

windfall profit   A profit arising, usually suddenly or unexpectedly, as a result of matters not directly connected with the normal business of the company or organisation concerned.

winding-up   The closing-down of a business, either voluntarily or by order of the court, with the selling-off of its assets and payments of its debts.

working capital   The capital readily available to a company for the day-to-day running of its business. It is what remains when current liabilities are deducted from current assets.

work study   The analysis of how jobs are done and the measurement of the time taken to do them, carried out in order to increase efficiency and productivity and to establish standard levels of performance. Also known as time and motion study.

yield gap   The difference between what is received in dividends from ordinary shares and the yield from fixed-interest shares.

zero-rated   A term denoting goods on which the purchaser pays no VAT and on which the seller can claim back any VAT he or she has already paid.

27.2 Computing

(See also 27.7: Word processing).

access   To gain control of a computer system or to retrieve data from a storage device (e.g. main memory) or peripheral unit (e.g. magnetic disk drive).

access time   The time taken to retrieve data or information from a storage device. Access times can vary according to the type of storage device used, e.g. access time from a magnetic disk is shorter than from magnetic tape.

acoustic coupler   A device which converts electrical pulses from a key-operated machine to sound (acoustic waves) for transmission and reception along telephone lines to and from a computer, permitting computers to be connected with a terminal by a modem and telephone handset.

address As information is entered into a computer, each place in which the information is stored has an address. That address alters as information is moved around. An address is itself a number.

ALGOL Algorithmic Orientated Language. A high level computer programming language used especially for scientific and mathematical applications.

analogue computer A type of computer in which varying electrical currents or voltages, etc. are used to represent other quantities (e.g. forces, speeds) proportionally in working out problems.

applications software A computer program or set of programs designed to carry out specific tasks (e.g. a business application, a game, word processing).

archive (1) To archive is the process of storing data files on a computer in a retrievable form (e.g. hard or floppy disk). (2) Archives are files stored on hard or floppy disk, usually data files rather than software.

ASCII American Standard Code for Information Interchange. An international standard computer code in which eight binary bits are combined to represent letters, numbers and symbols on a computer keyboard. Most VDUs and printers use this code.

assembler A computer program which converts a symbolic language program automatically into a machine language program which can then be directly executed by the computer.

assembly language A programming language in which each statement corresponds to a machine language instruction. It is usually given some form of mnemonic (e.g. BASIC, COBOL).

audio response A spoken reply from a computer, using a pre-defined limited vocabulary.

backing storage Storage media, such as magnetic disks, apart from the computer's main memory. Data and programs held in backing storage have to be transferred into the core store before use.

back-up copy A copy made of the working disk so that, in the event of accident to the working disk, all data is not lost completely.

BASIC Beginner's All-purpose Symbolic Instruction Code. A high level programming language designed for use in a number of various forms for microcomputers.

batch processing The method of processing data by computer which groups together a collection of transactions and processes them as a single unit (a batch) rather than as individual items.

baud rate A measure of the number of bits per second travelling from one part of a computer system to another, or between computers.

binary A method of counting using only two alternative values: 1 or 0, on or off.

bit An acronym for *binary digit*. The smallest unit of information used in a computer, having one of two values, 1 or 0. The CPU of a computer is often described according to the number of bits that it can process or access at one time (e.g. a 32 bit CPU).

bootstrap A method of inputting data prior to the loading of a computer program in order that the program can be loaded.

buffer (1) Memory space in a printer which stores the characters for printing. A printer with a buffer memory can perform more complex printing functions than one that will only print characters as they are fed from the computer. (2) An area where data can be temporarily stored whilst being transferred from one unit to another.

bug An error or defect in a computer system or computer program.

byte An acronym for *by eight*. The most common unit of computer storage, a byte (a group of eight bits) is equivalent to one character, symbol or two numerical digits. One byte contains enough information to represent one ASCII character.

cathode ray tube/terminal (CRT) A screen similar to a television screen which displays text from a computer. As keys are struck by the operator, letters or symbols appear on the screen.

central processing unit (CPU) The part of the computer system which co-ordinates the whole system, where all parts of the computer system are linked together and where the calculations and manipulation of data take place.

chip A single integrated circuit formed on the surface of a piece of silicon etched with tiny electronic circuits. It is between 1 and 5 cm in length and can have between 6 and 40 external connections.

COBOL Common Business Orientated Language. A high level computer programming language designed for use in business applications and the manipulation of business data, using terms which are related to ordinary English words.

code A machine language representation of a character.

cold start A complete restart of a computer following major failure or breakdown.

computer output microfilm (COM) Sometimes called computer output microfiche. Instead of producing paper output, COM systems reduce the same information to microfilm (or microfiche).

compatibility The ability of two devices, whether hardware or software, to work in conjunction, e.g. if a magnetic disk used on one computer can be read by another computer, the two computers are said to be compatible.

corruption The unintended alteration or mutilation of computer data during processing, storage or transmission.

CP/M Control Program for Microprocessors. A widely used disk operating system for microcomputers.

crash When computer hardware or software malfunctions, or when a program which is running cannot be completed or re-started, a computer system is said to have crashed.

cursor A marker on a VDU indicating the point at which text should be entered. Appearances can vary, some cursors are boxes, triangles or underlines, and some flash on and off.

data Numbers or characters which provide the building blocks for information. Data is normally deemed to be input into a computer in order that information can be output.

database An organised collection of files of information that has been systematically recorded. The files can be interconnected and form the base of an organisation's data processing system, with specific reference to information retrieval.

data processing Clerical, arithmetical and logical operations on data. In the context of information technology, data processing implies the use of a computer in its operations.

debug To test a computer program or routine and to isolate and correct errors to get rid of bugs or faults.

default The value of a variable which is used by a computer system, unless it is specifically altered by the keyboard to use another value.

density The amount of storage space on a magnetic disk.

direct access The ability to access data in a storage and retrieval system directly without having to scan any part of the storage file first. Each record's storage location is completely unconnected with any other record storage.

disk A flat circular medium used for magnetic backing storage of information and programs. A disk is divided into recording tracks and sub-divided into sectors.

disk capacity The amount of storage space on a disk.

disk drive An electro-mechanical device which houses a magnetic disk effecting necessary movement and writing to or reading from the disk.

disk operating system (DOS) Software that manages the storage and retrieval of information on disk and controls the operation of all activities relating to the use of magnetic disks in a computer system.

dot matrix printer A printer capable of producing work at high speed which uses a series of electrically hammered moving pins to create characters made up of a pattern of dots. Printed output material is not considered to be of letter quality.

double density disk   A magnetic disk with twice the storage capacity of a standard disk of the same dimension.

down   In computing terms, a system is said to be down when it is not operating.

download   The transference of data or programs from one computer to another, e.g. from a mainframe to a microcomputer.

downtime   A period when computer equipment is not operating because of malfunction, maintenance, etc.

dump   The transfer of data from one computer storage area to another or, more usually, to output.

dumping   The copying of contents of a storage area onto another medium usually for the purpose of security or checking.

external storage   Any storage medium which is portable (e.g. magnetic disks).

facsimile transmission   (See p 223).

field   A section of a computer record designated for the storage of specific information. A fixed field has a defined, unvarying length, whereas a variable field can be assigned different length values.

fifth generation computer   The coming generation of computers with greatly increased processing power which facilitates the running of user-friendly artificial intelligence software.

file   An organised and structured collection of information recorded as a unit with an identifying name.

fixed head   Read/write heads in a CPU or disk drive which are kept stationary.

fixed head disk   A disk memory with one read/write head for track on the disk.

floppy disk   A thin disk made of a flexible material with one or both sides coated to accept magnetic recording, usually either 5¼ inches or 8 inches in diameter. Also known as a **magnetic disk**.

flowchart   A graphical representation showing the sequence of events and choices which need to be made in the solution of a problem, using symbolic shapes and usually, although not exclusively, relating to a computer program.

flowcharting   A method of representing a series of events with lines which represent inter-connection and symbols which represent events or processes. Systems flowcharts represent the relationship between events in a data processing system. Program flowcharts show the logical components of a computer program.

foreground   A facility of some computers whereby high priority tasks can be carried out whilst those of low priority are also being carried out in the background.

format (1) To format is to arrange data or text according to specific instructions. (2) An arrangement of data, which may refer to the layout of a printed document, the order of instructions in a program or the arrangement of data in a computer file.

formula A term used in spreadsheet software. If several columns of figures have to be totalled, or a percentage of each calculated, a formula can be set up to do this and then run.

FORTRAN Formula Translator. A high level computer programming language used specifically for scientific, technical or mathematical applications.

fourth generation computers The majority of contemporary computers.

hard copy Permanent output from a computer and usually synonymous with print on paper.

hard disk A magnetic disk hermetically sealed to prevent contamination by dust and moisture offering large storage capacity and used for the bulk storage of computer data.

hard sectoring The marking of sector boundaries on a magnetic disk by the punching of holes in the disk. All available space can be used for data storage.

hardware The magnetic, electrical, mechanical and electronic components which make up a computer.

hash Data which is nonsense.

head A device which reads and records or erases information on a computer storage medium.

hexidecimal code A data code which uses the base 16 as compared with base 2 for binary code and base 10 for decimal code.

high level language A computer programming language which allows a user to employ instructions close to his/her own familiar language rather than machine code. The higher the level of the language, the nearer the language is to English language.

high resolution The fineness of detail distinguishable in an image and often referred to the screen of a VDU.

icon An image on the screen of an advanced microcomputer resembling a familiar office object (e.g. document, tray) and representing a work area in the computer. The work area is accessed by moving the cursor to the icon and then pressing a key to call up that work area.

image printer Using optical technology, a printer which will compose an image of a complete page from digital input, the final copy being produced as print on paper.

immediate access store   A storage area in a computer into which information can be written and from which it can be instantly read no matter where it is in the store.

incompatibility   If a program capable of running on one computer cannot be run on another computer, the software is said to be incompatible.

input   The putting in of information to a computer by an operator from a keyboard and therefore being information received by a computer.

input device   A piece of equipment which allows data and instructions to be entered into a computer's memory (e.g. keyboard, terminal, light pen, MICR, OCR).

integrated   In reference to computer packages, sometimes called a suite, the linking together of a database, spreadsheet, word processing and graphics which can interact actively.

integrated circuit   See **chip**.

intelligent terminal   A terminal which has some processing or computing capabilities independent from the computer it is connected to.

interface   The connecting link between two parts of a computer system, e.g. the cable that runs between a word processing terminal and its disk drive.

internal storage   The internal **read only memory** of a computer where programs and data are stored.

joystick   A device in the form of a unit with a small stick which moves the cursor on a VDU.

laser disk   A form of video used to access information held on a disk rather than on a tape. The disk is read by decoding patterns produced by a laser light reflected off the disk's surface.

laser printer   A printer using a laser light source to write on paper which is then passed through an ink powder. Ink is attracted to the area on the paper which has been written on and excess powder is removed. The ink is then fixed by chemical treatment or heat.

liquid crystal display (LCD)   Liquid crystals can be switched from an opaque to a transparent state when interposed between a light source and an observer. LCD is often used on calculators.

load   To enter information or a program into a computer from a storage device.

log on/off   To initiate or terminate on-line interaction with a computer.

loop   A series of instructions within a computer program which are performed continuously until a condition which has been pre-determined is met, when the computer will exit from the loop and carry on with the next instruction in the original program.

low level language   A computer language which is very close to the computer's own machine code. Each low level language instruction has its own direct machine code equivalent.

machine code   A binary code used in machine language for a machine's basic instructions which are directly acceptable to the CPU of a computer system.

machine language   A language used by a computer for internal communications with its related parts and the language in which a computer performs arithmetic and editing functions.

macro code   An instructional code capable of generating several machine instructions. Also known as macro.

magnetic card   A piece of cardboard or plastic with a magnetisable surface on which data can be recorded.

magnetic disk   See **floppy disk**.

mainframe   The CPU of a large computer installation with many terminals attached and distinguishing the computer from a minicomputer or microcomputer.

megabyte   1048576 bytes, frequently referred to as one million bytes and used to measure storage capacity of a computer or CPU.

memory   A device in the CPU of a computer which can store information for extraction by the computer when required. Memory is measured in **bytes**.

microcomputer   A category for the smallest computers which uses a microprocessor as its processing element, having sufficient peripherals and memory to link with the outside world and store information.

microprocessor   Sometimes a synonym for microcomputer but more correctly the central processor in which all elements of a control unit are contained on a single chip.

minicomputer   A medium-sized computer, smaller than mainframe but larger than micro, with either general or specialised usage including process control, often used by a medium sized company to keep records, payroll, stock, etc.

modem   An acronym for *modulator/demodulator*. A device for converting a digital signal from a computer into an analogue signal which can then be transmitted along a standard telephone line.

mouse   A device which can be rolled across the surface of a graphics table. When a button on the mouse is depressed, the computer will address the item in the mouse position. Commonly used with **icons**.

MS DOS A commercial name for a **disk operating system**.

network A computer system where a number of components at a physical distance from each other can be interconnected by telecommunications channels.

off-line A terminal or other computer component not connected to or controlled by a CPU.

on-line A terminal or other component directly connected to the CPU in a computer system and which will interact directly with the central processor.

operating system A collection of programs contained in a computer used to control the sequencing of processing of other programs from the operation of various input and output devices.

optical character recognition (OCR) A technique in which information in the form of characters, numbers or symbols is read by an optical scanning device, or optical character reader, which converts the information into computer readable form.

PASCAL Program Appliqué à la Sélection et la Compilation Automatique de la Littérature. A large multi-disciplinary database compiled by the French Centre Nationale de la Recherche Scientifique. Sometimes referred to as a high level language used for general programming work.

peripheral Any unit of a computer (e.g. disk drive, joystick, light pen, card reader, magnetic tape unit, printer) which connects in different ways to the central processor and memory and which forms input and output devices.

program A set of instructions which a computer carries out in sequence enabling the computer to operate and carry out specific tasks.

programming language The language in which coded instructions are written for a computer.

random access memory (RAM) Memory into which information can be written and from which it may read in a random access fashion. The size of a computer's random access memory is a measure of the computer's power.

read The copying of information from a storage medium, or the electronic retrieval of information.

read only A term used in reference to memory and magnetic disks. If a disk has been write protected, its contents can be read but nothing can be written to it. This facility provides a safeguard against the accidental erasure of data, information and programs stored on a disk.

read only memory (ROM) A store of memory from which

information can only be read or copied. Usually it is a permanent store holding software which is permanently or firmly in place. Sometimes referred to as firmware.

real time A computer system is said to be operating in real time if the system operates synchronously, responding to a request from a terminal and the processing of information which is fed in takes place straightaway.

retrieval The way in which a computer searches for particular files or parts of files in response to a request from a user and loads those files to the cursor or screen.

sequential access The storage and retrieval of records and information which has been recorded in sequence (e.g. on magnetic tape). Information to be accessed is searched for in an order of start to finish, until the required text is encountered. Also known as serial access.

sequential storage The storage of records in an order where the next available space after the storage of the previous record is used.

serial The travelling of electrical patterns of bits down a wire to a computer, one after the other. Often referred to as serial bit stream.

serial interface An interface in which access time involves a waiting time where serial bit transmission is used.

serial storage Storage on a magnetic device in which words appear in sequence often inferring that access time will include a waiting time.

shared facility A computer system in which several pieces of equipment use the same facility (e.g. a disk drive, a printer). Also known as shared resource.

shared logic A computer system consisting of work stations made up of keyboards and VDUs which are connected to a CPU, usually with a hard disk. The terminals operate under central control.

soft copy Computer output on a medium which cannot be read by an observer e.g. floppy disk or computer output as displayed on the screen of a VDU.

software A generic term for programs, operating systems, packages and compilers which are used to direct the operations of a computer or other hardware and which can be run on computer hardware, consisting of patterns of binary information.

speech generation The production of human speech by a computer using a limited vocabulary where often the computer can read back the information given to it.

split screen The displaying of more than one image on the screen of a VDU. Areas of the screen are referred to as 'windows'.

spreadsheet An application program which provides a matrix into which data can be entered and manipulated and intended for use in forecasting and financial planning.

storage   Another word for memory in a computer system, or the medium on which information can be stored.

system   An organised set of computer components which interact to allow the processing of data.

systems analyst   A person trained in the investigation, analysis and design of computer systems (often for business applications) who can provide solutions to the most effective way of processing data.

systems analysis   The task of analysing computer systems and determining how a computer system can be made more efficient (normally used for business applications).

systems software   Software used to run the operating system of a computer. Also known as operating software.

tape   An input or output storage device for a computer. There are two kinds of tape: paper and magnetic.

terminal   A peripheral device consisting of a keyboard and screen, linked to a computer used to input data and receive output from the computer, or for sending and receiving data over a communications channel.

time sharing   A computer system that allows many terminals or users to concurrently share a central computer, each user having the impression that he or she has the sole use of the computer.

touch screen   A terminal with a screen which is sensitive to the touch of the user. Positions touched usually using a finger or a light pen are recorded by the computer as a signal allowing data to be input or a command to be followed.

variable   (See under Word Processing p 366).

visual display unit (VDU)   A cathode ray tube on which the output of a computer can be displayed.

Winchester disk   A form of backing storage for a computer consisting of a magnetic disk in an hermetically sealed container which is very powerful. Sometimes referred to as a rigid or **hard disk**.

window   A feature of some advanced microcomputer systems in which the VDU screen is split into sections, called 'windows', enabling the operation of different sections of the memory to be seen at the same time.

working disk   A back-up copy of a disk is made and stored in a safe place and the original disk becomes the working disk, i.e. the disk which is being worked on at the present time. If for any reason the working disk is damaged, the back-up disk can be used to make another working copy.

27.3 Legal

abstract of title A summary of the title deeds and documents for unregistered land.

accessory One who aids or participates in a crime, but not as principal.

act of bankruptcy The action of a creditor which allows a debtor to present a bankruptcy petition to the court.

actus reus The guilty act as part of a criminal offence. Compare with **mens rea**.

ancient lights The right to light of windows which have enjoyed twenty years of unobstructed access to light, binding the owner of an adjacent property against building or planting so as to obstruct the light.

arbitration The settling of a dispute by a person or group agreed upon by the opposing parties in order to obtain a decision which is equitable.

artificial person An entity, such as a registered company or society, which is seen in the eyes of the law as a person, as opposed to a natural person i.e. an individual.

adjudication The act of a court in pronouncing judgment.

administrator One empowered by a court to take charge of the personal estate of a deceased person, in default of an executor.

affiliation order An order of a magistrates court requiring the alleged father of an illegitimate child to make payments to maintain the child.

age of consent The age at which a person is legally competent to give consent to certain acts, in particular marriage and sexual intercourse.

airspace The part of the atmosphere above a piece of land which in English and international law belongs to the owner of the land.

appellant A person who appeals to a higher tribunal or court for a previous decision to be changed.

arrestable offence (1) A criminal offence for which there is a mandatory fixed penalty. (2) A criminal offence carrying a prison sentence of at least five years for a first offender. A warrant is not necessary for arrest.

assignment The legal transfer for assigning of rights; the writing by which a transfer is made.

attest To testify or bear witness to; to affirm by signature or oath; to give proof of.

bankruptcy The state of one whom the court has adjudged insolvent and whose affairs are compulsorily administered in order to distribute any assets among the creditors.

beneficial owner   One entitled to the use of land or income from the land.

battery   An attack using force against a person, e.g. beating, wounding, or, irrespective of causing harm, threatening by touching clothes or body.

bona fide   Evidence of good faith.

bond   A written obligation to pay a sum or to perform a contract.

bylaw   (1) The law of a local authority or private corporation. (2) A supplementary law or an inferred regulation.

care order   A court order which entitles a local authority to care for a child in spite of claims made by a parent or guardian.

casus belli   (1) An occurrence which gives rise to war. (2) Grounds for a quarrel.

caveat   A warning; a notice given by an interested party in a case so as to halt proceedings until the party is given a hearing.

chattel   Any kind of property which is not freehold.

circumstantial evidence   Evidence of circumstances providing indirect or inferential evidence of a fact but not direct proof of it.

civil action   A court case which is not a criminal prosecution; a case brought by a person or party against another party for an alleged wrong in order to obtain compensation.

cohabit   To live together as if husband and wife.

collateral security   An additional and separate security for repayment of money borrowed.

collusion   A secret agreement to deceive, especially one made between parties apparently in conflict in a lawsuit.

committal   The act of sending a person to court or to prison, usually temporarily.

common law   The unwritten law of England which is embodied in reported cases and commentaries and administered by the royal courts.

common law marriage   A marriage recognised as such by long association and repute, not by a marriage ceremony.

completion   In conveyancing, the final stage in the sale of a property, when ownership is transferred from the seller to the purchaser.

commute   To convert into a lighter penalty, as in the commutation of a sentence.

concurrent sentences   Prison sentences for two or more offences which are served simultaneously, not consecutively.

consecutive sentences   Prison sentences for two or more offences which are served one after another, not concurrently.

consideration A thing given or done or abstained from by one person in agreement with another, in exchange for that other person giving, doing or abstaining from something. It is an essential element in making an agreement legally binding, e.g. a contract.

contempt of court (1) In criminal law, conduct obstructing or tending to obstruct the administration of justice. (2) In civil law, disobedience of an order of court, or breach of an undertaking given to the court.

contract A legally binding agreement between two or more parties.

conveyancing The transference of property from the seller to the purchaser.

copyright The sole right to reproduce a literary, dramatic, musical, or artistic work—also to perform, translate, film or record such a work.

corroboration Oral or written evidence given in court which confirms other evidence given.

coverture The condition of a married woman as legally deemed under the protection of her husband.

debenture A written acknowledgment of a debt; the form in which loans are made to companies.

decree absolute In divorce, a decree which terminates a marriage and which takes effect immediately.

decree nisi In divorce, a conditional decree which becomes a **decree absolute** unless cause be shown to the contrary.

deed of covenant (See under Business p 308).

deed poll A deed executed by one party, especially one by which a person changes his or her name.

de facto Actual, if not rightful.

de jure By right, legally.

dies non A day on which judges do not sit, or one on which normal business is not transacted.

domicile A person's legally recognised place of residence.

easement The right to use something, particularly land, not one's own, or to prevent its owner from making an inconvenient use of it.

ejection (1) Expulsion of a possessor from his or her property, resulting in an action of ejection to recover it. (2) An action to remove persons illegally occupying property.

encumbrance (1) A debt secured over land. (2) A legal claim on an estate.

estoppel A conclusive admission which cannot be denied by the party whom it affects.

exchange of contracts In conveyancing, the point at which the purchaser and the vendor exchange signed identical copies of the sale of contract, making the sale legally binding.

execution (1) The carrying out by a law officer of e.g. a citation or contract. (2) The carrying out of a criminal sentence. (3) The authentication of a deed.

fee simple Unconditional inheritance or ownership of land.

fee tail An estate which may descend only to the direct heirs of the owner and cannot be disposed of by the immediate possessor.

femme sole An unmarried woman (spinster, widow or divorcée).

foreclosure The process by which a mortgagor, failing to repay the money lent on the security of an estate, is compelled to forfeit his right to redeem the estate.

freehold The right to hold property or land free of duty.

garnishee A person warned not to pay money owed to his or her direct creditor because the latter is indebted to the **garnisher** (who gives the warning).

'gazump' To raise the price of property after accepting an offer from a buyer but before the contract has been signed.

ground rent Rent paid to a landlord for the use of the ground for a specified term, usually ninety-nine years.

habeus corpus A writ requiring a jailer to produce a prisoner in person and to state the reasons for his or her detention.

hearsay evidence Evidence given by a witness based on the oral statements of someone else and not on his or her own knowledge.

hereditament Any property that may pass to an heir.

hire purchase agreement A credit agreement in which a hired article becomes the property of the hirer after a stipulated number of payments.

in camera Court proceedings conducted in the judge's private chambers, not in open court.

incorporation The formation of a company or other association which has a personality distinct from its members.

indictable offence An offence that could be tried on indictment in the Crown Court.

indictment The written accusation against one who is to be tried by jury.

injunction A writ by which a court stops or prevents some unfair or illegal act being done.

in loco parentis A term describing the role of a guardian or custodian who cares for children on behalf of their parents.

interlocutory Describing an intermediate stage before a final decision, e.g. interlocutory injunction, interlocutory proceedings, i.e. occurring at a hearing before the full court trial takes place.

intestate Without having made a valid will.

jointly and severally Describing two or more persons legally associated in obligation or ownership.

joint tenancy Property held by two or more persons as joint tenants.

laches Negligence or undue delay by a plaintiff in bringing an action to court to enforce his or her equitable right.

leading question A question so put as to suggest the desired answer, allowed only in cross-examination.

leasehold A tenure in land or property on a lease, for a fixed term.

letters of administration The authority granted to a person to administer or distribute the personal estate of a deceased person, in default of an executor.

libel A defamatory and untrue publication or statement in permanent form, such as print or film.

lien A right to retain possession of another's property until he or she pays a debt.

liquidation The process of dissolving a company. It can be initiated by members or creditors of the company, or by a court order.

litigant A person engaged in a lawsuit.

litigation The action of carrying on a lawsuit.

lump sum award Damages paid as a single sum of money and not in several smaller amounts.

maintenance In divorce, payment made either in a lump sum or in instalments to support children or the other spouse.

malfeasance An illegal deed, especially of an official.

mandamus A writ or command issued by a higher court to a lower.

mandate A right given to a person to act in the name of another.

manslaughter Unlawful homicide without intent or with mitigating circumstances.

mens rea The criminal intention that a defendant must be proved to have had when committing a crime if he or she is to be convicted.

misfeasance The negligent or improper performance of a lawful act.

mitigation Lessening the severity of a penalty or the seriousness of the offence.

mortgagee One to whom a mortgage is made or given.

mortgagor One who mortgages his or her property.

naturalise To grant the privileges of natural-born citizens to an alien.

negotiable instruments Documents which can be transferred from one person to another upon endorsement, e.g. cheques, promissory notes, bills of exchange.

next friend The person appointed to act in a legal action for a minor or a mental health patient.

notary public An officer, usually a solicitor, authorised to certify deeds, contracts, copies of documents, affidavits, etc.

obiter dictum A remark made by a judge in giving judgment which is not of central importance to the case but may be used in the future as persuasive authority.

patent (letters patent) An official document conferring an exclusive right or privilege, such as the sole right for a term of years to the proceeds of an invention.

peppercorn rent A trivial or nominal rent which by agreement the tenant does not pay to a landlord but which preserves the legal title of the landlord.

perjury The breaking of an oath; the crime committed by one who, when giving evidence on oath or affirmation as a witness in a court of justice, gives evidence which he or she knows to be false.

petition A written application to a court for some judicial action.

power of attorney A power given to one person by another to act on his or her behalf.

precedent A previous judicial instance or proceeding that is used as an authority for making the same decision in later cases.

prima facie Describing evidence sufficient to support the bringing of a charge, or a case supported by such evidence.

pro indiviso Describing rights which two or more persons hold in common.

pro rata Proportionately.

promissory note A written promise to pay a sum of money on some future day or on demand.

promoter One who takes part in the setting up of a new company.

putative Reputed, commonly supposed to be, e.g. as applied to a marriage supposed invalid by canon law but entered into in good faith by at least one of the parties, or to the alleged father of an illegitimate child.

quasi contract An implied contract.

quid pro quo Something done in exchange for something else.

receivership The state of a bankrupt company or of property which is the subject of litigation when a court has appointed a receiver to administer the affairs of the company or property.

recognisance A legal obligation entered into before a magistrate to do, or not to do, some particular act; money pledged for the performance of such an obligation.

respondent A defendant, especially in a divorce suit.

salvage (money) Compensation, usually assessed by the court, which is made to persons other than the ship's company for preserving a ship or cargo from danger of loss.

search The examination of records and registers to find encumbrances affecting title to property.

sequestration A writ allowing a court to seize control of a person's property.

sine die Without a day having been appointed,—pertaining to a meeting or other business indefinitely adjourned.

slander Injurious defamation by spoken words or by looks, signs or gestures.

statute law Law in the form of statutes, i.e. (in Britain) contained in the Acts of Parliament.

sue To take legal action, e.g. instituting a suit or making a claim.

summary offence An offence that must be tried before magistrates.

suspended sentence A sentence not served unless another crime is committed.

testator One who leaves a will.

title deeds Documents proving ownership of land and the terms of ownership.

tort Any wrong, not arising out of contract, for which there is a remedy by compensation or damages.

treasure trove Ownerless objects of intrinsic or historical value found hidden, which are the property of the Crown (in England, gold and silver only).

undischarged bankrupt A bankrupt who has not been given an order of discharge by the court and who is thus liable to certain restrictions and disqualifications.

venue (1) The county where a crime is alleged to have been committed. (2) The place where the cause is tried.

waiver A written statement formally indicating the abandonment or resignation of legal rights.

ward of court A minor in the care of a guardian who has been appointed by the court or the parents.

wardship The jurisdiction of the High Court to make a minor a ward of court.

warranty An undertaking in a contract which is additional to the main purpose of the contract, breach of which may lead to a claim for damages.

wasting assets Property in the estate of a deceased person which is declining in value and which cannot be replaced or renewed.

without prejudice A disclaimer used in correspondence and other documents indicating that if settlement of a case is not reached, the statements it relates to cannot be used as evidence without the agreement of both parties.

27.4 Medical

abrasion An injury in which the surface of the skin or lining of a part of the body has been lost or scraped off.

abscess A collection of pus in a cavity formed by the destruction of normal body tissue.

Achilles tendon A large tendon, which can be felt in the lower part of the back of the calf, and which runs down to the heel bone.

acne A common skin condition affecting in particular the face, back and chest, and consisting of small pus-filled boils and blackheads.

acupuncture The insertion of fine needles into particular parts of the body for the treatment of disease or the relief of pain.

adenoids Glandular tissue at the back of the nose, which is normally large in children and may cause breathing and hearing problems. Adenoids normally shrink as the child gets older.

adrenalin A hormone, the release of which is stimulated by factors such as emotion, pain and stress. The effect of adrenalin is to cause the heart's output to increase and blood to be redirected to tissues whose requirements are high in times of stress.

agoraphobia A fear of being in a large open space.

AIDS An illness caused by a virus which destroys the body's immune system. Thus infections and certain tumours can no longer be dealt with by the body and can overwhelm the patient, causing death. It is spread by sexual intercourse and by contact with infected blood, e.g. through the sharing of needles by drug addicts. Many carriers of the virus have not yet developed signs of the illness.

allergy A condition in which a substance causes symptoms in a susceptible individual not normally caused in the majority of people (e.g. skin rashes, diarrhoea, asthma).

amniocentesis A test performed to detect possible abnormalities in an unborn baby, in which a sample of the fluid surrounding the baby in the womb is removed through a needle inserted into the mother's abdomen.

anaemia A low level of haemoglobin in the blood due to deficiency of iron or vitamins.

analgesic A drug which relieves pain.

angina Pain felt usually in the chest on exertion or in response to emotion, caused by narrowing or blockage of one or more of the blood vessels which supply the heart.

anorexia nervosa A serious condition especially common in adolescent and young women in which loss of appetite and aversion to eating leads to marked weight loss. Emotional factors are thought to play a part in the development of this condition.

antibody A substance produced by the body as a defence against e.g. infection by a bacteria or virus, enabling the body to fight the infection.

antibiotic A drug which will destroy or inhibit the growth of bacteria and certain other micro-organisms which cause infectious disease.

arthritis Inflammation in one or many joints causing pain and restriction of movement.

asbestosis An incurable lung disease caused by inhaling asbestos particles.

asthma A breathing disorder in which the bronchial tubes are intermittently narrowed, causing breathlessness and a wheezing noise as air is expired through the narrowed tubes.

atherosclerosis Fatty deposits in the walls and the inside of blood vessels leading to hardening of arteries and their narrowing and blockage, thereby reducing blood supply to tissues.

athlete's foot A fungus infection of the skin of the feet, occurring especially between the toes and leading to redness, itching, soreness and cracking.

bacteria Micro-organisms which may be free-living or parasitic and which may or may not cause disease.

biopsy The removal of a piece of tissue for microscopic examination and subsequent diagnosis.

blood group This refers to hereditary differences in red blood cells and is important when blood transfusion is required; blood given to an individual must have red blood cells of that individual's group or a serious reaction will occur.

blood pressure The pressure of blood flow in the arteries consisting of two readings; one taken when the heart is contracting (systolic) and one taken when the heart is relaxed (diastolic).

bronchitis Inflammation in the bronchial tubes due to irritation from such agents as smoke or infection.

bulimia Compulsive eating of excessive quantities of food in response to emotional factors. Self-induced vomiting may occur.

cancer Excessive growth of abnormal cells which multiply more quickly than normal body cells, causing destruction of surrounding tissue and spreading to other parts of the body.

carcinogen A substance which causes cancer.

carcinoma A type of cancer arising in the surface layers of an organ or tissue.

cardiac Pertaining to the heart.

catheter A hollow tube, e.g. a urinary catheter which is a flexible tube passed from the outside into the bladder, allowing urine to be removed when a patient is unable to initiate or control urination.

cerebro-vascular accident A condition in which blood supply to an area of the brain is interrupted by a haemorrhage or arterial blockage, causing paralysis, loss of sensation or other symptoms, depending on the part of the brain affected. Also called a stroke.

chemotherapy Treatment of disease with drugs.

cerebral Pertaining to the brain.

cervical smear test A screening test for cancer of the cervix or neck of the womb, performed by examining under the microscope cells obtained from the cervix in a vaginal examination. The test picks up cell changes which may in time lead to cancer development at a treatable stage.

chiropractor A practitioner who believes that disease is caused by abnormalities of nerves and who is skilled in manipulation, in particular of the spine, in order to restore the normal function of nerves.

cholesterol A fat-like substance found in animal fats, oils and egg yolks. Raised levels in the blood are associated with atherosclerosis.

chromosomes Rod-shaped structures, 46 of which occur in the nuclei of all cells of the human body, 23 being passed on from each parent. Chromosomes carry on them the genes or hereditary factors which determine the characteristics of the person.

colic A strong involuntary contraction of the muscle of the bowel or of an abdominal organ which causes severe pain to be felt.

colostomy A surgical procedure in which the rectum and anus, which have been affected by disease, are bypassed and a new opening of the colon is created on the surface of the abdomen through which excrement is passed.

congenital Present at birth.

claustrophobia A fear of being shut up in a confined space.

coma A deeply unconscious state.

coronary thrombosis A 'heart attack' in which one or more arteries to the heart become blocked, causing loss of blood supply and therefore loss of oxygen to the heart muscles' supply by the artery. If the area involved is extensive, the heart will be unable to function and death will result. Lesser degrees of damage will heal.

cyst A bag-like structure containing fluid or semi-solid material.

delirium A state of diminished awareness in which a patient may be confused, restless, and may experience hallucinations or illusions.

dementia A condition in which intellectual functions such as memory, ability to learn new things, awareness of time, surroundings and people are gradually and irreversibly lost and deterioration of personality and behaviour occurs.

dermatitis Inflammation of the skin in response to irritation.

diabetes A disease, caused by lack of the hormone insulin, in which the level of glucose in the blood is abnormally high, causing symptoms ranging from increased thirst and passing more urine to coma and death.

dialysis A method by which waste products from protein breakdown can be removed from the blood when the kidneys, which normally perform this function, have failed.

dyslexia Impaired ability to read owing to malfunction in that part of the brain concerned with understanding the written word.

dysmenorrhoea Cramping pain in the lower abdomen felt at the time of mentrual periods.

ectopic pregnancy A pregnancy in which the fertilised egg becomes implanted somewhere other than the womb (often in the Fallopian tube).

embolism A condition in which a solid particle or air bubble becomes lodged in an artery, causing interruption of blood flow.

emphysema A condition in which there is increase in size of the smallest airways in the lungs, causing transfer of oxygen from the lungs to the bloodstream to be less efficient. The term also describes the presence of air in the tissues caused by, e.g. a penetrating chest wound.

epidural An injection of local anaesthetic into the lower spine causing loss of painful sensation in the lower part of the body, thus making it possible to perform surgery without a general anaesthetic.

epilepsy A disturbance in the brain caused by abnormal electrical activity and leading to 'fits' in which there may be symptoms such as loss of consciousness, jerking of limbs, and unusual sensations.

fibrositis Pain and stiffness of muscles and soft tissues usually of the neck, shoulders and trunk; of uncertain cause.

fracture A break, usually of a bone. A green-stick fracture is an incomplete break which occurs only in children.

gangrene The death of tissues of the body due to inadequate blood supply.

gastric Pertaining to the stomach.

gastro-enteritis An infection of the gastro-intestinal tract from the stomach downwards, causing vomiting, diarrhoea and abdominal pain.

glandular fever   A disease particularly affecting young adults due to a virus infection, leading to enlargement of the lymph glands and a large variety of symptoms including sore throat and extreme tiredness.

haemoglobin   The iron-containing part of the red blood cell which combines with oxygen.

haemophilia   A hereditary condition, almost always affecting males, in which a factor essential for blood clotting is present in a concentration lower than normal, and leading to excessive bleeding from minor injuries.

haemorrhoids   Dilated veins around the anus. Also known as piles.

hepatitis   Inflammation of the liver often caused by virus infection or excessive alcohol consumption. It may or may not be accompanied by jaundice.

hernia   The abnormal protrusion of an organ or part of it through an opening in surrounding structures. Hernias are often noticed as a lump in the groin, where the abdominal cavity lining, containing intestine, may protrude through the abdominal muscle.

herpes   A variety of virus which often infects the skin or nerves, causing a rash with characteristic blisters. It may affect the face (cold sores), the genitals (genital herpes), or cause shingles elsewhere on the body.

homeopathy   The treatment of disease with minute amounts of substances which themselves cause the symptoms which characterise the disease.

hormones   Chemical substances produced in the body which regulate the function of certain tissues and organs.

hypertension   Raised blood pressure.

hysterectomy   Surgical removal of the uterus or womb.

ileostomy   A surgical procedure in which the colon, rectum and anus are bypassed because of disease and an opening of the ileum or small bowel is created on the surface of the abdomen, through which excrement is passed.

immunity   A state of being not susceptible to an infection, usually because a past infection has stimulated production by the body of antibodies which remain and destroy the infecting organisms if they are encountered again.

inflammation   The response of tissues or organs to injury or infection, characterised by redness, swelling, pain and heat.

jaundice   A yellow appearance of the skin and whites of the eyes which occurs in liver-disease or where there is obstruction to the outflow of bile from the liver.

leukaemia A variety of cancer affecting the blood, in which there is production of large numbers of abnormal white blood cells at the expense of red cells and platelets (which help blood-clotting). Characteristic symptoms are bleeding, anaemias and susceptibility to infections.

lumbago Low back pain from any cause.

lymph Fluid found in the lymphatic vessels (which run alongside blood vessels), the function of which is to fight infections and develop immunity to them.

malignant A term used to describe cancer which, untreated, is likely to progress and result in death.

mastectomy Surgical removal of the breast as part of treatment for breast cancer.

meningitis An infection of the *meninges*, the tissue covering the brain and spinal cord.

menopause The cessation of menstrual periods occurring around the age of 45-50. Also called the 'change of life'.

metabolism The chemical changes which occur in the body in order to maintain life, involving the conversion of food to energy and the breakdown and repair of tissues.

metastatic A term describing the spread, usually of cancer, from the source to other areas of the body.

micro-organism A minute living organism, usually too small to be seen with the naked eye (e.g. bacterium, virus, fungus or yeast).

migraine A throbbing headache, often on one side of the head, thought to be caused by dilation of cerebral arteries, sometimes associated with other symptoms, such as disturbance of vision or sensation and vomiting.

Mongol A person with what is now usually known as Down's Syndrome, in which an extra chromosome is present in body cells. The syndrome is characterised by a typical appearance, mental retardation and other congenital abnormalities.

multiple sclerosis A disease of the nervous system which may cause abnormalities of sensation, movement and co-ordination, and eyesight problems, all of which may be temporary in the initial stages but are subject to variable and progressive deterioration over the years.

muscular dystrophy A disease which is usually inherited and which causes wasting of muscles and progressive weakness.

narcotic A drug which induces very deep sleep to the point of unconsciousness.

neurosis A disorder of the mind usually caused by stress and anxiety in the patient's environment and characterised by severe and persistent anxiety.

osteopath A practitioner who attributes disease to disorder of the skeletal system and who applies suitable manipulation with the aim of correcting it.

pacemaker A battery-operated electrical device which is inserted into the body to stimulate the heart to beat in the presence of disease which has caused abnormal slowing of the heart.

paranoid Having an unreasonable belief that people wish or are doing harm to one.

paraplegia Paralysis of the legs and lower part of the body affecting movement and sensation and usually also leading to inability to urinate and defecate.

Parkinson's disease A disorder of the nervous system due to damage to the brain caused by, e.g. atheroscelerosis, infections or drugs. Characterised by muscular stiffness and rigidity and bodily shaking.

pertussis Whooping cough.

phlebitis The inflammation of a vein, usually just under the skin.

placebo A harmless and inactive substance given instead of a real drug; a dummy tablet which may work in the same way as an active tablet where a patient believes it will do so.

pleurisy Infection or inflammation of the surface coating of the lungs.

pneumonia Infection or inflammation of the lung tissues.

prognosis The likely outcome of an illness.

prolapse A falling down or out of place; a term often used of the womb, where pelvic muscles have become weak and no longer hold it up; it may therefore come down and be felt as a lump in the genital region. Also used of an inter-vertebral disc; a slipped disc is also called a prolapsed disc.

prophylaxis Preventative measure against disease.

psoriasis A skin disease characterised by redness and scaling of skin.

psychopath A person with an antisocial personality, unconcerned about the effect of his or her actions on others.

psychosis Serious mental illness, due to disturbance within the brain, in which the patient loses touch with reality and may have abnormal beliefs and hallucinations.

psychosomatic A term used to describe illnesses in which emotional factors produce physical symptoms.

quadriplegia Paralysis of all four limbs.

radiotherapy Treatment of disease, often cancer, by X-rays and other forms of radiation.

renal Pertaining to the kidney.

rubella German measles.

scarlet fever An infectious disease caused by a bacterium, the streptococcus, and consisting of a sore throat and a rash. It has become less common since the advent of penicillin treatment and nowadays is easily treatable.

schizophrenia A serious mental illness, of unknown cause, which leads to a variety of symptoms including disintegration of the personality, abnormal beliefs, hallucinations and paranoia.

sciatica Pain felt in the buttock and back of the leg caused by pressure on the sciatic nerve, often from a slipped disc in the lower spine.

senility A term describing changes occurring in old age, often referring to **dementia.**

shingles A common disease caused by the herpes virus, the symptoms of which are pain and a blistering skin rash in a confined area on one side of the body, the area being that supplied by a particular nerve in which the virus has lain dormant.

spina bifida A congenital abnormality in which the normal uniting into a tube of the spinal bones in the foetus does not occur throughout the length of the spine. The spinal cord may be exposed and damaged.

spastic A term used to describe involuntary muscular rigidity.

steroids Chemicals naturally occurring in the body, of which there are a wide variety including hormones and cholesterol. Artificially produced as drugs, they have a powerful action against inflammation, though used in excess they can lead to serious side-effects.

stroke See **cerebro-vascular accident.**

tennis elbow Inflammation in the tendons on the outer side of the elbow, possibly causing severe pain and difficulty in gripping and turning movements; not necessarily associated with tennis playing.

teratogen Anything which causes damage to a developing foetus in the womb.

thrombosis Clotting of blood within blood vessels.

thrush An infection caused by a yeast, affecting in particular the mouth, vagina, groin and skin folds.

tinnitus Ringing in the ears.

tracheostomy An artificial opening from the trachea (the windpipe) to the surface of the neck, created to allow a patient to breathe in circumstances where breathing is obstructed above the trachea.

tumour A lump of new tissue growing independently of surrounding tissue. It may or may not be cancerous.

ulcer An open sore, deeper than an abrasion.

urticaria An itchy, bumpy rash caused by allergy, also called nettle rash or hives.

varicose veins Abnormally dilated veins near the surface of the skin.

vasectomy Male sterilisation achieved by dividing the *vas deferens* on both sides, thereby preventing sperm leaving the body in the ejaculate.

verucca A wart; a small lump caused by a slow-growing virus.

virus A minute micro-organism which lives in cells as a parasite, causing a wide range of infectious diseases and also certain tumours.

27.5 Printing

acknowledgments The prelim in a book in which the author or editor thanks those who assisted in the preparation and publication of the book.

all edges gilt (aeg) Describing a book having the top, side and bottom trimmed edges of the pages coloured gold.

art paper Paper coated with a composition containing china clay, used for printing illustrations, especially fine-screen (i.e. 150 lines per inch) half-tones.

artwork Illustrations and other decorative material suitable for reproduction.

ascender The part of a letter which extends above the body of the letter. Contrast with **descender**.

bibliography (1) The study, description or knowledge of books, in regard to their outward form, authors, subjects, editions and history. (2) A descriptive list of books. (3) A book containing such a list.

bleed In bookbinding, the extent to which an illustration extends beyond the trimmed size of a page in order to ensure that the print will run off the page after trimming.

blind blocking Blocking which produces a recessed surface which is not enhanced by the use of ink or metal foil.

blocking In bookbinding, impressing letters or a design on a book cover using ink or metal foil. Contrast with **blind blocking**.

blurb A brief description of a book, printed on the jacket or the back of the book.

bold (face) Describing any style of typeface printed with very heavy strokes.

break off An instruction to a printer to begin text on the next line rather than run it on to the present line. Also called take over.

bulk The estimated thickness of a book, enabling the jacket to be designed with the correct width of spine.

camera-ready copy (CRC) Typescript copy which does not need to be typeset but which is ready for photographing. It is often produced on a word processor with a daisy wheel printer or a laser printer.

cancel A new reprinted leaf to be substituted for a suppressed leaf (containing a major error) after the book is printed.

caps An abbreviation for capitals (**upper-case** letters).

case The hard covers of a book i.e. the front, back and spine.

cased Machine-bound in hard covers.

cast-off An estimate of the length of copy, including number of words, illustrations, etc., expressed in the number of pages the copy will fill when printed.

catchword/phrase (1) A word or phrase in the text, e.g. an entry in a dictionary, which is repeated at the top of the column containing the entry. (2) A word or phrase repeated at the beginning of a textual note at the bottom of the page.

cedilla A mark placed under the letter 'c' to indicate an s-sound (in French and Portuguese), and in other languages, e.g. Turkish, to denote other sounds.

cold composition/type Typesetting by photographic methods i.e. filmsetting or photocomposition or by typewriter. Contrast with **hot-metal typesetting**.

collate (1) To place in order, as sheets of a book for binding, and to examine with respect to completeness and sequence of sheets. (2) To examine and compare books, and especially old manuscripts, in order to ascertain information about the history of composition and publication.

collotype A form of gelatine process in book illustration and advertising.

colophon An inscription at the end of a book or literary composition, often naming the author and scribe or printer, with place and date of execution, etc., as on a modern title-page.

compositor A person who sets up type.

copy Material to be printed (e.g. typescripts, photographs, line drawings).

copy preparer A person who marks up typescripts with the typographical specifications chosen by the designer.

cropping Cutting off or masking the areas of an illustration which are not to be reproduced.

dedication A prelim containing the author's inscription of the book to another person.

descender The part or 'tail' of a letter which comes below the line of type. Contrast with **ascender**.

diacritical marks Accents, cedillas and other marks attached to letters to indicate modified sound, value, etc.

diaeresis Two dots placed over the second of two adjacent vowels to show that each is to be pronounced separately (e.g. naïf).

displayed Describing typed matter, such as long quotations, set on separate lines, indented and preceded and followed by extra space to distinguish it from the rest of the text.

dummy A sample of a proposed job made up with the actual material and cut to correct size to show bulk, style of binding, etc.

duodecimo A book formed of sheets folded so as to make twelve leaves, usually written 12mo.

edition The number of copies of a book printed at a time, or at different times without significant alteration.

edition de luxe A splendid and expensive edition.

elite In typography, a measurement of length referring to twelve typewritten characters to the horizontal inch.

ellipsis Three dots indicating the omission of a word or words.

em The square of the body of any size of type. The 12 point em is the standard unit of typographic measurement.

em rule A rule which occupies the width of an em or the square of any size of type.

en Half of an em.

en point A point which is placed in the middle of a piece of type as wide as an en so that it is printed with space on either side.

en rule A rule which is half the width of an em rule.

endmatter The parts of a book which follow the text (e.g. appendices, bibliography, index).

endnotes Notes which come at the end of the relevant chapter or at the end of the book instead of being printed at the foot of the relevant page.

endpaper A folded sheet at the beginning or end of a book, one leaf of which is pasted to the binding, leaving the other as a flyleaf.

epigraph A quotation or motto at the beginning of a book or a chapter.

erratum/errata slip A list of corrections or errors in writing or printing tipped in to a book.

flyleaf A blank leaf at the beginning or end of a book.

folio (1) A sheet of paper folded in half. (2) A book made up of such sheets. (3) A manuscript leaf. (4) The particular number of such a leaf (e.g. folio 12).

format   Strictly, the size of a trimmed page, but generally used to distinguish the form, shape and style in which a book is produced.

fount   A complete assortment of types of one size and design, with all that is necessary for printing in that design. Also called (especially in the US) font.

full out   Describing a passage which is not indented but adjoins the left or right margin.

furniture   The pieces of wood, metal or plastic, of various lengths and widths, put round pages of type to make margins and fasten the matter in the chase.

galley proof   A proof of text matter before it is made up into pages. Also called a slip proof.

gathering   A folded section of pages comprised of one sheet or part of a sheet. Also called a signature.

half-title   The first printed page of a book, containing only the title and preceding the title-page. Also called a bastard title.

half-tone   A photographic process which represents light and shade by dots of different sizes, the image being photographed through a screen.

hanging indentation   Describing the first line of a paragraph which is printed full out left, with the next lines indented. Also called reverse indent.

headline   The line at the top of a page containing the title of the book or a chapter title.

histogram   A statistical graph in which frequency distribution is shown by means of vertical columns (see p 77).

hot-metal typesetting   Used to describe machines or methods using type made from molten metal (e.g. monotype, linotype).

imposition   The assembling of pages prior to printing so that they will be in the right order when the sheet is folded.

impression   A single printing of a book. A reprint having only minor corrections is a new impression.

imprint   The name and address of the publisher and the printer, and the date and place of publication of a book. The publisher's imprint appears on the title-page, the printer's on the verso or on the last page of a book.

indentation/indention   The blank space at the beginning of a line printed further in from the margin than subsequent lines.

insert   Printed matter placed in a book and not secured in any way.

inset   A printed section placed inside another before binding.

kern The part of a type that projects beyond the body and rests on an adjoining letter.

landscape A book or illustration having the longer sides at head and foot. Contrast with **portrait**.

layout A plan of a job showing position of type, illustrations and specifying type sizes and type faces.

leading Additional spacing between lines of type.

lemma A headword at the start of a textual note.

letterspacing Adding small spaces between characters, usually capitals or small capitals, to enhance the appearance of a line.

ligature A type of two or more letters joined together, e.g. æ, ff, fl.

line drawing A drawing comprised of black lines and solid and tint areas, without variable tones.

literal A wrong letter in printed or typed matter resulting from a mistake made by the typesetter.

lower-case The small letters of the alphabet.

make up The arrangement of composed types into columns or pages, including the insertion of illustrative matter, captions, headlines, notes, etc.

masking Covering the areas on the edge of a photograph which are not to be reproduced.

measure The width of a column or page of type, usually expressed in 12 point (or pica) ems.

Monotype A machine that casts and sets type letter by letter; a reproduction made by this process.

octavo (1) Having eight leaves to the sheet, usually written 8vo. (2) A book, or the size of a book, made up of such sheets.

offprint A reprint of a single article from a periodical.

offset lithography The most common form of photolithography, the process of lithographic printing from a photographically prepared plate using greasy ink; a rubber blanket receives the printed image and transfers it to paper.

opening The two pages exposed together when a book is opened.

overrunning Rearranging lines of type within a paragraph when a correction makes a line shorter or longer, achieved by moving words from one line to another and altering the spacing between them.

Ozalid A method of proofing film-set matter onto chemically treated paper; a reproduction made by this process.

page-on-galley proofs Proofs of pages which have not been imposed.

paste-up A layout in which galley proofs are pasted down to pages and outlines are drawn to show the size and position of illustrations.

perfect binding An unsewn book binding in which the backs of the gathered sections are sheared off and the leaves held in place by glue.

photogravure A method of photo-engraving in which the design etched on the metal surface is sunk into the surface, not relief.

pica In typography, a measurement of length, referring to ten typewritten characters to the horizontal inch.

pitch The number of characters that will fit into one inch of a line of text, typically 10, 12 or 15 when the typed text is monospaced.

plate (1) An engraved piece of metal used for printing. (2) An impression printed from it, an engraving. (3) An illustration separately printed, usually on different paper, and insetted in a book.

point A measurement of type sizes: 72 points to the inch.

portrait Describing the shape of a book or illustration with a height greater than its width. Contrast with **landscape**.

prelims The preliminary pages of a book, comprising the half-title, title, dedication, contents, etc.

print run The number of copies printed at a single printing.

proof One or more early impressions printed for the purpose of correcting errors. Also called a pull.

proportional spacing The spacing of typewritten characters in proportion to their size. Standard typewriters produce letters of uniform width, e.g. a capital L is given the same space as a lower case l, irrespective of their size.

pullout/foldout A folded sheet insetted into a book which, when unfolded, opens out beyond the pages of the book.

quarto (1) Having the sheet folded into four leaves or eight pages, usually written 4to. (2) A book, or the size of a book, made up of such sheets.

range To align, e.g. characters, lines of type.

recto The right-hand page of an open book. Contrast with **verso**.

reprint To print a new impression, especially with little or no change; an offprint.

repro pull A reproduction proof, of a quality good enough to be suitable for reproduction photographically.

retouching Work done by hand, especially on a photograph by pencil-work on the negative, to enhance the image or remove imperfections.

rough A rough sketch to give an impression of the original, or a drawing which needs to be redrawn.

rule A continuous printed line.

running head A headline which changes from page to page.

saddle stitched To stitch, normally with wire, through the back fold of insetted work.

sans serif   A style of typeface without serifs.

screen   A grid, of various gauges, through which images are photographed. The result, in which the image is broken up into dots, is called a **half-tone**.

serif   The finishing stroke at the top and bottom of a letter.

set   To arrange type by hand into words and lines.

sheet   A sheet which has not been folded.

signature   (1) A letter or figure at the foot of the first page (and usually on one or more successive pages) of each sheet in a book, indicating the order in which the sheets should be bound. (2) A folded section of pages comprising one sheet so marked.

solid   Describing type set without the insertion of spaces (leading) between the lines.

sort   One character of type.

special sort   An unusual character, or a character which is not part of the standard fount.

specification   The detailed description of typeface size, style, etc. which the designer determines for each book. Also called a type spec.

specimen   A specimen page giving examples of all the typographical styles, sizes, headings, etc. that a printer will encounter in setting a particular book.

spread/double-page spread   A table, illustration, etc. which extends across an opening.

stet   To restore text after marking for deletion, an instruction indicated to the printer by a row of dots below the text which is to be restored.

strip in   To join the ends of two pieces of film or paper.

tint   A mechanical tint: a pattern of dots, hatching, etc. or a solid panel in a second colour, which a draughtsman, blockmaker or printer can apply to an illustration.

tip in   Pasting a pullout, plate, errata slip, etc. to the adjoining page, rather than binding it in with the other pages.

transpose   To change the order of characters, words, paragraphs, etc.

turnovers   All the lines in a paragraph except the first.

type area   The area on a page occupied by the text and the notes (it may or may not include the headline and page number).

typeface   The printing surface of a type cut into one of a variety of styles.

umlaut   In German, the two dots placed over a letter representing a vowel change brought about by a vowel or semivowel, especially i, j, in the following syllable.

unit   The body width in which letters are cast in the Monotype method, calculated as one em = 18 units, or one en = 9 units.

upper-case Capital letters.

variant/variant reading One or more words and/or punctuation marks in an early version of a text which differ from the final version.

verso The left-hand page of an open book. Contrast with **recto**.

web printing Printing on a reel of paper as distinct from printing on individual sheets. Reeled paper is normally cut and folded on the printing press.

widow The last line of a paragraph when it appears at the top of a page.

wordbreak The division of a word at the end of a line.

wrap-round A small group of pages, such as half-tones, folded around a signature so that half precede the signature and the rest follow it.

x height The height of a lower-case x (i.e. a letter without an ascender or descender), used to gauge the height of a particular typeface.

27.6 Stock Exchange

above par Describing a share or bond the market price of which is greater than its face value.

account A division of the Stock Exchange calendar; an account usually runs for two weeks (ten working days).

accepting house (See under Business p 306).

account day The day on which the bargains done in the course of an individual account are settled, usually the second Monday after the end of the account.

accumulative dividend A dividend which has not been paid out to shareholders and is therefore included in a company's liabilities.

after-hours dealings Dealings conducted after the official close at 3.30 pm and which thus become the first deals done on the following day of business. Also known as early bargains.

aftermarket The trading of bonds immediately after they have been issued.

agent A trader who acts for an investor.

alpha securities The largest industrial shares, called 'blue chip' stocks before the Big Bang.

application form The document, issued by a company as part of its prospectus, for use by the public to apply for shares in the company.

arbitrage   Buying stocks and shares in one country or market and selling them in another, in order to profit from price differences.

Articles of Association   (See p 116).

assets   A business's property or resources, such as buildings, machinery, stock, cash, debts, and goodwill.

asset-stripping   The practice of taking over a company (usually one with a poor financial record) and selling off its assets in order to make a profit.

authorised capital   The maximum amount of money that a company is allowed to raise by issuing shares to the general public. This amount is shown in the company's Memorandum of Association.

backwardation   A situation which occurs when the bid price and offer price of a market maker deviate enough to allow an immediate profit to be made by simultaneously buying and selling.

banker's acceptance note   A letter of credit or draft which is backed by a bank.

bargain   Any deal or transaction taking place on the Stock Exchange.

bear   A Stock Exchange dealer or other trader who sells shares, commodities, etc. in the hope that prices will fall before he or she is due to deliver. He or she can then buy them at a lower price and in this way make a profit. A market in which prices are falling is called a **bear market**. Compare with **bull**.

bearer bond   A bond which has no registration of ownership and which is thus held by whoever possesses it.

bed and breakfast   Sale and repurchase of the same stock at an agreed cost to establish a capital loan or loss for tax purposes, whilst retaining beneficial ownership.

beta securities   Since the Big Bang, the name for secondary shares (more active than gamma securities).

bid   An approach by one company to purchase another.

bid price   The price at which a market maker will buy.

Big Bang   The name given to the changes in the system and rules of the London Stock Exchange which came into effect on 27 October 1986, involving (among other things) the abolition of the distinction between stockbrokers and stock-jobbers, and of fixed commissions.

bond   A security issued by a government or a commercial organisation on which the holder receives a rate of interest usually fixed until the repayment date.

bonus issue   Extra shares issued free of charge by a company to its shareholders in proportion to the size of their current holdings. This is paid for from company reserves, and is done so that the company's share capital will more closely reflect the value of its assets.

boom market A period of rising prices, increased business activity, higher demand and increased profits.

broker A dealer or agent buying and selling (or arranging contracts for others to buy and sell) insurance, stocks and shares, shipping, etc.

brokerage The charge made by a broker for the work done in arranging a contract. It is usually calculated as a percentage of the value of the contract. More specifically, it is the charge made by a stockbroker for buying or selling shares on a client's behalf.

broker/dealer After the Big Bang, a member of the Stock Exchange able to carry out the functions previously performed by both stockbrokers and stock-jobbers (but only allowed to act in one or the other capacity in any particular deal).

bull A Stock Market dealer or other trader who buys shares, commodities, etc. in the hope that prices will rise before he or she is due to receive them. He or she can then resell them at the higher price and in this way make a profit. A market in which prices are rising is called a **bull market**. Compare with **bear**.

bulldog bond A bond denominated in sterling which is issued in the British market by a person not resident in Britain, usually guaranteed by a foreign government.

call An instalment of the total payment for newly-issued shares.

call option An option to buy shares or commodities at or within a specified time and at an agreed price.

capital (1) The total financial resources of an individual or organisation. (2) The total amount of money collected by the person(s) starting a company.

capitalisation issue An issue of shares which results from the conversion of a company's money reserves into share capital by means of a bonus issue. Also known as a free or scrip issue.

capital markets The money market which deals in securities which are generally medium or long-term, not short-term.

cash and new The amount paid by a seller for the privilege of postponing delivery of stocks and shares. Also known as **contango**.

CD Certificate of deposit. A certificate issued by a bank, usually for up to 90 days' maturity, which is negotiable and earns interest.

checking An automated facility offered by the Stock Exchange which matches up both parties to a bargain.

clearing system An institution which handles transactions and accepts securities for safe keeping.

close The time when a trading session ends.

closing prices The buying and selling prices of stocks and shares when the Stock Exchange finishes business for the day.

commercial paper Short-term bonds (i.e. up to 270 days) which are unsecured against the assets of the issuer.

commission Payment made to an agent or sales representative for business done, usually a percentage of the value of that business (e.g. of sales made).

common stock The American term for ordinary shares.

compensation fund The fund which the Stock Exchange maintains to reimburse investors when a member firm fails to meet its obligations.

consideration The monetary value of a Stock Exchange transaction.

contango See **cash and new**.

convertible bond A bond on which the holder exercises the option, usually for a limited time, to convert into the shares of the company which issued it, or the parent company.

coupon A dated slip (usually one of several) accompanying a bond. When it is presented to the company on the stated date it entitles the holder to a dividend or to interest due on the bond.

cum (1) Used in expressions (e.g. *cum cap.* capitalisation issue, *cum div.* dividend issue, *cum rights* rights issue) to indicate that the buyer is allowed to participate in the issue specified. (2) The abbreviation for 'cumulative' (e.g. cumulative preference share).

cumulative preference share A share with a fixed and guaranteed rate of dividend. If a company cannot afford to pay in a particular year, the dividend accumulates. Holders of cumulative preference shares must be paid in full before any payment is made to other shareholders.

current yield The return of a financial asset to a holder, expressed as the interest rate or coupon on the market price. Also known as interest yield or running yield.

debenture A particular type of loan to a company, or the document describing it. Debentures are not part of the company's share capital. They carry a fixed rate of interest (which must be paid whether the company makes a profit or not) and are usually redeemable on a set date.

deferred ordinary shares Shares whose holders are entitled to part of the company's profits only after all other shareholders have been paid.

direct placement Placing an issue of securities with a financial institution without the use of an underwriter.

discount The amount below the issue price at which a stock is trading.

discretionary account An account for which buying and selling can be undertaken without first obtaining the consent of the client.

dividend/dividend yield A proportion of a company's profits paid to shareholders. It is usually expressed as a percentage of the face value of the shares.

drop-lock A bond which automatically changes rates, changing to fixed-rate interest if the rates drop below a predetermined point.

dual capacity A situation, enabled by the Big Bang, which allows member firms of the Stock Exchange to act as agents and principals.

eligible liabilities In British banking, the liabilities that may be allowed in calculating the reserve-asset ratio.

equity The total assets of a company after liabilities are taken into account.

eurobonds Securities on which the named currency is not the currency of the country in which they have been issued.

eurodollar American currency held by an American not resident in the US, usually as a deposit with the foreign branch of an American bank or with a bank outside the US.

euronote Short-term notes (i.e. issued from three months to six months) structured as a medium-term loan in which the underwriter agrees to issue notes on request.

ex coupon Security without the right to the coupon, or the interest rate, on the bond.

face value The value printed on a share or similar document. It may be higher or lower than the market value.

Fed funds Deposits by member banks in the US Federal Reserve System, which consists of a board of governors, twelve Federal Reserve Banks and thousands of privately-owned banks who combine to control the supply of money and credit.

firm order An order to buy or sell a security that can be effected within the time allowed without further confirmation.

fixed interest security A security or bond which offers an annual guaranteed interest payment (e.g. UK gilts). There is usually a fixed date on which the bond is redeemed.

floating rate interest An interest rate which changes on a pre-determined regular basis to reflect changes in market rates, usually calculated at a certain number of points above the bank rate (e.g. floating-rate CDs, bonds or notes).

foreign bond A bond which a foreign borrower issues in the domestic market of a particular country and which is denominated in the currency of that country.

forward contract/delivery A contract for the settlement of a financial instrument or commodity on a mutually agreed date in the future. Unlike a **futures contract**, it is not standardised.

futures contract   A standardised contract for the sale or purchase of a fixed quantity of commodity, financial instruments, cash, etc. at a future date.

gamma securities   Stocks which are relatively inactive.

gilt-edged securities   Securities such as government stocks which are regarded as very safe investments, issued to fund the deficit between a nation's taxes and revenues and government spending. Their fixed rate of interest is comparatively low, but repayment is guaranteed. Also known as gilts.

hedging   Attempting to prevent losses caused by fluctuations in market prices, e.g. offsetting the cost of a purchase by selling a balancing amount before having to pay for the purchase.

insider dealing   Buying and selling shares in a company on the basis of 'inside' knowledge, e.g. confidential information about the company's financial position. The Stock Exchange disapproves of insider dealing and has taken steps to outlaw it.

issue price   The gross price placed on an issue of securities before commissions are deducted, expressed as a percentage of principal amount.

issuing house   An institution which arranges the details of an issue of stock or shares as well as the compliance required by the Stock Exchange with its regulations governing the listing.

jobber   See **market maker**.

liability   Something which is owed to someone else. Typical liabilities include money owed to suppliers, money due to be paid to shareholders, money owed in tax to the Inland Revenue, and money—in the form of a loan or overdraft—owed to the bank.

LIBOR   London Interbank Offered Rate: the interest rate offered by banks in the London eurodollar market, used as a point of reference for many international loans and floating-rate issues.

LIFFE   London International Financial Futures Exchange. Market where financial futures and options on financial futures (e.g. bonds, interest rates and currencies) are traded.

listed security/stock   A security (formerly called a quoted company) which has complied with certain requirements of the Stock Exchange and which is listed in the Stock Exchange Daily Official List.

longs/long-dated securities   A security which is not due to be redeemed for at least fifteen years.

mandate   The authorisation of the borrower to proceed with loan or bond issue under the terms agreed with the lead manager.

margin   Same as **spread**.

market maker   A Stock Exchange member who buys and sells stocks i.e. a broker/dealer. Before the Big Bang, this was the function of a stock-jobber, who was not allowed to deal with the public.

market order   An order to be executed immediately which is given to a broker or agent to buy or sell at the best price obtainable.

market valuation   The current value of a company or security, computed by multiplying the current price by the current number of shares issued.

maturity date   The time at which a loan or bond becomes due for payment.

member firm   A firm of broker/dealers which is a member of the Stock Exchange.

middle price   The price which is halfway between the two quoted in the Stock Exchange Daily Official List, or the average of the buying and selling prices offered by a market maker.

money market   Discount houses, banks, accepting houses and other financial institutions engaged in buying, selling, lending and borrowing money for profit.

net worth/assets   The total value of assets (both fixed and current) minus the current liabilities.

new time   Trading on the Stock Exchange for the next account period in the last two days of the present one.

nominal price   The estimated price for a security when no deals were done during a trading session.

nominal yield   The interest which can be earned on the face value of a bond. See also **current yield**.

nominee   A person named by and operating on behalf of another person, usually to preserve that person's anonymity.

note   A certificate of indebtedness usually used for short-term issues.

offer price   The price at which a market maker will sell, the best offer being the lowest obtainable from all the market makers who are quoting.

opening   The official start of a trading session, at which time an opening price is recorded.

option   The right to buy (**call option**) or sell (**put option**) at a specified price, at or within a specified time, whatever happens to the market price.

OTC   Over-the-counter: trading conducted outside stock exchanges.

par   The value stated on the front of a share, etc.

partly paid   Security on which a part of the issue price has been paid, with the remainder to be paid at a specified rate.

portfolio A collection of investments made by a person or institution.

preference shares Shares which give the owner the right to receive a fixed dividend each year before ordinary shareholders receive any profit. If the company goes into liquidation, preference shareholders receive their share capital before ordinary shareholders if sufficient funds are available.

preferred ordinary shares A type of share ranking between ordinary shares and preference shares in the 'queue' to receive payment of a dividend.

premium The amount paid for a share over and above its par value.

primary market The new market for a new issue of securities. Once dealing starts, the market is a secondary one.

principal A sum of money on which interest is paid.

prospectus A document giving details about a company and inviting the public to buy shares in the company. A copy must be sent to the Registrar of Companies beforehand.

proxy (1) A document authorising a person to act on another person's behalf (e.g. by voting on behalf of a shareholder at a company meeting). (2) A person who has been authorised to act in this way.

put option An option to sell shares or commodities at (or within) a specified time and at an agreed price. The option is usually acquired by paying a proportion of the value of the items.

quotation (1) A statement of the price and conditions relating to a (possible) business transaction. Often shortened to **quote**. (2) The listing of a company's shares in the official Stock Exchange publication (and the buying and selling of its shares in the Stock Exchange). To obtain such a quotation, usually regarded as a valuable privilege, a company must meet certain requirements (especially relating to giving information about itself).

redemption yield Annualised (or semi-annualised) yield which takes account of the flow of coupon payments on a stock as well as the amounts of profit or loss incurred on repayment of the principal on redemption.

repurchase agreement An agreement in which a security is sold and later bought back, the difference between the selling and repurchase prices being partly in lieu of interest. The seller is thus provided with cash during the interval.

reserves (1) Part of a company's profits which is retained within the company for various possible uses (i.e. not paid out to shareholders in the form of a dividend). (2) Amounts of gold and foreign currencies held by a country. They can be used to pay foreign debts, influence exchange rates, etc. (3) Amounts of cash held by banks and immediately available to customers.

roundtripping An action which enables a company to borrow and lend at a profit by taking advantage of a short-term rise in market rates to a higher level than its own rates of borrowing.

samurai bond The Japanese term for a bond issued in Japan by a foreign institution which is denominated in yen and purchasable by non-residents of Japan.

scrip issue Same as **capitalisation issue** and **bonus issue**.

SEAQ Stock Exchange Automated Quotations: an electronic system in operation since the Big Bang which displays the quotations of market makers.

securities Financial assets, such as shares or bonds, which can be bought and sold.

short The sale of a security which is not in the possession of the seller in the expectation that a profit can be made from falling prices between the selling and the delivery dates.

shorts/short-dated securities Securities which are due to be redeemed within five years.

split The process by which the number of shares in an issue is increased and the nominal value decreased so that the net effect to holders is nil. Utilised to make shares more marketable.

spread (1) In the bond markets, the difference between the selling and the buying price. (2) In the futures markets, the simultaneous sale and purchase of the same instrument for delivery in different months, and of different contracts in the same month.

stag A person who applies for new shares in the belief that they will be over-subscribed and that he or she will be able to sell his/her allotment immediately for a good profit.

stock-jobber See **market maker**.

stop-loss order An order to buy or sell at a certain price, either above or below the market price at the time the order was given.

straddle The practice of purchasing a futures contract in one market while simultaneously selling it in another.

straight bond A fixed-rate bond without conversion (i.e. not converted into gold or dollars at a fixed price).

subordinated debt In the event of liquidation, a debt that can be claimed by an unsecured creditor only after the claims of other debts have been met.

swap An agreement between two counter-parties to exchange debt obligations to enable each party to take advantage of differing interest rates or currency opportunities.

switching (1) Moving from one stock to another to take advantage of expected changes in interest rates and/or expectations, or of anomalies which may have developed. (2) Liquidating a position in the futures market while at the same time re-establishing the position in another future on the same commodity or financial instrument.

syndicate The body of managers, underwriters and selling agents of a bond.

talisman The acronym for Transfer Accounting, Lodgement for Investors, Stock Management for Jobbers: a service established in 1979 which automated much of the settlement of UK securities listed on the Stock Exchange.

tap stock A UK government bond, issued through the government broker, which can be adjusted to influence the gilts market.

traded options Options which can be traded throughout their life and exercised on the expiry date by the eventual holder.

transfers The form on which the seller of a security authorises the removal of his or her name from the register and the substitution of the name of the buyer.

turnover value The total monetary value of transactions, computed by multiplying the price by the number of shares traded.

underwriter/underwriting (1) A member of Lloyd's who accepts the risk of insuring by guaranteeing payment from his or her personal wealth in return for a share of the premium. (2) A person or institution who agrees to take up a proportion of a share issue should the investment public apply in an insufficient amount, in return for a fee.

unlisted companies Companies not listed in the Stock Exchange Daily Official List but which may be included in the USM.

USM Unlisted Securities Market. The market for the buying and selling of those shares, etc. which are not on the Stock Exchange's official list (i.e. which cannot be bought and sold on the Stock Exchange).

unsecured creditor A creditor who is entitled to payment only after secured creditors have been paid in full. If there is money left over for this, unsecured creditors are treated equally and paid in proportion to the amounts of their loans.

warrant A document issued by a company to a stockholder giving him or her the right to buy further stock at a stated price, either before a given date or at any future date.

Yankee bond A bond issued by a foreign entity in the US which is registered with the Securities and Exchange Commission.

yearling British stock which is issued by municipal authorities and which matures within a year.

yield/yield gap The difference between what is received in dividends from ordinary shares and the yield from fixed-interest shares.

zero coupon bond A bond issued without an interest coupon but at a discounted price: it will give a computed interest by the time it is redeemed at face value.

27.7 Word processing

(See also 27.2: Computing)

alphanumeric Describing any combination of letters of the alphabet and Arabic numerals which can be processed by a computer.

background A facility of some computers whereby low priority tasks can be performed whilst those of high priority are also being performed in the foreground.

bi-directional printing The printing of lines both right to left and left to right, eliminating the need for a return to the beginning of the line.

block In computing, a group of records or information units handled as a single unit and stored in adjacent locations on magnetic tape or disk. In many magnetic storage devices only complete blocks can be accessed or transferred.

boilerplate A passage of text used repeatedly in various contexts which can be inserted in different files.

centring Locating a heading or other words of text equidistant between the left and right margins.

central processing unit (CPU) The part of a computer system which co-ordinates the whole system, where all parts of the system are linked together and where the calculations and manipulation of data takes place.

character A generic expression for a letter of the alphabet, a number, a symbol or a punctuation mark printed or displayed on a screen.

character set The collection of numbers, letters, symbols and graphics that can be generated by a particular system.

command key A special key or set of keys on a keyboard which has been defined to carry out certain tasks (e.g. underscoring, saving data).

communicating word processors Word processors connected via a network to allow very rapid office-to-office and/or business-to-business communication of text.

communications   A peripheral piece of hardware enabling a word processor to communicate with other equipment.

conditional page break   A facility on most word processors that once the page length has been determined for a file, the word processor can be programmed to insert its own page break.

control key   A key on a computer keyboard which when depressed with a variety of other keys gives additional facilities for the manipulation of files.

cpi   Characters per inch. The number of characters to every horizontal inch of typing, usually 10, 12 or 15. Also known as **pitch**.

create   The term given to the setting up of a new file in computing or word processing.

cursor   A marker on a VDU indicating the point at which text should be entered.

cut and paste   Marking the text to be repositioned (cut) and moving it to a new location (paste). A labour-saving feature when large blocks of text have to be moved.

daisy wheel   The name given to a print where the type head is circular and the characters are attached round it on the ends of stalks.

daisy wheel printer   A printer having a wheel which rotates at speed until the required character is brought before a hammer. The character is then struck by the hammer against the ribbon. Daisy wheels are interchangeable to facilitate different typefaces and produce letter-quality printout.

dictionary   A library; a file of text with special applications (e.g. a spelling dictionary).

discretionary hyphen   A hyphen inserted between syllables of a word which runs on from one line of text to the next and which is automatically deleted when the line length is changed.

display format   The total number of characters visible on screen, expressed either as the total number or as the number of lines and characters in each line.

distributed logic   Computer systems where logic or intelligence are distributed in the system rather than located centrally e.g. some word processing systems link intelligent terminals which may make shared use of other resources such as storage, printer.

document   A medium and the data recorded on it. Most commonly refers to print on paper.

document based system   A word processing program where each file is produced as a whole document and not divided on screen into pages.

document merge   A facility of most word processors to join together two separate documents making one final document. If more than two documents are integrated, the process is referred to as document assembly.

dual pitch printer A printer which has the facility to switch from one type size to another by the movement of a switch.

edit The process of removing or inserting information by an operator when a record is passed through a computer.

erase To delete or obliterate a file or an item of data.

error detection A facility of communications which ensures that text has not been corrupted during transmission.

flag Information which can be added to computer data in order to characterise the data or to provide information about it. Sometimes called a marker, point or a tag.

footer A page number, catchword or other short piece of text printed at the bottom of each page, below the last line of text.

format The layout or arrangement of the text on screen or on paper.

free-form text database A facility of some word processing programmes whereby files can be organised in a specified manner and then any word or combination of words can be located, the items identified being scrolled in a window on screen.

function key One or more keys on a keyboard which allow a user to issue a series of commands with one key depression, provided that the keys have been allocated special functions.

global search A feature which activates the cursor to find every occurrence of a pre-determined character, word or phrase in a file.

global search and replace An editing function in word processing where the cursor will search for each occurrence of a particular character, word or phrase and replace it with another pre-determined character, word or phrase.

glossary Any set of frequently used passages of text (**boilerplates**).

header A page number, catchword or other short piece of text printed at the top of each page, above the first line of text.

help menu A facility which enables a WP operator to find information on available commands and their syntax without leaving the program in use and without having to refer to the manual.

impact printing A means of printing where the characters are formed on the paper by means of a hammer striking the ribbon (e.g. dot matrix printers, line printers).

insert The addition of a word, phrase or paragraph to any text that has already been produced.

insert mode Any text that is typed at a keyboard which is added to the version already appearing on the visual display unit.

justified text   Text which has an even right margin equal to the left margin and where the right hand margin appears vertically straight.

justify   To adjust the positions of words on a page, distributing additional space in lines so that the right margin forms a straight vertical and parallel edge to the left margin.

letter quality   The term usually refers to output from a printer where the printing is indistinguishable from that typed on a good electric typewriter.

letter quality printer   Any printer that can produce print of the same quality as a good electric typewriter.

line feed   A facility of most printers to automatically move the paper up through the printing mechanism one line at a time.

line graphics   A facility which enables some word processors to draw boxes or other horizontal or vertical lines round a passage of text.

list processing   A facility which enables word processors to automatically merge predetermined lists of data (e.g. names and addresses) in a standard passage of text, creating a new document.

logic-seeking   Describing a printer which automatically skips over blank spaces in the text and so prints faster.

mail merge   The process of combining a document file and a mailing list in word processing for the production of a standard letter.

mark (block)   A function which enables an operator to cut and paste passages of text by inserting special code markers at the beginning and end of a passage.

matrix printer   A printer in which each character is made up of a series of dots produced by a print head pushing a pattern of wires against a ribbon and onto the paper which also moves across the paper.

menu   A list of possible options or facilities presented to the user from data or word processing software on a computer.

merge   The combining of information from two or more sources (e.g. address lists or mailing lists with document files or form letters).

mnemonics   In word processing, a code of a few characters which initiates commands (e.g. erasing a file, moving a block, re-formatting a page).

mode   Any operating function on a word processor.

multi-access   Describing a system which enables several operators to use it simultaneously.

non-impact printing   Printers which do not require physical impact for printing characters on paper (e.g. ink jet printing and electrostatic printing).

numeric Describing a field or character only able to contain or indicate a numeral.

numeric keypad A keyboard containing only numerals.

output Information transmitted by a computer or its storage devices to a screen or printer. It may be in the form of print on paper, punched cards or paper tape.

output device A device capable of receiving information from a central processor or peripheral unit which translates computer information into another medium (e.g. a VDU, printer).

overwrite The writing of data into a computer's memory where data previously held in a location is replaced with the new data.

page The amount of text which can be displayed on screen, or a passage of text divided from another by a page break.

pagebased system A feature of some word processing programs where each file is produced in pages making up a whole document. The hard copy output is the same as it appears on the screen of a VDU.

page break An internal command which informs the printer to start a new page.

page control A feature which allows a WP operator to address the length of the typing page to suit the display of text, or omit pages of typed text which will still be numbered chronologically within the document, for the later insertion of diagrams or drawings.

page feed A facility of most printers to roll up the paper one page at a time through the printing mechanism.

pagination (1) The numbering of pages in a document. (2) A word processing function used to create and number pages.

pitch The number of characters per horizontal inch of typing (e.g. 10, 12 or 15). Also known as **cpi**.

printer An output device from a computer which produces hard copy (text on paper) concerned with speed, quality and price.

print out The reproduction of text (printed paper output) on paper which a computer produces via a printer.

print pause A command facility which stops the printer for paper change, ribbon change, paper jam, etc. automatically.

prompt A computer initiated message to the operator used to indicate that particular information is required before the program can proceed any further.

protocol A set of standards which govern a format of communications to be exchanged between two devices in a communications system.

queue The processing of jobs or items (e.g. data awaiting action, execution or transmission). If terminals in a multi-user system send a file for printing simultaneously, the files will be queued and printed in rotation.

recall   Transferring stored text to enable it to be edited or printed.

records management   A facility of some word processors which allows for the sorting, editing, storage, etc. of data which may not be related to text.

reformat   A feature whereby after the insertion, modification or deletion of text in a file, the format of the file can automatically be readjusted to give a good finished copy within the pre-set margins or line length.

repagination   Automatic alteration of page numbering and size—a feature which is normally used after the editing of text, particularly in document-based systems.

required hyphen   A hyphen in a compound word or expression which is not automatically deleted when the length of a line is altered.

reverse printer   A printer capable of printing right to left, and left to right. Also known as a bi-directional printer.

ruler line   A line across the top or bottom of a VDU screen which indicates the margin positions and the tabulation which has been set.

run   The execution of a computer program, suite of programs or routine.

save   A term used to refer to the storing of data on storage media (e.g. on magnetic disks).

scan   The examination of material e.g. a word processing document, a page of a document or the conversion of data into machine readable form.

scroll   The movement of text up and down or across a VDU so that the user can view the whole of a document or, on systems that display only half pages, the whole of a page.

search   An examination of information in computer file to find the occurrence of a character, word or phrase.

search and replace   A facility in which every occurrence of a specified character, word or phrase is replaced with a pre-defined character, word or phrase. Also known as global exchange or global search and replace.

shared logic   A computer system consisting of work stations made up of keyboards and VDUs which are connected to a CPU, usually with a hard disk. The terminals operate under central control.

sort   The arrangement of items of information into a meaningful order, often into alphabetical, numerical or chronological order.

spelling check   In word processing, a program which uses a standard or specialised dictionary which can be added to by the user. When the program is run, the text is checked for spelling errors which the user can correct.

stand-alone   A piece of equipment which can operate independently of any other equipment e.g. a work station which can operate on its own without being connected with a CPU is a stand-alone system. Often a category for word processors which are self contained and require no additional equipment.

standard paragraphs   Text that is frequently used, stored and available for insertion into assembled documents.

standard text   A facility which enables the operator to store and recall rapidly and easily words and phrases and often paragraphs that are used frequently.

stationery   In word processing, single-sheet stationery describes the standard A4 format, fed into a printer sheet by sheet. Continuous stationery consists of a long strip of paper perforated at the end of each sheet and, at the sides with sprocket holes, allowing it to be fed into a printer by a tractor feed.

status line   The line at the top or bottom of the screen which gives details of the work being performed (e.g. file name, page, line and column numbers, line spacing).

stop code (switch code)   A special character identifying the location in the text at which data can be later inserted automatically.

strikeover   A facility to type one character over another character, so that both characters (letters, numbers, symbols or a combination of these) appear in one type space.

string   A group of items which are arranged in sequence according to a set of pre-defined rules (e.g. a set of consecutive characters in a computer memory).

string search   A facility sometimes referred to as the find facility; when a string of characters is typed to the search, the file will be searched for where that string appears. Also known as search facility.

text editing   The editing of text, which may be carried out on any form of computer from a mainframe with appropriate software to a dedicated word processor.

text editor   Software which manipulates the text of computer programs themselves.

text processing   Computer editing and subsequent production of text. Often used as a synonym for word processing, although text processing more commonly refers to the handling of very large quantities of text.

thermal printer A method of printing using paper coated with a dye that darkens at predetermined temperatures to produce a copy of an image.

tractor feed A piece of equipment which attaches to a printer using continuous stationery: two belts of circular studs catch the sprocket holes in the stationery to feed it through.

unconditional page break A feature of word processing programs where the operator works through a document checking page breaks and putting in unconditional page breaks where necessary.

underscore The underlining facility on word processing software.

variable block A piece of information that can be substituted for another piece of information if requested by the user. Often referred to as a variable.

visual display unit (VDU) A cathode ray tube, which looks similar to a television screen and which displays text from a computer.

word count facility Found on some document-based word processing systems, the number of words typed at any one time appears on the screen.

word processing The electronic storage, editing and manipulating of text using an electronic keyboard, computer and printer where text is stored on a magnetic medium except for final output which is in the form of print on paper.

word processor (WP) An electronic device used for the storage, editing and manipulation of text and consisting of a keyboard, an internal memory or storage, external storage, logic and printer. There are three main types: stand-alone, shared logic and distributed logic.

wordwrap A term referring to the way in which a partially typed word is automatically moved to a new line if the length of the word proves too long to fit into the existing line. Also known as wraparound.

write protect The covering of the exposed part of a floppy disk where information can be written to or read from, by a tag so that information can no longer be written on to the disk, but the reading of information from the disk is not interfered with.

write protect tag A tag used to prevent data being written onto a magnetic disk.

27.8 Foreign words and phrases

à bas Down, down with! *(Fr)*
ab initio From the beginning *(L)*

à compte   On account; in part payment *(Fr)*
ad finem   To the end *(L)*
ad gustem   According to taste *(L)*
ad hoc   For this special purpose *(L)*
ad infinitum   Without any apparent end *(L)*
ad interim   In the meanwhile *(L)*
ad libitum   At pleasure; as much as/in any way that one desires *(L)*
ad nauseam   To a sickening degree *(L)*
ad rem   To the point; to the purpose *(L)*
ad verbum   Word for word; literally *(L)*
affair d'amour/affaire de cœur   A love affair *(Fr)*
aficionado   An ardent follower, fan *(Sp)*
à fond   To the bottom; thoroughly *(Fr)*
agent provocateur   One paid to associate with a person, party or group, with the purpose of leading them to commit acts which will make them liable to punishment *(Fr)*
à la carte   According to the menu, each dish priced separately *(Fr)*
alter idem   Another precisely similar *(L)*
amor vincit omnia   Love conquers all things *(L)*
ante meridiem   Before noon *(L)*
à point   To the point; exactly right; opportunely *(Fr)*
apologia   A defence; justification *(L)*
au fait   Expert, knowledgeable about something *(Fr)*
au gratin   With breadcrumbs *(Fr)*
au pis aller   At the worst *(Fr)*
autre temps, autre mœurs   Other times, other manners *(Fr)*
avant-garde   Very modern; ahead of (artistic) fashion *(Fr)*
bête noir   What one hates most *(Fr)*
bona fide   In good faith; genuine *(L)*
bona vacantia   Unclaimed goods *(L)*
bonhomie   Easy good nature *(Fr)*
carpe diem   Enjoy the present day; seize the opportunity *(L)*
carte blanche   Freedom of action; (literally) a blank paper *(Fr)*
cause célèbre   A very famous trial *(Fr)*
caveat emptor   Let the buyer beware; at the buyer's risk *(L)*
ceteris paribus   Other things being equal *(L)*
chacun à son goût   Each to his own taste *(Fr)*
cherchez la femme   Look for the woman; there's a woman at the bottom of it *(Fr)*
cogito ergo sum   I think, therefore I am *(L)*
comme il faut   As it should be *(Fr)*
compos mentis   Of sound mind *(L)*

cordon bleu   Blue ribbon; a cook of the highest excellence *(Fr)*

corpus delicti   The body, substance or foundation of the offence *(L)*

cosi fan tutte   That is what all women do; women are all like that *(It)*

coup de main   A sudden enterprise or effort *(Fr)*

crème de la crème   The very best *(Fr)*

cri de cœur   A cry from the heart *(Fr)*

cui bono?   For whose benefit is it?; who gains by it? *(L)*

de bonne grâce   With good grace; willingly *(Fr)*

de haut en bas   From top to bottom; contemptuously *(Fr)*

déjà vu   A feeling of having previously experienced something as it happens *(Fr)*

Deo gratias   Thanks to God *(L)*

de rigueur   Absolutely necessary because of etiquette, fashion, etc. *(Fr)*

Dieu et mon droit   God and my right *(Fr)*

dolce far niente   Sweet doing-nothing; sweet idleness *(It)*

double entendre   A word or phrase with two meanings, one straightforward and one subtle or indecent *(Fr)*

dramatis personae   The characters of a drama or play *(L)*

dulce et decorum est (pro patria mori)   It is sweet and glorious (to die for one's country) *(L)*

dum spiro, spero   While I breathe, I hope *(L)*

ecce homo   Behold the man *(L)* (The words of Pontius Pilate)

embarras de richesses   Too much of a good thing *(Fr)*

enfant terrible   A child whose sayings embarrass his elders; a person who embarrasses his colleagues in a similar way *(Fr)*

en masse   In a body; all together *(Fr)*

en passant   In passing; by the way *(Fr)*

entente cordiale   A friendly agreement or relationship between states *(Fr)*

errare est humanum   To err is human *(L)*

esprit de corps   Regard for the honour of the body to which one belongs *(Fr)*

et ego in Arcadia   I too have lived in Arcadia; I too had that experience *(L)*

et tu, Brute!   You too, Brutus? *(L)* (Caesar's alleged exclamation when he saw Brutus amongst his assassins)

eureka!   I have found (it)! *(Gr)* (Archimedes' alleged exclamation when he thought of a way to determine the purity of the gold in the King of Syracuse's crown)

ex cathedra   From the episcopal or papal throne or professional chair; with high authority *(L)*

exempli gratia By way of example *(L)*
ex libris From the books of/library of *(L)*
fait accompli An accomplished fact; a thing already done *(Fr)*
faux pas A mistake; social blunder *(Fr)*
festina lente Hasten gently; hurry slowly *(L)*
furor loquendi/scribendi A rage for speaking/writing *(L)*
genius loci The guardian spirit of the place *(L)*
gloria in excelsis Glory to God in the highest *(L)*
grande dame A lady of aristocratic manner and forceful personality *(Fr)*
hasta mañana Until tomorrow *(Sp)*
hic sepultus Here (is) buried *(L)*
hoi polloi The masses; the rabble; the vulgar *(Gr)*
honi soit qui mal y pense Shame to him who thinks evil; the shame be his who thinks ill of it *(L)*
ibidem (ibid.) In the same place, thing or case *(L)*
idée fixe A fixed idea; an obsession *(Fr)*
in extremis At the point of death or in desperate circumstances *(L)*
in flagrante delicto In the very act; (literally) while the crime is blazing *(L)*
infra dignitatem (infra dig) Beneath one's dignity *(L)*
in re In the matter of *(L)*
in statu quo In the former state *(L)*
inter alia Amongst other things *(L)*
inter nos Between ourselves *(L)*
in toto Entirely *(L)*
in vino veritas In wine is truth; wine brings out the truth *(L)*
ipso facto By that very fact; thereby *(L)*
joie de vivre Joy of living *(Fr)*
Kirche, Küche, Kinder Church, kitchen, children *(Ger)*
laissez faire A general principle of non-interference *(Fr)*
le beau monde The fashionable world *(Fr)*
magnum bonum A great good *(L)*
magnum opus A great work; someone's greatest achievement *(L)*
maître d'hôtel A house-steward, major-domo, a manager or head-waiter of an hotel *(Fr)*
mala fide With bad faith; treacherously *(L)*
mal à propos Ill-timed *(Fr)*
mea culpa By my own fault *(L)*
memento mori Remember death; a reminder of death *(L)*
mens sana in corpore sano A sound mind in a sound body *(L)*
mirabile dictu Wonderful to tell *(L)*

modus operandi   Manner of operation; way of going about a job *(L)*

morituri te salutamus   We who are about to die salute you *(L)* (The greeting given by the gladiators to the emperor)

mot juste   The word which exactly fits the context *(L)*

nemine contradicente (nem con)   Without opposition, with no-one speaking to the contrary *(L)*

nemo me impune lacessit   No-one provokes me with impunity *(L)* (the motto of Scotland)

nihil ad rem   Nothing to the point *(L)*

nil desperandum   Never despair *(L)*

noli me tangere   Don't touch me *(L)* (the words of Jesus quoted from John's Gospel, but now often used as a general warning against interference)

nom de guerre   A pseudonym; (literally) a war name *(Fr)*

non sequitur   A remark or action unconnected with what has gone before; a conclusion that does not follow logically from the premises *(L)*

nota bene (NB)   Mark well; take good note *(L)*

nouveau riche   One who has only lately acquired wealth; an upstart *(Fr)*

obiter dictum   A thing said by the way; a cursory remark *(L)*

onus probandi   The burden of proving *(L)*

O tempora! O mores!   Oh the times! Oh the manners/customs!; What times! What conduct! *(L)*

pari passu   With equal pace; together *(L)*

per ardua ad astra   By steep and difficult ways to the stars; the way to the stars is not easy *(L)*

per diem   By the day *(L)*

persona non grata   An unacceptable person *(L)*

pièce de résistance   The best or most important item; the substantial course at dinner *(Fr)*

pied-à-terre   A dwelling kept for temporary, secondary or occasional use, usually in a city *(Fr)*

pis aller   Makeshift; the worst or last shift *(Fr)*

plus ça change, plus c'est la même chose   The more that it changes the more it is the same thing, i.e. no superficial or apparent change alters its essential nature *(Fr)*

post meridiem   After noon *(L)*

prima facie   At first sight *(L)* See also under Legal p 332.

pur sang   Of pure blood; total *(Fr)*

qui s'excuse s'accuse   He who excuses himself accuses himself; whoever makes too many or unnecessary excuses lays himself open to suspicion *(Fr)*

quid pro quo (See under Business p 313).

quod erat demonstrandum (the thing) which was to be proved or demonstrated *(L)*

raison d'être The reason for the existence of something *(Fr)*

rara avis A rare person or thing; (literally) a rare bird *(L)*

res judicata A case or law suit already decided *(L)*

rien ne va plus (Literally) nothing goes any more—used by croupiers to indicate that no more bets may be placed *(Fr)*

sang froid Coolness of behaviour; calmness; (literally) cold blood *(Fr)*

sans souci Without care or worry *(Fr)*

savoir faire Knowledge of what to do and how to do it *(Fr)*

semper idem Always the same *(L)*

se non è vero, è ben trovato If it is not true, it is cleverly invented *(It)*

solvitur ambulando It is solved in walking, i.e. the problem is solved by actually doing it, by practical experiment *(L)*

sub judice Under (legal) consideration *(L)*

suum cuique Let each have his own *(L)*

taedium vitae Weariness of life *(L)*

tant mieux/pis So much the better/worse *(Fr)*

tempus fugit Time flies *(L)*

terra incognita An unknown country *(L)*

tour de force A feat of strength or skill *(Fr)*

tout court Quite brief(ly), without preface; simply or brusquely *(Fr)*

ultima ratio regum The last argument of kings—the cannon, war *(L)*

urbi et orbi To the city (Rome) and the world; to everyone *(L)*

uti possidetis The principle of letting e.g. belligerents keep what they have acquired; (literally) as you possess *(L)*

vade mecum A handbook or pocket-companion; (literally) go with me *(L)*

veni, vidi, vici I came, I saw, I conquered *(L)* (The words of Julius Caesar)

ventre à terre Flat out; at full speed; (literally) belly to the ground *(Fr)*

verbatim (et literatim) Word for word (and letter for letter) *(L)*

videlicet (viz) To wit, namely *(L)*

vigilante An unofficial peacekeeper or protector of a group; member of a vigilance committee *(SP)*

vivat rex/regina Long live the king/queen *(L)*

vox populi, vox Dei The voice of the people is the voice of God *(L)*

28 ABBREVIATIONS IN COMMON USE

(1) *It is now usual to spell abbreviations, especially of scientific terms and names of international organisations, without stops. In the list below, the stops are generally omitted, but it should be understood that in most cases neither method of writing (with or without stops) is wrong.*

(2) *Abbrevaitions for the names of societies and associations are given, but abbreviations for the designations of those belonging to any particular organisations—as Associate, Fellow, Associate Fellow, Member, or Associate Member—are not specifically included.*

A Associate . . . see note (2) above; amateur; Academician; argon; ampere; angstrom; atomic (in **A-bomb**); denoting the first, or a high, class (as in **A-road**); advanced (in **A-level**); Austria (IVR)

Å Ångström

a are (metric measure); accepted; acre; active; afternoon; *annus* year; *ante* before

ā, āā in prescriptions, *ana* (Gr), i.e. of each a like quantity

AA Automobile Association; Alcoholics Anonymous; anti-aircraft

AAA Amateur Athletic Association; American Automobile Association

AAM air-to-air missile

AAQMG Assistant Adjutant and Quartermaster General

AAS *Academiae Americanae Socius* Fellow of the American Academy

AB able-bodied seaman; *Artium Baccalaureus* Bachelor of Arts

ABA Amateur Boxing Association

Abb. Abbess; Abbot; Abbey

abbr., abbrev. abbreviated; abbreviation

ABC Associated British Cinemas; American Broadcasting Corporation; Australian Broadcasting Corporation

abd abdicated; abridged

ABFM American Board of Foreign Missions

ab init *ab initio* from the beginning

abl ablative

ABM anti-ballistic missile

Abp Archbishop

abr abridged; abridgment

ABS Associate of the Building Societies Institute; Association of Broadcasting Staff

abs, absol. absolute(ly)

abs re *absente reo* the accused being absent

ABTA Association of British Travel Agents

AC aircraft(s)man; Aero Club; Alpine Club; *ante Christum* before Christ; (or **ac**) alternating current (*elect.*); Companion of the Order of Australia

Ac actinium

A/C, a/c account

ACA Associate of the Institute of Chartered Accountants

ACAS Advisory, Conciliation and Arbitration Service

acc (or **acct, a/c**) account; accountant; (or **accus**) accusative; according

ACGB Arts Council of Great Britain

ACP African, Caribbean and Pacific

ACT Australian Capital Territory

act. active; acting

ACTT Association of Cinematographic Television and Allied Technicians

ACU Association of Commonwealth Universities

ACW aircraft(s)woman

AD *anno Domini* in the year of the Lord; Dame of the Order of Australia

ad (or **advt**) advertisement; after date; *ante diem* before the day

ADC aide-de-camp; (or **AD and C**) advise duration and charge

ad fin *ad finem* at, towards, or to, the end

ad inf *ad infinitum* to infinity

ad init *ad initium* at or to the beginning

ad int *ad interim* in the meantime

adj   adjective; adjourned; adjustment
Adjt   Adjutant
Adjt-Gen   Adjutant-General
ad lib   *ad libitum* at pleasure
ad loc   *ad locum* at the place
Adm   Admiral
admin   administration
ADP   automatic data processing
adv   advent; adverb; *adversus* against;
   advocate; advisory
ad val   *ad valorem* according to value
advt   advertisement
ae, aet   *aetatis* of his age, aged (so many
   years)
AEA   Atomic Energy Authority (UK)
AEB   Associated Examining Board
AEC   Atomic Energy Commission (US)
AEI   Associated Electrical Industries
AERE   Atomic Energy Research
   Establishment
AEU   Amalgamated Engineering Union
AF   Associate Fellow . . . see note (2)
   above; Admiral of the Fleet; audio
   frequency
AFA   Amateur Football Association
AFC   Air Force Cross
AFG   Afghanistan (IVR)
AFL-CIO   American Federation of
   Labor and Congress of Industrial
   Organizations
AFM   Air Force Medal
AG   Adjutant-General; (or **A-G**)
   Attorney-General; *Aktiengesellschaft*
   (Ger) joint stock company
Ag   *argentum* silver
AGM, agm   annual general meeting
AGR   advanced gas-cooled reactor
agr, agric   agriculture
Agt   Agent
AH   *anno Hegirae* in the year of
   Hegira—i.e. from the flight of
   Mohammed (AD 622, 13 Sept)
Ah   ampere hour
AHA   Area Health Authority
AHS   *anno humanae salutis* in the year of
   human salvation
AI   artificial insemination
AIBD   Association of International
   Bond Dealers
AID   artificial insemination by donor;
   Agency for International Development
   (US)
AIDS   acquired immune deficiency
   syndrome

AIH   artificial insemination by husband
AK   Knight of the Order of Australia
AL   Albania (IVR)
Al   aluminium
Al(a)   Alabama
Alas   Alaska
Alba   Alberta
Alcan   Aluminium Company of Canada
Ald   Alderman
alg   algebra
alt   alternate; altitude; alto
Alta   Alberta
AM   Associate Member . . . see note (2)
   above; *Artium Magister* Master of Arts;
   (or **am**) *ante meridiem* before noon;
   Anno Mundi in the year of the world;
   Ave Maria Hail Mary; amplitude
   modulation; Member of the Order of
   Australia
Am   americium
Am, Amer   America; American
AMC   American Motors Corporation
AMDG   *ad majorem Dei gloriam* to the
   greater glory of God
AMMA   Assistant Masters' and
   Mistresses' Association
ammo   ammunition
amp   ampere
amt   amount; air mail transfer
amu   atomic mass unit
an.   *anno* in the year; anonymous; *ante*
   before
anal   analysis; analogy
anat   anatomy
anc   ancient(ly)
ANC   African National Congress
Ang   *Anglice* in English
anme   *anonyme* (Fr) limited liability
anon   anonymous
ans   answer
antiq   antiquities; antiquarian
Anzac   (a soldier serving with the)
   Australian-New Zealand Army Corps
Anzus   (the alliance between)
   Australia, New Zealand and the United
   States
AO   Army Order; Officer of the Order
   of Australia
AOB   any other business
AOCB   any other competent business
AOC-in-C   Air Officer
   Commanding-in-Chief
AOF   Ancient Order of Foresters
aor   aorist

373

AP Associated Press

APEX Association of Professional, Executive, Clerical and Computer Staff

apo apogee

Apoc Apocalypse; Apocrypha(l)

app appendix; apparent(ly); apprentice

appro approval; approbation

approx approximate(ly)

APR annual percentage rate

Apr April

APRC *anno post Romam conditam* in the year after the founding of Rome (753 BC)

AQ achievement quotient

aq *aqua* water

Ar argon

Ar, Arab Arabic

ar *anno regni* in the year of the reign

ar, arr arrive(s); arrival

ARA Associate of the Royal Academy

ARAMCO Arabian-American Oil Company

ARC Agricultural Research Council

arccos inverse cosine

arch archaic; architecture

archaeol archaeology; archaeological

Archd Archdeacon; Archduke

archit architecture

arcsin inverse sine

arctan inverse tangent

arg *argentum* silver

arith arithmetic(al)

Ariz Arizona

Ark Arkansas

ARP Air Raid Precautions

ARR *anno regni regis* or *reginae* in the year of the king's or the queen's reign

arr arranged; arrive(s); arrival

art article; artificial; (or **arty**) artillery

AS Anglo-Saxon; *anno salutis* in the year of salvation; Assistant Secretary

As arsenic

ASA Amateur Swimming Association; American Standards Association

asap as soon as possible

ASC American Society of Cinematographers

Asda Associated Dairies

Asdic an acronym from Allied (or Anti-) Submarine Detection and Investigation Committee, used for a particular device for locating submerged objects

ASE Amalgamated Society of Engineers; Association for Science Education

ASEAN Association of South-East Asian Nations

ASF Associate of the Institute of Shipping and Forwarding Agents

ASH Action on Smoking and Health

ASLEF Associated Society of Locomotive Engineers and Firemen

ASM air-to-surface missile

ASP accelerated surface post

Ass, Assoc Association

Asst Assistant

AST Atlantic Standard Time

ASTMS Association of Scientific, Technical and Managerial Staffs

astr, astron astronomy

astrol astrology

AT Alternative Technology

ATA Air Transport Auxiliary

ATC Air Training Corps; air traffic control; automatic train control

ATM automated teller machine

atm atmosphere

at no, at numb atomic number

Att Attic (Greek); Attorney

Att-Gen Attorney-General

attrib attribute(d); attributive(ly)

Atty Attorney

ATV Associated Television

at wt atomic weight

AU (or **ÅU**) Ångström unit (now usu. Ångström; abbrev. Å); astronomical unit

Au *aurum* gold

AUC *anno urbis conditae* or *ab urbe condita* in the year from the building of the city—Rome (753 BC)

AUEW Amalgamated Union of Engineering Workers

Aufl *Auflage* (Ger) edition

Aug August

AUS Australia, including Papua New Guinea (IVR)

AUT Association of University Teachers

aut, auto automatic

Auth Ver, AV Authorised Version

AV audio-visual

av *annos vixit* lived (so many) years

av (or **ave**) avenue; average

AVM Air Vice-Marshal

avoir, avdp avoirdupois

AWOL absent, or absence, without official leave

AWRE   Atomic Weapons Research Establishment
ax   axiom
az   azimuth

B   Baron; British; Bachelor; boron; bel; black (on lead pencils); Belgium (IVR)
2B, 3B   same as **BB, BBB** (on lead pencils)
b   born; book; bowled; breadth
BA   *Baccalaureus Artium* Bachelor of Arts; British America; British Association (for the Advancement of Science); British Academy; Buenos Aires; British Airways; Booksellers' Association (of Great Britain and Ireland)
Ba   barium
BAA   British Airports Authority
BABS   beam, or blind, approach beacon system
BAC   British Aircraft Corporation
Bach   Bachelor
BACIE   British Association for Commercial and Industrial Education
BACS   Bankers' Automated Clearing Service
BAFTA   British Academy of Film and Television Arts
BAgr(ic)   Bachelor of Agriculture
BAI   *Baccalaureus in Arte Ingeniaria* Bachelor of Engineering
bal   balance
BALPA   British Airline Pilots' Association
B and B   bed and breakfast
B and FBS   British and Foreign Bible Society
BAOR   British Army of the Rhine
Bap, Bapt   Baptist
bap, bapt   baptised
Bar   Barrister
bar   baritone
BArch   Bachelor of Architecture
Bart   Baronet
Bart's   St Bartholomew's Hospital, London
BASF   *Badische Anilin und Soda-Fabrik* (German chemical company)
BAT   British-American Tobacco Company
bat, batt   battalion; battery
BB   Boys' Brigade; double, or very, black (on lead pencils)
bb   books

BBB   triple black, blacker than **BB** (on lead pencils)
BBBC   British Boxing Board of Control
BBC   British Broadcasting Corporation (orig. Company)
BBFC   British Board of Film Censors
BC   before Christ; Board of Control; British Columbia; Battery Commander
BCAL   British Caledonian (Airways)
BCC   British Council of Churches
bcg   bacillus of Calmette and Guérin, an attenuated strain of the tubercle bacillus, used for inoculation
BCh   *Baccalaureus Chirurgiae* Bachelor of Surgery
BCL   Bachelor of Civil Law
BCom(m)   Bachelor of Commerce
BCS   British Computer Society
BD   Bachelor of Divinity
bd   bound
BDA   British Dental Association
Bde   Brigade
BDH   British Drug Houses
BDI   *Bundesverband der Deutschen Industrie* (Ger) Federation of German Industry
BDS   Bachelor of Dental Surgery
bds   boards
BE   Bachelor of Engineering; Board of Education
Be   beryllium
B/E, be   bill of exchange
BEAB   British Electrical Approvals Board
BEAMA   British Electrical and Allied Manufacturers' Association
BEd   Bachelor of Education
Beds   Bedfordshire
BEF   British Expeditionary Force
bef   before
Belg   Belgian; Belgium; Belgic
BEM   British Empire Medal
Benelux   a name for Belgium, the Netherlands and Luxembourg
BEng   Bachelor of Engineering
Berks   Berkshire
B ès L   *Bachelier ès Lettres* (Fr) Bachelor of Letters
B ès S   *Bachelier ès Sciences* (Fr) Bachelor of Sciences
bet.   between
BeV   billion electron-volt(s) (in USA, where billion means 1000 million, same as **GeV**)
bf   brought forward

BFPO   British Forces Post Office
BG   Bulgaria (IVR)
bhp   brake horse-power
BHS   British Home Stores
Bi   bismuth
Bib   Bible
Bibl   Biblical
bibl   bibliotheca (=a library, book-collection, or catalogue)
biblio, bibliog   bibliography
BICC   British Insulated Callender's Cables
BIFU   Banking Insurance and Finance Union
BIM   British Institute of Management
biog   biography
biol   biology
BIPM   *Bureau International des Poids et Mesures* (Fr) International Bureau of Weights and Measures
BIR   British Institute of Radiology
BIS   Bank for International Settlements
bis   bissextile (=having a day added, as a leap year)
bk   book; bank; bark
bkg   banking
bkt   basket
BL   Bachelor of Law; Bachelor of Letters; British Legion; British Leyland; British Library
bl   barrel; bale; (or **B/L**) bill of lading
BLAISE   British Library Automated Information Service
bldg   building
BLESMA   British Limbless Ex-Servicemen's Association
BLit(t)   *Baccalaureus Lit(t)erarum* Bachelor of Literature or Letters
BLLD   British Library Lending Division
BLMC   British Leyland Motor Corporation
BLRD   British Library Reference Division
Blvd   Boulevard
BM   Bachelor of Medicine; British Museum; Brigade Major
BMA   British Medical Association
BMEWS   ballistic missile early warning system
BMJ   British Medical Journal
BML   British Museum Library
BMus   Bachelor of Music
BMW   *Bayerische Motoren Werke* (Ger) Bavarian motor works

Bn   Baron
bn   battalion
BNEC   British National Export Council
BNFL   British Nuclear Fuels Limited
BNOC   British National Oil Corporation
bo   branch office; buyer's option; (or **BO**) body odour
BOA   British Optical Association
BOC   British Oxygen Company
BOCM   British Oil and Cake Mills
Bol   Bolivia
bor   borough
BOSS   Bureau of State Security (South Africa)
bot   botany; bought; bottle
BOTB   British Overseas Trade Board
Boul   Boulevard
BP   British Pharmacopoeia; British Petroleum; Baden-Powell; be prepared
Bp   Bishop
bp   boiling-point; bills of parcels; bills payable; (or **b pl**) birthplace; *bonum publicum* the public good
BPC   British Printing Corporation; British Pharmaceutical Codex
BPharm   Bachelor of Pharmacy
BPhil   *Baccalaureus Philosophiae* Bachelor of Philosophy
BQ   *bene quiescat* may he (or she) rest well
BR   British Rail; Brazil (IVR)
Br   bromine
Br   Brother
br   bank rate; branch; brig; brown; bridge
Braz   Brazil; Brazilian
BRCS   British Red Cross Society
BRD   *Bundesrepublik Deutschland* (Ger) German Federal Republic
b rec   bills receivable
Bret   Breton
Brig   Brigadier
Brig-Gen   Brigadier-General
Brit   Britain; Britannia; British; Briton
Bro   Brother
Bros   Brothers
BRS   British Road Services
BS   Bachelor of Science or of Surgery; Blessed Sacrament; balance sheet; (or **bs**) bill of sale; British Shipbuilders
BSA   Building Societies Association; Birmingham Small Arms

BSAC British Sub Aqua Club
BSC British Steel Corporation; British Sugar Corporation
BSc Bachelor of Science
BSI British Standards Institution; Building Societies Institute
BSM British School of Motoring
BS(S) British Standards (Specification)
BST British Summer Time; British Standard Time
Bt Baronet
BT British Telecom
BTA British Tourist Authority
BTEC Business and Technical Education Council
Btu British thermal unit
bu. bushel(s)
Bucks Buckinghamshire
Bulg Bulgaria; Bulgarian
BUNAC British Universities North America Club
BUPA British United Provident Association
bus., bush. bushel(s)
BV *Beata Virgo* Blessed Virgin; *bene vale* farewell
BVM The Blessed Virgin Mary
BVM(&)S Bachelor of Veterinary Medicine and Surgery

C carbon; Conservative
°C degree(s) Celsius, centigrade
c centi-; *caput* chapter; cent; centime; *circa* about; caught
¢ cent(s)
© copyright
CA Chartered Accountant (Scotland); County Alderman
Ca calcium
ca *circa* about; cases
CAA Civil Aviation Authority
CAB Civil Aeronautics Board (USA); Citizens Advice Bureau
cad cash against documents
CAI computer-aided instruction
CAL computer-assisted learning
cal calorie
Cal, Calif California
Cam, Camb Cambridge
Cambs Cambridgeshire
CAMRA Campaign for Real Ale
CAN customs assigned number
Can Canada; Canadian; Canon; Canto

C and A Clemens and August (clothing stores)
C and G City and Guilds (of London Institute)
C & W country and western music
Cant Canterbury; Canticles
Cantab *Cantabrigiensis* of Cambridge
Cantuar *Cantuaria* Canterbury; *Cantuariensis* of Canterbury
CAP Common Agricultural Policy
cap capital; *caput* chapter; *capitulum* head, chapter; *capiat* let him (or her) take
caps capitals (in printing)
Capt Captain
CAR Central African Republic
Car. *Carolus* Charles
car. carat
CARD Campaign Against Racial Discrimination
Card. Cardinal
Cards Cardiganshire
CARE Co-operative for American Relief to Everywhere
Caricom Caribbean Community and Common Market
CASE Confederation for the Advancement of State Education
CAT College of Advanced Technology; computer-aided typesetting
cat. catechism; catalogue
Cath. Catholic
cath. cathedral
CB Companion of the Order of the Bath; confined (or confinement) to barracks; Citizens' Band (radio); cash book
CBC Canadian Broadcasting Corporation
CBE Commander of the Order of the British Empire
CBI Confederation of British Industry
CBM Californian Business Machines
CBS Confraternity of the Blessed Sacrament; Columbia Broadcasting System
CC County Council; Cricket Club; closed circuit (transmission); Companion of the Order of Canada; Chamber of Commerce
cc cubic-centimetre(s); *capita* chapters; carbon copy
CCA current cost accounting
CCCP see **USSR**

CCF Combined Cadet Force

CCPR Central Council of Physical Recreation

CCS Corporation of Certified Secretaries

CD *Corps Diplomatique* (Fr) Diplomatic Corps; Civil Defence; contagious disease(s)

Cd cadmium

c/d carried down

CDN Canada (IVR)

Cdr Commander

CDSO Companion of the Distinguished Service Order

CDV Civil Defence Volunteers

CE Civil Engineer; Council of Europe

Ce cerium

CEDO Centre for Education Development Overseas (formerly **CREDO**)

CEGB Central Electricity Generating Board

CEI Council of Engineering Institutions

cel celebrated

Celt. Celtic

cen central; century

CEng Chartered Engineer

cent *centum* a hundred; century; central

CENTO Central Treaty Organisation

CERN *Conseil Européen pour la Recherche Nucléaire* (Fr) European Organisation for Nuclear Research

cert certainty; (or **certif**) certificate; certificated; certify

CET Central European Time

cet par *ceteris paribus* other things being equal

CF Chaplain to the Forces

Cf californium

cf calf (book-binding)

cf *confer* compare

cf (and) i cost, freight, and insurance

CFAFr Communauté Financière Africaine franc

CFPFr Communauté Française du Pacific franc

cg centigram(me)(s)

cg centre of gravity

CG(L)I City and Guilds (of London) Institute

CGPM *Conférence Générale des Poids et Mesures* (Fr) General Conference of Weights and Measures

CGS (or **cgs**) centimetre-gramme-second (unit or system); Chief of the General Staff

CGT capital gains tax; *Confédération Générale du Travail* (Fr) General Confederation of Labour

CH Companion of Honour; *Confederatio Helvetica* Switzerland (also IVR)

Ch Chief; China; Church; Champion

ch central heating; chaldron; chapter; child

Chamb. Chamberlain

Chanc. Chancellor; Chancery

Chap. Chaplain; Chapter

CHAPS Clearing House Automated Payments System

Chas Charles

ChB *Chirurgiae Baccalaureus* Bachelor of Surgery

chem chemistry; chemical

Ch Hist Church History

Chin. China; Chinese

ChJ Chief-Justice

ChM *Chirurgiae Magister* Master of Surgery

choc chocolate

Chr Christ; Christian

chron chronicle; chronology; chronological

CI Channel Islands

CIA Central Intelligence Agency (USA)

Cia *Compagnia* (It) Company

CID Criminal Investigation Department; Council of Industrial Design

CIE *Córas Iompair Éireann* (Ir) Transport Organisation of Ireland

Cie *Compagnie* (Fr) Company

cif cost, insurance, freight

CIGS Chief of Imperial General Staff (now **CGS**)

CII Chartered Insurance Institute

CIM Commission on Industry and Manpower

C-in-C Commander-in-Chief

CIPFA Chartered Institute of Public Finance and Accountancy

CIPM *Comité International des Poids et Mesures* (Fr) International Committee of Weights and Measures

CIR Commission on Industrial Relations

cir, circ *circa, circiter, circum* about

circs circumstances

CIS Chartered Institute of Secretaries

CIT Chartered Institute of Transport

cit citation; citizen

civ   civil; civilian
CJ   Chief-Justice
Cl   chlorine
cl   centilitre(s); *cum laude* with praise; class; clause
class   classical; classification
CLitt   Companion of Literature
CLR   computer language recorder
CLT   computer language translator
CM   Certificated Master: Corresponding Member; Common Metre; *Chirurgiae Magister* Master of Surgery; Member of the Order of Canada
Cm   curium
cm   centimetre(s)
CMG   Companion of the Order of St Michael and St George
CMI   computer-managed instruction
Cmnd   Command Paper
CMRST   Committee on Manpower Resources for Science and Technology
CMS   Church Missionary Society
CNAA   Council for National Academic Awards
CND   Campaign for Nuclear Disarmament
CNR   Canadian National Railway
CNS   central nervous system
CO   conscientious objector; Colonial Office (before Aug. 1966); Commonwealth Office (from Aug. 1966; see also **FCO**); Commanding Officer; Criminal Office; Crown Office
Co   cobalt; Company; County
c/o   care of
coad   coadjutor
Cod.   Codex
COD, cod   cash (or collect) on delivery
co-ed   co-educational
C of A   Certificate of Airworthiness
C of E   Church of England; Council of Europe
C of I   Church of Ireland
C of S   Church of Scotland; Chief of Staff
cog   cognate
cog   centre of gravity
COGB   Certified Official Government Business
COHSE   Confederation of Health Service Employees
COI   Central Office of Information
COL   computer-oriented language

Col   Colonel; Colorado
col   column
coll   college; colleague; collector; colloquial
collat   collateral(ly)
colloq   colloquial(ly)
Colo   Colorado
COM   computer output microfilm
Com   Commander; Commodore; Committee; Commissioner; Commonwealth; Communist
com   common; comedy: commerce; committee; commune
Comdr   Commander
Comdt   Commandant
COMECON   Council for Mutual Economic Aid, or Assistance (Communist Nations)
comm   commentary; commander; communication
Commissr   Commissioner
commn   commission
Commy   Commissary; Communist
comp   comparative; compositor; compare; compound; compounded
compar   comparative; comparison
COMSAT   Communications Satellite (USA)
Com Ver   Common Version
Con   Consul
con   *contra* against; *conju(n)x* consort; conclusion; conversation; convenience
conc   concentrated; concentration
Cong   Congress; Congregation(al)
conj   conjunction; conjunctive
Conn   Connecticut
conn   connection; connected; connotation
cons   consonant
Consols   Consolidated Funds
cont, contd   continued
contr   contracted; contraction
contr bon mor   *contra bonos mores* contrary to good manners or morals
conv   conventional
co-op   co-operative
Cop, Copt   Coptic
Cor   Corinthians; Coroner
Cor Mem   Corresponding Member
corol, coroll   corollary
Corp   Corporation; Corporal
corr   corrupted; corruption; correspond
Cor Sec   Corresponding Secretary
CoS   Chief of Staff

cos cosine
CP Clerk of the Peace; Common Pleas; carriage paid; College of Preceptors; Communist Party; Cape Province (S. Africa)
cp candle-power; compare
CPA Chartered Patent Agent
CPAC Consumer Protection Advisory Committee
CPAG Child Poverty Action Group
CPC Clerk of the Privy Council
CPI, cpi consumer price index; characters per inch
Cpl Corporal
cpp current purchasing power
CPR Canadian Pacific Railway
CPS *Custos Privati Sigilli* Keeper of the Privy Seal; (or **cps**) characters per second
CPSA Civil and Public Services Association
CPU central processing unit
CR *Carolus rex* King Charles; *civis romanus* a Roman citizen; *Custos Rotulorum* Keeper of the Rolls
Cr chromium
cr credit; creditor; crown
CRAC Careers Research and Advisory Centre
CRE Commission for Racial Equality
cres, cresc crescendo; crescent
CRMP Corps of Royal Military Police
CRO cathode-ray oscillograph; Commonwealth Relations Office (until 1966); Criminal Records Office
CRT cathode-ray tube
CS Court of Session; Clerk to the Signet; Civil Service; Christian Science; Chemical Society; orthobenzylidene malononitrile, an irritant 'gas' synthesised (1928) by *C*orson and *S*toughton; Czechoslovakia (IVR)
Cs caesium
c/s cycles per second (hertz)
CSE Certificate of Secondary Education
CSEU Confederation of Shipbuilding and Engineering Unions
CSIRO Commonwealth Scientific and Industrial Research Organisation
CSO community service order
CSP Council for Scientific Policy; Chartered Society of Physiotherapists
CST Central Standard Time
CSU Civil Service Union

CSV community service volunteer
CSYS Certificate of Sixth Year Studies
C/T credit transfer
Ct Connecticut
ct cent; carat
CTC Cyclists' Touring Club
CTOL conventional take-off and landing
CTT capital transfer tax
Cu *cuprum* copper
cu, cub cubic
CUP Cambridge University Press
cur, curt current (this month)
cusec cubic feet per second
CV, cv *curriculum vitae* (see Dict), or *cursus vitae* course, progress, of life
cva cerebrovascular accident
CVO Commander of the (Royal) Victorian Order
CWO, cwo cash with order
cwr continuous welded rail
CWS Co-operative Wholesale Society
cwt hundred-weight(s)—**c** (*centum* a hundred), **wt** (weight)

D deuterium; Federal Republic of Germany (IVR)
3-D three-dimensional
d day; diameter; *dele* delete; dead; died; deserted; degree; *denarius* or *denarii* a penny or pence (before 1971): duke
DA District Attorney; Diploma of Art
D(A)AG Deputy (Assistant) Adjutant-General
Dan Daniel; Danish
D and C dilatation and curettage (an operation which cleans out a body-cavity, esp. the womb)
DATEC data and telecommunications
dau daughter
dB decibel
DBE Dame Commander of the Order of the British Empire
DC *da capo* (It) return to the beginning (*mus*); District of Columbia; (or **dc**) direct current (*elect*): District Commissioner
DCL Doctor of Civil Law; Distillers Company Limited
DCM Distinguished Conduct Medal
DCMG Dame Commander of the Order of St Michael and St George
DCS Deputy Clerk of Session

DCVO Dame Commander of the (Royal) Victorian Order

DD *Divinitatis Doctor* Doctor of Divinity

dd, D/D days after date; day's date; direct debit

DDD *dat, dicat, dedicat* gives, devotes, and dedicates; *dono dedit dedicavit* gave and dedicated as a gift

DDR *Deutsche Demokratische Republik* (Ger) German Democratic Republic (also IVR)

DDS Doctor of Dental Surgery

DDT dichlorodiphenyltrichloroethane, an insecticide

DE Department of Employment

DEA Department of Economic Affairs

Dec December

dec deceased

dec, decl declaration; declension

DEd Doctor of Education

def definition; (or **deft**) defendant

deg degree(s)

Del Delaware

del delegate; (or **delt**) *delineavit* drew it

demon, demons demonstrative

DEng Doctor of Engineering

dent dental; dentist; dentistry

DEP Department of Employment and Productivity

Dep, Dept, dep, dept department; deputy

dep deposed; depart(s); departure

der, deriv derivation; derived

derv diesel engine fuel oil (from *d*iesel *e*ngined *r*oad *v*ehicle)

DES Department of Education and Science

DesRCA Designer of the Royal College of Art

DEW distant early warning

DF Defender of the Faith; Dean of the Faculty

DFC Distinguished Flying Cross

DFM Distinguished Flying Medal

dft defendant; draft

DG *Dei gratia* by the grace of God

dg decigram(me)(s)

dh *das heisst* (Ger) that is to say

DHSS Department of Health and Social Services (formerly Security)

dial dialect

diam diameter

DIC Diploma of the Imperial College

dict dictator; dictionary

diff different; difference

DIG Disabled Income Group

DIH Diploma in Industrial Health

dil dilute

DIN *Deutsche Industrie Normen* (Ger) German Industrial Standards

DIng *Doctor Ingeniariae* Doctor of Engineering

Dip Diploma, as eg **Dip Ed,** Diploma in Education, **Dip Tech,** Diploma in Technology

Dir Director

dis discontinued

disc discount; discoverer

diss dissertation

dist distance; distinguish; district; distilled

div divide; division; divine; divorced; dividend

DIY do-it-yourself

DJ disc-jockey

DK Denmark (IVR)

DL Deputy Lieutenant

dl decilitre(s)

DLit(t) *Doctor litterarum* or *litteraturae* Doctor of Letters or Literature

DM Deutsche Mark (Federal German currency)

dm decimetre(s)

DMus Doctor of Music

DMZ demilitarised zone

DNA deoxyribonucleic acids

DNB Dictionary of National Biography

do *ditto* (It) the same (aforesaid)

DOA dead on arrival

dob date of birth

DOC District Officer Commanding

DOE Department of the Environment

DOG Directory of Opportunities for Graduates

DOM *Deo optimo maximo* to God, best and greatest; *Dominus Omnium Magister* God the master of all; dirty old man

Dom *Dominus* Lord; Dominion

dom domestic

DOMS Diploma in Ophthalmic Medicine and Surgery

Dor Doric

doz dozen

DP Displaced Person; data processing; duly performed (the work of the class)

DPH Diploma in Public Health

DPh, DPhil *Doctor Philosophiae* Doctor of Philosophy
DPM Diploma in Psychological Medicine
dpm disintegrations per minute
DPP Director of Public Prosecutions
dpt department
Dr Doctor; debtor; drummer; driver; drachma (Greek currency)
dr dead reckoning; dram; drawer
DS *dal segno* (It) from the sign (*mus*); disseminated sclerosis
ds, D/S days after sight
DSC Distinguished Service Cross
DSc *Doctor Scientiae* Doctor of Science
DSM Distinguished Service Medal
DSO Distinguished Service Order
dsp *decessit sine prole* died without issue
DT data transmission; (or **dt, DT's, dt's**) delirium tremens
DTh *Doctor Theologiae* Doctor of Theology
DTI Department of Trade and Industry
DV *Deo volente* God willing
dvp *decessit vita patris* died in father's lifetime
dwt pennyweight—**d** (*denarius* a penny), **wt** (weight)
dyn dyne; dynamo; dynamometer

E East; English; Spain (IVR)
E energy
E and OE errors and omissions excepted
eaon except as otherwise noted
EAPS European Association of Professional Secretaries
Ebor *Eboracum* York; *Eboracensis* of York
EBU European Broadcasting Union
EC East Central; Established Church; European Community; Electricity Council
EC $ East Caribbean dollar
ECE Economic Commission for Europe
ECG electrocardiogram (-graph)
ECG(D) Export Credits Guarantee (Department)
ECO English Chamber Orchestra
ECSC European Coal and Steel Community

ECT electroconvulsive therapy
ECTU European Confederation of Trade Unions
ECU English Church Union; European currency unit
Ed Editor
ed, edit edited; edition
EdB Bachelor of Education
EDC European Defence Community
EDF European Development Fund
Edin Edinburgh
edit edited; edition
EDP electronic data processing
EDS English Dialect Society
EE errors excepted
EEC European Economic Community
EEG electroencephalogram (-graph)
EET Eastern European Time
EETS Early English Text Society
EFL English as a foreign language
EFT electronic funds transfer
EFTA European Free Trade Association
EFTPOS electronic funds transfer at point of sale
eg, eg, ex gr *exempli gratia* for example
EGU English Golf Union
EI East Indies
EIS Educational Institute of Scotland
El Al Israeli airline (lit. 'towards the sky')
elec, elect electric; electricity
ELT English language teaching
EMA European Monetary Agreement
EMF European Monetary Fund
emf electromotive force
EMI EMI Limited (formerly Electrical and Musical Industries Limited)
Emp Emperor, Empress
EMS European Monetary System
emu electromagnetic unit
enc(s) enclosure(s)
ENE east-north-east
ENEA European Nuclear Energy Agency
Eng England; English
eng engineer; engraver; engraving
Ens Ensign
ENSA Entertainments National Services Association
ENT Ear, Nose and Throat
Env Ext Envoy Extraordinary
EOC Equal Opportunities Commission
eod every other day

EP extended play (record): electroplated
Ep Epistle
EPA European Productivity Agency
EPIC Exchange Price Information Service
EPNS electroplated nickel silver; English Place-Name Society
EPU European Payments Union
ER *Elisabeth Regina* Elizabeth, Queen
ER(I) *Edwardus Rex (Imperator)* Edward, King (and Emperor)
ERNIE *e*lectronic *r*andom *n*umber *i*ndicator *e*quipment (computer)
ESA European Space Agency
Esc escudo (Portuguese currency)
ESE east-south-east
ESL English as a second language
ESN educationally subnormal
ESP extra-sensory perception
esp, espec especially
Esq, Esqr Esquire
ESRC Economic and Social Research Council
ESRO European Space Research Organisation
ESSO Standard Oil
EST Eastern Standard Time; electric shock treatment
est established; estimated
ESU English-Speaking Union
ET Arab Republic of Egypt (IVR)
ETA estimated time of arrival
et al *et alii, aliae,* or *alia* and others; *et alibi* and elsewhere
etc, &c *et ceteri* or *cetera* and the others, and so forth
ETD estimated time of departure
et seq or **sq** (sing), *et sequens* **et sqq** (pl) *et sequentes* or *sequentia* and the following
ETU Electrical Trades Union
ety, etym etymology; etymological
EU Evangelical Union
Eu europium
Euratom *Eur*opean *Atom*ic Energy Community
eV electron-volt
ex examined; example: exception; executive; export
Exc Excellency
exc except; exception
ex div *extra dividendum* without dividend
ex gr *exempli gratia* for the sake of example
ex lib *ex libris* from the books (of)—as on bookplates

ex officio by virtue of his office (Lat)
exp export; exponential
exr executor
exrx executrix
ext extension; externally; extinct; extra; extract

F Fellow . . . see note (2); Fahrenheit; fluorine; France (IVR)
F force
f following; farthing; feminine; fathom; foot; forte; folio
f frequency
FA Football Association; Faculty of Actuaries
Fa Florida
fam familiar; family
FAO Food and Agriculture Organisation
FAS Fellow of the Society of Arts; Fellow of the Antiquarian Society
fas free alongside ship
FBA Fellow of the British Academy
FBI Federal Bureau of Investigation
FCA Fellow of the Institute of Chartered Accountants
FCO Foreign and Commonwealth Office (**FO** and **CO** combined in 1968)
fcp, fcap foolscap
FD *Fidei Defensor* Defender of the Faith
Fe *ferrum* iron
Feb February
fec *fecit* did it, or made it (sing.)
fem feminine
FET field-effect transistor
feud feudal
ff *fecerunt* did it, or made it (pl); folios; following (pl)
ff fortissimo
FH fire hydrant
FIAT *Fabbrica Italiana Automobile Torino* (It) Italian Motor Works in Turin
Fid Def *Fidei Defensor* Defender of the Faith
FIDO Fog Investigation and Dispersal Operation; Film Industry Defence Organisation
fi fa *fieri facias* that you cause to be made (a writ of execution)
FIFA *Fédération Internationale de Football Association* (Fr) International Association Football Federation

FIFO first in, first out
fig figure; figurative(ly)
FIS Family Income Supplement
fl *floruit* flourished; florin
Flor, Fla Florida
fl oz fluid ounce(s)
FM frequency modulation; Field-Marshal
Fm fermium
fm fathom
FO Foreign Office (see **FCO**); Field Officer; Flying Officer
fo, fol folio
fob free on board
FOC father of the chapel
foc free of charge
FOE Friends of Europe; Friends of the Earth
for free on rail
FP fireplug; former pupil; Free Presbyterian
fp forte-piano; freezing-point
FPA Family Planning Association
FPS foot-pound-second
Fr francium; franc; Father; France; French; Friar; Friday
fr fragment; franc; frequently
frat fraternise; fraternity
FRCP Fellow of the Royal College of Physicians (**Edin,** of Edinburgh; **Lond,** of London; **Irel,** of Ireland)
FRCPS Glas Fellow of the Royal College of Physicians and Surgeons of Glasgow
FRCS Fellow of the Royal College of Surgeons (**Ed,** of Edinburgh; **Eng,** of England; **Irel,** of Ireland)
F(R)FPSG (formerly) Fellow of the (Royal) Faculty of Physicans and Surgeons of Glasgow (now **FRCPS Glas**)
FRG Federal Republic of Germany
FRPS Fellow of the Royal Photographic Society
FRS Fellow of the Royal Society (**E,** of Edinburgh)
FSF Fellow of the Institute of Shipping and Forwarding Agents
FT Financial Times
ft foot, feet; fort
fth, fthm fathom
fur furlong(s)
fut future
fz sforzando (*mus*)

G Gauss; giga-
G constant of gravitation, the factor linking force with mass and distance
g gram(me)
g acceleration of gravity
GA General Assembly
Ga gallium; Georgia
Gael Gaelic
gal, gall gallon(s)
G and S Gilbert and Sullivan
GATT General Agreement on Tariffs and Trade
gaz gazette; gazetteer
GB Great Britain (also IVR)
GBE (Knight or Dame) Grand Cross of the British Empire
gbh grievous bodily harm
GBS George Bernard Shaw
GC George Cross
GCA ground control(led) approach system or control apparatus
GCB (Knight) Grand Cross of the Bath
GCE General Certificate of Education
GCH (Knight) Grand Cross of Hanover
GCHQ Government Communications Headquarters
GCM General Court-Martial; (or **gcm**) greatest common measure
GCMG (Knight) Grand Cross of the Order of St Michael and St George
GCVO (Knight or Dame) Grand Cross of the (Royal) Victorian Order
Gd gadolinium
GDI gross domestic income
gdns gardens
GDP gross domestic product
GDR German Democratic Republic
Ge germanium
GEC General Electric Company
Gen Genesis; (or **Genl**) General
gen gender; genitive; genus; general
gent gentleman
Geo Georgia; George
geog geography
geol geology
geom geometry
Ger German
GeV giga-electron-volt (the equivalent of a thousand million electron-volts, same value in Europe as **BeV** in USA)
GHQ General Headquarters
GI government (or general) issue (US Army); hence, common soldier
Gib Gibraltar

GIGO   garbage in, garbage out
Gk   Greek
GKN   Guest, Keen and Nettlefold
Gl   glucinum (now beryllium)
Glam   Glamorganshire
GLC   Greater London Council
Gld   guilder (Dutch currency)
GLORIA   Geological Long Range
   Asdic
Glos   Gloucestershire
GM   George Medal; (or **G-M**)
   Geiger-Müller counter; General Motors
gm   gram(me)
GMBATU   General, Municipal,
   Boilermakers and Allied Trades
   Union
GmbH   *Gesellschaft mit beschränkter
   Haftung* (Ger) limited liability company
GMC   General Medical Council
GMT   Greenwich Mean Time
GMWU   General and Municipal
   Workers Union (now **GMBATU**)
GNP   gross national product
GOC   General Officer Commanding
Gov   Governor; (or **Govt**) Government
GP   General Practitioner; Gallup poll;
   Gloria Patri glory to the Father
GPO   General Post Office
GR   Greece (IVR)
Gr   Greek
gr   grain; grammar; grouse; gunner
gram   grammar
GR(I)   *Georgius Rex (Imperator)* George,
   King (and Emperor)
GS   General Staff; General Service;
   Geological Society; Grammar School
GSM   gram(me)s per square metre
GSO   General Staff Officer
GSP   Good Service Pension
GT   *gran turismo* used of a fast motor-car
   built for touring in style
GUM   *Gosudarstvenni Universalni Magazin*
   (Russ) State Universal Store
GUS   Great Universal Stores

H   hydrogen; Henry; hydrant; hospital;
   hard (on lead pencils); Hungary (IVR)
2H   same as **HH** (on lead pencils)
h   hour
h   height
HA   Heavy Artillery
Ha   hahnium
ha   hectare; *hoc anno* this year

HAC   Honourable Artillery Company;
   high-alumina cement
h and c   hot and cold (water laid on)
Hants   Hampshire (*Hantshaving,* orig.
   name of county)
HB   hard black (on lead pencils)
hbar   hectobar
HBM   His (or Her) Britannic Majesty
HC   Heralds' College; House of
   Commons; Holy Communion
HCF   (or **Hon CF**) Honorary Chaplain
   to the Forces; (or **hcf**) highest common
   factor
HCM   His (or Her) Catholic Majesty
HE   His Excellency; His Eminence; high
   explosive; horizontal equivalent
He   helium
Heb, Hebr   Hebrew; Hebrews
HEH   His (or Her) Exalted Highness
her   heraldry; *heres* heir
Herts   Hertfordshire
HF   high frequency
Hf   hafnium
hf   half; **hf-bd** half-bound; **hf-cf**
   half-calf; **hf-mor** half-morocco
HG   His (or Her) Grace
Hg   *hydrargyrum* mercury
HGV   heavy goods vehicle
HH   His (or Her) Highness; very hard
   (on lead pencils)
HIDB   Highlands and Islands
   Development Board
Hi-Fi, hi-fi   high fidelity
HIH   His (or Her) Imperial Highness
HIM   His (or Her) Imperial Majesty
HIS   *hic iacet sepultus* here lies buried
hist   historian; history; historical
HJ(S)   *hic jacet (sepultus)* here lies
   (buried)
HK   House of Keys (Isle of Man); Hong
   Kong (also IVR)
hl   hectolitre(s)
HM   His (or Her) Majesty
HMA   Headmasters' Association
HMAS   His (or Her) Majesty's
   Australian Ship
HMC   His (or Her) Majesty's Customs;
   Headmasters' Conference
HMCS   His (or Her) Majesty's Canadian
   Ship
HMG   His (or Her) Majesty's
   Government
HMI   His (or Her) Majesty's Inspector,
   Inspectorate

HML His (or Her) Majesty's Lieutenant

HMP *hoc monumentum posuit* erected this monument

HMS His (or Her) Majesty's Ship or Service

HMSO His (or Her) Majesty's Stationery Office

HMV His Master's Voice (gramophone company)

HNC Higher National Certificate

HND Higher National Diploma

Ho holmium

ho house

Hon Honourable; Honorary

Hons Honours

Hon Sec Honorary Secretary

hor horizon; horology

hort, hortic horticulture; horticultural

HP hire-purchase; High Priest; half-pay; (or **hp**) horse-power

HQ headquarters

HR House of Representatives; Home Rule

Hr Herr

hr hour

HRE Holy Roman Emperor or Empire

HRH His (or Her) Royal Highness

HRIP *hic requiescit in pace* here rests in peace

HS *hic situs* here is laid

HSE Health and Safety Executive; *hic sepultus* (or *situs*) *est* here is buried (or laid)

HSH His (or Her) Serene Highness

HSS *Historiae Societatis Socius* Fellow of the Historical Society

HT high tension

HTV Harlech Television

Hunts Huntingdonshire

HWM high water mark

Hz Hertz (cycles per second)

I iodine; Island, Isle; Italy (IVR)

I electric current

IA Institute of Actuaries

Ia Iowa

IAAF International Amateur Athletic Federation

IAAS Incorporated Association of Architects and Surveyors

IAEA International Atomic Energy Agency

IAM Institute of Advanced Motorists

IAS Indian Administrative Service

IATA International Air Transport Association

IB Institute of Bankers

IBA Independent Broadcasting Authority

ib, ibid *ibidem* in the same place

IBM International Business Machines (computer manufacturers)

IBRD International Bank for Reconstruction and Development (World Bank)

IC integrated circuit

i/c in charge

ICA Institute of Contemporary Arts; Institute of Chartered Accountants

ICAO International Civil Aviation Organisation

ICBM intercontinental ballistic missile

ICE Institution of Civil Engineers; internal combustion engine

ICFC Industrial and Commercial Finance Corporation

IChemE Institution of Chemical Engineers

ICI Imperial Chemical Industries

ICJ International Court of Justice

ICL International Computers Limited

ICMA Institute of Cost and Management Accountants

ICRC International Committee of the Red Cross

ICS Indian Civil Service (in Republic of India, **IAS**)

ID Intelligence Department; identification; infectious diseases

Id Idaho

id *idem* the same

IDA International Development Association

IDD International direct dialling

IDN *in Dei nomine* in the name of God

IDV International Distillers and Vintners

i.e., ie *id est* that is

IEC International Electrotechnical Commission

IEE Institution of Electrical Engineers

IF intermediate frequency; insufficient funds

IFC International Finance Corporation

IHC, IHS for the Greek capitals **IHC** (**H,** capital eta (= **E**) and **C,** a form of sigma (= **S**)), first two and last letters of *Iesous* Jesus, often misread as *Jesus Hominum Salvator* Jesus Saviour of Men

ihp   indicated horse-power
IL   Institute of Linguists; Israel (IVR)
ILC   irreversible letter of credit
ILEA   Inner London Education Authority
Ill   Illinois
ill   illustration; illustrated
ILN   Illustrated London News
ILO   International Labour Organisation or (its secretariat) International Labour Office
ILP   Independent Labour Party
IMechE   Institution of Mechanical Engineers
IMF   International Monetary Fund
imit   imitative
IMM   Institution of Mining and Metallurgy
Imp   Imperial; *Imperator* Emperor
imp   (or **imperf**) imperfect; (or **imper**) imperative; *imprimatur* let it be printed; (or **impers**) impersonal
IMunE   Institution of Municipal Engineers
In   indium
in   inch(es)
inc   including; incorporated
incl   including; included
IND   same as **IDN**; India (IVR)
Ind   Indiana; Independent
ind, indic   indicative
indecl   indeclinable
indef   indefinite
indiv   individual
Ind Ter   Indian Territory
inf   *infra* below; infantry; infinitive
infra dig   *infra dignitatem* beneath one's dignity
init   *initio* in the beginning
in lim   *in limine* on the threshold, at the outset
in loc   *in loco* in its place
in loc cit   *in loco citato* in the place cited
in pr   *in principio* in the beginning
INRI   *Jesus Nazarenus Rex Judaeorum* Jesus of Nazareth King of the Jews
Inst   Institute
inst   instant—the present month; institute
InstP   Institute of Physics
instn   institution
int   interest; interior; interpreter; international; integral

Intelsat   International Telecommunications Satellite Consortium
interj   interjection
Interpol   International Criminal Police Commission
interrog   interrogation; interrogative(ly)
in trans   *in transitu* in transit
intrans   intransitive
intro, introd   introduction
inv   *invenit* designed it; invented; invoice
IOB   Institute of Building
IOC   International Olympic Committee
IoJ   Institute of Journalists
IOM   Isle of Man
IOU   I owe you
IOW   Isle of Wight
IPA   Institute of Practitioners in Advertising; International Publishers' Association; International Phonetic Alphabet
IPC   International Publishing Corporation
IPCS   Institution of Professional Civil Servants
IQ   Intelligence Quotient
iq   *idem quod* the same as
IQPS   Institute of Qualified Private Secretaries
IQS   Institute of Quantity Surveyors
IR   Iran (IVR)
Ir   iridium; Irish
IRC   International Red Cross
IRA   Irish Republican Army
IRB   Irish Republican Brotherhood
IRBM   intermediate range ballistic missile
Irel.   Ireland
IRL   Ireland (IVR)
IRQ   Iraq (IVR)
ISBN   International Standard Book Number
ISCh   Incorporated Society of Chiropodists
ISD   international subscriber dialling
ISF   Institute of Forwarding and Shipping Agents
Is(l)   island
ISO   Imperial Service Order; International Organisation for Standardisation
ISS   International Social Service
ISSN   International Standard Serial Number

ISTC Iron and Steel Trades Confederation
IT Information Technology
It Italian; Italian vermouth
ITA Independent Television Authority (now **IBA**)
ita initial teaching alphabet
ital italic; Italian
ITN Independent Television News
ITO International Trade Organisation
ITT International Telephone and Telegraph Corporation
ITU International Telecommunications Union
ITV Independent Television
IU international unit
IU(C)D intra-uterine (contraceptive) device
IUPAC International Union of Pure and Applied Chemistry
IUPAP International Union of Pure and Applied Physics
IVR International Vehicle Registration
IW Isle of Wight

J joule; Japan (IVR)
J Judge; Justice
JAL Japan Air Lines
Jan January
Jas James
JC *Juris Consultus* Jurisconsult; Jesus Christ; Justice Clerk
JCD *Juris Civilis Doctor* Doctor of Civil Law
JCR junior common room
JFK John Fitzgerald Kennedy
JHS same as **IHC**
JMB Joint Matriculation Board
Josh Joshua
JP Justice of the Peace
Jr, Jun, Junr Junior
JUD *Juris Utriusque Doctor* Doctor both of Canon and of Civil Law
Jul July
Jun June; Junior
junc junction
jurisp jurisprudence

K Kelvin (thermometer scale); kelvin; *kalium* potassium; kilobyte
k kilo-
Kan Kansas

KB Knight of the Bath; Knight Bachelor; King's Bench
KBE Knight Commander of the Order of the British Empire
KC King's Counsel; King's College; Kennel Club
KCB Knight Commander of the Bath
KCMG Knight Commander of the Order of St Michael and St George
KCVO Knight Commander of the (Royal) Victorian Order
Ken Kentucky
KG Knight of the Order of the Garter
kg kilogram(me)(s)
KGB *Komitet Gosudarstvennoi Bezopasnosti* (Russ) Committee of State Security
KGCB Knight of the Grand Cross of the Bath
kilo kilogram(me); kilometre
kk *kaiserlich-königlich* (Ger) Imperial-Royal
KKK Ku Klux Klan
KL Kuala Lumpur
KLH Knight of the Legion of Honour
KLM *Koninklijke Luchtvaart Maatschappij* (Du) Royal Dutch Airlines
KM Knight of Malta
km kilometre(s)
kn knot (nautical, etc, measure)
KO, ko knock out; kick off
K of L Knight of Labour
kpg, kph kilometres per gallon, hour
Kr krypton
kr kreutzer; krone
Ks Kansas
KT Knight of the Thistle
Kt Knight Bachelor
kV kilovolt
kW kilowatt
kWh kilowatt-hour
Ky Kentucky

L Lake; Latin; Liberal; lumen; learner (driver); *libra* pound; Luxembourg (IVR)
L symbol for inductance; luminance
l litre (the abbreviation, though the accepted one, is undesirable as liable to be misread); latitude; league; left; long; (or **lb**) *libra* pound
l length
LA Law Agent; Literate in Arts; Los Angeles; Library Association

La lanthanum; Louisiana
Lab Labour
lab laboratory
LAC Licentiate of the Apothecaries' Company
LAMDA London Academy of Music and Dramatic Art
Lancs Lancashire
lang language
LAR Libya (IVR)
LASER *l*ight *a*mplification by *s*timulated *e*mission of *r*adiation
Lat Latin
lat latitude
lb *libra* pound (in weight)
lb, lbw leg before wicket
LBC London Broadcasting Company
lc lower-case (in printing); *loco citato* in the place cited; left centre; letter of credit
LCCI London Chamber of Commerce and Industry
LCD liquid crystal display
LCh, LChir *Licentiatus Chirurgiae* Licentiate in Surgery
LCJ Lord Chief-Justice
LCM, lcm least common multiple
Ld Lord
Ldp, Lp Lordship
LDS Licentiate in Dental Surgery
LDV Local Defence Volunteers (later Home Guard)
LEA Local Education Authority
LEAP Life Education for the Autistic Person
lect lecture
LED light emitting diode
leg legal; legate; legislature
Leics Leicestershire
LEPRA Leprosy Relief Assocation
lex lexicon
LF low frequency
LGU Ladies Golf Union
lh left hand
LHD *Litterarum Humaniorum Doctor* Doctor of Humane Letters
LI Long Island; Light Infantry
Li lithium
Lib Liberal
lib *liber* book
lib cat library catalogue
Lieut Lieutenant
LIFO last in, first out
LILO last in, last out
Lincs Lincolnshire

liq liquid
lit literal(ly); literature
lith, litho, lithog lithograph; lithography
Lit Hum *litterae humaniores* humane letters, the humanities
Lit(t)D *Litterarum Doctor* Doctor of Letters
LJ Lord Justice
LLB *Legum Baccalaureus* Bachelor of Laws
LLCM Licentiate of the London College of Music
LLD *Legum Doctor* Doctor of Laws
LLM *Legum Magister* Master of Laws
LM long metre
lm lumen
ln natural logarithm
LNG liquefied natural gas
LOB Location of Offices Bureau
loc cit *loco citato* at the place quoted
L of C line of communication
log logarithm
lon, long longitude
Lond London
Lonrho *Lon*don *Rho*desian (industrial conglomerate)
loq *loquitur* speaks
LP long-playing (record); Lord Provost; low pressure; Labour Party
LPG liquefied petroleum gas
LPO London Philharmonic Orchestra
Lr lawrencium; lira (Italian currency)
LRAM Licentiate of the Royal Academy of Music
LRCP Licentiate of the Royal College of Physicians (**Edin,** of Edinburgh; **Lond,** of London; **Irel,** of Ireland)
LRCS Licentiate of the Royal College of Surgeons (**Ed,** of Edinburgh; **Eng,** of England; **Irel,** of Ireland)
LSA Licentiate of the Society of Apothecaries
LSD lysergic acid diethylamide (a hallucinatory drug)
L.S.D. *librae, solidi, denarii* pounds, shillings, pence
LSE London School of Economics
LSO London Symphony Orchestra
LT low tension
Lt Lieutenant
LTA Lawn Tennis Association
Lt-Col Lieutenant-Colonel
Ltd limited liability

Middx   Middlesex
mil, milit.   military
Min   Ministry
min   mineralogy; minimum; minute
Minn   Minnesota
MIRV   Multiple Independently Targeted Re-entry Vehicle (type of missile)
misc   miscellaneous; miscellany
Miss   Mississippi
MIT   Massachusetts Institute of Technology
MJ   megajoule(s)
MJI   Member of the Institute of Journalists
MK   (on cars) mark
Mkk   markka (Finnish currency)
MKS   metre-kilogram-second unit, or system
MKSA   metre-kilogram-second-ampere unit, or system
ml   millilitre(s)
MLA   Member of Legislative Assembly; Modern Language Association
MLC   Member of Legislative Council; Meat and Livestock Commission
MLitt   *Magister Litterarum* Master of Letters or Literature
Mlle   *Mademoiselle* (Fr) Miss;—pl **Mlles** *Mesdemoiselles.*
MLR   minimum lending rate
MM   (Their) Majesties; Martyrs; Military Medal
MM.   *Messieurs* (Fr) Gentlemen, Sirs
mm   millimetre(s)
Mme   *Madame* (Fr) Mrs;—pl **Mmes** *Mesdames*
MN   Merchant Navy
Mn   manganese
MO   Medical Officer
Mo   molybdenum; Missouri
mo   month
MOD   Ministry of Defence
mod   modern; moderate
mod con   modern convenience
MOH   Medical Officer of Health
mol   mole (unit)
mol wt   molecular weight
Mon   Monmouthshire; Monday
Monsig   Monsignor
Mont   Montana; Montgomeryshire
mos   months
MOS(T)   metal oxide silicon (transistors)
MOT   Ministry of Transport

MP   Member of Parliament; Military Police; Metropolitan Police; Municipal Police (US); mounted police
mp   mezzo-piano; melting-point
MPDS   Market Price Display Service
mpg, mph   miles per gallon, hour
MPharm   Master of Pharmacy
MPS   Member of the Pharmaceutical Society; Member of the Philological Society
MR   Master of the Rolls
Mr   Mister; Master
MRA   Moral Rearmament
MRC   Medical Research Council
MRCA   multirole combat aircraft
MRG   Minority Rights Group
Mrs   Mistress (fem of **Mr,** Mister)
MS   manuscript; Master of Surgery; *Memoriae Sacrum* Sacred to the Memory; milestone; multiple sclerosis
Ms   see Dictionary
ms   millisecond(s); (or **M/S**) months (after)
MSC   Manpower Services Commission
MSc   Master of Science
MSF   medium standard frequency
msl   mean sea-level
MSS   manuscripts
MST   mountain standard time
MSW   Medical Social Worker
MT   Mechanical Transport; mean time
Mt, mt   mount
MTh   Master of Theology
mth   month
Mts, mts   mountains
mus   music; museum
MusB(ac)   Bachelor of Music
MusD(oc)   Doctor of Music
MusM   Master of Music
mv   merchant vessel; motor vessel; muzzle velocity
MVO   Member of the Royal Victorian Order
MW   medium wave
Mx   Middlesex
myth   mythology; mythological

N   nitrogen; newton; North, Northern; Norway (IVR)
n   name; noun; *natus* born; neuter; noon; nano-
Na   *natrium* sodium

NAAFI Navy, Army, and Air-Force Institute(s) (providing canteens for the armed forces)

NABM National Association of British Manufacturers

NACRO National Association for the Care and Resettlement of Offenders

NALGO National and Local Government Officers' Association

N and Q Notes and Queries

NASA National Aeronautics and Space Administration (USA)

Nat National

nat *natus* born

nat hist natural history

NATO North Atlantic Treaty Organisation

nat ord natural order

Nat Phil natural philosophy

Nat Sci Natural Science(s)

NATSOPA National Society of Operative Printers, Graphical and Media Personnel

NATTKE National Association of Television, Theatrical, and Kinematographic Employees

Nat West NatWest, National Westminster Bank

naut nautical

nav naval; navigation

NAVAR combined navigation and radar system

Nazi *Nazionale Sozialisten* (Ger) German National Socialist Party

NB New Brunswick; North Britain; North British; North bag (in postal sorting); (or **nb**) *nota bene* note well, or take notice

Nb niobium

NBC National Broadcasting Company (USA)

NBL National Book League

NBS National Bureau of Standards (USA)

NC New Church; numerical control; North Carolina

NCB National Coal Board (now British Coal)

NCCL National Council for Civil Liberties

NCO non-commissioned officer

NCR National Cash Register Company; no carbon required

ncv no commercial value

Nd neodymium

ND, NDak North Dakota

nd no date, not dated

NDPS National Data Processing Service

NE north-east; New England

Ne neon

NEB New English Bible; National Enterprise Board

Neb, Nebr Nebraska

NEC National Executive Committee; National Exhibition Centre

NED New English Dictionary (now **OED**)

NEDC National Economic Development Council (Neddy)

NEDO National Economic Development Office

neg negative

NEI *non est inventus* has not been found

nem con *nemine contradicente* no one contradicting

nem diss *nemine dissentiente* no one dissenting

NERC Natural Environment Research Council

Neth Netherlands

neut neuter

Nev Nevada

New M New Mexico

N/F no funds

NF Norman French; Northern French; National Front; Newfoundland (also **Nfd**)

NFER National Foundation for Educational Research

NFS National Fire Service

NFT National Film Theatre

NFU National Farmers' Union

NFWI National Federation of Women's Institutes

NGA National Graphical Association

NH New Hampshire

NHBRC National House-Builders' Registration Council (or Certificate)

NHI National Health Insurance

NHS National Health Service

NI Northern Ireland; national insurance

Ni nickel

NIRC National Industrial Relations Court

NJ New Jersey

NKVD *Narodny Komitet Vnutrennikh Del* (Russ) People's Committee of Internal Affairs

NL   Netherlands (IVR)
NLRB   National Labor Relations Board (USA)
NM, N Mex   New Mexico
n mile   international nautical mile
NNE   north-north-east
NNW   north-north-west
NO   New Orleans; natural order
no   (or **No**) *numero* (in) number; not out
nom, nomin   nominative
non-coll   non-collegiate
non-com   non-commissioned
Noncon   Nonconformist
non obst   *non obstante* notwithstanding
non pros   *non prosequitur* does not prosecute
non seq   *non sequitur* it does not follow
non-U   not upper class
NOP   National Opinion Poll
nop   not otherwise provided
Northants   Northamptonshire
Northd   Northumberland
Nos, nos   numbers
Notts   Nottinghamshire
Nov   November
NP   Notary Public; New Providence; (or np) new paragraph
np   no place (of publication)
NPFA   National Playing Fields Association
NPG   National Portrait Gallery
NPL   National Physical Laboratory
npl   noun plural
nr   near
NRA   National Rifle Association
NRDC   National Research Development Corporation
NS   New Style; Nova Scotia
ns   nanosecond(s); not specified; nouns
NSB   National Savings Bank
n sing   noun singular
NSPCC   National Society for Prevention of Cruelty to Children
NSRA   National Small-Bore Rifle Association
NSW   New South Wales
NT   New Testament; Northern Territory; National Trust
NTDA   National Trade Development Association
ntp   normal temperature and pressure
NTS   National Trust for Scotland
NU   name unknown

NUGMW   National Union of General and Municipal Workers
NUI   National University of Ireland
NUJ   National Union of Journalists
NUM   National Union of Mineworkers
NUPE   National Union of Public Employees
NUR   National Union of Railwaymen
NUS   National Union of Students; National Union of Seamen
NUT   National Union of Teachers
NV   New Version
NV(A)LA   National Viewers' and Listeners' Association
nvd   no value declared
NW   north-west
NWT   North-west Territory (Canada)
NY   New York (city or state)
NYC   New York City
NYO   National Youth Orchestra
NZ   New Zealand (also IVR)

O   oxygen; Ohio
o/a   on account of
O&C   Oxford and Cambridge (Schools Examination Board)
O & M   organisation and method
OAP   Old Age Pension or Pensioner
OAPEC   Organisation of Arab Petroleum-Exporting Countries
OAS   on active service; Organisation of American States
OAU   Organisation of African Unity
ob   *obiit* died
obdt   obedient
OBE   Officer of the Order of the British Empire
obj   object; objective
obl   oblique; oblong
obs   obsolete; observation
o/c   overcharge
OC   Officer Commanding; Officer of the Order of Canada
OCF   Officiating Chaplain to the Forces
OCR   optical character recognition or reader
Oct   October
oct   octavo
OCTU   Officer Cadet Training Unit
OD   Ordnance Datum or Data
O/D   overdrawn

OE Old English
OECD Organisation for Economic Co-operation and Development
OED Oxford English Dictionary
OF Old French; Oddfellow
off. official; officinal
OFT Office of Fair Trading
OHMS On His (or Her) Majesty's Service
OK see Dictionary
Okla Oklahoma
OM Order of Merit; Old Measurement
OMR optical mark recognition
ono or near(est) offer
Ont Ontario
Op Opera; Opus
op out of print; opposite; operation
op cit *opere citato* in the work cited
OPEC Organisation of Petroleum-Exporting Countries
opp opposed; opposite
Ops Operations; Operations Officer; Operations room
OR other ranks; operations research
Or, Ore, Oreg Oregon
ord ordained; order; ordinary; ordnance
orig origin; original(ly)
OS Old Style; Ordinary Seaman; outsize; Ordnance Survey
O/S outstanding
osp *obiit sine prole* died without issue
OT Old Testament; occupational therapy
OTC Officers' Training Corps
OU Open University
OUP Oxford University Press
Oxbridge *Ox*ford and Cam*bridge.*
Oxf Oxford
OXFAM *Ox*ford Committee for *Fam*ine Relief
Oxon *Oxonia* Oxford; *Oxoniensis* of Oxford; Oxfordshire
oz ounce(s) (15th cent. It *ōz,* abbreviation of *onza*)

P phosphorus; parking; President; Prince; pedal; Portugal (IVR)
P power
p new penny; new pence; piano; pico-; page; participle
P&P postage and packing
PA Press Association; Publishers

Association; personal assistant; Public Address (system)
Pa protactinium; pascal
Pa, Penn Pennsylvania
pa past
p.a. (or **pa**) per annum; participial adjective
PABX private automatic branch exchange
Pal Palestine
pam pamphlet
Pan Panama
Pan Am Pan-American (World Airways Incorporated)
P and O Peninsular and Oriental (Steamship Navigation Co)
pa p past participle
par paragraph; parallel; parish
pass passive
pa t past tense
Pat Off Patent Office
PAYE Pay As You Earn (Income Tax)
PB Pharmacopoeia Britannica; Plymouth Brethren
Pb *plumbum* lead
PBX private branch exchange
PC Police Constable; Privy Councillor; *Patres Conscripti* Conscript Fathers
pc postcard; per cent
pce piece
PCS Principal Clerk of Session
Pd palladium
pd paid
PDI pre-delivery inspection
PDR People's Democratic Republic
PDSA People's Dispensary for Sick Animals
PE Protestant Episcopal; physical education
p/e price-earnings ratio
PEC photoelectric cell
ped pedal
PEI Prince Edward Island
PEN Poets, Playwrights, Editors, Essayists, and Novelists
Pen Peninsula
Penn, Pa Pennsylvania
PEP Political and Economic Planning; personal equity plan
per period; person
per an per annum
per cent see Dictionary
perf perfect

per pro *per procurationem* by the agency (of)

Pers Persian

pers person; personal

Pes peseta (Spanish currency)

PF Procurator Fiscal; Patriotic Front

Pf pfennig (German currency)

pf piano-forte

PG paying guest

Pg Portugal; Portuguese

PGA Professional Golfers' Association

phar, pharm pharmaceutical; pharmacopoeia; pharmacy

PhB *Philosophiae Baccalaureus* Bachelor of Philosophy

PhD *Philosophiae Doctor* Doctor of Philosophy

Phil Philadelphia; philology; philological; philosophy; philosophical

phon, phonet phonetics

phonog phonography

phot photography

phr phrase

phys physiology; physics; physician

PIA Pakistan International Airlines

PIB Prices and Incomes Board

pinx *pinxit* painted it

PL Poet Laureate; Public Library

pl plural

PLA Port of London Authority

PLC, plc Public Limited Company

PLO Palestine Liberation Organisation

PLP Parliamentary Labour Party

PLR public lending right

plu, plur plural

plup pluperfect

PM Past Master; (or **pm**) *post meridiem* after noon; Postmaster; (or **pm**) *post mortem* after death; Prime Minister; Provost-Marshal

Pm promethium

pm premium

PMG Postmaster-General; Paymaster-General

PMO Principal Medical Officer

Pmr Paymaster

PMRAFNS Princess Mary's Royal Air Force Nursing Service

pn promissory note

PNdB perceived noise decibel

PO Post Office; Petty Officer; Pilot Officer

Po polonium

po postal order; pole

pod pay on delivery

Pol Econ Political Economy

pop population; popular

POP Post Office preferred

pos, posit positive

POUNC Post Office Users' National Council

POW prisoner of war

PP parish priest; present pupil; past President

pp pages; *per procurationem* by proxy (also *per pro* for and on behalf of); pianissimo; past participle

ppc picture post-card

PPE Philosophy, Politics and Economics

PPI Plan Position Indicator; printed postage impression

PPS *post postscriptum* a later additional postscript; Parliamentary Private Secretary

PQ Province of Quebec

PR prize ring; Puerto Rico; proportional representation; *Populus Romanus* the Roman people; public relations

Pr Prince; priest; Provençal

pr pair; per; present; price

PRA pre-recorded address; President of the Royal Academy

Preb Prebend; Prebendary

pref preface

prep preparation; preparatory; preposition

Pres President

pres p present participle

pret preterite

Prin Principal

PRN *pro re nata* for special occasion arising

PRO Public Relations Officer; Public Record Office

pro professional; prostitute; probationary

prob probably

Prof Professor

pron pronoun

PROP Preservation of the Rights of Prisoners

prop proper(ly); proposition; property

Prot Protestant

pro tem *pro tempore* for the time being

Prov Proverbs; Provincial; Provost

RAC Royal Automobile Club; Royal Armoured Corps; Royal Agricultural College

Rad Radical

rad radian; *radix* root

RADA Royal Academy of Dramatic Art

RADC Royal Army Dental Corps

RAE Royal Aircraft Establishment

RAEC Royal Army Educational Corps

RAeS Royal Aeronautical Society

RAF Royal Air Force

RAM Royal Academy of Music; random access memory

ram relative atomic mass

RAMC Royal Army Medical Corps

RAN Royal Australian Navy

R and A Royal and Ancient (Golf Club) St Andrews

R and B rhythm and blues (type of popular music)

R and D research and development

RAOC Royal Army Ordnance Corps

RAPC Royal Army Pay Corps

RAS Royal Astronomical Society; Royal Asiatic Society

RAVC Royal Army Veterinary Corps

RBA Royal Society of British Artists

RBS Royal Society of British Sculptors

RC Roman Catholic; Red Cross; Royal College of Art

RCA Royal Canadian Academy; Radio Corporation of America

RCAF Royal Canadian Air Force

RCM Royal College of Music; Regimental Court-Martial

RCMP Royal Canadian Mounted Police

RCN Royal Canadian Navy

RCOG Royal College of Obstetricians and Gynaecologists

RCP Royal College of Physicians

RCS Royal College of Surgeons; Royal Corps of Signals; Royal College of Science

RCT Royal Corps of Transport

RCVS Royal College of Veterinary Surgeons

RD Rural Dean; Naval Reserve Decoration; (or **R/D**) refer to drawer

Rd Road; rand (S African currency)

RDC Rural District Council

RDI Designer for Industry of the Royal Society of Arts

RDS Royal Dublin Society

RE Royal Engineers; Royal Society of Etchers and Engravers; Royal Exchange

re with reference/regard to

Réau Réaumur's thermometric scale

rec *recipe* take; record; receipt

recd received

REconS Royal Economic Society

ref referee; reference

Ref Ch Reformed Church

reg, regd registered

Reg Prof Regius Professor

regt regiment

rel relating; relation; relative

rel d relative density

REME Royal Electrical and Mechanical Engineers

rep representative; republic; report; reporter

rept receipt; report

retd retired; returned

Rev revise(d); revision; (or **Revd**) Reverend

rev revolution

Rev Ver Revised Version

RF *République française* (Fr) French Republic; radio frequency

RFC Rugby Football Club

RFU Rugby Football Union

RGG Royal Grenadier Guards

RGN Registered General Nurse

RGS Royal Geographical Society

Rgt Regiment

RH Royal Highness

rh right hand

RHA Royal Horse Artillery; Royal Hibernian Academy; Road Haulage Association; Regional Health Authority

rhet rhetoric; rhetorical

RHF Royal Highland Fusiliers

RHG Royal Horse Guards

RHistS Royal Historical Society

RHM Rank Hovis McDougall

RHS Royal Humane Society; Royal Horticultural Society; Royal Historical Society; Royal Highland Show

RI Royal Institute of Painters in Water Colours; Rhode Island; religious instruction; Indonesia (IVR)

RIA Royal Irish Academy

RIAM Royal Irish Academy of Music

RIBA   Royal Institute of British Architects

RIC   Royal Irish Constabulary; Royal Institute of Chemistry

RICS   Royal Institution of Chartered Surveyors

RIGB   Royal Institution of Great Britain

RIP   *requiescat in pace* may he (or she) rest in peace

RIPHH   Royal Institute of Public Health and Hygiene

RJET   remote job entry terminal

RL   Lebanon (IVR); Rugby League

RLO   returned letter office

RLS   Robert Louis Stevenson

Rly, rly   railway

RM   Royal Mail; Royal Marines

RMA   Royal Military Academy, Sandhurst; Royal Marine Artillery

RMetS   Royal Meteorological Society

RMO   Resident Medical Officer

RMP   (Corps of) Royal Military Police

RMS   Royal Mail Steamer; Royal Microscopical Society

RN   Royal Navy

Rn   radon

RNAS   Royal Naval Air Service(s)

RNIB   Royal National Institute for the Blind

RNLI   Royal National Lifeboat Institution

RNR   Royal Naval Reserve

RNVR   Royal Naval Volunteer Reserve

RNZAF   Royal New Zealand Air Force

RNZN   Royal New Zealand Navy

ro   *recto* on the right-hand page

ROC   Royal Observer Corps

ROI   Royal Institute of Oil Painters

ROM   read only memory

Rom   Romans

rom   roman (in printing)

Ro-Ro   roll-on-roll-off

RoSPA   see **RSPA**

RP   Reformed Presbyterian; Regius Professor; Received Pronunciation; Royal Society of Portrait Painters

RPA   radiation protection adviser

RPI   retail price index

RPM   retail price maintenance

rpm, rps   revolutions per minute, second

RPO   Royal Philharmonic Orchestra

RPS   Royal Photographic Society

RR   Right Reverend

RRE   Radar Research Establishment

RRP   recommended retail price

RS   Royal Society

RSA   Royal Society of Antiquaries; Royal Society of Arts; Royal Scottish Academy or Academician; Republic of South Africa

RSC   Royal Shakespeare Company

RSE   Royal Society of Edinburgh

RSFSR   Russian Soviet Federated Socialist Republic

RSG   Regional Seats of Government

RSL   Royal Society of Literature

RSM   Regimental Sergeant-Major; Royal Society of Medicine; Royal School of Music

RSO   railway sub-office; railway sorting office; rural sub-office; radiological safety officer; Resident Surgical Officer

RSPA, RoSPA   Royal Society for the Prevention of Accidents

RSPB   Royal Society for the Protection of Birds

RSPCA   Royal Society for the Prevention of Cruelty to Animals

RSS   (or **SRS**) *Regiae Societatis Socius* Fellow of the Royal Society; Royal Statistical Society

RSV   Revised Standard Version

RSVP   *répondez s'il vous plaît* (Fr) reply, if you please

RT   radiotelephone, -phony

RTE   *Radio Telefís Éireann* (Ir) Irish Television

Rt Hon   Right Honourable

RTO   Railway Transportation (or Traffic) Officer

RTPI   Royal Town Planning Institute

Rt Rev   Right Reverend

RTZ   Rio Tinto Zinc Corporation Limited

RU   Rugby Union

Ru   ruthenium

RUC   Royal Ulster Constabulary

R-unit   Röntgen unit—unit of measurement of X-ray radiation

RV   Revised Version

RWS   Royal Society of Painters in Water Colours

Ry, ry   railway

RYA   Royal Yachting Association

RYS   Royal Yacht Squadron

RZS   Royal Zoological Society (**E,** of Edinburgh)

S sulphur; square; stokes; siemens; South; Sabbath; Saint; society; sun; Sweden (IVR)

s second(s)

$ dollar

SA South Africa; South America; South Australia; Salvation Army; sex-appeal; *Société anonyme* (Fr) limited liability company; Society of Arts; Society of Antiquaries (**Scot,** of Scotland)

sa *secundum artem* according to art; *sine anno* without date

sae stamped addressed envelope

Salop Shropshire

SALT Strategic Arms Limitation Talks

SAM surface-to-air missile

SARAH Search and Rescue and Homing

SAS *Societatis Antiquariorum Socius* Fellow of the Society of Antiquaries; Scandinavian Airlines System; Special Air Service

Sask Saskatchewan

Sat Saturday

S.A.T.B. soprano, alto, tenor, bass

SAYE save as you earn

Sb *stibium* antimony

SBN Standard Book Number

SC *senatus consultum* a decree of the Roman senate; Special Constable; Supreme Court; Staff College; Staff Corps; South Carolina

Sc scandium

sc *scilicet* namely; *sculpsit* (he) sculptured (this); (or **s. caps, sm. caps**) small capitals (in printing)

s/c self-contained

ScB *Scientiae Baccalaureus* Bachelor of Science

ScD *Scientiae Doctor* Doctor of Science

SCE Scottish Certificate of Education

SCF Save the Children Fund

Sch schilling (Austrian currency); school

sci fa *scire facias* that you cause to know

sci- fi science fiction

scil, sciz, *scilicet* namely (cf **viz**)

SCL Student of Civil Law

SCM Student Christian Movement; State Certified Midwife

Scot Scotland; Scottish

ScotBIC Scottish Business in the Community

SCR senior common room

Script Scripture

SCUBA self-contained underwater breathing apparatus

sculp, sculpt *sculpsit* (he) sculptured (this); sculpture; sculptor

SD, S Dak South Dakota

sd *sine die* without a day (fixed)

SDA Scottish Development Agency

SDC single data converter

SDLP Social and Democratic Labour Party

SDP social, domestic and pleasure; Social Democratic Party

SDR special drawing rights

SE south-east; Society of Engineers

Se selenium

SEAC South-East Asia Command

SEATO South-East Asia Treaty Organisation

Sec, Secy Secretary

sec secant; *secundum* in accordance with; second; section

sec leg *secundum legem* according to law

sec reg *secundum regulam* according to rule

sect section

SED Scottish Education Department

Sem seminary; Semitic

SEN State Enrolled Nurse

Sen Senator; senior

Sep, Sept September; Septuagint

seq *sequens* following (pl **seqq,** *sequentes* or *sequentia*)

SERC Science and Education Research Council

Serg, Sergt Sergeant

Sess Session

SF science fiction; Sinn Fein; signal frequency; Finland (IVR)

SFA Scottish Football Association; Sweet Fanny Adams (= nothing at all)

SFr Swiss franc

sfz sforzando

SG Solicitor-General

sg specific gravity

SGHWR steam-generating heavy water reactor

SGP Singapore (IVR)

SHAEF Supreme Headquarters of the Allied Expeditionary Force

SHAPE Supreme Headquarters Allied Powers Europe

shv *sub hoc verbo* or *sub hac voce* under this word

SI Système International (d'Unités)
Si silicon
sic so written
sig signature
sin sine
sing singular
SIPRI Stockholm International Peace Research Institute
SIS Secret Intelligence Service
SJ Society of Jesus
SL Solicitor at Law; Sergeant-at-Law; (or **S Lat**) South latitude
SLADE Society of Lithographic Artists, Designers, Engravers and Process Workers
sld sailed
slp *sine legitima prole* without lawful issue
SM Short Metre; Sergeant-Major
Sm samarium
Smith. Inst. Smithsonian Institution
SMLondSoc *Societatis Medicae Londiniensis Socius* Member of the London Medical Society
SMM *Sancta Mater Maria* Holy Mother Mary
SMMT Society of Motor Manufacturers and Traders
SMO Senior Medical Officer
SMP School Mathematics Project
smp *sine mascula prole* without male issue
Sn *stannum* tin
sn *secundum naturam* according to nature
SNCF *Société Nationale des Chemins de Fer français* (Fr) French national railways
SNO Scottish National Orchestra
SNP Scottish National Party
SO Staff Officer; Signal Officer; standing order; special order
so seller's option
Soc Society
SOGAT Society of Graphical and Allied Trades
Sol, Solr Solicitor
sol solution
Sol-Gen Solicitor-General
sop soprano
SOS see Dictionary
Sp Spanish
sp *sine prole* without issue; spelling; species (pl **spp.**)
SPCK Society for Promoting Christian Knowledge
SPG Special Patrol Group

sp gr specific gravity (now relative density)
SPQR *Senatus Populusque Romanus* the Senate and People of Rome
SPR Society for Psychical Research
sps *sine prole superstite* without surviving issue
spt seaport
SPUC Society for the Protection of the Unborn Child
sp vol specific volume
sq (or **Sq**) square; *sequens* following (in pl **sqq**, *sequentes* or *sequentia*)
sqn squadron
SR Southern Region
Sr senior; Sir; Señor; strontium
sr steradian
SRC Science Research Council; Student Representative Council
SRCh State Registered Chiropodist
SRI *Sacrum Romanum Imperium* Holy Roman Empire
SRN State Registered Nurse
SRS (or **RSS**) *Societatis Regiae Socius* Fellow of the Royal Society
SRU Scottish Rugby Union
SS Saints; *Schutzstaffel* (Ger) Hitler's bodyguard
ss steamship; screw steamer
SSAFA Soldiers', Sailors' and Airmen's Families Association
SSC Solicitor before the Supreme Court (Scotland); *Societas Sanctae Crucis* Society of the Holy Cross
SSD *Sanctissimus Dominus* Most Holy Lord (the Pope)
SSE south-south-east
SSM surface-to-surface missile
SSN Standard Serial Number
SSRC Social Science Research Council
SST supersonic transport
SSW south-south-west
St Saint; Strait; Street
st stone (weight)
Staffs Staffordshire
STD subscriber trunk dialling
std standard
Ste *Sainte* (Fr) fem of Saint
ster, stereo stereophonic; stereotype
ster, stg sterling
stet let it stand
STOL short take-off and landing
STP *Sanctae Theologiae Professor* Professor of Theology

stp   standard temperature and pressure
str   steamer
str   strong
STS   Scottish Text Society
STUC   Scottish Trades Union Congress
STV   Scottish Television; Single Transferable Vote
SU   strontium unit—unit of measurement of strontium radiation; Scripture Union; Soviet Union (also IVR)
sub   subject
subj   subject; subjunctive
subst   substitute; substantive
suf, suff   suffix
sup   superfine; superior; (or **superl**) superlative; supreme; *supra* above; supine; supplement
superl   superlative
supp, suppl   supplement
Supr   Supreme
Supt   Superintendent
Surg   surgeon; surgery
sv   *sub voce* under that heading; *sub verbo* under the word
SW   south-west; small women('s); short wave
SWALK   sealed with a loving kiss
SWAPO   South West Africa People's Organisation
SWG   standard wire gauge
syn   synonym

T   tritium
t   tonne (cf **l**, litre)
t   time
TA   Territorial Army
tal qual   *talis qualis* just as they come, average quality
tan   tangent
TASS   *Telegrafnoye Agentsvo Sovietskovo Soyuza* (Russ) telegraph agency of the Soviet Union; Technical, Administrative and Supervisory Section (of **AUEW**)
Tb   terbium
TB   tuberculosis
Tc   technetium
TCCB   Test and County Cricket Board
TCD   Trinity College Dublin; Twentieth Century Dictionary
TCL   Trinity College of Music, London
TCP   trichlorophenylmethyliodosalicyl (a proprietary germicide)

TD   Territorial Decoration; *Teachta Dála* (Ir) member of the Dail
Te   tellurium
tech.   technical; technology
TEFL   teaching English as a foreign language
tel   telephone
tel, teleg   telegram; telegraph
temp   temporal; *tempore* in the time of; temperature; temporary
Ten, Tenn   Tennessee
ten   tenor
Ter, Terr   Territory; terrace
term   termination
TES   Times Educational Supplement
TESL   teaching English as a second language
Test   Testament
Teut   Teutonic
Tex   Texas
Text Rec   *textus receptus* the revised text
TF   Territorial Force
tf   till forbidden
TFR   Territorial Force Reserve
TGWU   Transport and General Workers' Union
Th   thorium; Thursday
ThD   Doctor of Theology
theat   theatrical
theol   theology; theologian
THES   Times Higher Educational Supplement
THF   Trust Houses Forte
ThL   Theological Licentiate
Tho, Thos   Thomas
TI   Tube Investments
Ti   titanium
tid   *ter in die* thrice a day
TIF   *Transports Internationaux par Chemin de Fer* (Fr) International Rail Transport
TIR   *Transports Internationaux Routiers* (Fr) International Road Transport
TIROS   Television and Infrared Observation Satellite
Tl   thallium
TLS   Times Literary Supplement
TM   transcendental meditation
Tm   thulium
TN   trade name
TNT   trinitrotoluene (explosive)
TO   turn over; Telegraph-office; Transport Officer
Toc H   Talbot House
TPI   Town Planning Institute

tpr   teleprinter
TR   Turkey (IVR)
tr   transpose; transactions; translator; trustee; transfer
trans   transitive; translated; translation; transpose
TRH   Their Royal Highnesses
trig   trigonometry
Trin   Trinity
TSB   Trustee Savings Bank
TSO   town sub-office
TT   teetotal; Tourist Trophy; tuberculin tested
Tu, Tues Tue   Tuesday
TUC   Trades Union Congress
TV   television
TVA   Tennessee Valley Authority
TVP   texturised vegetable protein
TWA   Trans-World Airlines
TWI   Training within Industry
typ, typo   typographer; typography

U   uranium; Unionist; upper-class; Uruguay (IVR)
UAE   United Arab Emirates
UAR   United Arab Republic
UC, uc   upper case (capital letters)
UCAR   Union of Central African Republics
UCATT   Union of Construction, Allied Trades and Technicians
UCCA   Universities Central Council on Admissions
UCL   University College London
UDA   Ulster Defence Association
UDC   Urban District Council; Universal Decimal Classification
UDI   Unilateral Declaration of Independence
UDR   Ulster Defence Regiment
UDT   United Dominions Trust
UEFA   Union of European Football Associations
UF   United Free Church (of Scotland)
UFO   unidentified flying object
UGC   University Grants Committee
UHF   ultra high frequency
UJD   *Utriusque Juris Doctor* Doctor of both Laws (Canon and Civil)
UK   United Kingdom
UKAEA   United Kingdom Atomic Energy Authority
ULCC   ultra large crude carriers

ult, ulto   *ultimo* in the last (month); ultimate(ly)
UMIST   University of Manchester Institute of Science and Technology
UN   United Nations
UNA   United Nations Association
UNCTAD, Unctad   United Nations Commission for Trade and Development
UNEP   United Nations Environment Programme
UNESCO   United Nations Educational, Scientific and Cultural Organisation
UNICEF   United Nations International Children's Emergency Fund—now United Nations Children's Fund
UNIDO   United Nations Industrial Development Organisation
Unit   Unitarian
Univ   University; Universalist
UNO   United Nations Organisation
UNRRA   United Nations Relief and Rehabilitation Administration
UP   United Presbyterian; United Press
UPU   Universal Postal Union
UPW   Union of Post Office Workers
Uru   Uruguay
US   United States; United Service(s); Under-secretary
us   *ut supra* as above
US(A)   United States (of America) (also IVR); United States Army
USAF   United States Air Force
USCL   United Society for Christian Literature
USDAW   Union of Shop, Distributive and Allied Workers
USIS   United States Information Service
USN   United States Navy
USPG   United Society for the Propagation of the Gospel
USS   United States Ship or Steamer
USSR   (also **CCCP** (Russ)) Union of Soviet Socialist Republics
usu   usually
USW   ultrasonic waves; ultrashort waves
usw   *und so weiter* (Ger) and so forth
UT   Universal Time
Ut   Utah
ut dict   *ut dictum* as said
ut sup   *ut supra* as above
UU   Ulster Unionist
uv   ultraviolet

UVF   Ulster Volunteer Force
UWIST   University of Wales Institute of Science and Technology

V   vanadium; volt
V   symbol for electric potential difference
v   velocity; *versus* against; *vide* see; verb; verse; volume
VA   Royal Order of Victoria and Albert; Vicar Apostolic; volt-ampere(s)
Va   Virginia
vac   vacuum; vacation
VAD   Voluntary Aid Detachment
val   value
V and A   Victoria and Albert Museum
var   variant; variety; variable
var lect   *varia lectio* variant reading
VAT   Value-added Tax
Vat   Vatican
vb   verb
VC   Victoria Cross; Vice-Chancellor; Vice-Consul
VCR   video cassette recorder
VD   Venereal Disease(s); Volunteer (Officers') Decoration
vd   various dates; vapour density
VDC   Volunteer Defence Corps
VDQS   *Vins délimités de qualité supérieure* (Fr) wines of superior quality from approved vineyards
VDU   visual display unit
VE   Victory in Europe (1945)
veg   vegetable(s)
Ven   Venerable
VERA   versatile reactor assembly; vision electronic recording apparatus
verb sap   *verbum sapienti,* or **verb sat,** *verbum sat(is)* a word to the wise is enough
Vet, Veter   Veterinary
Vet Surg   Veterinary Surgeon
VF   voice frequency; video frequency
VG   Vicar-General; (or **vg**) very good
vg   *verbi gratia* for example
VHF   very high frequency
vi   verb intransitive
via   by way of
Vic   Vicar; Vicarage
Vict   Victoria; Victoria University
vid   *vide* see
vil(l)   village
VIP   Very Important Person
VIR   *Victoria Imperatrix Regina* (see **VRI**)

Vis, Visc   Viscount
viz   *videlicet* namely (z = mediaeval Latin symbol of contraction)
VJ   Victory over Japan (1945)
vl   *varia lectio* variant reading (pl **vvll**)
VLCC   very large crude carrier
VLF   very low frequency
VN   voucher number
vo   *verso* on the left-hand page
voc   vocative
vocab   vocabulary
vol   volunteer; volume
VP   Vice-President
VR   *Victoria Regina* Queen Victoria
VRD   Volunteer Reserve Decoration
VRI   *Victoria Regina et Imperatrix* Victoria, Queen and Empress
VRQ   verbal reasoning quotient
VS   Veterinary Surgeon; *volti subito* turn quickly
VSO   Voluntary Service Overseas
VSOP   very special old pale
Vt   Vermont
v t   verb transitive
VTO(L)   vertical take-off (and landing)
VTR   video tape recorder
Vul, Vulg   Vulgate
vul, vulg   vulgar
vvll   see **vl**
VW   *Volkswagen* (Ger) people's car
vy   various years

W   *wolframium* tungsten; watt; West; Welsh; women('s)
w   weak; with
WA   West Africa; Western Australia
WAAC   Women's Army Auxiliary Corps (now **WRAC**)
WAAF   Women's Auxiliary Air Force (earlier and later **WRAF**)
Wash   Washington
WASP   White Anglo-Saxon Protestant
Wb   weber
WBA   West Bromwich Albion Football Club; World Boxing Association of America
WBC   World Boxing Council
WC   water-closet; Western Central; Wesleyan Chapel
WCC   World Council of Churches
W/Cdr   Wing-Commander
WCT   World Championship Tennis
W/E   week ending

WEA   Workers' Educational Association
Wed   Wednesday
wef   with effect from
WEU   Western European Union
wf   wrong fount (in printing)
WFTU   World Federation of Trade Unions
wg   wire gauge
WHO   World Health Organisation
WI   West Indies; Women's Institute
Wilts   Wiltshire
Wis   Wisconsin
wk   week
WLF   Women's Liberal Federation
Wm   William
WMO   World Meteorological Organisation
WNP   Welsh Nationalist Party
WNW   west-north-west
WO   War Office (1964 absorbed in Ministry of Defence); Warrant Officer; walk-over
Worcs   Worcestershire
Wp, Wpfl   Worshipful
WP   Warsaw Pact; word processing
wp   weather permitting; word processing
wpb   wastepaper basket
wpm   words per minute
WR   Western Region
WRAC   Women's Royal Army Corps
WRAF   Women's Royal Air Force
WRI   Women's Rural Institute
WRNS   Women's Royal Naval Service
WRVS   Women's Royal Voluntary Service (previously **WVS**)
WS   Writer to the Signet
WSW   west-south-west
wt   weight
W Va   West Virginia

WVS   Women's Voluntary Service (now **WRVS**)
WWF   World Wildlife Fund
Wy, Wyo   Wyoming

X, Xt   Christ. (X = Greek *Ch*)
x   *ex* (Latin without), as in **x d,** ex dividend
Xe   xenon
Xm, Xmas   Christmas
Xn, Xtian   Christian

Y   yttrium; yen (Japanese currency)
y   year; yard
Yb   ytterbium
yd   yard
ye   the (the **y** not being a **y** but representing the old letter thorn, þ)
Yeo   Yeomanry
YHA   Youth Hostels Association
YMCA   Young Men's Christian Association
Yn   yen (Japanese currency)
Yorks   Yorkshire
yr   your; younger; year
yt   that (*y* as in **ye** above)
YTV   Yorkshire Television
YU   Yugoslavia (IVR)
YWCA   Young Women's Christian Association

ZA   South Africa (IVR)
zB   *zum Beispiel* (Ger) for example
Zn   zinc
ZPG   zero population growth
Zr   zirconium
ZST   Zone Standard Time

INDEX